12/01 gale 78⁰⁰

THE GREENHAVEN ENCYCLOPEDIA OF

THE RENAISSANCE

Other Books in the Greenhaven Encyclopedia Series

THE GREENHAVEN ENCYCLOPEDIA OF

THE RENAISSANCE

by Tom Streissguth

Konrad Eisenbichler, *Consulting Editor*

GREENHAVEN PRESS
An imprint of Thomson Gale, a part of The Thomson Corporation

Detroit • New York • San Francisco • New Haven, Conn. • Waterville, Maine • London

THOMSON

GALE

Christine Nasso, *Publisher*
Elizabeth Des Chenes, *Managing Editor*

© 2008 The Gale Group.

Star logo is a trademark and Gale and Greenhaven Press are registered trademarks used herein under license.
For more information, contact:
Greenhaven Press
27500 Drake Rd.
Farmington Hills, MI 48331-3535
Or you can visit our Internet site at http://www.gale.com

Cover photograph reproduced by permission of © Araldo de Luca/Corbis.

ISBN-13: 978-0-7377-3216-0 (hardcover)

ISBN-10: 0-7377-3216-4 (hardcover)

Library of Congress Control Number: 2007938127
Printed in the United States of America
10 9 8 7 6 5 4 3 2 1

Contents

Contents

G

H

I

J

K

L

M

Preface

On May 20, 1347, a small band of people gathered in the streets of Rome. Led by a man dressed in a full suit of armor, they marched to the Capitoline Hill, the heart of the ancient capital. They watched as the man climbed onto the crumbling foundation of a Roman monument. He spoke and gestured for hours, stirring the crowd to cheers. The wretched state of the city, he declared, was the fault of corrupt and greedy noble families who cared only for fighting each other and nothing for the pride or safety of the common people. The man pronounced the city overthrown and the ancient republic restored. Rome would again become the *caput mundi*, the center of the world.

Cola di Rienzo, the speaker perched on the ancient stone, was born into the humble family of a tavern keeper. As a boy he learned to read Latin and had spent many hours studying Rome's history and writing. The power and glory of Rome fascinated him, but when he looked at the city of the fourteenth century, he felt only anger. Medieval Rome was a shambles—a collection of miserable hovels and dangerous neighborhoods, surrounded by the crumbling temples, monuments, and aqueducts of the past. Wealthy families warred from their fortified towers, descending into the streets to murder their rivals and anyone who got in their way which on one dark day included Cola's own brother.

Di Rienzo was obsessed with the mission of restoring Rome to its former glory. In 1344 he began gathering friends and allies to overthrow the city authorities. After three years, he succeeded. Terrified of the mobs di Rienzo had at his back, the noble families fled to their country estates.

He had the support of powerful and important people, including Petrarch, a poet also fascinated by Roman history. Petrarch saw in di Rienzo a new Brutus—a fighter against tyranny (Marcus Junius Brutus had conspired to assassinate Julius Caesar in 44 B.C., believing Caesar a man determined to hold the powers of a dictator over Rome). Petrarch had made a lifelong study of Roman writers and had translated many of their manuscripts, several of which he had discovered himself. Although Rome had been a pagan city, he believed that it could serve as a model for pious Christians, and that the ancient books and monuments of Rome served as worthy inspirations for writers and artists of his own day.

Di Rienzo battled in vain. In 1354, the Roman mob turned against him, attacking and murdering him during a speech. His power in Rome had been fleeting, but the example of classical Rome endured for Petrarch and the generations that followed. Writing, art, sculpture, and architecture brought a Renaissance, or rebirth, of the ancient world of the Romans and Greeks. This creative flowering spread from Italy to the rest of Europe and brought forth the most famous works ever created on the continent.

The Renaissance in Italy

In the fourteenth century, scholars such as Petrarch and Poggio Bracciolini were combing the libraries of monasteries and cathedrals, where the ancient books of Plato, Aristotle, Livy, Vitruvius, Cicero and others had been copied down and preserved. Most of these books were written in Latin, the language of ancient Rome that still served as a universal language for the educated people of Europe. Some had been preserved by Arab scholars and had returned to Europe through the Moorish kingdom of Spain and the Islamic realms of the Middle East. Scholarship in the classics was further helped by the arrival of Greek scholars from the Byzantine Empire, who fled as the Ottoman Turks conquered their homeland in the middle of the fifteenth century.

A new scholarship emerged, as the books were studied and translated into the modern languages, such as French and Italian, that had evolved from Latin. In doing so, these scholars and editors were carrying out a revolution in thought. No longer were their efforts concentrated on the philosophy of Christianity, and the works of church fathers such as Saint Ambrose and Saint Augustine who had made the interpretation of the Bible their life's work. Instead, the ancient pagan authors and their approach to art and philosophy were found worthy of study. The doctrines of the Christian church that had dominated medieval society now competed with the sensibilities of ancient Greece and Rome.

In the fifteenth century the passion for ancient writers traveled from scholars to rulers. In describing the Florentine prince Cosimo de' Medici, the historian George Holmes wrote, "Cosimo … combined great wealth with a genuine interest in both classical literature and the arts. Cosimo fell under the spell of a belief in the spiritual value of truths to be gained from ancient literature.…"[1]

Humanists such as Cosimo de' Medici strived to lead a virtuous life, and to instill the virtues of ancient Rome and Greece in their own society through education and training of the young. A basic humanist education was believed to lay the proper foundation for studies in the fields of law and medicine and life as a worthy citizen. Wealthy families employed humanists to tutor their children, believing that knowledge of classical literature in its original language was the mark of a truly educated man or woman. Instead of learning and following church dogma, the scholars of the Renaissance posed questions and offered criticism of the church and of long-accepted public institutions. To the Renaissance humanist, the Middle Ages was a time of primitive art, science, and philosophy—a time that was drastically different, and less worthy, than their own.

This humanist trend in art began in Italy, with the works of Giotto di Bondi and Masaccio, who strived to portray the reality of the human form and human emotions in their works. It was present also in written works, such as the short stories written by Giovanni Boccaccio in his *Decameron*—a collection of one hundred tales of very human greed, lust, and folly. "Humanism" was taken up by the philosophers of Florence, such as Giovanni Pico della Mirandola, who combined many different faiths into a single all-encompassing worldview that he credited not to divine inspiration but to the creativity of authors, religious leaders, and philosophers.

At the same time, art and writing became more accessible. The streets and squares of Florence, Venice, Rome, and other cities displayed new monuments and statuary, created in the classical style. Latin texts were not just privileged to the few, but available to many through translation and through the new technology of printing. Books circulated widely in towns among aristocrats and members of the middle class. The works of an Italian author could be studied widely in Germany, France, the Netherlands, and England, while artists in those countries found it worth their trouble and expense to visit Rome and other Italian cities to study the art of the ancients. The French writer Michel de Montaigne wrote that "mixing with men is wonderfully useful, and visiting foreign countries to bring back knowledge of the characters and ways of those nations, and to rub and polish our brains by contact with those of others.... [There is] no better school for forming one's life than to set before it constantly the diversity of other lives, ideas, and customs."[2]

Artists of the Renaissance escaped their medieval role as craftsmen and artisans, who had been obedient to the rules of their guilds and working on commission from churches and wealthy patrons. Michelangelo Buonarroti and Leonardo da Vinci created an individual point of view and philosophy, and fully expressed this outlook in their works. The best artists took their place as equals of kings and popes, who vied for their artworks and their allegiance.

Many political and religious leaders took great pains to patronize artists and give their cities a cloak of classical grandeur meant to reflect the virtues of its leaders. Lorenzo de' Medici, the prince of Florence, and Popes Julius II and Leo X recruited the bests artists of their day, commissioned hundreds of important works, and paid their charges handsomely. The taste for art extended to the merchant class that strived to imitate the nobility by decorating their homes with paintings, sculpture, and architecture in the classical style.

State and Church in the Renaissance

The Renaissance was a time of artistic innovation and unruly, violent politics. The social and political turmoil was due to the expanding economy and the rise of new social classes. Merchants, artisans, and petty nobility all demanded attention to their interests. To quell this factionalism, the Renaissance prince ruled with arbitrary power, unchecked by elected assemblies or councils. He had the power to levy taxes, raise armies, arrest and punish opponents, and promulgate laws that in many cases served for his personal benefit. He relied on prestige and the fear of his subjects to secure his authority and, ultimately, establish a family dynasty. The tools of this task were diplomacy, military force, bribery, marriage, and assassination. A good prince knew the proper time and place to use all the weapons at his disposal; politics became not simply an exercise of power but a demanding profession at which certain men excelled and others did not.

Some Renaissance leaders emulated Rome in forming republics, and claiming that their power came directly from the consent of the people. The Renaissance republic, however, was far from a democracy. It was an oligarchy of leading merchants or nobles, who passed laws in assemblies and governed through councils, in which the term of office was brief, sometimes as short as two months. City republics, including Siena, Genoa. Florence, and Venice in Italy, controlled surrounding land and taxed its farmers, although granting no right of representation to peasants living outside the walls.

Secular power often vied with sacred authority, with the Catholic Church remaining the most powerful institution in Europe. The church offered eternal life to believers and threatened eternal damnation to sinners and heretics. It collected tithes and indulgences (remissions of punishment for sins) from practicing Catholics, took part in conflicts among the nations, and patronized artists and writers, who still dedicated many of their works to religious themes.

An Economic Rebirth

The Middle Ages waned as humanism flowered and as Europe experienced an economic revival. Safer roads and sea-lanes encouraged trade between southern and northern Europe. Banking houses, such as that of the Medici in Italy and the Fuggers in Germany, made loans and investments that increased credit and the circulation of money. The manufacturing of luxury goods, such as silk in Florence and glass in Venice, and foreign trade enriched even those without aristocratic titles to their name. The wealth accumulated by aristocratic families no longer was spent on defensive works and the arming of private militias. Instead, the display of art and good taste became paramount, and the patronage of a skilled artist in his court marked the Renaissance noble as someone worthy of admiration and respect.

The expanding economy and improving technology played a vital role in the innovations of Renaissance artists. In the words of Paul Johnson in his book *The Renaissance*:

> As wealth accumulated, those who possessed it gratified their senses by patronizing literature and the arts, and they were joined by sovereigns, popes and princes, who found ways of taxing the new wealth of their subjects. But wealth alone would not have produced the phenomenon we call the Renaissance.... Europe, in the later Middle Ages, was entering a period of ... intermediate technology. Especially in the Low Countries, Germany and Italy, thousands of workshops of all kinds emerged, specializing in stone, leather, metal, wood, plaster, chemicals and fabrics, producing a growing variety of luxury goods and machinery. It was chiefly the families of those who worked in these shops that produced the painters and carvers, the sculptors and architects, the writers and decorators, the teachers and scholars responsible for the huge expansion of culture that marked the beginnings of the early modern age.[3]

At the same time, scholars were taking to the roads, seeking out patrons and spreading their knowledge and their constant questioning of long-held ideas. The Medici brought the leading humanist scholars to their palaces in Florence, and employed them as tutors for their children. Niccolo Machiavelli, Sir Thomas More, and Desiderius Erasmus offered the example of Greek and Roman thinkers in solving practical problems of the world in which they lived. Universities in Bologna and Padua, Italy, educated the young in the new sciences of medicine and astronomy, and in the philosophies of Plato and Aristotle. Reasoning was applied to the study of ancient texts, which were studied in their original language, and the medieval scholastic method—which focused on theological debates—was gradually left behind. Students examined the works of ancient philosophers, rather than sacred texts, and concentrated on worldly poetry, ethics, rhetoric, and grammar. The cultural flowering in northern Italy inspired native sons such as da Vinci, Michelangelo, and Sandro Botticelli to incorporate classical concepts and mythology into their paintings and sculpture.

Renaissance art and humanism spread to the rest of Europe through the sixteenth century. The French kings Charles VIII and Francis I brought in artists and writers from Italy. The German painter and engraver Albrecht Dürer spent many years in Italy, observing the works of Italian painters and sculptors. The Hungarian king Matthias Corvinus hired Italian architects to raise new palaces and civic buildings in his capital of Buda. The Renaissance sensibility arrived in Spain, Portugal, Poland, Scandinavia, Bohemia, and northern Germany, having a far-reaching effect on writers and architects. The English Renaissance was marked by profound literature, including the plays of William Shakespeare, Ben Jonson, and Christopher Marlowe and the poetry of Edmund Spenser and John Milton, still considered among the greatest works ever written in the English language.

Reformation in the Church

The direct questioning of long-accepted ideas eventually reached the Christian hierarchy. In the late fourteenth century the church had been split in two, with rival popes claiming their title in Rome and in Avignon, a city of southern France. For a brief period, three men all claimed to be the true heirs to the Papacy, and the resulting bitter debate greatly damaged the church's reputation as an infallible medium between God and the faithful. Although the schism was resolved, the church fathers continued living as worldly, and immensely wealthy, monarchs, decorating their palaces with extravagant art, libraries, and collections and lusting for money, territory, and power to rival Europe's secular kings.

Repelled by the corruption of the church, dissidents began a close study of the New Testament and arrived at a novel concept of the church and the authority it should hold over believers. The German monk Martin Luther was inspired to create the doctrine of "justification by faith alone." Belief in Christian principles, according to Luther, should be left to the individual, and not made dependent on his good works or the purchasing of indulgences sold by the church. Luther broke with the Catholic Church and the pope, its leader, and created a Protestant sect that offered its believers a rival institution—one that served religious as well as political ends. The Protestant Reformation was taken up in northern Europe and in England, where King Henry VIII rode the wave of Protestantism to establish a new religion the Church of England and to declare independence from the pope and settle his divorce from his first queen, Catherine of Aragon. But Protestantism was resisted with great determination by Catholic rulers, such as the Habsburg leaders of the Holy Roman Empire. The conflict would endure for generations and bring about the devastating Thirty Years' War in the seventeenth century.

New Art and New Science

Renaissance artists developed a more naturalistic depiction of the world. The Florentine architect Filippo Brunelleschi virtually invented perspective, the accurate depiction of three-dimensional space on a flat, two-dimensional surface. Leonardo da Vinci, an artist of a later generation, gave his paintings great depth with the use of areas of varying light and shadow. Da Vinci also applied his personal study of human anatomy to figures in his painted canvases, and placed many of his subjects in a natural setting of mountains, rocks, and trees. In northern Europe, artists utilized new painting materials. In the

Netherlands, for instance, Jan van Eyck and others began using oil-based paints as a medium and stretched canvas as a surface—materials that gave painting a greater range of more naturalistic color. The Flemish painter Pieter Brueghel expanded the subject matter of art to the everyday world. Instead of saints and holy men, Brueghel depicted peasants, farmers, and ordinary city-dwellers going about their daily lives.

As artists took up new techniques and materials, mathematicians and astronomers relied on logic, reasoning, and observation to challenge long-held concepts of the natural world and the heavens. The earth lost its position as the center of the universe in the observations and writings of Nicolaus Copernicus, who rejected the geocentric system of the ancient Greek astronomer Ptolemy that had been accepted wisdom since the second century. The telescope allowed Galileo Galilei to observe the moons of Jupiter. Biologists began the systematic classification of plants and animals. Physicists explored the properties of gravity, light, and motion. A new approach to medicine and healing replaced traditional concepts of the "bodily humors" and the influence of the stars and planets on the human body. The scientific method employing observation, deduction, and reasoning, replaced the slavish devotion to the rigid systems of ancient Greek thinkers Aristotle (in the natural sciences) and Galen (in medicine).

Mannerism and the End of the Renaissance

The Renaissance began with a fragmented map of small states and principalities. It ended with a few national monarchies dominating the continent, after consolidating their authority of surrounding smaller and weaker principalities. Spain had been united by the marriage of Ferdinand II of Aragon and Isabella of Castile; the French kings extended their control to once-independent states such as Brittany. England under the Tudor dynasty, which ended with the reign of Elizabeth I, had become a major naval power and the seat of a far-flung colonial empire.

By the middle of the sixteenth century younger artists had fully accepted the naturalistic approach of the early Renaissance, and commonly took classical mythology as their theme. Artistic innovation slowed; the masterpieces of the High Renaissance, in the opinion of many, simply could not be surpassed. Artistic innovation declined as creators imitated their predecessors, adding only complex composition and exaggerated forms and emotion. Architects decorated their structures with elaborate forms and statuary, marring the simply geometrical beauty that Brunelleschi and others had strived for. This "Mannerism" spelled the end of the Renaissance and the "rebirth" of classical virtues, such as the balance of the elements of a picture or building. As humanism became a virtue of the past, a new period of Baroque art came into being, and the map of Europe was soon to be dominated by wealthy and powerful states such as France that saw their interests extended well beyond the old borders.

Over a short span of two centuries, men and women of the Renaissance created many of the world's greatest works of art, sculpture, architecture, music, and literature. Writers and scientists accepted the humanist worldview, while artists in the following generations imitated towering figures such as Michelangelo and Leonardo, and many others who still exert a powerful influence on artists of the twenty-first century. The Renaissance patron became a paradigm for collectors and connoisseurs of art in the modern world, while the princes of the age made a few halting steps toward the modern, republican form of government. In many ways, the history of modern Europe began with the Renaissance and still takes place in the shadow of its fascinating people and events.

Notes

1. George Holmes, *Renaissance*. New York: St. Martin's, 2006, p. 87.

2. Quoted in William James Bouwsma, *The Waning of the Renaissance, c. 1550–1640*. New Haven, CT: Yale University Press, 2000, p. 8.

3. Paul Johnson, *The Renaissance: A Short History.*, New York: Modern Library, 2000. pp. 15–16.

academies

Italian humanists and scholars revived the ancient Greek academy beginning in the middle of the fifteenth century. The academy was an informal group that met for teaching, discussion, lectures, readings, and debate. Most importantly for Renaissance scholarship, these groups were a way for newly discovered manuscripts to circulate in a time when printed books were rare and expensive commodities. The original *akademia* was a school founded by the Greek philosopher Plato in a sacred precinct outside the walls of Athens. In 1462, under the patronage of Cosimo de' Medici, the ruler of Florence, a Platonic Academy began meeting in a Medici villa. Medici appointed as head of the group the scholar Marsilio Ficino, whom Medici held in high regard as the collector and translator of many significant ancient-Greek texts. The Platonic Academy had its imitators in Florence and other cities.

By the middle of the sixteenth century, the academy was a common feature of large cities and university towns throughout Italy and was spreading to the rest of Europe. In some cases, the academies posed an apparent threat to the established authorities, in particular the Catholic Church. The Accademia Secretorum Naturae (Academy of the Secrets of Nature), began meeting in Naples in 1560. Under the direction of the scientist Giambattista della Porta, the academy welcomed members who wrote about or taught the natural sciences. The group soon came under suspicion by the Catholic Church from 1560, however, for teaching ideas counter to official doctrine. The academy was formally condemned by the church in 1580 and quickly disbanded.

To establish a Renaissance academy marked a patron or scholar as a person of advanced ideas, a devotee of the new humanism and scientific inquiry that was inspired by Greek and Roman writers. But in many cases the purpose of the academy was as much social as educational. Many academies had informal names, such as the *Confusi* (the Confused), the *Gelati* (the Frozen) and the *Infiammati* (the Inflamed). Members adopted rules, symbols, secret signs, and garb that proclaimed their membership and marked them off from the ordinary run of city-dwellers.

By the end of the sixteenth century, there were several hundred academies in Italy. In cities that were growing into regional and national centers, academies persisted and grew, while in minor cities they declined and eventually disappeared. Some academies concentrated on a single area of interest, such as language (the Florentine Academy) or art (the Academy of Design, also in Florence). The Accademia dei Lincei (Academy of the Lynxes) was founded in Rome in 1603 by Federico Cesi, who named this group for the sharp vision and observational powers of the lynx. The most famous member of this group was Galileo, who found support among its members for scientific theories found heretical by the church. This academy was revived in the eighteenth century and is now the national scientific institute of Italy. The Renaissance academy also has survived in France with the Academie Francaise and in England with the Royal Society, both founded in the seventeenth century.

SEE ALSO: education; Ficino, Marsilio; humanism; Medici, Cosimo de'

Agricola, Rudolf
(1444–1485)

A Dutch scholar and humanist, Rudolf Agricola was born in the town of Bafflo, in the Low Countries (comprising present-day Belgium, Luxembourg, and the Netherlands), as Rudolf Huysmann. He studied the works of Cicero and Quintilian at the universities of Erfurt in Germany and Louvain in Belgium, where he became a skilled critic and debater. In 1468, he began study at the University of Pavia, in northern Italy, and in 1475 joined the court of Duke Ercole of Ferrara, who also employed him as a musician. Agricola befriended the leading humanists of Italy, studying and disputing the works of ancient Latin and Greek authors. His first allegiance was to Germany and the Low Countries, however, and he left the duke's court in 1479 to spread his enthusiasm for classical authors to northern Europe. Agricola's restless life was typical of Renaissance scholars and humanists, many of whom wandered from one state, princely court, and university to the next in search of patrons and appointments.

Agricola is best known for his treatise *De inventione dialectica* (On Dialectical Invention), a manual for teachers of logic and rhetoric. After his death, this work grew popular with scholars and students throughout northern Europe. At the invitation of John of Dahlberg, the Bishop of Worms, in 1482 he became a lecturer at the University of Heidelberg in Germany. Over the years Agricola added Hebrew to his knowledge of Greek and Latin, and took up the study of the Old Testament in its original language. He traveled to Rome in 1485 to accompany the embassy of John of Dahlberg to Innocent VIII, the newly elected pope. On this journey Agricola was struck with an illness and died soon after returning to Germany.

Alberti, Leon Battista
(1404–1472)

An Italian painter, essayist, poet, philosopher, mathematician, musician, and architect, Alberti was one of the universal scholars of the early Renaissance. Born in Genoa, he was the illegitimate son of Lorenzo Alberti, a merchant of Florence who had been placed under a ban by the city. After moving from Genoa to Venice, Lorenzo Alberti established a bank. He soon entered a well-known academy in Padua run by Gasparino Barzizza, then studied law at the University of Bologna. He earned his doctorate in canon (church) law in 1428. Skilled in Latin, he wrote *Philodoxius* in Latin verse and fooled a publisher into claiming it to be the work of the ancient poet Lepidus.

In 1429 the Alberti family returned to Florence, where Leon began a study of architecture. He joined the Florentine court of Pope Eugenius IV, who had been driven out of Rome, and became canon of the cathedral of Florence. At some time in the 1430s he moved to Rome where, in 1432 he became an abbreviator, whose job was to prepare documents for the pope and his administration. Alberti wrote treatises on a variety of subjects. His works from this early period include *On the Advantages and Disadvantages of Letters*, biographies of the saints, and *Descriptio urbis*

Romae, a guide to the ancient ruins of Rome. In *De Componendis Cifris* he explores cryptography; in *I Libri della Famiglia* he instructs readers on domestic life and the education of children.

Alberti took a great interest in art and architecture, and was one of the first critics to write extensively on the emerging trends of the early Renaissance. His book *De Pictura* was a manual on the art of painting. Writing for the aristocratic patrons of art in Italy, Alberti expounded on the science of mathematics as the foundation for the art of painting. *De Pictura* contained a detailed explanation of linear perspective, as first developed by Filippo Brunelleschi, the architect who designed the dome of the cathedral of Florence. In Alberti's view, the true aim of the artist, whether painter or sculptor, was to create harmony by imitating nature to the best of his ability. This perspective represents an important break from the medieval sensibility that emphasized biblical themes and devotion to the Christian faith.

Alberti's appointments allowed him time and freedom to pursue his studies and writing. He was appointed as prior of San Martino in the town of Gangalandi, Tuscany, and in 1448 became the rector of the parish of San Lorenzo in Mugello. In 1447 he became an inspector of monuments for the pope, an appointment he held until 1455. He was employed as a musician as well as an architect, and was appointed by Pope Nicholas V to restore the papal palace and to design the Trevi Fountain. Alberti designed the facade of Santa Maria Novella in Florence, an important symbol of early Renaissance architecture, as well as the church of San Andrea and the church of San Francesco in Rimini, a work commissioned by Sigismondo Malatesta, the city's ruler. San Francesco married religious architecture with classical motifs, including a triumphal arch and a great dome in imitation of the ancient Pantheon of Rome (the dome was never completed, however, as work on the church ended with the death of Malatesta in 1466).

San Francesco was the first structure Alberti designed on the principles described in *De Re Aedificatoria*, his best-known work. *De Re Aedificatoria* held up ancient Roman architecture as a model for his Italian contemporaries, and propounded principles of architecture that Renaissance builders would follow for the next two centuries. Modeled on the work of Vitruvius, a Roman architect, *De Re Aedificatoria* covered town planning, building techniques, engineering, and aesthetics. The book spread the ideas of the Florentine Renaissance to the rest of Italy and remained a standard text on architecture until the eighteenth century. To historians Alberti represents the classic Renaissance humanist, the universal man who applied his talents and genius to many different fields and who strived to achieve a classical harmony and balance in his works.

SEE ALSO: architecture; Florence; humanism; Vitruvius

alchemy

Alchemy is the historic inquiry into the nature of matter, a research undertaken by many individuals in different cultures around the world. Alchemists were chemists, physicists, and philosophers, who had as their ultimate goal the transformation of ordinary matter into gold. They undertook experiments, speculated on the composition of matter, and wrote treatises that were notorious for their complexity and their obscure, often made-up language. During the Renaissance, the reputation of alchemy and alchemists declined. Some monarchs and church officials banned their work, and alchemists were subject to arrest and execution as magicians and heretics.

The ancient Greeks and Romans told of an ancient sage, the Egyptian Hermes Trismegitus, who was believed to have discovered many of the secrets of matter. Europe's medieval alchemists collected plants, minerals, soil, and other substances, combining them and altering them in a search of the "philosopher's stone," which would allow them to create gold or silver from more common materials. In the quest for curing illness, they also undertook a search for a universal panacea that would relieve deadly maladies and bring the sick back to health.

The alchemists applied principles of astrology, religion, and metaphysics in their books of formulas, attempting to arrive at universal principles that would explain their observations. Although they failed in their efforts to find the philosopher's stone, they did uncover useful compounds. In their research into the nature of light and illumination, the alchemist Hennig Brandt discovered phosphorus in 1669. Alchemical knowledge also contributed to industries such as dyeing, tanning, metalworking, and glassmaking.

Alchemists of the Renaissance drew on the medieval scholastic tradition of logic and argument, the knowledge of Arab herbalists and chemists, and the application of scientific research in industry and manufacturing. During the Renaissance, many philosophers and scientists wrote alchemical works. Sir Isaac Newton devoted more than thirty years to the investigation of alchemy, setting down experimental notes, transcribing and editing the works of others, and making up catalogs of sub-

A medallion bearing the likeness of Pope Alexander VI. THE LIBRARY OF CONGRESS.

stances and their properties. The German scientist Andreas Libavius wrote *Alchemia*, considered by many to be the first chemistry textbook. In some cases, the principles of alchemy provided a framework for influential systems of philosophy and knowledge. Paracelsus (1493–1541), considered by many as the greatest alchemist of the Renaissance era, created an all-encompassing chemical trinity, in which all earthly substances were grounded in salt (the principle of fixedness), sulfur (the principle of inflammability), and mercury (the principle of combining).

SEE ALSO: Paracelsus

Alexander VI
(1431–1503)

Pope from 1492 until 1503, Alexander VI is known as one of the most charismatic, but also one of the most corrupt and decadent, church leaders in history. He was born as Rodrigo Lancol in the town of Xativa, near Valencia, Spain. After his uncle Cardinal Alfonso Borgia was elected as Pope Calixtus III in 1455, Rodrigo adopted the family name of Borgia and was appointed as a bishop. Under his uncle's patronage he studied law at the University of Bologna and in 1456 was made a cardinal. He was widely praised for his ability, energy, and gift for conversation and persuasion. When Pope Innocent VIII died in 1492, Borgia emerged as a leading candidate to succeed to the Papacy. He won the election by bribing the cardinals who met to choose a successor and promising his rivals high positions in the Curia, the papal administration.

On reaching the papal throne, Alexander began conducting himself more like a worldly king than a religious leader, making alliances and fighting wars to increase the power and wealth of his family. In Rome he dealt with a crime wave by ordering criminals hanged in public and their houses razed. He ordered magnificent palaces to be built in the city, as well as the raising of fortifications and the improvement of roads and bridges. He invited scholars, musicians, and theater troupes to the papal court, and organized magnificent processions and ceremonies.

In the meantime, he bestowed high church offices on his favored children, three sons and a daughter by his mistress Vannozza dei Cattani. He made Cesare Borgia the archbishop of Valencia and Giovanni Borgia a cardinal as well as the Duke of Gandia, a realm in Spain. He arranged the marriage of his daughter Lucrezia to Giovanni Sforza.

While attempting to lay claim for the Borgias on papal lands, Alexander was opposed by the king of Naples, Ferdinand I, as well as the powerful Orsini clan of Rome. Ferdinand organized an alliance with Florence and Venice, while Alexander sought the help of Charles VIII, the king

of France, a monarch who had plans for the conquest of Naples. In 1493, however, Alexander made peace with Naples, arranging the marriage of his son Giuffre to a granddaughter of Ferdinand. In order to ensure his authority in Rome, Alexander created twelve new cardinals, and also bestowed the title of cardinal on his son Cesare.

On the death of Ferdinand I in 1494, Alexander allied again with Charles VIII and invited the French to invade Italy and conquer Naples. After the French army arrived, however, Alexander began to fear French domination of Italy and formed a league against Charles. This alliance defeated the French at the Battle of Fornovo. Alexander afterward sent his papal armies against the Orsinis, who remained his determined enemies.

Under Alexander's rule the papal administration became a ruthless agency of blackmail and murder. The church sold indulgences (remissions and pardonings of sin) as well as church offices to raise enormous sums of money, and the pope spent this wealth in supporting Cesare Borgia's military campaigns in northern Italy. While Rome became the scene of rampant violence, the Vatican itself was used as a luxurious place of entertainment and sumptuous orgies. Alexander also had a great appreciation for art, however, and brought the most renowned Renaissance artists of Italy, including Donato Bramante, Michelangelo Buonarroti, and Raphael, to work in Rome.

The last years of Alexander's life were spent in fighting a conspiracy among the Orsini and Colonna families against him. To defeat his opponents, Alexander swept members of the Orsini clan into dungeons while Cesare lured two of the plotters to a palace in the town of Senigallia, where the men were strangled. In August 1503, Alexander and Cesare suffered some form of mysterious poisoning at a Vatican banquet. Although Cesare survived, Alexander died a slow and gruesome death. By this time he was widely despised and feared; only four church officials attended his funeral Mass.

SEE ALSO: Borgia, Cesare; Borgia, Lucrezia

Alfonso V of Aragon (the Magnanimous) (1396–1458)

King of Aragon and Naples, and an important Renaissance patron of the arts and scholarship, Alfonso was the son of Ferdinand I of Aragon and the adopted son of Joanna II of Naples, who made him the hereditary king of her realm. This queen, who had no direct heir, allied with Alfonso against Louis III, a prince of Anjou, whom Alfonso defeated on the battlefield in 1421. In this way Naples, then one of the wealthiest states in Europe, was made part of the Spanish realm of Aragon. In 1423, however, Joanna and Alfonso broke off their alliance and in 1435 the queen abdicated the throne of Naples to Louis, who had the support of Pope Martin V.

To contest Naples, Alfonso hired the mercenary Braccio da Montone to lead his forces. Joanna's captain Muzio Sforza then defeated Alfonso and the queen officially named Louis III as her heir. After the death of Louis in 1434, Joanna named Rene of Anjou as her heir in her will. She died in 1435, leaving Naples as a prize for any ruler with the ambition and the manpower to capture it. Alfonso led his forces into Italy, capturing the important towns of Capua and Gaeta, but was then defeated and taken prisoner. A persuasive speaker, he convinced his captors in Milan to re-

lease him, then gathered another fleet and returned to Naples. He besieged the city in 1441 and finally captured it the next year. The pope formally recognized him as the king of Naples in 1443. Alfonso left the rule of Aragon to his wife and brother and lived in Naples. He beautified and improved the city, repairing aqueducts, paving streets, and building monuments. Alfonso introduced Italian Renaissance humanism to Spain and made Naples the center of the Renaissance by patronage of artists such as Francesco Laurana.

Alfonso founded the academy of Naples and commissioned from Laurana a triumphal arch for his entrance into the city in 1443, which formed part of the Castel Nuovo. An important patron of the arts and literature, Alfonso held the classical Roman writers in reverence and set an example for future princes of Italy, who considered patronage of great art and architecture a way of making their permanent mark on the states they ruled.

SEE ALSO: Naples

Alighieri, Dante (1265–1321)

Medieval poet who set his three-part work *The Divine Comedy* in Italian, breaking with the tradition of writing serious literary works in Latin, and who is considered the greatest poet of the Italian language. Born in Florence, Italy, he was a member of the minor aristocracy who traced their lineage to celebrated Crusaders and to the nobility of ancient Rome. Dante's clan sided with the Guelph faction, which supported the popes in their struggles with the Holy Roman Emperor. Dante was educated in monastic schools in Florence and also privately with Brunetto Latini, a renowned teacher of rhetoric. In 1289, he took part in the battle of Campoldino in

This fresco by Luca Signorelli depicts "Dante Meeting Manfred in Purgatory," a scene from the third canto of Dante's "Purgatorio."

which the Florentine Guelphs soundly defeated their rivals in the Ghibelline faction.

Dante was a devoted student of the ancient Roman poet Virgil as well as Cicero, a famous Roman politician and orator. Drawn to poetry, he studied the ancient Latin poets as well as the songs of the troubadours of Provence (southern France). He began composing love sonnets as a young man. An encounter with a young noblewoman, Beatrice Portinari, who struck him as an ideal of beauty and grace, inspired many of his poems. Her death at an early age in 1290 moved him to collect his poetry in *Vita Nuova*, or "New Life." The poems and prose passages of this book, which was completed by 1294, were written in Italian, and not Latin, and represent one of the earliest efforts by any Italian writer to express himself in the vernacular (everyday language) of his homeland.

Dante involved himself in the civil struggles that were then dividing Florence into two hostile camps. He joined the doctors and apothecaries guilds (guild membership was required for anyone who sought high public office), and a few years following the appearance of *Vita Nuova*, he became a member of the city council of Florence. When he traveled to Rome as Florentine envoy to Pope Boniface VIII in 1301, his opponents in the Guelph party who remained behind had him banished from the city, seized his property, and threatened him with execution should he ever return. For the remaining twenty years of his life, Dante lived in exile, wandering from town to town and never receiving a pardon from the city of Florence that would allow him to return. He lived in Verona, Bologna, and Paris, taking refuge in the homes of patrons and nobles who either admired his works or who shared his political beliefs. He became a supporter of Emperor Henry VII in the latter's drive to reunite the Italian city-states. In 1310 an invasion of Italy by Henry temporarily gave Dante hope for a return to Florence. These hopes were ended with the death of the emperor while on campaign in Tuscany in 1313. Dante's letters to Henry angered the Florentine leaders further; when the city offered him a pardon with certain strict conditions, Dante refused the offer and was afterward condemned to death.

While in exile, Dante wrote *De Vulgarii Eloquentia*, a treatise on Italian as a literary language, and *On Monarchy*, a work on politics in which Dante supported the idea of a king to unite and control the many squabbling political factions of Italy.

Il Convivio, or *The Banquet*, was a second collection of poems and commentaries. *The Divine Comedy*, which Dante began about 1306 and originally named simply *The Comedy*, tells the story of the author's imaginary voyage through Hell, Purgatory, and Paradise. The three books of the poem consist of more than fourteen thousand lines, contained within one hundred cantos. In the first two books of the work, he is guided by Virgil, the historical author of the epic poem *The Aeneid*; on the trip through Paradise he accompanies Beatrice, a distant love of Dante's youth to whom he dedicated all of his works. The poem is divided into three-line stanzas in a scheme known as *terza rima*, in which the first and third lines rhyme with the middle line of the previous stanza. *The Divine Comedy* is an allegory of an ordinary man's journey through life, and his striving to escape worldly sin and misery through reason, represented by Virgil, and the spiritual enlightenment and hope offered by God. Dante's work established the Tuscan dialect of Italian as a worthy language of poetry and other literary forms; the use of everyday language in his works and those of Giovanni Boccaccio greatly expanded the audience for poetry and prose. Dante's blend of religious and secular themes in his work also helped to bridge the medieval and humanist eras of European literature.

SEE ALSO: Boccaccio, Giovanni; Florence; literature

Anguissola, Sofonisba
(1532–1625)

A painter and portraitist, Sofonisba Anguissola was born in Cremona, Italy, the daughter of noble parents. She studied painting in Cremona and in 1554 traveled to Rome, where she met Michelangelo, who agreed to critique copies she made of his sketches. Social conventions prevented her from rendering mythical allegories or biblical subjects, which frequently contained nude figures, or large-scale historical works. As a result she specialized in portraits of family members and acquaintances in domestic settings. In 1559 she became a court painter for Elizabeth of Valois, the queen of Spain. At the royal court in Madrid she painted official portraits that found favor with the royal family as well as aristocratic patrons. King Philip II of Spain rewarded her with a generous pension. In 1580 she returned to Italy, settling in Genoa, where she set up a private studio and became one of the city's most prominent artists. As the first woman to win renown as a painter during the Renaissance, she inspired many younger women to pursue similar careers.

Anne of Brittany
(1477–1514)

Queen consorts of France and Duchess of Brittany, Anne was a wealthy patroness of Renaissance art and music who devoted her life to keeping Brittany independent of French control. Born in Nantes, a port city of the Breton coast, she was the daughter of Duke Francis II and Margaret of Foix. Brittany had remained independent of France even after the defeat of England by the French at the close of the Hundred Years' War. Although Brittany fought the French armies to a stalemate in 1488, by the Treaty of Verger that concluded this war Anne was not allowed to marry without the approval of the French king. The only surviving child of her parents, Anne inherited her father's title when he died in a riding accident and left no male heirs.

In the French kingdom the Salic law prohibited women from reigning; the arrival of an unmarried girl as the nominal head of Brittany set off a diplomatic crisis between Brittany and France. To head off the claims of the French, a marriage was arranged between the twelve-year-old Anne and Maximilian, the Habsburg emperor of the Holy Roman Empire, long an enemy of France. The wedding took place by proxy in December 1490, without the bride and groom actually meeting to take part in a ceremony; at the insistence of France the marriage was soon dissolved by a decree from the pope. The French king Charles VIII then began a siege of Anne's capital at Rennes, which ended with the city starving and capitulating and Anne agreeing to marry Charles. The wedding took place at the chateau of Langeais, in the face of angry protests from the Habsburg dynasty, which claimed the marriage to be illegal.

As a result of her marriage to Charles, Anne was crowned as the queen of France in February 1492. She gave birth to four children, all of whom died before reaching adulthood. When Charles died in 1498 Anne was married to his successor, Louis XII, but also returned to Brittany, where she allowed a parliament of representatives to meet. Although Louis claimed the right to govern her duchy, she defied French claims on Brittany until her death in 1514. She had two surviving daughters by Louis—Claude and Renee. By her will the duchy passed to her younger daughter Renee; however, Louis forced the issue of Breton independence by decreeing Claude as the rightful heir to Anne's title. By the marriage of Claude to Francis of Angouleme, who became King Francis I in 1515, Brittany passed on the control of France.

SEE ALSO: Charles VIII; Francis I; Maximilian I

An aerial view of Brunelleschi's "Il Duomo," the dome of the Cathedral of Santa Maria Del Fiore in Florence. THE BRIDGEMAN ART LIBRARY/GETTY IMAGES.

architecture

The architecture of the Renaissance drew on forms and techniques recovered from ancient Greece and Rome. This classical architecture came to light with the rediscovery of the Roman architect Vitruvius, whose book *On Architecture* revealed building techniques that had been lost in the Middle Ages. Vitruvius's work was translated into many languages and appeared in several new editions; *On Architecture* inspired new treatises by Renaissance writers striving to explain and inspire the use of classical proportions and harmony. These authors, including Leon Battista Alberti and Andrea Palladio, aspired to teach universal ideals, grounded in mathematics, classical philosophy, science, geometry and the art of perspective. They were translated and spread quickly throughout Europe as the taste for the classical ideal spread. By the time of the High Renaissance, appearance in the ancient style (*all'antica* in Italian) gave a church, private home, or palace the stamp of an aristocratic and intellectual elitism. Giorgio Vasari, in *The Lives of the Most Excellent Italian Painters, Sculptors, and Architects*, had the honor of coining the term *rinascita*, or "re-birth," a designation for the entire age of returning to classical ideals.

Italian architects were the first to abandon the medieval Gothic manner of designing sacred and secular buildings. The Italians saw the Gothic style as a strange and foreign importation, brought by northern barbarians and imposed on the heirs of the ancient Romans. Throwing off the old style was a point of pride; the education of many artists and architects included a pilgrimage to Rome to investigate and measure the remains of the ancient city. The work of Filippo Brunelleschi in Florence was an important harbinger of the new architecture of the Renaissance. Brunelleschi's architectural masterpieces included the Santo Spirito and San Lorenzo in Florence, and the dome of the city's cathedral. In the next generation, Donato Bramante, Giovanni Amadeo, Leon Battista Alberti, Andrea Palladio, Antonio da Sangallo, Raphael, and Michelangelo Buonarroti carried the classical ideal throughout Italy.

Their new style emphasized symmetry, the balance of different elements, and harmonious proportions. Plain surfaces and clear lines swept away the exuberant clutter of Gothic spires and sculpture. The classical arch and dome came into style; columns in the three ancient orders—Doric, Ionic, and Corinthian—gave the appearance of a classical temple, and revealed the basic geometry of a building. The facade and the interior of the building worked together, rather than being entirely separate elements as in the Middle Ages.

Church architecture was more consistent across the continent, with two major plans dominating—the basilica in the shape of a cross, with elongated nave and short transept, and the Greek cross. The Greek cross was admired for its balance and perfect proportions of the square and circle, but after the Catholic Reformation the church, in its effort to echo the virtues of the early Christians, returned to the traditional basilica plan.

Private architecture also assumed classical models. Roman homes, with severe street fronts, individual rooms coming off long corridors, and colonnaded interior courtyards, were imitated in majestic Renaissance palaces, with the Farnese Palace of Antonio da Sanagallo in Rome one of the best-known examples. Facades were regular and symmetrical, surmounted by a cornice, and centered on immense doorways that advertised the owner's wealth and prestige. The rooms were decorated with fresco paintings, another imitation of Roman style. Country homes adopted Roman features, such as grottoes, elaborate gardens, fountains, pools, and open-air courtyards.

Accompanying new ideas in architecture was the new science and art of town planning, which began to change Europe's urban landscape. Comprehensive plans cleared away the organic web of medieval streets and replaced it with logical grid plans (borrowed from Roman colonies), large and open public squares, and wide boulevards that served as an axis of traffic and commerce. Renaissance cities were also decorated with classical features such as columns, arches, and monumental statuary. The largest example of urban renewal was the city of Rome itself, where the dark and chaotic medieval neighborhoods were cleared away and the city knit together with wide avenues, with a practical purpose of accommodating the many religious pilgrims making their way to Saint Peter's Basilica.

Italian architecture and its classicism spread throughout the rest of Europe, where builders blended the new style with techniques and traditions of their own countries. Toward the end of the sixteenth century, classicism became an international idiom, used in the monumental buildings such as the Louvre palace in Paris, and the Escorial near Madrid.

The architecture of the sixteenth century used classical buildings as a mere starting point for new innovations. The leading figure of the new Mannerist style was Michelangelo Buonarroti, who designed the Campidoglio in Rome, a beautifully proportioned public square atop the Capitoline Hill, the heart of the ancient city. Churches and aristocratic palaces were built, structures that were unknown to the ancient Romans. In France, the Renaissance style was expressed in graceful chateaus, such as Chambord and Azay-le-Rideau, that replaced the fortresslike castles of the medieval age. In England, Inigo Jones applied classical design to royal palaces and private homes in the early seventeenth century.

SEE ALSO: Alberti, Leon Battista; Bramante, Donato; Brunelleschi, Filippo; Michelangelo Buonarroti; Palladio, Andrea; Vitruvius

Ariosto, Ludovico (1474–1533)

Italian poet whose *Orlando Furioso*, became one of the most famous literary works of the Renaissance. Born in the town of Reggio Emilio, the son of a military commander, Ludovico Ariosto moved to Ferrara while still a boy. He later studied law despite his preference for poetry. He was instructed in Latin and Greek by the scholar Gregorio da Spoleto, but on the death of his father in 1500 he became responsible for his nine siblings. Two years later, he became the commander of the town of Canossa.

As a young man, Ariosto found a needed patron in Cardinal Ippolito d'Este, who showed ignorance and contempt for his works and used him as a common servant. In 1516 Ariosto completed *Orlando Furioso*, an epic poem in forty-six cantos. He based the poem on *Orlando Innamorato*, an unfinished work of Matteo Maria Boiardo. It was a tale of romance and chivalry that borrowed themes and characters from the popular chansons de geste, epic romances of the medieval age. The poet takes on the role of a singing troubadour, describing the adventures of Orlando, a knight who fights the Saracens for the emperor Charlemagne and goes mad with love for the beautiful Angelica. In *Orlando Furioso* Ariosto showed great respect for chivalric poetry but also chided the chansons de geste for their old-fashioned attention to courtly manners. His work inspired several major poets to create imitations and leading painters to illustrate scenes from the poem.

Ariosto left the cardinal's household in 1518 and joined that of Alfonso I, the duke of Ferrara, whom he served as ambassador to Pope Julius II. The duke later appointed him governor of Garfagnana, a remote district in the Apennine Mountains. Ariosto was responsible for managing a lawless region infested with bandits, but had won such a reputation for his poetry that he was immediately released by a band of criminals after being kidnapped.

Known throughout Italy, Ariosto's poem found an even larger audience when it was published in its final form in 1532. Ariosto's other works include satires and stage comedies, including *La Cassaria* and *Il Suppositi*, modeled on the works of the ancient Romans Plautus and Terrence. The latter work was borrowed by William Shakespeare for his play *The Taming of the Shrew*.

SEE ALSO: Ferrara; Tasso, Torquato

Aristotelianism

Aristotelianism is the philosophy inspired by the Greek philosopher Aristotle, who was born in Stagira, a town of the Chalcidice region of northern Greece, in 384 B.C. A student of Plato, he founded the Lyceum, a school modeled after Platos' Academy in Athens. At the Lyceum, Aristotle instructed students in science, rhetoric, and natural philosophy. His most famous pupil was Alexander of Macedon, who established Greek lyceums in the many cities of Asia, the Middle East, and Africa that he conquered or founded. Medieval scholars began studying Aristotle's system of thought in the twelfth century, when his works were translated into Latin. Modern translations and the newfound interest in classical authors made the Aristotelian system a major branch of scholarship during the Renaissance.

Most of the writings of Aristotle that survived into the Middle Ages, and to modern times, were composed of teaching notes. They were written on scrolls that survived centuries of war, political chaos, and neglect to be preserved in European monasteries, where they were then transcribed and collected into editions, including *Nicomachean Ethics, Physics, Politics,* and *Poetics.* Aristotle's teachings were also preserved and studied by Islamic scholars, including Ibn Sina (Avicenna) and Averroes, whose commentaries spurred a revival of Aristotelian studies in Europe.

Aristotle attempted to encompass the entire natural world and all phenomena in his philosophy known as Aristotelianism, which included the studies of logic, rhetoric, poetics, natural science, politics, mathematics, and ethics. He classified all knowledge into a threefold system of science (*episteme*), conduct (*praxis*), and created works (*poesis*). Logic was the most important discipline as it provided a means of understanding science and the analytical processes through inductive reasoning.

Renaissance scholars throughout Europe presented Aristotle's theories as a foundation for studying the natural world and human conduct through the theoretical, practical, and productive sciences. Theoretical science (*theoria*) combined natural philosophy, or things that can be seen and are made up of matter, with the study of theology, mathematics, astronomy, and thought processes. Practical sciences analyzed ethics, politics, and human conduct. The practical sciences attempted to advance the cause of moral virtues, such as courage and moderation, by instilling such virtues in the young through education and then carrying them out through a well-reasoned system of laws and justice. According to Aristotle's teachings, the proper conduct and exercise of virtues will bring true happiness to society as well as the individual. The productive sciences included poetics, rhetoric, architecture, and medicine.

Aristotelianism further spread after the fall of Constantinople in 1453, when Greek exiles began arriving in western Europe.

For the first time, many of Aristotle's works were being studied in the original ancient Greek language that was slowly spreading with the revival of classical texts. In addition, translations were made into common languages such as Italian and French. New branches of Aristotelian studies were also forming, along with various schools of thought on how to organize Aristotle's texts and present his system of knowledge. Many of Europe's leading university lecturers devoted themselves exclusively to the study of Aristotle, with some strictly following the texts, and others applying the Aristotelian system to the ever-changing natural and social worlds they experienced. For example, Leonardo Bruni, an important translator of Aristotle's works, replaced the word-for-word translations of the medieval era with a freer translation more fit for study in Latin. Galileo Galilei and Philipp Melanchthon also incorporated Aristotelianism into their works. While some writers were content to simply annotate Aristotle's works, others probed deeper, posing questions and problems in an attempt to extract deeper universal meaning to their new systems of natural philosophy.

As the organizer of philosophical and scientific thought, Aristotle was the most important figure of the classical world for all Renaissance scholars, and his works provided the basic framework of all university studies. Aristotle's works were read in lecture halls in the three stages of *lectio* (lecture), *repetio* (repetition), and *disputatio* (disputation, or argument). The invention of printing in the mid-fifteenth century allowed Aristotle's works to be widely distributed to a literate public. Lavish print editions, with commentaries, indexes, and summaries along with questions for argument and examination, were the precursors to the modern school textbook.

SEE ALSO: Bruni, Leonardo; classical literature

Ascham, Roger (ca. 1515–1568)

A noted scholar of England, Ascham was born in Yorkshire and entered Cambridge University at the age of fourteen. He became so proficient in ancient Greek studies that he presented lectures on the subject to his fellow students, and won widespread admiration for his writing and speaking abilities. He completed his bachelor's degree at the age of eighteen and soon after was made a fellow of the university. Wearied by the constant study, writing, and lecturing, Ascham diligently applied himself as well to the sport of archery. His work *Toxophilus* was an essay on the manly, English sport, and imparted the lesson that practice, physical work, and sheer repetition is more useful in certain arts than mere theory. The essay, written in a straightforward English free of the pretentious language of other academics, won the favor of King Henry VIII, who granted Ascham a pension of ten pounds a year and hired him as a tutor to his daughter Elizabeth, later Queen Elizabeth I. Ascham instilled a love of the Greek and Latin classics in Elizabeth, and as a respected scholar he was appointed by Henry as a diplomat. He became Latin secretary to Queen Mary and continued in the position as secretary when Elizabeth succeeded her half sister to the throne of England. Ascham was a key figure in the teaching of classical literature in the English Renaissance. Late in his life he completed *The Scholemaster*, a famous treatise on the teaching of Latin.

SEE ALSO: Elizabeth I; Henry VIII

astrology

Astrology, the study of the planets and their position in order to predict future events, has its origins in ancient Babylonia. The basic principles of astrology as set out in the *Tetrabiblos* of Ptolemy, the Alexandrian astronomer of the second century, formed the basis of astrology as it was practiced in the Middle Ages. Planets, the "wanderers" of the night sky, were believed to have certain characteristics that had a corresponding affect on earth. Saturn, for example, was considered a cold, dry, and harmful planet, while the moon was viewed as warm, moist, and beneficial. The position of the planets relative to each other, and their motion along the ecliptic plane or zodiac, also came into play.

The complexities of this system made it a difficult and esoteric science, understandable only to educated men and out of the reach of commoners. An occult mystique surrounded astrologers, who seemed to have access to hidden knowledge of how the universe really worked. The church condemned astrology as heresy, and as the practice of magicians and charlatans. But astrology was strongly defended by medieval authors such as Guido Bonatti, the official astrologer of the city of Florence, who set out his opinions in the influential book *Liber Astronomicus*. At the mercy of a capricious natural world, and the workings of fate that were often difficult to explain, nobles and kings sought the assistance of astrologers, who promised to turn the wheel of fortune in their favor.

In the fifteenth century, the printing press began spreading astrology to a wider audience. In addition to his Bibles, Johannes Gutenberg produced almanacs that were widely imitated throughout Europe and that served to make the dangerous,

unpredictable natural world a little more predictable. Almanacs were calendars, with a schedule of holy days and saints' days, advice on planting and harvesting, weather forecasts, and prognostications of important events. Worldly predictions made almanacs suspect to kings and their ministers, however, and in many corners of Europe it became a crime to publish astrological data and predictions. The church remained adamantly opposed to astrology as an occult practice, and in 1586 Pope Sixtus VI condemned the practice in a famous papal bull (decree).

Nevertheless, nobles and royalty—and many of the popes—were devoted believers in astrology; many of them employed astrologers at their courts and made no important decisions without taking into consideration their advice. Important matters of state, and especially of war, never were decided without the advice of astrologers, who claimed to eliminate chance and misfortune with their complicated charts and obscure language. Lucas Gauricus was the official astrologer to Pope Leo X and Pope Clement VII. Philipp Melanchthon was a renowned German astrologer whose advice was often called upon. Catherine de Médicis, a queen of France, was devoted to astrology and employed Michel de Notredame, or Nostradamus, the most renowned astrologer of France. Nostradamus published an important work on astrology in 1555. At the respected universities of Pavia and Bologna, astrologers held professorships and vied with astronomers for student followers. Bologna, Milan, and Mantua were important centers of astrological research during the Italian Renaissance.

Traditional astrologers cast personal horoscopes based on the position of the planets at the time of one's birth. There were many variations of this practice. The English astrologer William Lilly practiced horary astrology: the prediction of events based on the time when a person poses a question, not when he or she is born. Lilly's accurate predictions gained him the support of King Charles II and a salary from the government of Oliver Cromwell. His predictions also got him in serious trouble with the authorities, who accused him of setting the 1666 Great Fire of London after predicting this event.

Astronomical observation brought about new theories of the true nature of the universe during the Renaissance; the Polish astronomer Nicolaus Copernicus theorized that the earth revolves around the sun, not the other way around. This heliocentric theory was a drastic change from traditional beliefs and initiated a gradual decline in the acceptance of astrology among scientists and philosophers. The philosopher Giovanni Pico della Mirandola was skeptical of astrology, but many astronomers, including Johannes Kepler and Tycho Brahe, offered their services as astrologers to nobles and princes. The influence of astrology among scientists waned at the end of the Renaissance and disappeared altogether in the Enlightenment, which followed.

SEE ALSO: astronomy; Brahe, Tycho; Melanchthon, Philipp; Pico della Mirandola, Giovanni

astronomy

Astronomy of the Middle Ages was grounded in the work of Ptolemy, a scientist of ancient Alexandria, whose work *The Almagest* set out the Ptolemaic system of an earth-centered universe. The Ptolemaic view was accepted by philosophers and sanctioned by the church, and his work was the foundation of studies and commentaries by the medieval scholars Georg von Peuerbach, Johann Müller (known as Regiomontanus), and Georg Joachim Rheticus. To verify their observations astronomers drew on the Alfonsine Tables that were set down in Toledo, Spain, in 1252, and that were based on the Ptolemaic system. The earth was the center of the universe around which the sun, planets, and stars revolved; the heavens were permanent and unchanging; a perfect harmony and balance existed in which, according to astrologers, celestial phenomena had their effect on events and people on the terrestrial globe.

As the skill of observers improved, however, the Ptolemaic system came under question. The Polish astronomer Nicolaus Copernicus, while using the Alfonsine Tables in 1504 in observing a conjunction of Mars and Saturn, found them inaccurate. Trusting in his own calculations, Copernicus began questioning the Ptolemaic system and concluded that a heliocentric (sun-centered) structure accounted more accurately for the motions of the planets. This theory was revolutionary and, in Copernicus's view, dangerous, as it questioned the accepted wisdom supported by the church for centuries. He did not allow his theory to circulate in print until the end of his life, although heliocentrism became a common topic of debate among clergy and scientists in the early sixteenth century. The Alfonsine Tables would be replaced by the Prutenic Tables of Erasmus Reinhold, which were based on the Copernican heliocentric universe.

In 1572, the Danish astronomer Tycho Brahe discovered a new star and, in 1577, a comet. Through these observations Brahe showed that the heavens were ever-changing, producing new objects and phenomena that were not accounted for in traditional astronomy. The invention of the telescope in the early seventeenth century allowed astronomers more accurate observations that led to improvements in the Copernican system. Using a telescope and colored lenses, in 1611 Christoph Scheiner observed sunspots—dark spots that appear at times on the sun—proving that the sun was a mutable body, and not a perfect sphere of fire or light. In studying the motion of Mars, Johannes Kepler concluded that the circular orbits of traditional astronomy were a mirage. Instead, according to Kepler, the planets moved in elliptical orbits, with the sun lying at one focus of the ellipse. According to Kepler's harmonic law, the orbital period of a planet varied with the distance of the planet from the sun. Astronomers would later use this law to calculate the dimensions of the solar system.

The complex equations theorized by Kepler and others replaced the fixed and unchanging doctrines of the past. Sir Isaac Newton introduced the law of universal gravitation, which explained the relationship between orbit and velocity. The Rudolphine Tables created by Tycho Brahe and Kepler in 1627 replaced the Prutenic Tables. Astronomy became a science, carried out through accurate observation. Renaissance astronomers dared to question traditional wisdom, even at the risk of losing their reputations and their lives. The Italian scientist Galileo Galilei, using a telescope, discovered the moons of Jupiter and the mountains and craters of the moon. For his theories on the nature of the solar system; and his discovery of worlds previously unknown, he was threatened by the Inquisition of the Catholic Church—a tribunal that punished heresy—and his works were censored. Nevertheless, the work of Galileo and others placed the tra-

ditional view of the heavens through a transformation, explaining the universe was a skill passing out of the hands of philosophers and the church and to a class of scientific specialists who rejected medieval traditions of astrology and religious doctrine altogether.

SEE ALSO: astrology; Copernicus, Nicolaus; Galilei, Galileo; Kepler, Johannes

Aurispa, Giovanni (ca. 1369–1459)

An Italian scholar and renowned book collector, Aurispa was born in the town of Noto, on the island of Sicily. In 1413 he traveled to the island of Chios, where he unearthed works by the ancient Greek scholars Sophocles, Euripides, and Thucydides that were still unknown in western Europe. On two occasions he visited the city of Constantinople, capital of the Byzantine Empire, to search for ancient Greek books and manuscripts. He gathered 238 volumes before returning to Italy in 1423, but finding himself without financial means, he had to pawn many of his finds. Among these ancient works were the plays of Sophocles and Aeschylus, the ancient epic known as the *Iliad*, and works of Xenophon and Plato. Aurispa taught Greek in Bologna and Florence, Italy, and became secretary to Pope Eugene IV in 1441. He was kept in this post by Eugene's successor, Nicholas V. Aurispa produced several Latin translations of ancient Greek writers, including Archimedes. He was a key figure in the rediscovery of classical literature in Renaissance Italy.

Austria

Austria during the Renaissance was a duchy of central Europe that had importance as the seat of the Habsburg dynasty.

In 1273, Count Rudolf of the Habsburg family was appointed king of Germany. Five years later his sons Albert and Rudolf became the rulers of Austria, a small domain along the Danube River. Habsburg archdukes reigned in Austria for more than six hundred years afterward. They brought new territories under their control through marital alliances. In the fifteenth century the Habsburg king Frederick III became Holy Roman Emperor, and from that point on the Habsburgs remained in possession of this title. Archduke Maximilian married a princess of Burgundy in 1477, bringing that wealthy realm of northwestern Europe under the Habsburgs' control. Through another marriage, Maximilian's son Philip reigned in Castile, Aragon, and Italian possessions. By the time of Emperor Charles V, the Habsburgs also were in control of Bohemia and Hungary, making their realm the largest in Europe.

Patronage of artists and scholars by the Habsburgs made Vienna an important center of the Renaissance in central Europe. The royal court attracted noted artists, sculptors, architects, and composers. Many Dutch composers were employed at the sixteenth-century courts of the Habsburgs. One of the notable Renaissance humanists to make his home in Austria was Enea Silvio Piccolomini, who was the royal poet laureate of Emperor Frederick III, later the emperor's secretary, and finally Pope Pius II in 1458. The University of Vienna, under the leadership of Conradus Celtis, drew scholars from throughout the empire. Celtis had the works of ancient authors translated into German, staged ancient Roman plays in Vienna, and founded a college for poets. He had come to the capital at the invitation of Maximilian I, who also commissioned work from Albrecht Dürer and several other German

masters. The Schloss Neugebaude, an imperial villa, and the Hofburg, the Habsburg palace in Vienna, were built in the classical style then popular in Italy.

SEE ALSO: Dürer, Albrecht; Habsburg dynasty

Aviz, House of

A ruling dynasty of Portugal that assumed power in 1385 with the coronation of Joao I, master of the Order of Aviz, as king. The Order of Aviz, symbolized by a green cross, was founded in the twelfth century to contend with the Moors, Islamic occupiers of the Iberian Peninsula. Under the kings of Aviz, Portgual became one of the wealthiest realms in Europe. Portuguese mariners explored the coasts of Africa, Asia, and the western hemisphere, laying claim to Brazil in South America and trading ports in the East Indies, India, and China.

The second ruler of the dynasty, Duarte I, the Philosopher, supported the founding of a school of navigation by his brother, Prince Henry the Navigator, at Sagres. Duarte allied Portugal with England by marrying Philippa of Lancaster, daughter of the English prince John of Gaunt. His son, Afonso V, succeeded him in 1438 at the age of six. After coming of age, Afonso attacked and conquered several important ports in North Africa, earning the nickname of "the African." Joao II, coming to power in 1481, dealt with rebellious nobles in his country who were being supported by the Spanish realm of Castile. To put an end to the conspiracies, Joao summoned three noblemen to his royal palace and murdered them.

Manuel I reigned from 1495 until 1521. This was an important time for overseas trade and the establishment of Portugal's far-flung colonial empire. Portuguese explorers traveled to Brazil, discovered routes across the Indian Ocean, and staked Portuguese claims in India. The style of Portuguese architecture known as Manueline was named after this illustrious king. Under Joao III, called the Grocer King, Portugal sent missions to China and Japan, colonized Brazil, and secured a monopoly in the rich trade of cloves, nutmeg, and cinnamon from the East Indies. Joao's successor Sebastian I died fighting in Morocco in 1578.

Sebastian never married and died without an heir, the vacancy leading to a violent struggle over the throne of Portugal. Anthony, grandson of Manuel I, claimed his right to inherit the throne in 1580 but was opposed by Philip II, king of Spain and a member of the Habsburg dynasty. Philip defeated Anthony at the Battle of Alcantara, after which Anthony retreated to the Azores Islands and Philip assumed power, ending the reign of the House of Aviz. Until 1640 Portugal and Spain would be united under the rule of the Habsburgs.

SEE ALSO: Henry the Navigator; Manuel I; Philip II; Portugal

Bacon, Francis
(1561–1626)

English philosopher and essayist, and a key voice and advocate of the Scientific Revolution that followed on the heels of the Renaissance. Bacon was born in London, the son of Sir Nicholas Bacon, Queen Elizabeth's Lord Keeper of the Great Seal, and Ann Cooke Bacon. He was the nephew of William Cecil, the chief counselor to the queen, and his family connections prepared him from an early age for a public career. At the age of twelve, he entered Trinity College, Cambridge, where he studied Aristotelianism but found it lacking in objectivity. In 1576 he traveled to France, where he stayed until 1579, upon the death of his father. Unable to prosper from his father's meager legacy, he studied law at Cambridge and became a barrister in 1582.

Bacon took a seat in the English parliament in 1584 and began seeking advancement and the patronage of the queen. His opposition to a scheme for raising taxes, however, brought him into Elizabeth's disfavor. He improved his prospects by allying himself with the Earl of Essex, a favorite of Elizabeth, and serving as Essex's counselor. In 1596 Bacon was appointed counsel to the Queen, but his financial situation did not improve and in 1598 he was arrested for debt. After a falling out with the Earl of Essex, Bacon was appointed to investigate Essex on the suspicion of treason. Essex was executed in 1601; Bacon explained his findings in the essay "A Declaration of the Practices and Treasons of the Earl of Essex."

On the death of Queen Elizabeth in 1603, James I, the first of the Stuart dynasty, ascended the throne of England. Bacon earned recognition from the crown for his help in condemning the Earl of Essex. He was bestowed a knighthood in 1603, became a solicitor in 1607, and was appointed clerk of the king's Star Chamber in 1608. In 1613 James named him attorney general, and in 1616 Bacon became a member of the king's Privy Council. In 1618 he attained the post of Lord Chancellor, in which he advised the king on

English politician and philosopher of science Sir Francis Bacon.

economic and political matters and also advocated the union of England and Scotland under a single monarch. At the same time, his continuing financial troubles brought him under suspicion of corruption. In 1621 Bacon was investigated and then forced out of office for taking bribes. He was fined forty thousand pounds, imprisoned in the Tower of London for several days, and banned from holding any official position in the future. After this fall from grace Bacon retired from public life and turned to studying and writing.

Bacon's works include *The Colours of Good and Evil, Meditationes Sacrae, The Advancement of Learning* (1605), and *Novum Organum*, published in 1620. His most famous work is a book titled *Essays*, a collection of writings that he began assembling in 1597 that span thirty years. In his essays and books Bacon describes a new method of deductive reasoning, urging scientists and philosophers to proceed on the foundation of observable facts instead of from popular religious or philosophical doctrines, whether they originated in the ancient or medieval world. Further, the scientist should avoid certain habits of mind, which Bacon called "Idols," that arose from their own nature, from their use of language, from their upbringing, and from the society in which they lived. In his view a rigorously factual investigation and controlled experiments would eventually lead to the discovery of general principles that governed all natural phenomena. In *De Augmentis Scientiarum*, published in 1623, Bacon separates duty to society from duty to God, and denies the idea that universal principles should govern human actions in their social, nonreligious lives. He recognizes the separation of science and religion, maintaining that faith could not be justified through the intellect and that scientific investigation could not

proceed on faith. This philosophy marked the end of an age in which strict religious doctrines bound European thinkers, writers, and scientists; and when philosophers constructed elaborate but artificial systems to explain the evidence of their senses.

New Atlantis is a novel Bacon wrote in the 1620s in which he creates a utopian society founded on scientific principles that bring about a variety of useful inventions: a way to preserve food by chilling it, a system of controlling the air temperature within closed rooms, and a method of speaking across long distances. Although he was no scientist, throughout his life Bacon sought to apply his philosophical principles to experiments to the best of his ability, using materials at hand. In 1626, while traveling on a cold winter's day, he was inspired by a new idea for preserving food. He had a woman kill and clean a chicken that he then stuffed with snow. Falling ill with pneumonia, he then ate the chicken in an attempt to ward off the illness and soon came down with a fatal case of food poisoning.

Bacon enjoyed little popularity during his lifetime, but his reputation grew posthumously through the seventeenth century, when many scientists relied on the philosophical foundation he had laid in their pursuit of scientific truth. The establishment of England's Royal Society in 1660 was largely inspired by Bacon's philosophy, which advocated benefitting the general public welfare through the advancement of science.

SEE ALSO: Aristotelianism; Elizabeth I; James I of England

Barocci, Federico (ca. 1526–1612)

One of the leading Italian artists of the early Baroque period. Born as Federico

Fiori in Urbino, he studied with his uncle, Bartolomeo Genga. Barocci moved to Rome in his twenties and, while training with a minor painter named Taddeo Zuccaro, came under the influence of Raphael. Barocci also studied the works of Correggio, who used warm colors in a graceful, flowing design. In Rome Barocci learned the demanding skill of copper engraving and also became a portraitist and fresco painter. In Rome he was commissioned to paint frescoes at the Vatican and also completed a *Last Supper* in the church of Santa Maria Sopra Minerva. While decorating a ceiling at the Vatican for Pope Pius IV, however, he came down with a case of food poisoning that he feared was a deliberate attack by jealous rivals.

Soon afterward Barocci retreated to Urbino, where for the rest of his life he remained under the protection and patronage of the Duke of Urbino, Francesco Della Rovere, for whom Barocci did a striking portrait. Barocci was an extremely slow and methodical painter, but his works show soft lights, a confident ability to draw and position figures, a full range of colors and an ingenious use of light, much in contrast to the darker and more somber works of many of his contemporaries, including the more widely acclaimed Michelangelo da Caravaggio. Among art historians, Barocci is known as much for his sketches and drawings as for his paintings, as the studies and cartoons he completed before putting his brush to canvas are as skillfully performed as his full-scale completed works. For his sketches, Barocci used the new medium of colored pastel, which has remained a favorite method of modern painters.

Devoted to the cause of the Catholic Church, Barocci was an ardent supporter of the Counter-Reformation, which was an attempt by the church to return Protestant lands to Catholic control. He became a member of the Capuchin religious order and completed two major altarpieces for the mystic preacher Saint Philip Neri: *The Visitation* and *The Presentation of the Virgin*. Barocci's *Martyrdom of St. Vitale* became a strong influence on Baroque painters of Italy and northern Europe in the age following his death.

SEE ALSO: Correggio; Michelangelo Buonarroti; Raphael

Bartolommeo, Fra (1472–1517)

Artist born in Savignano di Prato, near Florence in Tuscany. Showing talent as a boy, Bartolommeo was apprenticed to the workshop of Cosimo Rosselli, where his first works were influenced by Piero di Cosimo, Domenico Ghirlandaio, and Fra Filippo Lippi. He also made an intense study of the works of Leonardo da Vinci. In 1498 he created a famous portrait of Girolamo Savonarola, the Dominican friar who denounced in his sermons what he proclaimed to be the vain and degenerate works of Florentine artists. Bartolommeo took Savonarola's sermons to heart and brought many of his own works to the bonfires where books, art, and sculptures were destroyed. He joined the Dominican order in 1500, and became a monk in the convent of San Marco in Florence. He gave up painting until 1504, when his superior ordered him to run the monastery's workshop. Under the instruction of Raphael, he studied the use of perspective and color. He completed altarpieces for cathedrals in Lucca and Florence, Italy, and Besancon, France. In 1513 he moved to Rome, painted *Peter and Paul* and *St. Mark Evangelist*, considered by many to be his finest work. His paintings show a mastery of color, light, and texture, and he was especially masterful in painting clothing and intricate drapery.

Battiferra degli Ammannati, Laura (1523–1589)

Italian poet, known for several volumes of her writings as well as her marriage to Bartolomeo Ammannati, a renowned sculptor who worked closely with Michelangelo Buonarroti. She was born in Urbino, the illegitimate daughter of a wealthy man of the church, Giovanni' Antonio Battiferri, and his concubine, Maddalena Coccapani. First married to a professional musician, Vittorio Sereni, Laura was widowed in 1549. Some time in her youth she had met Ammannati, an up-and-coming artist who carried out commissions for the church and for the duke of Urbino, who hired him to decorate a country villa in the Umbrian town of Pesara.

Laura Battiferra's marriage to Ammannati was arranged by her influential father and took place in the spring of 1550, not long after the death of her first husband. The couple lived in Rome, where he worked on several important commissions. After the death of his patron, Pope Julius III, they moved to Florence, where Ammannati was taken into the court of Cosimo de' Medici. There, Battiferra earned her reputation as a poet. In 1560 her poems appeared in the *First Book of Tuscan Works*, a collection of several different poets from Florence and its surroundings. Inspired by the Italian poets Petrarch and Dante Alighieri, and the ancient Roman poets Ovid and Virgil, she wrote more than three hundred sonnets in which she used great skill in language and a wide-ranging knowledge of philosophy, mythology, and literature. A pious woman and a devout Catholic, she also created Italian translations of the penitential psalms in the 1560s and donated much of her wealth to the Society of Jesus, or the Jesuits.

Bellini, Gentile (ca. 1429–1507)

The son of Jacopo Bellini, Gentile was one of the most renowned Venetian painters of the Renaissance. Trained by his father, he closely followed Jacopo's painting style in his early works. In 1474 he began work on a cycle of historical paintings that would decorate the Chamber of the Great Council in the Doge's palace in Venice. For the Scuola Grande di San Lorenzo, Bellini painted another grand cycle, including *The Procession of the True Cross in the Piazza San Marco*, a work completed in 1496. These huge canvases contain hundreds of figures and highlight the splendor of the city of Venice. Bellini also made Venice the setting for paintings he made for the religious confraternity of San Giovanni Evangelista. These works, which include *Procession in St. Mark's Square* and *Recovery of the Holy Cross*, celebrate a holy relic owned by the school.

In 1479 the Doge of Venice sent Bellini as a diplomat to the court of Muhammad II, the sultan of the Ottoman Empire, who had requested a skilled painter. Muhammad defied Islamic traditions forbidding representations of the human form by having Bellini paint his portrait, a lifelike picture that became one of Bellini's most famous works. Bellini's reputation in the east gained him prestige in Venice and imbued his later works with elements of Islamic artistic style. Bellini was also known for his portraits of the doges of Venice and other nobility, including Caterina Cornaro, the queen of Cyprus.

Bellini, Giovanni
(ca. 1431–1516)

Considered the master of Venice Renaissance painting, Giovanni is the brother of Gentile Bellini and the son of Jacopo Bellini. He began painting in his father's workshop and was hired to work with his brother at the School of San Marco.

Bellini was hired by the Doge of Venice to manage the artwork and decoration of the ducal palace. He worked to preserve and restore paintings within the palace and painted an original series celebrating the history of medieval wars between the Holy Roman emperors and the popes. Bellini also executed many famous, richly detailed altarpieces in churches in Venice and Vicenza. Working in the new medium of oil paints, he was able to infuse a wider range of color and to shade one hue carefully into the next. A master of landscape art, Bellini added lush and beautifully detailed natural scenes as backgrounds to his subjects, a talent that was widely copied in the Venetian school and in particular by the painters Titian and Giorgione.

Bellini, Jacopo
(ca. 1400–1470)

A painter of Venice, Bellini was the elder of an important family of artists. His two sons Gentile and Giovanni also emerged as prominent artists; his nephew Leonardo Bellini was a painter of manuscripts. His daughter Nicolosia married Andrea Mantegna, one of Bellini's pupils and a noteworthy artist in his own right.

Jacopo Bellini was the son of a pewterer. He was born in Venice, where he studied with Gentile da Fabriano, a famous painter who had workshops in Venice and Brescia. In about 1414, Bellini followed Fabriano to Florence. While Bellini was still a student, classical art was inspiring several mature Florentine artists of the time, including Masaccio, Donatello, Lorenzo Ghiberti, and Paolo Uccello. This new approach left a permanent mark on Bellini and on the art and architecture of Venice.

After his apprenticeship Bellini returned to Venice, where by the late 1420s he was master of his own workshop. He swiftly established himself as the most renowned painter in the city. He was commissioned by the city of Verona to paint a large *Crucifixion* for the city's cathedral, a work that was later destroyed. In 1441, he entered and won a competition with the artist Antonio Pisanello to create a portrait of Leonello d'Este, the marquess of Ferrara. He designed an altarpiece for the funerary chapel of the Gattamalata family in Padua and also did large-scale works for two Venetian confraternities, San Giovanni and San Marco. All of these works greatly enhanced Bellini's reputation and all of them disappeared or were destroyed after his death. Art historians believe that his surviving painting *Sts. Anthony Abbot and Bernardino of Siena*, which is now housed in Washington's National Gallery, made up part of the Gattamalata altarpiece.

Bellini's works straddle the Late Gothic and Early Renaissance styles. He painted icons of the Madonna in the traditional Byzantine style that was popular for centuries in Venice. Although he held to this older style in depicting figures and drapery, and in the use of gilding, under the influence of the Florentine artist Leon Battista Alberti, Bellini also introduced the new technique of one-point perspective into his works. He trained younger artists, including Andrea Mantegna, in these new techniques that gave paintings depth and volume they had lacked in the Gothic style.

Two of Bellini's notebooks, containing more than two hundred sketches, were even better known to contemporary artists than his paintings. Left to his sons in Bellini's will, they were used for generations by Venetian artists as models in classical and biblical themes and as studies in techniques of perspective.

SEE ALSO: Bellini, Gentile; Bellini, Giovanni; Mantegna, Andrea

Bentivoglio, Giovanni II (1443–1508)

Ruler of the Italian city of Bologna who made important improvements to the city and reigned over a splendid Renaissance court. He was the son of the city's chief magistrate, Annibale I Bentivoglio, who was murdered in 1445 at the hands of a rival, Battista Canneschi. With Annibale's son still too young to rule the city; the people of Bologna sent to Florence for Annibale's cousin Sante, who reigned until his death in 1463. Then twenty years of age, Giovanni made himself *signore*, or lord of the city. He put his skill as a military commander to use on behalf of the more powerful cities of Florence, Naples, and Milan.

Bologna's court flourished during Bentivoglio's reign. He commissioned paintings for churches and civic buildings and also ordered the building of the Palazzo Bentivoglio, a magnificent town hall. In 1506, Bentivoglio was excommunicated and deposed by Pope Julius II, who had designs of his own on Bologna. He fled the city at the approach of the pope's army. After his sons attempted to retake the city, the citizens of Bologna rebelled against him and destroyed his property.

Bentivoglio was then captured by the forces of the French king Louis XII, and died in Milan as the king's prisoner.

SEE ALSO: Julius II

Boccaccio, Giovanni (1313–1375)

Born in Florence as the illegitimate son of Boccaccio de Chellino, a merchant, Giovanni Boccaccio felt a strong ambition to become a poet from a young age. His father was employed by the Bardi banking house; he tutored his son in Latin and intended to make him a man of business. In about 1328 father and son traveled to Naples, where Giovanni trained as a banker while his father served the king as an adviser in financial matters. This apprenticeship lasted six years and left Boccaccio with an ever-stronger desire to study classical literature and write poetry. Through his father's position at the Neopolitan court he met philosophers, writers, and scientists, and also developed expertise in the subject of classical mythology.

Boccaccio found an early inspiration in his unrequited love for a young noblewoman, whom he first saw on Holy Saturday 1336 in the Church of San Lorenzo in Naples. Named Fiammetta in his works, she was the daughter of the king of Naples, whose high-born position and marriage drove Boccaccio to write *Fiametta Amoroso*, an account of his frustrated passion. He also wrote *Filocolo*, a medieval romance on unrequited love that describes in vivid detail the people and society of Naples.

Although he was schooled in the classics and in Latin and Greek, Boccaccio felt at home in his native tongue and with the popular poetic forms of Italy. His *Filostrato* is a long poem composed in *octavo*, an eight-line scheme from the island of Sicily that was popular with singers and common Italian poets. Describing the tormented jealousy of a young lover, Troilus, this poem represents the first time any author had attempted to make the Italian language, and the *octavo* form, an element of serious literature. Both Geoffrey Chaucer and William Shakespeare borrowed the characters and story of *Filostrato* to create important works.

In 1340, with his father in dire financial straits due to the bankruptcy of the Bardi company, Boccaccio returned unhappily to Florence. There he wrote *Ameto*, an allegorical romance in *terza rima*, the form of three-line stanzas that was employed by Dante Alighieri in *The Divine Comedy*. With this epic poem, Boccaccio was maturing as a writer, creating more serious works with great psychological insight. In the *Elegy of Lady Fiammetta* he describes the plight of a woman abandoned by her lover and overcome by despair. The *Ninfale Fiesolano* is considered by many as his finest work of poetry.

Boccaccio traveled to Ravenna in 1346 and returned for a short time to Naples. By 1348 he was once again in Florence, where the Black Death—the bubonic plague that struck Europe in the fourteenth century—had arrived to claim more than half the population. The plague inspired Boccaccio's *Decameron*, a book of one hundred short tales told by a company of young men and women who take refuge in the countryside to avoid the plague. In the *Decamaron*, the company decides on a new theme each day that is then expounded and explored in stories told by each person. The stories cover the entire range of human experience and emotion; some are lighthearted, bawdy comedies while others relate the tragic and serious consequences for all-too-human desires and weaknesses. The cast of characters includes fools, clowns, heroes, villains, artists, monks, nobles, and merchants, all subject to the strange whims of fate and all struggling to apply reason and prudence to the situations they face.

The *Decameron* soon gained a wide readership throughout Europe, although the author himself later stated his regrets for having written it. In 1350 he hosted Francesco Petrarca, or Petrarch, in his home in Florence. Petrarch, a scholar and Latin author, had a strong influence on Boccaico, who had begun an encyclopedic work on classical mythology. In the following years, at the urging of Petrarch, he wrote a biography of Dante and helped to introduce Homer, the ancient Greek author of the *Iliad* and the *Odyssey*, to the readers of Florence. He also wrote a long series of biographies, *On Famous Women* and *On Famous Men*. In 1362, a monk related a prophecy of imminent doom to the author, who resolved to give up studying and writing in favor of the consolations of religion. In his later years he served Florence as a public lecturer on the works of Dante and as an ambassador to Prussia, Milan, and the papal court at Avignon. After failing to secure a position at the court of Naples, he returned to his native Tuscany to live out his years in the town of Certaldo.

In the *Decameron* and his poetry Boccaccio's ambition was to make Italian a literary language—equal to Latin in descriptive and expressive power. Although he was grounded in the ideas of the medieval period, he abandoned allegory for realism, and the very human outlook of his works, particularly the *Decameron*, portends the humanistic outlook of the Renaissance, when the traditional forms of epic poetry and chivalric romance were gradually left behind for the more personal expression of plays, lyric poetry, and novels.

SEE ALSO: Dante Alighieri; Florence; humanism; Petrarch

Bohemia

Kingdom of central Europe and a leading northern center of literature and scholarship during the Renaissance. The name of Bohemia comes from the Boii, a tribe of Celts that inhabited this region in the time of the Roman Empire. After the fall of the western Roman Empire in the fifth century, Bohemia was settled by Slavs from the east. The Przemyslid dynasty established itself with the reign of King Boleslav I in the ninth century, when the people of Bohemia converted to Christianity. From about this time, the kings of Bohemia were subject to the ultimate authority of the Holy Roman emperor, a fact that led to a number of religious and political conflicts during the Renaissance.

After the invasion of the Mongols in the thirteenth century, the western and northern borderlands of Bohemia were settled by large numbers of Germans. In 1310, King John I established the Luxembourg dynasty. Bohemia became an important center of learning in the middle of the fourteenth century with the founding of the University of Prague during the reign of Charles IV. Charles ascended to the throne of the Holy Roman Empire and brought Bohemia its greatest success, controlling several regions of Germany, the duchy of Luxembourg, Moravia to the east, and Silesia in what is now southern Poland.

Bohemia's tradition of scholarship and religious tolerance was put to the test early in the fifteenth century, when Jan Hus, the rector of the University of Prague, began expounding a doctrine of defiance of the Catholic authorities. Invited to the Council of Constance, Hus was taken prisoner, tried, and burned at the stake for his heretical views, a punishment that was carried out on the orders of Emperor Sigismund. The death of Jan Hus inspired a violent rebellion in Bohemia, known as the Hussite Wars, and also served as an inspiration to the Protestant movement of Martin Luther in sixteenth-century Germany. Although the anti-Catholic forces were eventually defeated, Bohemia decreed freedom of religion within its borders in a document known as the Basel Compact.

In 1526 with the death of King Louis in battle against the Turks, Bohemia was joined to the Habsburg Empire of Austria under its new king, the Habsburg monarch Ferdinand I. The Catholic emperors, as kings of Bohemia, often found themselves at odds with their subjects over religious doctrine. One such conflict between King Ferdinand II and the Protestants of Bohemia touched off the Thirty Years' War that would devastate central Europe from 1618 until 1648.

Bohemia was a nation quite open to the new artistic and intellectual movements of the Renaissance. Printing presses arrived in Prague, the Bohemian capital, by the 1470s, helping disseminate essays and poetry in Latin and scholarly works in the Czech language. Bohemian translators rendered ancient Latin and Greek texts, as well as the works of contemporary Renaissance authors such as Martin Luther and Erasmus, into the Czech language. The historian Daniel Veleslavina published works of history, travel, and geography; other scholarly works covered law, medicine, and botany; the astronomers Johannes Kepler and Tycho Brahe both lived and worked at the court of Rudolf II in Prague. More daring authors of Bohemia wrote satirical verses and parodies that ridiculed the emperor, the Catholic Church, and the nobility.

Boleyn, Anne
(ca. 1501–1536)

Queen of England and second wife to King Henry VIII, Anne Boleyn was born to the wealthy Sir Thomas Boleyn, the Earl of Wilshire. When still a young girl, she traveled and studied in the Netherlands and in Paris, where she served the French royal court as an interpreter and as a lady-in-waiting to the queen. When she returned to England, she entered the service of Catherine of Aragon, the first wife of Henry VIII.

As a young woman Anne became a headstrong and charismatic figure at court, and soon attracted the king's eye. Henry offered Anne her own staff of servants and showered her with attention, presents, and proposals of marriage. Worried over the succession and the survival of the Tudor dynasty, Henry was eager to have sons, which Catherine of Aragon had failed to provide. However, Pope Clement VII refused to grant Henry the divorce he sought from Catherine of Aragon. In 1531, Henry banished Catherine of Aragon, an action that elevated Anne to a powerful position at court as an adviser to the king. Under her influence, Henry broke with the Catholic Church and, with Anne's encouragement, established the Church of England, an institution free of the pope's authority. Henry and Anne were married in secret, and in 1533 Anne Boleyn was formally crowned as the new queen of England. Her rise to power and Henry's actions in disavowing the pope greatly encouraged Protestant reformers in Europe such as Martin Luther.

In September of that year the new queen gave birth to a girl, the future Queen Elizabeth I, who would maintain the primacy of the Church of England. Henry's many mistresses sparked bitter marital conflict, however, and Anne's failure to have a son also worsened his view of her. Henry turned his attentions to another court lady, Jane Seymour, while Anne quickly fell out of favor. In 1536 she was arrested and charged with adultery and treason. She was convicted and the marriage to Henry was officially annulled. A few days later she was beheaded in the Tower of London.

Borgia, Cesare
(1475–1507)

Scion of the powerful Borgia family, Cesare Borgia was born in Rome to Cardinal Rodrigo Borgia and the cardinal's obscure mistress Vannozza dei Cattani. Cesare's uncle Alonso was elected as Pope Calixtus III in 1455. His father Rodrigo became Pope Alexander VI in 1492. Soon afterward Cesare was made the archbishop of Valencia, and in the following year, at the age of eighteen, became a cardinal. As a young man he prepared to follow in his father's footsteps; the pope intended to establish a lasting family dynasty through his eldest son Giovanni, the Duke of Gandia. This gave rise to a violent jealousy on the part of Cesare, who saw greater power and glory in a career outside of the limitations of the church. For this reason, historians believe Cesare had a central role in the assassination of his brother in 1497. This event ended Cesare's career in the church. He became an ambassador for the pope in Naples and his father worked to arrange a useful marriage for him with Carlotta, the daughter of the king of Naples. In 1498 Cesare resigned his office, the first cardinal in history to do so, and became an ambassador for the pope to France, who was requesting a papal annulment of his marriage to Jeanne of France in order to marry Anne of Brittany. Cesare brought the papal bull (decree) annulling the marriage and was rewarded by Louis XII with the title of Duke of Valentinois (Valence).

The pope sent Cesare north to subdue the rebellious cities of northern Italy. Cesare brought an army of Swiss, Gascons, French, and Italians, he marched to the Romagna and established a base at Cesena. He conquered Imola, and Forli. As commander of the armies of the church, he formed the new state of Romagna. In 1500 he defeated Rimini and Pesaro, and in the next year he defeated Faenza, whose leader was sent to Rome as a prisoner and later murdered. Greatly feared throughout northern Italy, Cesare was rising in his father's estimation and arriving at his plan to establish a hereditary monarchy in central and northern Italy. Alexander named him gonfaloniere of the church (a prestigious post) and as the Duke of Romagna in 1501. Still opposed by several northern princes and condottieri (leaders of mercenary soldiers), four of them repented their resistance to him and captured the town of Senigallia for his benefit. Arriving in the city, Cesare lured them to his palace, where on New Year's Eve 1502 he ordered two of them to be strangled. Cesare sought to form an independent base of power to serve his own ambitions, independent from that of the Papacy, and to this end maneuvered, schemed, and bribed among the Italian nobles.

The widespread fear and hatred he inspired eventually proved his downfall, however. Both father and son came down with a fever in 1503; although Cesare recovered, Alexander VI died. The election of his enemy Giuliano della Rovere as Pope Julius II. This pope sought the return of captured cities in Romagna to the papal territories. Cesare was taken prisoner and abandoned by the king of France. The pope demanded the return of territories conquered by Cesare's armies. Cesare fled to Naples. Julius schemed with the rulers of Spain, Ferdinand and Isabella, to have Cesare arrested in Naples, then a Spanish possession, by the city's governor Gonzalo de Cordova. In 1506 he escaped from prison in Spain and fled to Navarre, ruled by his brother-in-law John III of Navarre, the brother of his wife Charlotte d'Albret. He died at the siege of Viana in 1507.

Cesare is best known as a model leader, the ideal of the Renaissance prince, in the eyes of Niccolo Machiavelli, the Florentine historian who believed Cesare's combination of ambition and cunning were best suited to rule in his times. The historian, serving as an ambassador for Florence, spent some time at Borgia's court in 1502–1503 and described his actions and tactics in his work *The Prince*. Borgia's conquest of Romagna and the murder of his rivals at Senigallia on New Year's Eve 1502 in particular earned Machiavelli's praise.

Borgia, Lucrezia (1480–1519)

The daughter of the Spanish cardinal Rodrigo Borgia and his mistress Vannozza dei Cattani, Lucrezia Borgia was born in the Italian town of Subiaco. In 1492 Rodrigo Borgia was elected as Pope Alexander VI, and the Borgia family became one of the most powerful—and ambitious—in Italy. In the next year the pope arranged the marriage of Lucrezia, aged thirteen, to Giovanni Sforza, a scion of the ruling family of Milan. Sforza's usefulness to the pope soon declined, however, and he was pressured to annul his marriage. He eventually agreed to a divorce on the grounds of his own impotence, but not before spreading tales that the pope wanted Lucrezia for his own mistress. A faction opposed to the Borgia family took up the slander, also spreading the rumor that Alexander VI as well as Cesare Borgia, Lucrezia's brother, were having incestuous relations with her. The pope arranged a second marriage for Lucrezia with Alfonso of Aragon, a member of the dynasty that ruled the city of Naples. Out of jealousy or political ambition, Cesare Borgia ordered his henchmen to attack Alfonso in Rome and then strangle him in his bed. Lucrezia was then betrothed to Alfonso d'Este, the prince of Ferrara. As the Duchess of Ferrara, she presided at a renowned Renaissance court of artists and poets, and was praised by those who knew her as a gracious and intelligent woman. The political turmoil surrounding the Borgia family sullied the reputation of Lucrezia Borgia, who would go down in history as an ambitious, conniving, and evil woman. Modern historians question many of the misdeeds attributed to her, however, and believe her worst attribute was to have passively served her brother and father as a useful political pawn.

Bosch, Hieronymus (1450–1516)

A Dutch painter known for his densely crowded canvases and striking imagery that reflects an intensely religious outlook and a fascination with sin, weakness, and corruption. Born as Jeroen van Aeken, the son of Anthonius van Aeken, he took the surname Bosch from the town of 's-Hertogenbosch, the place of his birth. The son and brother of skilled painters, he lived his entire life in this town, which then belonged to the Duchy of Burgundy.

His first commission, undertaken with his father and two brothers, was an altarpiece, offered by the Brotherhood of Our Lady to the local cathedral.

The Flemish school of painting to which Bosch belonged was known for realistic depictions of everyday life; it included such masters as Pieter Brueghel, who was a devoted student of Bosch paintings. Few details are known about the private life of Bosch, other than that he was a member of the strictly orthodox Brotherhood of Our Lady, a group that venerated the Virgin Mary. He lived at a time of change, when the familiar religious mores and artistic styles of the Middle Ages were being transformed into the humanism and experimentation of the Renaissance. His work can be seen as a morbidly pessimistic view of this changing world and a prediction that the new, irreligious age was condemning Christian believers to hell.

Bosch's fame earned him many commissions from nobility and royalty. His successful workshop produced paintings, altarpieces, triptychs (three-paneled pictures), and smaller works undertaken for local art patrons. For the Cathedral of St. Johns, in his hometown, he was awarded many commissions to design altarpieces, garments, and stained glass, none of which have survived to modern times. His paintings are Christian allegories, many on the theme of temptation and damnation, with the most famous example being *The Garden of Earthly Delights*. This vivid ensemble of strange forms, monsters, devils, mythological figures, and grotesques includes more than one thousand figures. Its three panels are the *Garden of Eden* on the left, *Hell* on the right, and in the center *The Garden of Earthly Delights*, which shows an allegorical scene of man's temptation and downfall. *The Garden of Earthly*

Delights and other paintings by Bosch hold up an unpleasant mirror to the vices and foolishness of humanity. Their intent is to shock with the wickedness revealed in human and animal forms, and inspire repentance on the part of the viewer. *The Temptation of St. Anthony* is one of his most famous works. *The Vision of Tondalys* is a painting of dreamlike images, in which the legs of a man sprout roots and people fly through the air. *The Ship of Fools* shows a group of people voyaging on a small boat, wasting their lives in insignificant and futile pursuits as the ship drifts far from their harbor. *Death and the Miser* depicts the last moments of a greedy man who has hoarded his wealth and who now must face death, personified as an eerie phantom that is coming through his door. Modern art historians see Bosch as an important precursor to the surrealist imagery popular in the early twentieth century. His paintings were popular among wealthy and noble patrons in the Netherlands, Austria, and Spain, and he has had many imitators up to the present day.

SEE ALSO: Brueghel family

Bosworth Field, Battle of

A decisive battle fought on August 22, 1485, during the Wars of the Roses, a dynastic civil war that took place in late-fifteenth-century England. The conflict between the houses of York and Lancaster had reached a crucial turning point with the death of Edward IV in 1483. After this event, the late king's brother Richard of Gloucester of the House of York, had his two nephews, including the heir apparent Edward, held in the Tower of London, where they were likely murdered. After their disappearance, Richard was proclaimed King Richard III. To contest the throne, his rival Henry Tudor, the Earl of Richmond, gathered an army of about five thousand men, consisting of French mercenaries and knights of Lancaster, and marched to the vicinity of Leicester in central England. There they faced Richard and the Yorkists, who mustered about twelve thousand, including a force of four thousand men under the command of Sir William Stanley and Thomas Stanley, Henry Tudor's stepfather. Henry Percy, the Earl of Northumberland, and the Stanleys held back their forces, however, and about an hour after the start of the battle, the Stanleys deserted to Tudor's army. Richard ordered a desperate raid on Tudor's company, but was killed in the skirmish. After marrying Elizabeth of York, the victorious Henry Tudor was crowned as Henry VII, the first king of the Tudor dynasty.

Botticelli, Sandro (1444–1510)

A Florentine artist and a leading painter of the Renaissance, Botticelli was born as Alessandro di Mariano Filipepi (the name "Botticelli" means "little barrel" in Italian, a nickname the painter borrowed from his elder brother). Historians know little about his youth except that he was the son of a tanner. He may have worked in a goldsmith's workshop, and may have been an apprentice of Fra Filippo Lippi. His early paintings were influenced by Masaccio, one of the most important late-medieval painters, as well as Andrea del Verrocchio.

In the 1470s, Botticelli opened his own workshop, and remained a citizen of Florence for the rest of his life.

He won commissions from the church of Santa Maria Novella (*The Adoration of the Magi*), and from the Medici family for portraits of Cosimo de' Medici, Cosimo's son Giovanni, and his grandson Giuliano.

Sandro Botticelli's masterpiece, "Birth of Venus." THE ART ARCHIVE/DAGLI ORTI. REPRODUCED BY PERMISSION.

Pope Sixtus IV summoned Botticelli to Rome to execute frescoes for the walls of the Sistine Chapel, where he painted *The Youth of Moses, The Punishment of the Sons of Corah*, and the *Temptation of Christ.* After returning to Florence, he worked on illustrations for Dante's epic poem *The Divine Comedy*, and his illustrations appeared in the first printed edition of the poem, in 1481.

Botticelli was schooled in traditional religious themes. His works include several famous Madonnas, and paintings of Saint Sebastian, and Saint Augustine. But the artist's most famous works borrow figures and themes from pagan mythology, and are characterized by strong and precise contour, soft colors, and mysterious settings. The canvases entitled *Primavera* (1478) and *The Birth of Venus* (1485) were painted for the villa of Lorenzo di Pier-

francesco de' Medici, a cousin of the Florentine despot Lorenzo the Magnificent. In both paintings appears the figure of Venus, the ancient Roman goddess of love and beauty. In these works Botticelli may have been influenced by the philosophy of Neoplatonism, which was popular among Lorenzo's court circle, and which attempted to reconcile classical paganism and Christianity.

In 1480, Botticelli joined several important artists, including Pietro Perugino, Domenico Ghirlandaio, and Filippo Lippi, to complete a series of frescoes for the villa of Lorenzo the Magnificent.

Botticelli's artistic style changed in his later works, when he began painting more staged, traditional settings and figures in stiffer, more formal poses. Botticelli grew conservative in his approach to painting, and filled his works with a sense of religious devotion and piety. At the same time he became an ardent supporter of the Dominican friar Girolamo Savonarola, who was lashing out at the self-indulgent luxuries of aristocrats and rulers of Florence. One of Botticelli's later works, a *Crucifixion*, shows arrows raining down on Florence. The artist may have added some of his own works to the famous bonfires that Savonarola held to destroy what he saw as sinful art and books that were corrupting the city.

Late in life Botticelli suffered from a physical disability that prevented him from working. He lost commissions and found himself struggling to survive. His manner of painting, which reminded many people of past medieval artists, went out of style. He was largely forgotten until the nineteenth century, when "pre-Raphaelite" painters of England discovered his mysterious allegories and dreamlike imagery. Since that time, Botticelli's style and works have made him one of the most familiar artists of the Italian Renaissance.

SEE ALSO: Medici, Lorenzo de'; painting

Bourbon dynasty

A royal house whose members ruled many states of Europe, including France, Navarre, Naples, Sicily, and Spain, which still has a Bourbon member as its ceremonial king. The most powerful branch of the Bourbons ruled France from 1589 until 1792, when King Louis XVI was overthrown and executed during the French Revolution.

The family was established as the hereditary lords of Bourbon and vassals of the Capetian dynasty that established the French monarchy in the late tenth century. In 1268, Beatrix of Bourbon married Prince Robert, the count of Clermont and

a son of King Louis IX. Charles of Bourbon, the last of the line, died in 1527; another branch of the family was ruling the duchy of Vendôeme. This family became lords of Navarre, a small kingdom on France's southern border with Spain, in 1555. In the meantime, the Protestant revolt against the Catholic doctrine and hierarchy was driving France to a full-scale civil war. To make peace with the Huguenots (Protestants) of France, Catherine de Médicis, the mother of the French king, arranged a marriage of her daughter Margaret to Henry, the Bourbon and Protestant prince of Navarre. On the wedding day, August 24, 1572, the Catholics of France took the festivities as an occasion for a wholesale slaughter of Protestants in the Saint Bartholomew's Day Massacre. Henry announced his conversion to the Catholic faith but in 1576 again declared himself a Huguenot. In 1584, after the death of the younger brother of the king, Henry of Navarre became next in line for the throne. In 1589, when the king of France was assassinated, King Henry III of Navarre became the first Bourbon king of France as Henry IV.

The arrival of a Protestant on the throne of France raised the ire of Catholics, who rallied around Henry's uncle, Cardinal Charles de Bourbon. Henry defeated Charles in battle in 1590, but was unable to seize Paris, a Catholic stronghold, with the forces at his disposal. For the sake of the French kingdom and a hope for a lasting truce, he converted once again to Catholicism, remarking that "Paris is worth a mass," and was formally crowned in 1594. In 1598 Henry passed the Edict of Nantes that recognized Catholicism as the official religion of France but also decreed tolerance for the Huguenots. The civil war now at an end, France grew into the most powerful, united kingdom in Europe. Henry and his successor Louis XIII built new roads and canals, promoted the growth of textiles and other industries in the north, reformed and improved French agriculture, and built the French army and navy into a military force second to none in the western world. The Bourbons, through a system of their intendants, dominated the French nobles and extended their absolute control over the kingdom's many counties, duchies, and the semi-independent domains of the nobility. Under Louis XIV, France fought several wars for more territory in the north and east; but when the king revoked the Edict of Nantes in 1685 an exodus of Protestants from northern France took place, weakening the kingdom's productive industries.

In 1700, when the king of Spain died without an heir, Louis contested the throne of Spain with the Habsburg dynasty of Austria. England, the Netherlands, and Austria formed a coalition against the ambitious French. A War of the Spanish Succession lasted until 1714, when Louis finally succeeded in placing his grandson on the throne of Spain, at the cost of nearly emptying the French treasury. At his death Louis had reigned longer than any other king in the history of Europe. Under his great-grandson, Louis XV, France lost several major wars in Europe and North America, further damaging the kingdom's finances and leading to the widespread unrest that brought about the French Revolution.

SEE ALSO: France; Henry IV

Bracciolini, Poggio (1380–1459)

A leading humanist and scholar of the Italian Renaissance, Poggio Bracciolini was born Giovanni Francesco Poggio Bracciolini in the village of Terranuova, in Tuscany. A scholar of Latin and Greek, he could write and speak in both of these languages. He was an expert copyist and a tireless collector of ancient manuscripts, bringing hundreds of unknown works to light for the first time, and inspiring a generation of scholars to make their own researches into the writing and philosophies of the ancients. As a young man he journeyed to Rome, where he became a papal secretary, serving first with Boniface IX. He traveled with the popes, in whose service he had access to the libraries of monasteries and churches where many books had been stored for centuries. While the popes were embroiled in the Great Schism that divided the Catholic Church between the rival popes and their supporters in Avignon and Rome, Bracciolini brought to light important discourses of the Roman orator Cicero. He painstakingly copied down hundreds of damaged fragments and manuscripts, including books of Vitruvius, Marcus Quintilian, Titus Petronius, Titus Maccias Plautus, and other Latin authors who had been completely unknown during the Middle Ages.

In 1452 Bracciolini left the service of the popes and returned to Florence. He had earned a reputation as a speaker and a writer of panegyrics (praise for the dead), as a translator, and a writer of essays on customs and morals, including *On the Vicissitudes of Fortune, On Nobility*, and *On Marriage in Old Age*. He was also known for satires and obscene fables written in beautifully expressive Latin, collected under the title *Facetiae*, as well as invectives, or essays that criticized members of the clergy for their hypocrisy and vice. He translated the works of ancient Greeks, including Xenophon, into Latin, then the universal scholarly language. His famous work, *De Varietate Fortunae*, is a meditation on the passing of ancient glories of Rome. He was an early archaeologist, studying the ruins of Rome and deciphering their mysterious inscriptions. In 1453 he headed the chancery of the Republic of Florence, becoming the city's official historian. While in office he wrote a history of the city, in imitation of the Roman historian Livy. Bracciolini's work remains one of the best sources of information on the early Renaissance in Florence.

Brahe, Tycho (1546–1601)

A Danish astronomer, Tycho Brahe was born into a noble and wealthy family, the son of a minister to the king of Denmark. He studied at the University of Copenhagen, where he prepared for a career in law. On August 21, 1560, however, he witnessed an eclipse of the sun. Observation and mathematical calculations had already predicted the eclipse, an achievement that inspired Brahe to pursue astronomy. Discouraged by the conflicts and disagreements in astronomical measurements, he set out to collect as much information as possible from a single observation point with the most accurate instruments available, and develop a more consistent and accurate system of astronomical observation.

Brahe built an observatory known as the Uraniborg on the island of Hven. There he developed his own model of the universe, the Tychonic system, which reconciled the conflicts in the old Ptolemaic (earth-centered) and new Copernican (heliocentric) systems. In 1572 he observed a suddenly bright star in the constellation Cassiopeia, and described his findings in *De Stella Nova*, which coined the term "supernova." This observation was important for its revolutionary concept that the heavens were not fixed and eternal, as in the traditional view. Tycho believed in a geocentric universe, in which the earth was fixed, the sun orbited the earth, and the planets orbited the sun. He believed that if the earth did move, then nearer stars should shift with respect to background stars; this "parallax shift" was indeed present but not visible at the time. (Brahe was the last major astronomer to work by the naked eye, without using a telescope.)

At odds with the king of Denmark over his theories, Brahe moved to Prague in 1597 and won the patronage of Emperor Rudolf II, who used him as a court astrologer. Brahe jealously guarded his astronomical measurements; after his death by unknown causes they fell into the hands of his assistant, Johannes Kepler. The circumstances of Brahe's demise have led some historians to conclude that Kepler murdered his employer out of professional jealousy. Whatever the truth of the matter, in the following years Kepler relied on Brahe's calculations to develop a set of new laws governing the motion of the planets.

SEE ALSO: Copernicus, Nicolaus; Galilei, Galileo; Kepler, Johannes

Bramante, Donato (1444–1514)

Italian architect, a leading figure of the late Renaissance whose palaces, monuments, and church architecture were inspired by the ancient ruins of Rome. Born as Donato di Pascuccio d'Antonio, the son of a farmer in the village of Monte Asdruvaldo, in the central mountains of Italy, he may have first worked under the patronage of Federigo da Montefeltro, the duke of Urbino. As a young painter, he was influenced by Piero della Francesca and Andrea Mantegna. His first known commission was a painted frieze for the Palazzo del Podesta in the city of Bergamo, which he completed in 1477. By the 1480s, he was living in Milan and working as the court architect of Ludovico Sforza. He was commissioned to decorate the Church of Santa Maria Presso San Satiro in Milan, in which he created a *trompe l'oeil* (trick of the eye) choir through the use of deep perspective. Bramante designed the cloisters (enclosed courtyards) for the Sant'Ambrogio church, and with Leonardo da Vinci he also worked on the Church of Santa Maria delle Grazie. He then traveled to Pavia, where he assisted in the design of the city's cathedral.

In 1499, Bramante fled Milan when a French army besieged and conquered the city, overthrowing the Sforza dynasty. He traveled to Rome, where he made a close study of the city's ancient ruins. The monumental architecture of the classical city influenced his design for the cloisters of Santa Maria della Pace, which he completed in 1504. In 1502 he designed the Tempietto, a small circular chapel in the courtyard of the Church of San Pietro in Montorio. This elegant and simple building was designed as a monument to Saint Peter, who was martyred on the spot. Its careful proportions give it a feeling of serenity and balance; the Tempietto has been studied by architects ever since as a perfect imitation of the antique style and one of the most famous buildings of the Renaissance.

Under the patronage of the popes, Rome was becoming a leading center of Renaissance art. Pope Julius II engaged Bramante as his official architect and put him in charge of the rebuilding of Saint Peter's Cathedral and working on the Vatican Palace. Bramante redesigned the facade of the palace as well as the Belvedere Court, which was built in a series of staircases and loggias (covered passageways) that run along a terraced hillside. Since the Belvedere was raised, however, later designs all but destroyed Bramante's original composition, and only a spiral staircase survives to the present day intact.

In 1505 Bramante prepared a design for Saint Peter's, intended to be the greatest basilica of Christendom and a worthy successor to the great Pantheon, a still-intact monument of ancient Rome. Bramante initially created Saint Peter's in the shape of a Greek cross, as a tribute to the fallen city of Constantinople and its Hagia Sophia cathedral. Work began in the next year but progressed slowly as the design was altered. Bramante and Julius became close companions and the pope bestowed on his favorite architect the office of *piombatore*, the aide responsible for sealing the pope's letters and documents. Some time after 1510 Bramante designed the Palazzo Caprini in the center of Rome, a building Bramante designed as his own dwelling and which was later acquired by the painter Raphael. The Palazzo Caprini contained a first floor of simple city shops and higher stories designed as an aristocratic palace. The design of the palace disappeared under later additions and alterations but the building served as a model for many Roman buildings in the following centuries. Bramante died in 1514; at Saint Peter's only four columns and arches meant to support a huge central dome were in place at the time of his death. The completion of the work was assigned to Michelangelo Buonarroti, who completed the monumental dome that has since become a familiar landmark of the Vatican and the city of Rome.

SEE ALSO: architecture; Julius II; Michelangelo Buonarroti

Brenz, Johannes
(1499–1570)

A German theologian and reformer, Brenz was born in the town of Weil and educated at Heidelberg. He became at magister, or master teacher, in 1518, and was known far and wide for his lectures on the Bible and on Christian theology. He was ordained as a priest in 1520 but by 1523 was no longer celebrating traditional Mass. Brenz supported the reform efforts of Protestant Church founder Martin Luther, whom he accompanied at Luther's famous disputation at Heidelberg in 1518. In 1525 Brenz published the *Syngramma Suevicum*, in which he supported the idea that Christ was physically present in the Christian sacramental offerings of bread and wine. In 1530 he attended the Diet of Augsburg. When the Holy Roman Emperor, Charles V took up arms against the Protestant Schmalkaldic League, Brenz was forced to flee for his life from the city of Hall. He took refuge in the castle of Hohenwittlingen, under the protection of Duke Ulrich of Württemberg, where he became a leading supporter of the Protestant Reformation. In 1552 he attended the Council of Trent, and in 1554 became provost of the cathedral of Stuttgart.

SEE ALSO: Luther, Martin; Reformation, Protestant

Bronzino, Agnolo
(1503–1572)

A painter of Florence, Agnolo di Cosimo earned his nickname of Bronzino from his dark, "bronzed" complexion. He was the adopted son of the painter Jacopo Pontormo, whose pupil he became and who had a strong effect on his style. He became the official court painter to Cosimo de' Medici, creating portraits of the duke and his family that were imitated throughout Europe long after the close of the Renaissance. He lived for two years in Rome, where he created religious paintings in the emotionally cold, brightly colored and precisely drawn "mannerist" style that was then in vogue. His famous works include *Venus, Cupid, Folly and Time*, an allegorical account of love that Cosimo de' Medici presented as a gift to King Francis I, and *Eleanora Toledo and Her Son*, a portrait of de' Medici's wife and son. He helped to found the Academy of Design in Florence in 1563.

Brueghel family

A family of Flemish painters who produced paintings and drawings largely inspired by the work of its patriarch, Pieter Brueghel the Elder. This artist is best known for his new way of rendering natural landscapes and his bucolic scenes of peasant life. Born in the town of Breda, Brueghel apprenticed with the painter Pieter Coecke van Aelst and joined the Antwerp painters' guild in 1551. Like many northern European artists, he traveled to Italy to study the new styles pioneered by southern painters. In Italy Breughel produced his first signed painting, *Landscape with Christ and the Apostles at the Sea of Tiberius*. On his way home to Antwerp, he crossed the Alps, where the dramatic mountain landscape inspired him to make studies of natural forms that he later incorporated into his works.

On his return to the Low Countries, Brueghel worked as an engraver for an Antwerp publisher, Hieronymus Cock. The workshop produced the prints that were fashionable in merchant and middle-class families unable to afford commissioning original paintings. A Brueghel drawing entitled *Big Fish Eat Little Fish* appeared in 1557, with the signature of the better-known Hieronymus Bosch substituted for Brueghel's to boost sales. Bosch, then a renowned Flemish painter, remained an important influence on Brueghel, and the younger painter directly imitated him in his 1558 series of engravings entitled *Seven Deadly Sins* as well as allegorical paintings, including *The Triumph of Death* and *The Fall of the Rebel Angels*.

Brueghel's *Combat of Carnival and Lent*, completed in 1559, was his first signed painting. The painter was still modeling his work on Bosch, but also using stronger colors and arranging elements in the picture to achieve a careful balance of shapes and lines. The *Netherlandish Proverbs* and *Children's Games*, as well as the *Combat of Carnival and Lent*, were crowded canvases of multiple scenes and symbolic characters, all standing for the foibles and follies of the everyday world. In this manner Brueghel also painted *Dulle Grief* and *The Triumph of Death*, a gloomy landscape of fire, murder, and death that some historians believe was inspired by the religious civil wars then consuming much of northern Europe. *The Tower of Babel*, painted in 1563, is based on a biblical parable showing the folly of human ambition and the pretension to greatness.

Brueghel moved to Brussels, Belgium, in 1563. In the last few years of his life, he painted his most famous pieces, including *The Road to Cavalry* and *The Blind Leading the Blind*. Brueghel won a commission to paint a series of pictures of the seasons and months. Five of these paintings have survived to the present day and have become icons of the northern Renaissance: *Hunters in the Snow, Dark Day, Hay Harvest, Wheat Harvest*, and *Return of the Herd*. In beautifully rendered and vividly colored compositions, these paintings show man in harmony with a beneficent nature. Brueghel in these paintings left behind the religious context of medieval painting, and rendered the world in its natural visible state without the interference of religious doctrine and symbolism. Because of this approach to his art many consider Brueghel to have been the first truly "modern" painter.

Completed in 1566, Brueghel's *Massacre of the Innocents* was the painter's view of the tyranny of Spain's occupation of the Netherlands. Brueghel gained his reputation as a painter of peasant life through two of his most famous pictures, *Peasant Dance* and *Peasant Wedding Feast*. In these paintings Brueghel made the human figures more prominent, using expressions, poses, and colors to convey elemental human characteristics: joy, greed, hunger, stupidity, innocence, exuberance, and boredom. *Peasant Wedding Feast* shows not only Brueghel's masterful skill at rendering forms, but also an uproarious sense of humor and great sympathy for the universal condition.

One of Brueghel's late works, *Land of Cockaigne*, is a return to medieval allegory. The painter renders a knight, a peasant, and a merchant, all of them slightly off balance and falling victim to their weaknesses. *Magpie on the Gallows*, painted about the same time, shows a gallows rising above a scene of peasants celebrating in a field.

Brueghel's son, known as Pieter Brueghel the Younger (1564–1638), made his living producing copies of his father's works. Jan Brueghel the Elder (1568–1625) was known for his peaceful floral landscapes and still lifes. Both men were boys when their father died.

SEE ALSO: Bosch, Hieronymus

Brunelleschi, Filippo (1377–1446)

The most renowned architect of Florence, Filippo Brunelleschi decorated the city with imposing architecture that has endured as a symbol of Renaissance genius. The son of a prominent notary, he joined the Silk Guild of Florence as a boy. Showing great talent in the demanding arts of metalworking, he was welcomed into the city's guild of master goldsmiths and won commissions to execute silver altarpieces for the cathedral of Pistoia. His reputation as a sculptor also was spreading through the city and in 1401 he was invited to enter a competition to design the bronze doors of the new Baptistery in Florence. Unable to decide between the entries of Brunelleschi and his rival Lorenzo Ghiberti, the judges invited both men to execute the doors, a commission that Brunelleschi turned down out of wounded pride. His dramatic rendering of the sacrifice of Isaac survived, however, and is now housed in a Florentine museum.

Discovering a passion for architectural design, Brunelleschi joined his friend Donatello in a journey to Rome in 1402 to explore the city's ancient ruins. From his explorations and measurements of ancient Roman structures, he developed a system of ideal mathematical proportions; he was also one of the first artists to work out the principles of linear perspective. He had the opportunity to apply his system of geometrical harmony in his first important architectural commission, the design of the Foundling Hospital in Florence.

Brunelleschi's portico for this building was the first Renaissance structure to make use of classical elements such as columns and capitals.

The design earned widespread admiration in Florence and led to Brunelleschi's next important commission, a sacristy for the Basilica of San Lorenzo. At the same time, Brunelleschi was studying the design of a dome for the Basilica of Santa Maria del Fiore, the central cathedral of Florence. Begun in the fourteenth century, the structure was now finished except for the dome, which would have to span a diameter of 130 feet, a scale well beyond any dome attempted since the time of the ancient Romans. The builders and architects of Florence had no idea how to construct such a dome; raising a wooden scaffolding to support it while building—the conventional method at the time—was considered impossible. In 1419 Brunelleschi defeated his rivals in winning the commission, then solved the problem of the dome by designing a rounded cone, made of inner and outer shells supported by vertical and horizontal stone ribs. The architect designed not just the dome but also the machines and support structures used to raise it, as well as a lantern that was added after the dome was finished in 1436. The work on Santa Maria del Fiore is considered to be the architect's greatest architectural and engineering achievement.

Brunelleschi's other notable works include the Pazzi Chapel, in the church of Santa Croce, and the basilica of Santo Spirito, a church raised in an artisans quarter on the southern banks of the Arno River. This church was unfinished at the time of the architect's death; its facade was eventually completed in a later Baroque fashion that awkwardly clashes with the careful proportions of the interior.

56
notice it's a city building

Brunelleschi's floor design, in the form of a Latin cross with three naves, resembles that of San Lorenzo. Both churches became emblematic of the classical proportions and elegant style of Renaissance church architecture.

Fascinated by problems of engineering, Brunelleschi also turned his attention to the design of fortifications (for the city of Pisa), aqueducts (near Assisi), and riverboats for use on the shallow Arno. Brunelleschi's genius for design as well as engineering allowed him to establish the occupation of architect as an independent profession, free of the medieval restrictions of builders' and masons' guilds. He was honored at his death with burial in Santa Maria del Fiore, still the most prominent structure in Florence.

SEE ALSO: architecture; Ghiberti, Lorenzo

Bruni, Leonardo (1369–1444)

Scholar, historian, and leading citizen of Florence, Leonardo Bruni was born in the town of Arezzo. He studied law and the classics, taking inspiration from the historians and orators of ancient Greece and Rome. An ardent supporter of the Florentine republic, in 1401 he praised the city in a *Panegyric to the City of Florence*. In 1405 he attained the important post of apostolic secretary to Pope Innocent VII. He was elected as the chancellor of Florence in 1410 but resigned within a year and returned to Rome as a papal secretary. In 1415, after Pope John XXIII was ousted from office, Bruni returned to Florence.

In the meantime, Bruni's scholarship was bringing to light the works of Plato, Aristotle, Plutarch, and Demosthenes, whom he translated from Greek into Latin, making them accessible to many students and scholars for the first time. Bruni wrote popular biographies of the Italian poets Petrarch and Dante, the Roman orator Cicero and the Greek philosopher Aristotle. He is best known for *History of the Florentine People*, which was inspired by the books of the Roman historian Livy. Writing in Latin, he began this work in 1415 and continued on it until his death nearly thirty years later. Unlike the medieval chroniclers, who relied on legends and hearsay, *History of the Florentine People* drew on primary sources and important public and private documents.

In his works of history, Bruni was the first scholar of the Renaissance to describe a period of ignorance and superstition after the collapse of the western Roman Empire, an age followed by his own more sensible and enlightened times. (This gave rise to the concept of the "Middle Ages," a phrase coined by Bruni's contemporary Flavio Biondo to describe the period in Europe from A.D. 500 to 1500 that has endured to the present day.) Bruni also pioneered the movement of "humanism," a secular study of art and philosophy that made no reference to faith and that lay outside the strict boundaries of religious doctrine. As a political leader he advocated a streamlined and more democratic government for Florence; his *De Militia* supported the founding of a citizen army for the republic to replace the rapacious and unreliable mercenaries known as condottieri. He was made an honorary citizen of the city, exempt from taxation and other forms of service, for penning the *History of the Florentine People*, which the city government published in 1442. In 1427, he again attained the post of chancellor, which he held until his death in 1444.

Bruno, Giordano
(1548–1600)

Italian philosopher who was executed for his teachings and beliefs that were contrary to Catholic doctrine. Born in Nola, in the Kingdom of Naples, Bruno was the son of a soldier. He was a prodigy as a scholar and joined the Dominican Order, becoming a priest in 1572. He studied a wide range of philosophies and also took a keen interest in astronomy and mathematics, training himself to prodigious feats of memory that led many to suspect him of dabbling in the occult arts. He took up the Hermetic tradition, based on the writings of the ancient seer Hermes Trismegistus, a renowned figure since the Middle Ages and a representative of ancient Egyptian wisdom and magic. Bruno also studied the works of Saint Thomas Aquinas, a leading medieval scholar; Marcilio Ficino, a Renaissance Neoplatonist, or follower of Aristotelianism; and German philosopher Nicholas of Cusa. Bruno grew familiar with the heliocentric universe proposed by Nicolaus Copernicus, but took it a dangerous step further by teaching that the universe was infinite, and that the earth was only one among an infinite variety of worlds with no particular importance. This ran counter to Christian doctrine.

Accused of heresy by the order of friars called Dominicans, Bruno left Naples in 1576 for Rome, then traveled to Geneva, where he joined the Protestant Calvinist sect but was excommunicated for slandering the philosopher Antoine de la Faye. In 1579 he left Geneva, unhappy with the strict Calvinist methods, and became a professor of philosophy at Toulouse, France. Under constant scrutiny wherever he went, he spent time in Paris and then London, where he worked in the service of French ambassador Michel de Castelnau. In England his published works and his promotion of the Copernican system offended some. He also came under suspicion for a powerful mnemonic system of memory that he described in his works *The Shadow of Ideas*, *The Art of Memory*, and *Circe's Song*. In 1584 he completed two of his most important works, *On the Infinite Universe and Worlds* and *The Expulsion of the Triumphant Beast*. Bruno arrived in Prague in 1588. He was excommunicated there by Lutheran Church officials and had to flee the city. He returned to Germany in 1591. At the invitation of a Venetian noble, Giovanni Mocenigo, he moved back to Italy and became a memory tutor to Mocenigo. The two were soon at odds over Bruno's unyielding philosophy and abrasive personality. Mocenigo denounced Bruno, who was arrested in May 1592 and charged with heresy and blasphemy. He was transferred to Rome and imprisoned, finally tried for his negative views on Catholic dogma, including the rites of the Mass and the nature of the Trinity, for practicing magic, and for his heretical belief in a multiplicity of worlds. He was found guilty after a trial that lasted seven years and burned at the stake in 1600.

Byrd, William
(1540–1623)

Prolific English composer whose works are believed to have begun the Baroque style of harpsichord and keyboard music. Born in Lincolnshire, he joined the Chapel Royal as a boy and apprenticed to Thomas Tallis. Under the Catholic queen Mary I, this institution, which produced and performed music by appointment to the monarchy, was flourishing. Talented composers from all over the continent of Europe were invited to take up posts in the Chapel Royal, and Byrd contributed his own compositions from a young age. At the death of Mary and the succession of the Protestant queen Elizabeth I, Byrd and his Catholic sympathies were out of favor. He left the Chapel Royal and, in 1562, was appointed as an organist at Lincoln Cathedral. He returned to the Chapel Royal, where he was appointed to a salaried position, in 1572 and remained as a composer and organist. Byrd and Tallis were granted a lucrative license to print music in 1578. Over the next few years, they published several major collections of songs, including two in English: *Psalmes, Sonets and Songs* in 1588 and *Songs of Sundrie Natures* in 1589. Two collections of Latin motets (polyphonic choral compositions), under the title of *Cantiones Sacrae*, were published in 1589 and 1591. These were among the first song collections ever to be brought out in print. Byrd also published an important collection of his keyboard pieces, entitled *My Lady Neville's Book*. Discouraged by the anti-Catholic laws and politics of London, Byrd moved to a small village, Stondon Massey, in 1593 and remained there until his death. He published two sets of *Gradualia* after the turn of the seventeenth century, which were motets intended for performance during Catholic services. Writing and publishing this music was an act of daring in Protestant England where Catholic worship was still banned by law. After the "Gunpowder Plot" of 1605, in which Catholics were suspected of attempting to destroy the English parliament, Byrd's *Gradualia* and all of his Catholic church music was banned. Nevertheless, Byrd himself took part in illegal Catholic services, most of which were held in private homes, and continued to provide music to be performed during the Latin Mass. He also wrote stage songs, madrigals, and keyboard works that were collected in the *Fitzwilliam Virginal Book*, and various shorter works for voice and strings.

SEE ALSO: Elizabeth I; England; music

Caboto, Giovanni (John Cabot) (ca. 1450–ca. 1498)

Italian explorer known in English as John Cabot, born in either Gaeta or Genoa, Italy. The son of a merchant, he moved at a young age to Venice, where he married, raised a family of three sons, and lived off the Asian spice trade. In 1490, Caboto moved to Spain, where he became acquainted with Christopher Columbus and sought patronage from the monarchs of Spain and Portugal for a new voyage of discovery to the Spice Islands. Failing in this endeavor, he moved to England, where he settled in the port of Bristol and began petitioning King Henry VII for support of an expedition westward across the Atlantic Ocean. Caboto believed a more northerly route would prove shorter than those pioneered by the Portuguese around Africa, or the southerly route taken by Columbus, who mistakenly believed he had reached the East Indies in 1492. In 1496, Henry officially authorized the voyage with letters patent, while several merchants of Bristol agreed to sponsor it. Caboto set out that year but turned back after experiencing bad weather and conflict with his crew. In 1497, on his second expedition, he reached some unknown point on the eastern coast of North America, declaring it "New Found Land," then proceeded 900 miles (1448km) down the coast. He returned to Europe on a more southerly route, touching land again in Brittany. In 1498 Caboto set out with a larger fleet of five ships, with the intention of reaching Japan and China.

This expedition disappeared with all hands, and no clue to its fate has yet been found.

SEE ALSO: Columbus, Christopher

Callimachus (ca. 280 B.C.–245 B.C.)

An ancient Greek scholar and librarian, Callimachus was known in the Renaissance for his poetry and for a lost work known as the *Pinakes*, or Lists, a guide to the collection of the Library of Alexandria. Born in North Africa, Callimachus may have belonged to a noble family, although historians know few details of his life. He was well educated as a youth and eventually made his home in Alexandria, a city on the Mediterranean coast of Egypt established by Alexander the Great, and which became the center of Greek scholarship, science, and philosophy. Callimachus joined the court of Ptolemy II, the king of Egypt, and also became a member of the Museum, the Alexandrian school of philosophy and science that was built by Ptolemy I, founder of Egypt's Ptolemaic dynasty.

The hundreds of thousands of scrolls at the Alexandrian Library had been gathered from all corners of the Greek world and were meant to include every important literary, historical, philosophical, and scientific work in the world. Callimachus organized the collection and compiled the Lists to include the names of the books and some information about the lives of their writers. The authors were arranged according to their field, such as law, poetry, history, mathematics, or rhetoric, and listed in alphabetical order, as were their works.

His poetic works, unlike the "Lists," survived in the form of fragments and quotations into the Renaissance. *Aetia* was a group of narrative poems describing legendary figures and events, while *Iambi* was a collection of shorter poems, some of them describing the scholars and students Callimachus knew or heard about in Alexandria. He was also the author of a short epic, *Hecale*, and a collection known as *Hymns*. As a scholar, he wrote short studies in various fields of knowledge and collected them into the *Epigrams*. Callimachus engaged in a famous and long-standing debate with one of his own students, Apollonius of Rhodes, over the proper form and length of poetry, with Callimachus ridiculing the traditional longer epic poems and Apollonius mocking his rival's preference for shorter forms. Jealous of Apollonius's securing the job of librarian, Callimachus endlessly needled Apollonius for his pretentious and old-fashioned manner of writing. The work of Callimachus in the Library of Alexandria provided a foundation for later studies of ancient Greek writers; his debate with Apollonius over the nature of poetry was also well remembered and provided scholars and authors of the Renaissance with one of their most common points of debate.

SEE ALSO: classical literature

Calvin, John
(1509–1564)

Protestant theologian and founder of Calvinism, a religious movement that had far-reaching effects on European thought and culture. Born Jean Cauvin in Noyon, a town in the Picardy region of northern France, Calvin was the precocious son of a lawyer who began studies at the University of Paris at the age of fourteen. He studied law, theology, as well as ancient languages, including Greek, Latin, and Hebrew. After earning a doctorate, he moved to Geneva, in what is now the French-speaking region of Switzerland. Around 1533 Calvin rebelled against the Catholic hierarchy and took up the cause of the German Protestants. He attempted to have the city fathers adopt a new religious creed to be sworn to by all citizens of Geneva. Expelled from the city for his religious activism, he moved to Strasbourg, Germany, where he became a preacher in a Huguenot (French Protestant) church. In 1541, after several of his followers won election to the city council of Geneva, he was invited to return to the city, where he remained for the rest of his life.

Calvin believed in a direct interpretation of scripture, without any human commentators shaping the experience for the faithful. He believed in subordinating civic government to religious authorities, and in reforming the church through his own interpretation of the will of God. His work *Institutes of the Christian Religion* had a far-reaching effect on the Christian church in Europe. First published in 1536, the *Institutes* explained basic Protestant doctrines, such as the rejection of the authority of the pope and the doctrine of justification by faith, which was first put forth by Martin Luther, former Catholic monk and founder of the Protestant Reformation. Calvin believed in only two of the traditional Catholic sacraments: baptism and Holy Communion; he disagreed with Martin Luther in not believing in the physical presence of Christ in the offering of bread and wine, a strictly Catholic belief. The Holy Spirit, in Calvinist doctrine, could only be apprehended through the spirit, and never through the senses; there was no place in a Calvinist church for graven images or human saints.

Calvin also advanced the notion of predestination: the idea that the fate of the soul is determined before birth, and that worldly actions, no matter how pious or virtuous, can do nothing to change it. The world was made up of the visible church and the invisible church, which included those select individuals who were chosen by God to follow the righteous path to salvation and paradise. The visible church was made up of the elect on earth, who owed their first loyalty to their religion and who lay above and beyond the control of secular authorities.

Calvin believed that religious doctrine should govern secular life. In 1559 he founded the Academy of Geneva, to educate the young in worldly subjects with a strong grounding in faith. Seeking to create an ideal Christian community, he also employed a body known as the Consistory of Geneva as the city's religious court and enforcer of correct doctrine and observance. The consistory prohibited frivolous entertainments—dancing, gambling, and card-playing—as well as Catholic worship; under Calvin, the consistory also had the right to excommunicate participants, which had once belonged to the civil authorities. Calvin established four officers of his reformed theocratic government: ministers to preach and administer the sacraments; doctors to teach the citizens and train ministers; elders who would enforce strict regulations on morals and public behavior; and deacons, who oversaw the charitable institutions such as hospitals and poorhouses.

In Geneva Calvin preached the virtues of thrift, sobriety, and industry. He embraced the economic changes sweeping across Renaissance Europe, where a medieval agrarian society was giving way to an early industrial age in which trade and money took precedence.

In the meantime, opponents of Calvinist thought in Geneva were harshly suppressed. Libertine and atheist Jacques Gruet, who publicly berated Calvin and satirized him in verse, was arrested, tortured, and executed for heresy. The consistory also tortured and executed suspected witches. Calvin's most notable victim was Michael Servetus, a Spanish Anabaptist who had sworn enemies among Catholic and Protestant leaders. When Servetus was recognized in Geneva attending one of Calvin's sermons, he was arrested. With Calvin's support and approval, the council of Geneva tried him for heresy and had him burned at the stake.

Calvin's church gradually spread into northern Europe through a network of preachers, many of them French Huguenots, whom he had trained and guided in Geneva. His ultimate legacy was a harsh and unyielding Puritan outlook that guided its followers in their public and private behavior, and also brought many of its followers into open conflict with the authorities who governed them.

SEE ALSO: Luther, Martin; Zwingli, Huldrych

Camoes, Luis Vaz de (1524–1580)

Probably the best-known Portuguese poet and dramatist, author of *Os Lusiades* (*The Lusiades*), the national epic of Portugal. Camoes was born in Lisbon to an adventurer, Simao Vaz de Camoes, a member of the poor gentry. Simao died on a voyage to India shortly after the birth of his son, who would be schooled in monasteries and at Coimbra, the leading university in Portugal. In 1543, after completing his studies, he joined the royal court at Lisbon. He was banished from the court in 1548 for falling in love with a lady-in-waiting to the queen. He was further exiled from Lisbon for an insulting characterization of the king represented in one of his plays. He enlisted in the Portuguese army and fought against the Moors in North Africa, where he lost an eye defending the Mediterranean port of Ceuta. Returning to Lisbon, he was soon in trouble over a fight with a member of the king's household. He was arrested but released from prison on a pledge that he made stating he would serve in the Portuguese colonies in Asia.

Glad to leave the intrigues and backstabbing at court, Camoes sailed for India in 1553. He served honorably for three years, taking part in expeditions against the Malabar Coast and Arab ports along the Red Sea. He won a commission as an officer in the colony of Macau, a small island territory that Portuguese navigators had seized off the coast of China. Some time before or during these adventures he began writing *The Lusiades*, which recounts the voyages of Vasco da Gama and extols Portugal as a daring nation of explorers and colonizers.

Recalled to India to answer charges of theft, he was shipwrecked in the waters off the mouth of the Mekong River, in Southeast Asia. He survived to return to Goa, a state on the Malabar Coast, then sailed to Portugal's African colony of Mozambique. Destitute and nearly starving, he returned to Portugal with only *The Lusiades* to his name in 1570. He published the poem to popular acclaim and was rewarded by the

king of Portugal with a small pension. The poem was translated into several languages and served as an inspiration for the exploration and settlement of new lands in Asia and Brazil, the Portuguese colony in South America. Camoes also wrote plays and poetic works, including sonnets and lyric poetry that was collected and published under the title *Rimas* shortly after his death. His love poems took inspiration from the work of ancient writers as well as his contemporaries, including the Italian poet Pietro Bembo.

SEE ALSO: de Gama, Vasco; Portugal

Caravaggio, Michelangelo da (1573–1610)

Italian painter whose expressive works overthrew the classical traditions of the Renaissance with dark and striking imagery that would be widely imitated during the Baroque period that followed. Born in the town of Caravaggio to a carpenter, he was orphaned as a boy and served as an apprentice to the painter Simone Peterzano in Milan. He then traveled to Rome, where he struggled for a time as a painter of still lifes and flowers in a small and little-known painter's workshop.

In Rome Caravaggio's career turned when he gained the patronage of Cardinal Francesco del Monte, who had admired and bought the artist's realistic painting *Cardsharps*. This and other early paintings, including *Boy Bitten by a Lizard*, *Concert of Youths*, and *The Fortuneteller*, dealt with worldly scenes and ordinary people—an entirely new genre. But Caravaggio brought this interest in street life and everyday experience to his religious art, beginning with works depicting Saint Matthew (*The Calling of St. Matthew* and *The Martrydom of St. Matthew*). These paintings used commoners as models and placed sanctified biblical stories and miraculous occurrences in a familiar setting, making a break with the idealized figures and surroundings of past artists. Caravaggio also showed little respect for the gods of classical mythology; his portrait *Bacchus*, completed in 1595, shows the Greek god of wine and revelry as an insolent teenager draped in a bedsheet. His paintings had elongated, oddly posed figures and areas of deep shadow and startlingly bright color, used to highlight the personalities and themes of the work. This technique, called tenebrism, would be taken up by artists who followed him during the Baroque period.

The Saint Matthew series won Caravaggio fame and future commissions, including *The Deposition of Christ* and *Death of the Virgin*. This last painting distressed his patrons with his depiction of the Virgin Mary as a plain, fleshy, and noticeably pregnant woman. Caravaggio was accused of degrading religion and the saints, but his revolutionary new style, full of dramatic effects of light and posing, also attracted a legion of admirers, especially among fellow painters.

Caravaggio's turbulent private life got him into frequent trouble with the law. In 1600 he was arrested for fighting with an officer at the Castle Sant' Angelo in Rome, and in 1603 he was charged and jailed for libel after writing derogatory poetry about a rival painter. Several instances of disturbing the peace occurred in the next few years. In 1606, he got into a violent argument over a game of tennis that quickly turned into a sword fight in which Caravaggio killed his rival, Ranuccio Tomassoni. Threatened with arrest, he fled Rome and wandered through southern Italy and Naples, then under the control of Spain.

Caravaggio arrived in Sicily and in 1608 sailed for Malta, where his portrait of Alof de Wignacourt, head of the Knights of Malta, earned him the title of honorary knight of the order, and a payment of two Turkish slaves. A sword fight with one of the Knights then landed him in prison, from which he escaped; now pursued by the authorities of Malta as well as Rome, he wandered through Sicily and then reached Naples, where he was found by his Maltese pursuers and beaten senseless.

Through these events Caravaggio continued to produce expressive and startling religious imagery. The *Madonna of Loreto* shows the Virgin appearing before an old man and woman, whose bare feet are insolently turned toward the viewer of the painting. One of his last works, *The Resurrection of Lazarus*, shows Christ raising Lazarus from the dead; according to some accounts, Caravaggio exhumed a recently buried corpse to use as a model.

Severely injured after the assault in Naples, Caravaggio left Naples for Port' Ercole, where he was arrested by Spanish police who mistook him for another wanted man. He was released, only to come down with a pestilential fever from which he died within a few days. Three days later after his death, he received a formal pardon from the pope for the killing of Ranuccio Tomassoni in Rome.

SEE ALSO: Tintoretto, Jacopo; Titian; Veronese, Paolo

Carpaccio, Vittore (ca. 1460–1525)

The painter Vittore Carpaccio was born into a humble family of seafarers and fishermen and lived his entire life in Venice, Italy. He was a student of Lazzaro Bastiani and also studied under Gentile Bellini, although Bellini outshone him in prestige and commissions from the city's rulers and nobility. In 1501 the Doge of Venice commissioned paintings from Carpaccio for the Doge's Palace, where the painter's *Lion of St. Mark* can still be viewed. Carpaccio painted for religious schools and confraternities of Venice and is best known for *The Legend of St. Ursula*, a series of nine paintings completed about 1490 for Saint Ursula, a Venetian fraternity of merchants. His most famous paintings are large panoramic works, carefully drawn to glorify the city and its history, and without the intensity of religious and personal feeling that became fashionable among later Venetian painters. He depicted the lives of the saints in painting cycles of *Life of the Virgin, Life of St. Stephen, Life of St. George,* and *Life of St. Jerome.* His other famous works include *Ten Thousand Martyrs of Mount Ararat, St. Sebastian,* and *The Holy Pilgrim.* He set his paintings in the streets and homes of the town where he lived, and in this way his works provide a realistic look at the Venice of the Renaissance.

Cartier, Jacques
(1491–1557)

A French explorer and the first European to navigate the interior of Canada, Cartier was born in the port of Saint Malo in Brittany, then a duchy independent of the king of France. He earned a reputation as an able mariner and, in 1534, set out on his first voyage of exploration with two ships and 120 crew members. He made short work of the Atlantic crossing, arriving off the coast of Newfoundland after a voyage of just twenty days. He sailed north to the Strait of Belle Isle, and explored what are now known as Prince Edward Island and the Magdalen Islands. After returning south as far as the mouth of the Saint Lawrence River, and taking two Iroquois boys named Domagaya and Taignoagny hostage, he returned to France. Cartier was

then rewarded with a commission to return to North America. He set out with his young Iroquois guides and three ships in May 1535, and sailed up the Saint Lawrence, still determined to find a northerly route to the Spice Islands as well as a legendary land of blond men and mineral riches the local Indians knew as Sanguenay. The expedition sailed past the site of Quebec, where Cartier reunited the boys with their father, Chief Donnaconna, and then sailed as far as a large village of Huron Indians, Hochelaga at a site named Mont Royal (Montreal) by Cartier. The expedition wintered along the river, but many members took sick from scurvy. The company was saved by the use of white cedar bark, a remedy provided by Domagaya.

On a third voyage, in 1541, Cartier sailed with five ships to the mouth of the River Cap Rouge. He had brought farmers and convicts to establish a productive farming settlement; his instructions were to assist Jean-Francois de la Rocque in his attempt to found a permanent North American colony for the French king. Cartier built a winter fort at Charlesbourg-Royal, skirmished with the Hurons, and waited for de la Rocque to make his appearance. The settlement was decimated by scurvy and Indian attacks; Cartier finally abandoned it in the spring of 1542. While sailing off the coast of Newfoundland, he finally crossed paths with de la Rocque but decided to return immediately to France. On returning to France after this voyage, he settled in a country house near Saint Malo. Cartier's exploration of the Saint Lawrence and surrounding land opened this region to settlement and colonization by France; the French-speaking province of Quebec has since this time kept its ties to France despite the dominance of the rest of eastern North America by English-speaking settlers from Great Britain.

SEE ALSO: Caboto, Giovanni

Castagno, Andrea del (ca. 1421–1457)

A notable painter of Florence, Castagno was born as Andrea di Bartoldi Bargilla. As a young man he was known for a mural in the Palazzo del Podesta, an important civic building, showing the execution of rebels. In the 1440s Castagno traveled to Venice, where he completed a series of frescoes in the church of San Zaccaria, as well as *Last Supper* and a *Passion of Christ* cycle for the convent church of Saint Apollonia. These frescoes showed great skill in the handling of perspective, which Castagno had learned through a study of the paintings of Masaccio.

Castagno eventually returned to Florence, where he painted fresco cycles in the churches of Saint Apollonia and Saint Annunziata, and in a private estate, the Villa Carducci. He was best known in Florence for a portrait of Niccolo da Tolentino, a condottiere (mercenary) who had led the city's forces to an important victory. The portrait was completed over Tolentino's tomb within the Duomo, the cathedral of Florence. Castagno drew his inspiration from contemporary and ancient sources, making a study of Roman wall paintings as well as the striking new style of Donatello's lifelike sculpture. He realistically depicted the human figure, giving it a sculptural volume, realistic proportions, and dramatic expressions and movement that became characteristic of later Florentine painting, and notably in the works of Michelangelo.

SEE ALSO: Florence; painting

Castiglione, Baldassare (1478–1529)

A diplomat and author whose famous *Book of the Courtier* described the ideal Renaissance gentleman. Castiglione was born into a noble family of Lombardy in the town of Casatico, near the town of Mantua in northern Italy. As a young man he attended the court of the Sforza family, rulers of Milan, and served during a campaign against an invading Spanish army in 1503. He became a diplomat for Duke Francesco Gonzaga of Mantua, and in 1504 joined the court of Duke Guidobaldo Montefeltro of Urbino, who sent him as an ambassador to King Henry VII of England. Castiglione also joined an expedition sent by Pope Julius II against Venice and for his service was rewarded with the title of Count of Novellata. He became an ambassador to the papal court after the election of Pope Leo X. In Rome he struck up a friendship with the Italian artist Raphael, who painted a well-known portrait of the author. In 1521 Castiglione attained a position in the church: He was sent as an ambassador to Spain by Pope Clement VII, where he attended to Charles V, king of Sapin and Holy Roman Emperor. When Charles's army attacked Rome, Castiglione came under suspicion for not informing the pope of the disastrous attack beforehand. Castiglione defended his actions and was exonerated.

In 1528 Castiglione published *Il Cortegiano*, known in English as the *Book of the Courtier*. The book was based on the author's experiences at the ducal court of Urbino. In a series of lively dialogues and conversations, based on those he heard at the court, he expounds on the training and manners of the proper gentleman. Castiglione sees the courtier as a new type of man, one educated in the arts and literature and trained for military service. The courtier, in his view, should act with self-control and the dignified ease that comes from long experience of the world and training in a wide range of fields. This idea represents an important change from the medieval chivalric knight, who fought in service to a feudal overlord and solicited the affection of an idealized and unattainable lady.

The *Book of the Courtier* was translated into French, English, German, and Spanish. It was held in high regard in royal courts of France and England, and played a key role in introducing the humanistic outlook of the Italian Renaissance to northern Europe. The author is also known for an elegy he wrote for his friend Raphael on the painter's death in 1520, and letters that reveal in detail his life as diplomat and courtier.

SEE ALSO: Leo X; Raphael; Sforza, Ludovico

Catherine of Siena, Saint (1347–1380)

A mystic and visionary, and a noted literary figure of the early Italian Renaissance, Catherine Benincasa was born in the Tuscan town of Siena to a wool dyer. She experienced religious visions as a child and withdrew to a tiny room in her father's house, taking little food, practicing self-mortification, sleeping on a hard wooden plank, and living the life of a religious hermit. After joining the Dominican order at the age of eighteen she gradually ended her solitude, tending to the poor and the sick, even as the city was struck by a deadly outbreak of plague. She attracted a small crowd of devoted followers and became famous throughout the city and its surroundings for her virtue and saintliness. She was often called on to mediate disputes and involved herself in the wars be-

tween the church and several cities of northern Italy that had banded together to rebel against papal authority. When Pope Gregory XI raised an army to threaten Florence, one of the rebel cities, she traveled to the papal court in Avignon, France, to mediate the conflict. After arriving in Avignon, she urged the pope to return his court to Rome, against the opposition of French cardinals who were then dominating the church administration.

After the death of Gregory, his successor Urban followed her advice and returned to Rome, but the church was soon split between two candidates; Catherine supported Urban, elected by the cardinals of Rome, against Clement, supported by the French. Catherine diligently wrote to the men involved in this Great Schism, attempting through sheer force of personality and eloquence to heal the breach. Impressed by her insight and the force of her personality, Urban invited her to live in Rome, where she died in 1380. Her literary works include several hundred letters written to the popes and princes of Europe and the *Dialogue of Divine Providence*. Catherine was revered throughout Europe for her asceticism and her devotion to the church, as well as her startling and energetic involvement in worldly affairs. She was canonized by Pope Pius II in 1461.

Catholicism

In the Middle Ages, Christians of western Europe looked to the pope, the bishop of Rome, as the earthly leader of their faith. The "catholic" church meant the entire community of believers, whose lives were guided by church doctrine, and whose heresies and sins were punished by church authorities. Catholicism knit Europeans together at a time when political authority was weak, and when most people knew little of the world outside their village or feudal domain. Although the Holy Roman Emperors would challenge the popes for power in Italy, in the rest of Europe the Catholic hierarchy remained an unquestioned authority; the seven sacraments administered by a priest marked the most important events in an individual's life, and the calendar of holidays, saints' days, feasts, and fasts guided believers through the seasons of the year.

The Catholic Church grew into a wealthy institution from the tradition of the tithe, a donation of 10 percent of one's goods or income to the church. In Rome, the popes lived in luxurious palaces and presided over the Curia, the papal headquarters. Catholicism was a complex hierarchy of cardinals, archbishops, bishops, and local priests, who administered the sacraments and guided the members of the parish. The church was a cultural as well as religious institution. Catholic doctrine guided artists in their works, universities were founded under the authority of the church, and scholars devoted their writings to interpretation of the Bible and the works of the early church fathers.

The authority of the popes, however, posed a direct challenge to secular rulers who were attempting to consolidate their authority and create national governments. The kings of France had a long standing feud with the church over the authority of the pope to appoint bishops. Eventually, a French faction would take the Papacy out of Rome entirely and establish a new Catholic capital in the French city of Avignon. This Babylonian Captivity led to a split in the church and to several men all claiming to be pope at the same time. To resolve the problem, church members held a series of councils; this conciliar movement, which claimed that an assembly of church leaders held ultimate authority over the pope himself, became another source of debate and division.

In the Renaissance, as communication improved, as the Bible was translated into new languages, and as scholarship brought to light ancient philosophies, the Catholic Church found its doctrines and authority challenged. Jan Hus, a fifteenth-century reformer from Bohemia, founded a national church that paid no allegiance to the pope. Martin Luther, a German priest of the early sixteenth century, directly challenged the pope, accusing his church of corruption, worldliness, and godlessness. Hus, Luther, and other reformers sought to return Christianity to its roots, and restore the simple faith and religious devotion of the apostles and the early Christians. Luther's reform took Christians out of the Catholic Church entirely, and denied the authority of popes, bishops, and priests over the lives of believers.

The Catholic Church fought this Protestant Reformation with religious trials and threats of excommunication, which denied the sacraments to a heretic and barred his entry into heaven. The church also fought heresy with the Inquisition, a religious court, and the Index, a list of prohibited books. Catholicism was coming into conflict with many new currents of philosophy as well as scientific investigation. Astronomers such as Galileo Galilei and Nicolaus Copernicus had to be cautious about advancing theories that conflicted with accepted church doctrine.

In the century following Martin Luther's Reformation movement, civil and international wars were fought in Europe between Catholics and Protestants, with northern Europe largely breaking away, and southern Europe remaining loyal to papal authority. Although the Renaissance popes were the most powerful individuals in Europe, with immense treasuries and armies at their disposal, they were looked on as just another center of power, contending for land, taxes, and political authority with all the other rulers of the continent. The Papacy, in the hands of many Renaissance popes, became an instrument of amassing wealth and prestige and advancing the interests of their families.

The movement known as the Counter-Reformation was in full swing by the end of the Renaissance. The Council of Trent, which first convened in 1545, passed decrees against the Protestant movement, clarified Catholic doctrine, and attempted to set down uniform guidelines for the administration of the church. Although the Council of Trent was meant to reassert Catholic primacy, the church struggled for centuries to implement the decrees in the far-flung domains that still accepted the Catholic Church as the true Christian authority. The rise of powerful nation-states brought the church directly into conflict with kings over the appointment of bishops, the ownership of income-producing land, the authority of the religious courts, and other matters, while secular authorities sought to assert themselves as the final law of the land.

The most beneficial legacy of the Renaissance Catholic Church was its patronage of artists and their work. Under the commission of church authorities, artists such as Giotto, Michelangelo, Masaccio, and others raised artists well above their traditional status as mere artisans. The Renaissance popes made possible the new classicism in architecture, the monumental sculptures of Rome and other cities, and the innovations in painting, woodworking, engraving, and metalworking, all done in the service of the church. Even as the Protestant movement was splitting the church down a lasting divide, the popes were creating an enduring artistic legacy in cities all over Europe.

Cellini, Benvenuto (1500–1571)

Sculptor, jeweler, and goldsmith, Cellini was a leading craftsman and artist of the Italian Renaissance who described a turbulent and violent life through a famous autobiography. Born in Florence to a well-to-do landowning family, he was apprenticed to a goldsmith but fled the city after getting into a scrape with the law. He journeyed to Siena, the rival of Florence, then to the more distant city of Bologna, where he became an accomplished musician as well as a professional jeweler and metalsmith. At the age of nineteen he settled in Rome, where he became a musician at the court of the pope and an artisan in wide demand for delicately wrought medals, miniatures, and jewelry—some of the finest and most valuable works of art of his age. An accomplished soldier, he fought valiantly in the pope's armies during a siege of Rome, but could not subdue his violent nature in the face of challenges to his freedom or his honor on the part of friends, patrons, or the authorities.

He fled Rome after killing the man who had murdered his brother, engaging in a sword fight with a notary, and developing a sworn enemy of the son of Pope Paul III. On returning to the city, he was arrested on a charge of embezzlement and imprisoned in the Castel Sant' Angelo, the ancient fortress that stood high on the west bank of the Tiber River near the pope's palace at the Vatican.

Enraged at his captivity and his treatment in Rome, Cellini returned to Florence. There he completed *Perseus Holding the Head of Medusa*, a famous sculpture that stood for centuries in the main square of Florence, and which many historians rank next to the greatest works of Donatello and Michelangelo. When Florence went to war with Siena, Cellini was hired to strengthen the walls and defenses of the city, a task that he carried out with great skill and that earned him a pardon for the many accusations against him of violence, theft, and immorality.

Cellini created a celebrated gold medallion of Pope Clement VII, who employed him as a diemaker at the papal mint. He also created works on commission for Cardinal Pietro Bembo, King Francis and Alessandro de' Medici, the duke of Florence. Cellini objects were rare treasures jealously fought over by European kings and nobility, and remain objects of rivalry and veneration to this day among museums all over the world.

The artist's most renowned work, however, was an autobiography that he began writing in the 1550s. The author goes into great detail about his art, his many love affairs and rivalries, his dealings with nobility and rival artists, and his love of violence to settle any and all disputes. He interrupts his many strange, sometimes supernatural, adventures with extravagant praise of himself and his art, giving the impression of a chimeric, rough-edged character who outshines and outmaneuvers all who surround him. Cellini's autobiography became a classic and one of the most important written works to originate during the Renaissance.

Cereta, Laura
(1469–1499)

Renaissance author, humanist, and feminist. Born in Brescia, the eldest child of a

noble family, Cereta wa[s] lent education and tutor[ing] ally offered only to sons. She s[pent] of her youth in a convent, where learned Latin and Greek and made a study of the ancient writers Cicero, Virgil, and Pliny. She returned home at the age of eleven and began the study of mathematics and science with her father. Married to a merchant at the age of fifteen, she carried on her studies and her correspondences with scholars and writers from her new home in Venice. After the death of her husband from the plague, she devoted herself completely to the writing of letters, essays, and speeches, and also gave public readings of her essays. She may have also won an appointment as a professor of philosophy at the University of Padua. In 1488, she boldly defied convention by circulating a collection of her letters under the title of *Epistolae Familiares*. These letters had been sent to friends and acquaintances; they covered the topics of women's rights and social position, the institution of marriage, the right of women to an education, and women's political ability and their attainments as artists. She criticized the institutions of marriage and housekeeping as stultifying and condemned women's predilection for jewelry, fine dress, and cosmetics. She was roundly criticized for presuming to be the equal of men in intellectual ability, however, and after the *Epistolae Familiares* ceased trying to circulate her works. Her interest in overcoming social barriers to women in the field of education and scholarship laid the groundwork for the more widely published feminist writing after the Renaissance.

Cervantes, Miguel de
(1547–1616)

Spanish novelist and playwright whose work *Don Quixote* has become a world-

MIGUEL DE CERVANTES SAAVEDRA.
Natural de Alcalá de Henares, ingenio original y admirable en el habla Castellana, y Autor de la inmortal Fabula del Quixote. Murió en Madrid á los 68 a.º en el de 1615.

An engraving of Miguel de Cervantes.

renowned epic, laying an important foundation for modern literature and the novel. Born in Alcala de Henares, a town near Madrid, Cervantes was the son of a physician and minor noble. He left Spain as a young man and journeyed to Rome, where he entered the service of a cardinal. In Rome he discovered the literature of ancient Latin authors, and was inspired by the idea of reviving the literature of antiquity.

Cervantes enlisted with a Spanish garrison in the city of Naples, Italy, then under the control of a Spanish royal dynasty. He sailed with the fleet that battled the Ottoman Turks at the Battle of Lepanto, off the western coast of Greece, in 1571. He was wounded by gunfire in the battle and lost the use of his left hand—an in-

jury that remained a source of great pride throughout his life. He returned to active service and sailed in expeditions against the Turks in Greece and Tunis, a North African port.

In 1575 he set out for Spain from Naples. In the waters off the northern coasts of Catalonia, Cervantes's ship was attacked and he was captured by Algerian pirates, who brought him to the city of Algiers and sold him into slavery. He was held for five years until his parents ransomed him and brought him back to Spain.

Civilian life in Spain led him into a number of poorly paid positions as a civil servant. He worked as a purchasing agent for the fleet assembled against the English, known as the Spanish Armada, and as a tax agent, whose duties included the collection of taxes for the royal treasury. He suffered arrest and two short prison terms for misconduct and debt; historians believe that during one of these imprisonments he began writing *Don Quixote*.

He had begun his literary effort with *La Galatea*, a short novel, in 1585. In 1597 he was accused of mishandling money as a tax collector and was jailed in the royal prison of Seville. In 1607 Cervantes settled in Madrid, where he remained for the rest of his life. He wrote the *Exemplary Novels* in 1613, and a second part to *Don Quixote* in 1615. He recounted his misadventures as a slave in Algiers in two plays, *The Traffic of Algiers* and *The Baths of Algiers*.

Don Quixote first appeared in 1605. It was a tale of a poor Spanish nobleman, who relives the glories of the chivalric age through a fertile imagination and the companionship of a simple and devoted companion, Sancho Panza. Don Quixote is in constant quest to fight injustice, defend his honor, and win the hand of the fair maiden Dulcinea.

The novel attracted a wide audience through down-to-earth language, realism, sharply drawn characters, and its vivid depiction of the many ironic encounters that arise from the hero's delusions. The book is seen as a break with the chivalric romances that were the dominant form of literature in medieval Europe, and in this way paves the way for the modern novel and its basis in everyday experience and the inner emotional and spiritual life of its characters. *Don Quixote* has been translated into dozens of languages and printed in more than five hundred editions and remains a landmark of Western literature.

SEE ALSO: Lepanto, Battle of; Shakespeare, William

Charles V
(1500–1558)

King of Spain and Holy Roman Emperor, Charles governed the largest realm in Europe since the time of Charlemagne. He was the son of Philip I the Handsome (the Duke of Burgundy) and Joanna the Mad of Spain. He was grandson of Ferdinand of Aragon and Isabella of Castile, the joint rulers of Spain, and of Maximilian I, Habsburg emperor of the Holy Roman states. Born in Ghent, he was raised by an aunt, Margaret of Austria. Charles inherited the Netherlands, a part of Burgundy, on the death of his father in 1506, but ruled through Margaret, who served as his regent until 1515. On the death of Ferdinand II in 1516, Charles became the first monarch of a united Spanish kingdom that included Aragon, Navarre, Castile, Granada, Naples, Sicily, and Sardinia, and that also governed colonies established by Spanish explorers and adventurers in the Americas. As an outsider, Charles was at

A 1548 portrait of Charles V by famed Venetian artist Titian, "The Emperor Charles V Riding at Muhlberg." © GIANNI DAGLI ORTI/ CORBIS. REPRODUCED BY PERMISSION.

first unpopular in Spain, where he levied heavy taxes and appointed Flemish outsiders to govern.

In 1519, on the death of his grandfather Maximilian, Charles was elected as the Holy Roman Emperor, governing an area that included Austria and other territories in central Europe. His election frustrated the ambitious King Francis I of France, who also had claimed the title. This encounter laid the seeds of a long rivalry between the two rulers that would endure for decades. In 1522, finding the huge realm too much for a single man to rule, Charles gave up direct rule of his territories in Austria to his brother Ferdinand.

Charles still disputed control of Burgundy and Navarre with Francis I; at the same time, Italy was contested between the pope and foreign kings seeking to extend their influence to wealthy city-states such as Milan and Florence. The emperor allied with Pope Leo X and went to war against Francis I in 1521. Charles's army won an important victory at the Battle of Pavia in 1525, capturing Francis and bringing him to Spain, where the French king was forced to sign the Peace of Madrid. This treaty freed Milan from French control and ended France's claims to Burgundy. When he returned to France, however, Francis claimed he had signed the treaty under duress and renounced it. He formed an alliance against Charles that included King Henry VIII of England, Pope Clement VII, and the cities of Venice, Milan, and Florence. Charles responded with an invasion of Italy. His armies brutally sacked the city of Rome in 1527 and took the pope hostage. The Treaty of Cambrai in 1529 temporarily ended the conflict bctween the emperor and the French king; soon afterward Charles also signed the Peace of Barcelona with the pope. In 1535, Charles installed his son Philip as the Duke of Milan in defiance of Francis, who was again claiming the city. The war continued until 1538, then resumed in 1542 with Francis allying with Suleiman I, sultan of the Ottoman Empire, and Charles allying with Henry VIII.

In 1530, after reaching a peace agreement with Pope Clement VII, Charles was officially crowned the Holy Roman Emperor by the pope. The Spanish conquests in the New World had brought him prestige and a fortune in silver. Charles strongly believed in the Christianizing mission of the conquistadores; in Europe, he saw his own holy mission in the fight against Protestantism that was threatening the authority of the pope and emperor in Germany and in the Low Countries. In

1521, at the Diet of Worms, Charles had condemned the teachings of Martin Luther, the German monk who was leading the revolt against the Catholic Church, known as the Protestant Reformation. Charles sent inquisitors and troops to ruthlessly put down Protestant rebellion and worked to ally the princes of Germany with the Catholic Church and against the Protestant movement. In 1531 his Protestant opponents responded by organizing the Schmalkaldic League against him. The league allied with France against Charles; its officers seized Catholic properties, expelled Catholic leaders, and forcibly converted many German cities to Protestantism.

At the Council of Trent in 1545, Charles persuaded several German princes to join his crusade against Protestantism. With his opponents divided over strategy, he decisively defeated the Schmalkaldic League at the Battle of Mühlberg in 1546. In 1555 the Peace of Augsburg finally established a lasting compromise between Catholics and Protestants. By this treaty, the religion of each realm would be that of its prince. In the next year Charles abdicated his throne. His brother Ferdinand replaced him as the Holy Roman Emperor and his son Philip II became king of Spain. Charles entered a monastery in Yuste, Spain, where he died in 1558.

Charles VIII
(1470–1498)

King of France whose most important legacy was an invasion of Italy that threw the political world of the Italian Renaissance into turmoil for generations. Born in the castle of Amboise, he succeeded Louis XI to the throne of France in 1483 at the age of thirteen. The young king, who had little formal education and could barely read, was soon dealing with a rebellion of his cousin Louis of Orléans and France's powerful nobles, who were attempting to stymie the authority of the king in their lands. One revolt of the duke of Brittany endured for four years before Charles finally defeated it in 1488. Although he had been betrothed to the daughter of Emperor Maximilian I, Charles believed it wiser to marry the duke's daughter Anne, and in this way bring Brittany at last under royal control.

Looking for further conquests, Charles turned to the wealthy kingdom of Naples, for which the rulers of the French Angevin dynasty had a long-standing claim. In 1494, he made an alliance with Ludovico Sforza of Milan and led a French army into northern Italy. With a powerful force of Swiss mercenaries and seventy cannons at their disposal, the French marched through Tuscany, defeating Florence, and by February 1495 had reached Naples, where Charles deposed the Neapolitan king Alfonso and had himself crowned king. Soon afterward Milan, Venice, the Spanish king Ferdinand of Aragon, the pope, and the Holy Roman Emperor joined forces and defeated the French at the Battle of Fornovo. Charles was driven out of Italy, but the fight for power and influence in Italy among France, Spain, and the Holy Roman Empire lasted well into the sixteenth century. In the meantime, the chaotic condition of the Italian city-states encouraged many prominent Italian artists and writers to leave their homes and seek protection and patronage, a movement that had the effect of spreading humanism and the classical ideals of the Renaissance up and down the Italian peninsula.

SEE ALSO: Ferdinand II of Aragon; France; Italy; Naples

cities

Europe during the Renaissance developed a thriving urban society. In this era, city life made a break with that of the countryside; the peasants and townspeople had less in common and were less dependent on each other for food, trade, and defense. Renaissance cities served as economic as well as cultural centers, where the new scholarship, art, and literature thrived. The most densely urbanized parts of the continent were northern Italy, the Low Countries (modern Belgium and the Netherlands), southern England, northern France, and southern Germany. The continent's largest urban centers were Venice, Florence, Amsterdam, Paris, and London. All of these cities had diverse social groups, including a merchant class, a wealthy aristocracy, skilled artisans, and the poor, a class that included migrants from the countryside.

The physical appearance and layout of cities varied greatly from one region to the next. Most had fortifications, such as towers and walls, and gates that were used to control the flow of traffic and closed at night. Within the walls, palaces, cathedrals, and town halls rose highest above the streets and squares. Cities were divided into neighborhoods, most of them identified with a particular economic activity. Some cities had a large population of farmers, who lived within the walls but worked in fields just outside, or else held plots of open, cultivable land at the city's edge.

Within the walls, a broad range of social classes met on the streets. Dress distinguished the rich from the poor, the working class from the men and women of leisure and those connected with the courts. The crowds included itinerant peddlers, foreign merchants and, in university towns, students from far and wide, who formed an often-unruly faction tending to disturbances and disorder. With chaotic, unplanned street systems, Renaissance cities were choked with foot and vehicle traffic, and many city-dwellers lived in crowded, unsafe, and unsanitary homes, built high above the street. In the Middle Ages, these conditions had forced many outside and into the street during the day, making the medieval town a scene of public spectacle and entertainment. In the Renaissance, public life and entertainment began moving indoors, and took the form of musical concerts, plays, dances, gambling houses, and other diversions.

While medieval nobles and princes had ruled feudal towns independently of monarchs, many Renaissance cities had elected assemblies and councils that governed their affairs. The larger city-states in Italy, such as Milan, Florence, and Venice, also had authority over a surrounding region, including smaller cities and towns. These cities established separate authorities to deal with public health, sanitation, fire prevention, public hospitals and charity wards, policing, tax collection, and defense. An important trend in the Renaissance was the loss of autonomy by provinces and their capitals—the old medieval patchwork of small principalities—as national monarchies consolidated their power in capital cities, such as Paris, Madrid, and London. The local princes who had held sway in their autonomous and fortified cities lost both power and importance, while the artisan and merchant classes gained prestige with the establishment of guilds, mutual protection societies, and increase in trade.

Religious, social, political, and professional clubs knit the urban population together. Confraternities were secular associations meant to carry out the works of the church. Political groups formed to contend for power; guilds worked for the interests of artisans, merchants, and artists. Academies brought together noble patrons, scholars, and students, for the exchange of ideas. All of these groups had their bylaws and elected leaders, and carried out a vital function for ordinary individuals, who were powerless to effect change or further their interests on their own.

The Protestant Reformation—the rebellion against the Catholic Church initiated by Martin Luther—had a drastic effect on Renaissance urban life. The Reformation divided many towns along religious lines. Protestants reduced the role of the church in civic life, ended any civic authority of the clergy, ended monastic life, and made worship more a private and personal affair. Catholic regions kept their sense of religious brotherhood, public festivals and holidays, and the regular assembly of Mass. To enforce Catholic orthodoxy, the church established inquisitions in many regions to root out heretics and apostates, enforcing a uniform religious faith with the use of prisons, torture, and public executions.

The cities were nodes of exchange, in a system of trade that was expanding rapidly with the improvement of communication and transportation. Certain cities had industrial specialties, such as textile making in the Low Countries, ironworking in the Rhine valley, and banking in northern Italy. Port cities were centers of maritime industries: shipbuilding, warehousing, sail making, rope making, and provisioning armaments. In some cities professions were performed within certain nationalities and ethnic groups; throughout Europe the Jews were limited in the professions they could follow, often herded into walled ghettoes, or prohibited from cities altogether.

Toward the end of the Renaissance, economic stagnation took hold in southern Europe as trade shifted to the north and costly wars drained treasuries and the cities of men and material. Although Spain drew an immense amount of money from its colonies in the Americas, its ambitious kings bankrupted their realm through costly wars in Italy and the Low Countries. Heavily taxed and with their productive members levied into the royal armies, the cities of Spain saw their industries and commerce decline. The Thirty Years' War devastated cities in central Europe and Germany, while Venice and Genoa had to deal with the rising Ottoman Empire, whose corsairs and navies were closing the Mediterranean to European merchants altogether.

Nevertheless, the crowded, walled city had become a fixture in the landscape of Europe, and continued to draw immigrants from the countryside. Urban population would continue to increase after the Renaissance, and the city's role as a center of education, the arts, and an economic and cultural exchange between nations would remain.

classical literature

The works of the ancient Greeks and Romans survived the fall of the western Roman Empire and the chaos of the early Middle Ages. In monasteries of Europe and the British Isles, scribes carefully copied these books by hand and preserved them in small libraries. Medieval scholars knew the works of the Greek philosopher Aristotle, and the Roman historians Livy, Sallust, and Julius Caesar. Virgil's *The Aeneid* was considered the finest work of epic poetry, and the themes and characters of the *Metamorphoses of Ovid* inspired many medieval poets and artists.

The Italian poet Petrarch was the leading medieval scholar of classical literature, and the first to seek out and collect unknown ancient works, including the speeches of the Roman orator Cicero. Petrarch drew on classical ideas in his own works of history and poetry. He devoted much of his work to revising and editing manuscripts that had gone through many changes in the centuries since they were written. In his editing of the Roman historian Livy, for example, Petrarch made notes and suggestions wherever the meaning or language was not clear, and brought out corrected editions of his own.

In the early fifteenth century, collecting ancient manuscripts became a popular pastime of writers and scholars. Poggio Bracciolini spent years browsing through the libraries and monasteries of northern Europe. The poet Angelo Poliziano mastered ancient Greek, a rare feat in the early Renaissance, when the language was all but unknown in western Europe. Poliziano's scholarship was the most thorough and skilled of his times. He carefully traced the history of the books he examined, comparing the different versions in an attempt to arrive at the language of the archetype, or original work. This method of collation was an important advance over emendation, in which scholars applied their own interpretations to the original manuscripts and made additions and deletions directly to the text according to whim.

The invention of printing in the mid-fifteenth century proved a great boon to classical scholarship. Books no longer had to be transcribed by hand, and could be printed in large, uniform editions. Printing these editions in copies of hundreds gave rise to a much larger audience and widespread knowledge of ancient works. By the sixteenth century nearly all of the currently known works of ancient Latin authors were in print. In addition, the study and revival of classical Latin played a key role in the flowering of art, philosophy, law, and science in Renaissance Europe.

Most of the new books were in Latin, while the ancient Greek writers appeared in new Latin translations as the works of Herodotus, Thucydides, Sophocles, and Aeschylus and Ptolemy began turning up in the fifteenth century. Giovanni Aurispa, an enthusiastic manuscript hunter, traveled to Byzantium to search out unknown works, while Greeks fleeing the assault of the Turks (who overthrew the Byzantine Empire in 1453) came west with their ancient literature. Inspired by the story of the library of Alexandria, Pope Nicholas V sought to establish its modern rival in the Vatican and commissioned the translation of Greek works into Latin. In the 1470s, the library was finally created by Pope Sixtus IV, who made an immense collection of nearly four thousand books and manuscripts available to scholars.

In northern Europe, classical scholarship of the sixteenth century went beyond the discovery and explanation of the ancient texts. Scholars of the Netherlands and Germany applied the actions and ideals of ancient rulers and philosophers to the events taking place in their own day, especially the many conflicts brewing around the Protestant Reformation. The ideas of Aristotle, Marcus Aurelius, Plato, and Demosthenes entered the intellectual mainstream and were taken up by philosophers, poets, playwrights, and university lecturers. The ancient Greeks and Romans became widely regarded as the intellectual forebears of European civilization, even as the formerly universal Catholic Church was torn by dissent and movements for reform.

SEE ALSO: Aristotelianism; Aurispa, Giovanni; humanism; Nicholas

Clement VII
(1342–1394)

"Antipope" whose election brought about the Great Western Schism. Born Robert of Geneva, the son of the Count of Geneva, he was appointed bishop of Therouanne in 1361 and of the city of Cambrai in 1368. In 1371 he became a member of the College of Cardinals, the body that elects the pope. As a cardinal he led a brutal campaign against the town of Cesena, where the townspeople were resisting direct control of the pope. He put down the rebellion but a massacre he ordered of several thousand inhabitants earned him the nickname of "Butcher of Cesena." After this event, he was elected pope by a committee of French cardinals after the death of Gregory XI, but the election was contested by another candidate, Urban VI. Allied to the French king, Clement left Rome to establish a rival papal court and administration in Avignon, in what is now southern France. This commenced the Great Schism that did lasting damage to the church. With rival popes enthroned at Avignon and Rome, all of Christendom was forced to choose sides. The authority of the church hierarchy was thrown into doubt, inspiring the first stirrings of a movement for reformation of the church. Clement had the support of France, Scotland, Spain, and the Kingdom of Naples, as well as several states in the Holy Roman Empire, but he was unable to heal the breach in the church that continued for another generation after his death.

Clitherow, Margaret (1556–1586)

A Catholic martyr who lived and died in the northern English city of York, sometimes referred to as the Pearl of York. She was the daughter of Thomas Middleton, a chandler who would become the sheriff of York in 1564. She was raised as a Protestant, marrying a prosperous butcher, John Clitherow, who was a devout Protestant but whose close brother was Catholic. Margaret converted to Catholicism at the age of eighteen. During the reign of Elizabeth I, England was returning to the Protestant Anglican church established under Elizabeth's father Henry VIII. Strict laws enforcing attendance at the Anglican parishes landed her in prison for two years for her defiance. She made her home a center of Catholic resistance to the religious laws and Protestant domination. She took in Catholic priests and held secret Masses in hidden chambers in her home, and sent her own son abroad to a Catholic school.

In the meantime the English government had passed laws banning priests from the realm, and against protecting any Catholic or taking part in Catholic fasts, prayers, confessions, or religious ceremonies on penalty of death. In 1586, her husband John Clitherow was summoned to appear before the magistrates of York to explain his wife's activities; during the investigation hiding places in her home were found, along with the robes of Catholic priests. Margaret was arrested and charged with harboring fugitive priests and attending a Catholic Mass. On refusing to plead her case or call any witnesses in her defense, in order to spare her children and servants, she was sentenced to be crushed to death. The sentence was carried out on March 25, 1586. Her happy bearing and refusal to confess to any crime at the place of her execution made her into one of the most prominent martyrs of Catholicism.

SEE ALSO: Catholicism; Elizabeth I; England

clothing

New styles of dress evolved in the Renaissance, when men and women became acutely aware of clothing fashion. Throughout Europe, the cut, color, and material of clothes became important indicators of status, profession, and wealth. The clothing industry flourished, including a busy international trade in textiles and the creation of weaving and cloth-making workshops. New technologies allowed manufacturers to weave and dye clothing in larger quantities and at a faster pace. A general improvement in economic conditions allowed members of the middle class more disposable income to spend on clothing and ornaments. The changing style of clothing proved troublesome to the authorities, however, and new sumptuary laws limited the display of certain fabrics and colors, in order to more clearly differentiate the classes and keep society orderly.

Clothing and luxury industries thrived in Italy, where Florence and Lucca became prosperous silk-weaving centers that imported their raw material through the port of Venice. The Lucchese clothing industries also imported eastern fashion with their raw silk, adopting patterns and motifs of Chinese and Mongol clothing. Florence was known for its floral patterns. Italian damask, velvet, lace, satin, and taffeta were sold throughout the continent, and for those who could afford it, these luxury materials replaced heavy wool and simple linens as clothing material. The war in northern Italy, in which French and

German armies played an important role, also served to spread Italian fashion and material to northern Europe.

Throughout Europe, taste in clothing ran to heavy fabrics, elaborate drapery, close-fitting garments that emphasized the shape of the body, and head coverings. The fanciest clothes were lined with fur, ermine, or mink, and decorated with silver buttons, jewelry, fine lace, and gold thread. Men wore elaborate costumes that represented their authority and masculinity. The long robes and surcoats (overcoats) of the medieval era went out of style and was replaced by the doublet that was fitted and belted at the waist, and which accentuated the shoulders. Lower legs were covered with hose. The ruff was a lace ornament worn around the neck; the codpiece drew attention to the genitals. Men commonly wore swords at their side or carried small pistols or daggers for self-defense.

Women's fashions changed even more drastically than that of men. Hemlines dropped to the ground, and the full figure was magnified by several layers of clothing. Accessories grew in importance; women wore a variety of adornments, jewelry, and headgear. Men and women sported earrings, gloves, and rings. Women wore veils and wigs, which also became more popular for men at the close of the Renaissance.

Northern Europeans had a taste for padded sleeves and doublets, which made the figure more plump and rounded, which was the ideal of Renaissance beauty. German clothing was known for its puffs at the shoulders and knees, feathered hats, and slashing: two layers of cloth were placed one over the other, with the outer layer slashed to reveal the contrasting colors and material of the inner one. According to one tradition, the victory of the Swiss over the armies of Charles the Bold in 1476 brought about the rage for slashed clothing. The Swiss soldiers had taken clothing from the defeated on the battlefield, slashing the garments with their swords in order to improve the fit. For many, slashing was a way to defy sumptuary laws decreeing that commoners should wear clothing of only one color.

For artisans and the lower classes, clothing was simpler, and more utilitarian. Men wore linen breeches and woolen jackets; women wore skirts that reached to the ground and bodices overlaid with cloaks in cold or rainy weather. There were no ornaments and most clothing was black, gray, or brown in color.

Toward the end of the Renaissance Spanish clothing fashion took hold throughout Europe. Dark colors and especially black were favored, and the cut of clothes grew more straight and linear (the modern suit jacket evolved from late Renaissance clothing in the Spanish style). Women's upper bodies became more tightly constricted, while the Spanish also gave the world the farthingale, a hoopskirt that completely concealed the shape of the legs. The farthingale was combined with puffy sleeves and lace ruffs that completely covered the neck, giving women the appearance of a richly clothed fortress.

In England, tight sleeves and narrow bodices were fashionable. In the late sixteenth century, Queen Elizabeth I became the leading fashion arbiter among the English. The queen was ever conscious of the effect of appearance and ornament on those she dealt with, and set the standard of English Renaissance costume for women, with simple bodices, narrow waists, full-length skirts, and elaborate lace embroidery.

The Protestant movement greatly simplified the color and cut of clothing as well, and in some regions banished color altogether in favor of simple, unornamented black or white. To modestly cover the hair, women wore a variety of headdresses that harkened back to medieval times, including the bonnet and the wimple.

In southern Europe and Italy, the classes remained more sharply differentiated by their dress. At the height of fashion were the nobility, who held luxurious clothing as one of the bastions and symbols of superiority over the lower classes. But matching the nobility, especially in the city of Venice, were the courtesans whose business it was to cater to wealthy aristocrats and powerful men. Courtesans set the fashion tone with lavish gowns, elaborate headgear, glittering jewelry, alluring makeup, and high-heeled shoes—making them indistinguishable from the women of the nobility. Eventually the Venetian authorities took action and prohibited courtesans from wearing precious gems, gold, silver, silk, or necklaces and rings of any kind.

Clouet, Francois (1515–1572)

French portrait painter and miniaturist, born in Tours as the son of the artist Jean Clouet. He learned painting from his father and was brought to the court of King Francis I at a young age. He followed in his father's footsteps by winning an appointment as the king's court painter in about 1540. After the death of the king, he remained at the French court as the painter of King Henry II, Francis II, and Charles IX. He is best known for two portraits, *Elizabeth of Austria* and *The Apothecarist Pierre Quthe*, as well as the work known as *Lady in Her Bath*, a work that took the court and the art world by storm and set off a rage for bath portraits that remained a staple of the late Renaissance and early Baroque periods. These three works were the only paintings Clouet signed. He also executed paintings of Catherine de Médicis, Francis I, Mary Queen of Scots, and Charles IX. Clouet was a skilled draftsman and a painter with a special ability to reveal the emotion and character of his subjects in his works. His fame spread widely among the nobility of France and Clouet found his work in high demand throughout his life.

SEE ALSO: painting

Colleoni, Bartolomeo (1400–1475)

Italian mercenary born in Solza, northern Italy. His father, Paolo Colleoni, was a local nobleman who was killed by his own cousins in a dispute over an estate. Bartolomeo trained as a soldier in the city of Piacenza and then became a professional soldier. He fought in southern Italy for Alfonso of Aragon, who was disputing the throne of Naples with the Angevin dynasty. He then joined the army of Venice, where he quickly rose within the ranks. He led the Venetian army to victories against the city's arch rival, Milan. After Venice and Milan reached a truce, Colleoni entered the service of Milan, where he was arrested for suspected treason by the Visconti family, the reigning lords of the city. He returned to Venice, where he was made captain-general of the army. Venice rewarded him with profitable estates and lands and, on his death, honored his memory with an impressive statue of himself created by Andrea del Verrocchio that still stands.

Colonna, Vittoria
(1490–1547)

Italian poet and noblewoman, a significant friend and patron of Renaissance authors and artists. The daughter of a nobleman who held the title of Grand Constable of Naples, she was born in Marino, an estate of her father Fabrizio Colonna near Rome. Her marriage to Francesco D'Avalos, the marquis of Pescara, was arranged when she was just four years old. The wealth and prestige of her family attracted several more offers of marriage, but she met and fell in love with D'Avalos and finally married him when she was nineteen. Shortly after the ceremony in Naples, her husband enlisted with the armies of Emperor Charles V, who was fighting the French in northern Italy. D'Avalos was taken prisoner in Italy in 1512 and spent the next dozen years campaigning throughout Italy, while Colonna remained at his estate on the island of Ischia. After the Battle of Pavia in 1525, when D'Avalos was offered the throne of Naples for turning against Charles V, she persuaded him to turn down the offer. D'Avalos died soon afterward of wounds suffered in battle.

Grieving and determined to remain a single widow, Colonna devoted the rest of her life to the support of religious orders, the reform of the Catholic Church, and her poetry. Her verses in praise and memory of Francesco D'Avalos would be collected in 1538 under the title *Rime de la Divina Vittoria Colonna Marchesa di Pescara*. Her later poetry turned to religion and her spiritual life; she was an outspoken advocate of reform in the Catholic Church but would not accept Protestantism. She lived in Rome, Orvieto, and Ferrara, where she helped to establish a monastery, and became a patron and close friend of artists, including Michelangelo, and the writers Baldassare Castiglione and Pietro Bembo.

SEE ALSO: Michelangelo Buonarroti

Columbus, Christopher
(1451–1506)

Italian navigator who led the first European expeditions to the coasts and islands of the Caribbean Sea and South America. Born in Genoa as Christoforo Colombo, he was the son of a weaver, Domenico Colombo, and Susanna Fontanarossa. He received some education and learned Latin and Greek, and may have apprenticed with his father as a weaver. But finding a stronger taste for adventure and the sailor's life, Columbus joined the fleet of Rene of Anjou, a contestant for the throne of Naples, and then enlisted as a sailor for his native city of Genoa, at that time one of Europe's wealthiest merchant cities. He was wounded off the coast of Portugal in 1476; taking shelter in Lisbon, he joined his brother, who was a mapmaker, and began conceiving the idea of a western expedition to the East Indies.

The conquest of Constantinople by the Ottoman Turks in 1453, as well as the control of ports along the coast of North Africa and the Red Sea by Arab princes, made the land route to Asia hazardous to the health and wealth of European merchants. In the late fifteenth century, Portuguese navigators were exploring new routes to East Asia around the southern limit of Africa. Some time during his training and experience as a sailor, Columbus hit on the idea of a westerly route through unknown seas that would, he hoped, provide a much quicker route to the spices, silks, and other valuables of China, India, and the Spice Islands (of what is now Indonesia). Using the calculations of ancient navigators and geogra-

Christopher Columbus at the court of Ferdinand and Isabella, displaying some of the results of his voyage. THE LIBRARY OF CONGRESS.

phers, however, Columbus underestimated the circumference of the earth, a mistake that led him to the false notion that the westerly route would be faster and easier.

Historians generally credit Norwegian Vikings as the first European navigators to reach North America. However, the Viking expedition of around 1000 A.D. that established a small settlement in what is now Newfoundland was unknown to the rest of Europe and failed to establish a permanent settlement. In 1485, Columbus first proposed a new voyage to the west to the king of Portugal, John II. He asked for a fleet of three ships and a reward of 10 percent of all income from new land he discovered. The offer was rejected, after which Columbus turned to Ferdinand and Isabella, the monarchs of a newly united kingdom of Spain. He would sail from the port of Seville south to the Canary Islands,

then head due west and remain on that course until reaching Japan. Columbus believed he would enjoy clear sailing all the way to Asia.

At the time the kingdom of Spain was struggling with debts and in dire need of trade and gold; the relatively weak Spanish fleets, however, had no hope of overcoming the Portuguese, who were building and strengthening trading ports throughout Asia. Although the king and queen of Spain were advised to reject Columbus's voyage by navigators who claimed he was misjudging the distance to Asia, they rewarded him with a pension to prevent him from sailing for any rival nation and finally agreed to support his expedition in 1492. Columbus was named "Admiral of the Ocean Sea" and was promised a generous portion of money earned from any new Spanish ports or colonies.

The first expedition of three small ships set out in August 1492, taking five weeks to sail from the Canary Islands to a small island in the Bahamas Columbus called San Salvador, on October 12. The expedition continued to Cuba and Hispaniola, where the flagship Santa Maria ran aground. On Hispaniola Columbus founded a small settlement, La Navidad, where he left behind thirty-nine sailors.

The success of his first expedition earned Columbus acclaim in Spain and an agreement by Ferdinand and Isabella to support a second, much larger expedition of seventeen ships, which left in September 1493. This time the admiral landed on Dominica and Guadeloupe, then turned north and sailed through the long chain of small islands now known as the Lesser Antilles. The fleet passed the Virgin Islands and landed at Puerto Rico, but on encountering a hostile Carib village Columbus ordered his ships to Hispaniola, where he founded the settlement of Isabela. The expedition touched at Cuba and Jamaica before returning to Spain in the early fall of 1494.

A third expedition left Spain in May 1498. Columbus reached Trinidad and the coasts of what is now Venezuela. His harsh management of his own sailors and mistreatment of natives, however, led to his arrest by the governor of Hispaniola. Columbus was put in chains and returned to Spain a prisoner along with two of his brothers. He was summarily relieved of all duties as governor of the lands he had discovered, and denied any profit from the income attained from the new Spanish colonies.

Still determined to find a passage to the Spice Islands, Columbus managed to win his freedom and convince Ferdinand and Isabella to support a fourth voyage.

This fleet set out in May 1502. On arriving at Hispaniola, he was defied by the Spanish governor of Santo Domingo. His fleet then sailed to the coast of Honduras in Central America and then southward to Panama, where it encountered a fierce storm. Returning to Jamaica, his fleet was wrecked in another storm, and Columbus was forced to remain on Jamaica for more than a year awaiting rescue. The governor of Hispaniola, now the admiral's sworn enemy, finally sent help and Columbus succeeded in returning to Spain in November 1504.

Columbus has been hailed for more than five centuries as an intrepid navigator—and criticized for the harsh treatment he meted out to his sailors as well as Native Americans, whom he considered subhuman barbarians in desperate need of conversion to the Christian religion. His voyages began the era of exploration and colonization of North and South America by Europeans, an undertaking that greatly enriched and transformed Europe. He grew bitter at the imprisonment he suffered at the hands of his patrons in Spain, however, and died still unaware of the western hemisphere, and convinced he had found a faster route to Asia.

SEE ALSO: da Gama, Vasco; exploration; Ferdinand II of Aragon; Isabella I of Castile

commedia dell'arte

A form of improvisational theater that originated in Renaissance Italy, and that entertained outdoor audiences with a familiar cast of colorful, dramatic and comic characters. Commedia dell'arte was performed by itinerate troupes of players, each of whom specialized in a particular character. The plots were familiar to actors as well as audiences and usually involved the misadventures of two lovers who were continually frustrated in their desire for marriage and respectability. The plays, known as *canovacci*, were frequently interrupted by music, dancing, magic acts, juggling, and acrobatics. The characters and plot devices endured in many later forms of art, from serious opera to pantomime and Punch and Judy puppet shows.

The characters and plot of commedia dell'art often revolve around the Innamorati or Lovers, whose romance sparks much of the plot. Arlecchino (Harlequin) is a crafty and untrustworthy servant, who is constantly scheming to take advantage of the other characters. A pair of noisy sticks that he carries around the set gave rise to the expression "slapstick," meaning rough physical comedy. Brighella, a servant or innkeeper, is free with advice to the lovers of the play, and is also skilled at the arts of magic and fortunetelling. Il Capitano represents authority, a man with an impressive and courageous front who is in fact a cowardly incompetent. Il Dottore, the doctor, makes a show of his scientific knowledge, but like Il Capitano he always suffers a comeuppance at the end of the play. The rich miser, Pantalone, acts the aristocrat, and wears an impressive suit of clothes as well as a prominent money belt. He lords it over the other characters but is quite fearful of losing his money as well as his position. Zanni, a slow and stupid servant, is a buffoon who would rather sleep than work and who has few redeeming qualities.

The characters of commedia dell'arte had particular clothing, gestures, speech, and movement. Their masks evoked their inner characters as well, with Pantalone sporting the long hooked nose of a miser and Zunni the simple unadorned white robes of a servant. Some actors gained international renown for their skill at portraying stock characters and improvising dialogue, and the most prestigious commedia troupes were invited to royal and aristocratic courts for command performances. The plays were not high drama or serious theater, but rather popular entertainment that drew laughs with bawdy repartee and noisy pratfalls. During the Renaissance it spread to northern Europe, where the characters were adapted to local tastes. Commedia dell'arte troupes roamed until the tradition began to die out in the eighteenth century.

confraternities

The confraternity was an organization of the Christian faithful who did not belong to the church, but who banded together in order to live by Christian precepts and doctrine. The confraternities met for worship, for the instruction of the public and the young, for performing works of charity and visiting the sick, for organizing public processions, for the patronage of writers and artists, and for the celebration of weddings, funerals, and other important events. In some towns, a majority of men and many women belonged to a confraternity. By some estimates as many as one out of every five city-dwellers during the Renaissance belonged to such a group. Confraternities were most popular in Catholic Europe; Protestantism rejected the practice of confraternities and their adherence to traditional Catholic doctrines. Confraternities originated modern charities and the system of public welfare in Europe, on the basis of religious belief and worship, and also played a role in the reforms of the church hierarchy.

The confraternities originated in the Middle Ages, when the religious orders allowed lay people to join them as auxiliary members. Most confraternities were made up of urbanites who belonged to a growing middle class of merchants and artisans. In city politics, they became a force to be reckoned with, often opposed to ruling dynasties and the interests of the nobility. Some confraternities were small and secretive, and modeled themselves on the apostles of the New Testament. Others were larger and more public, welcoming anyone who qualified to enter their ranks. They were a familiar presence in cities containing churches, meeting houses, and dining halls for the use of their members. A few, such as the Brotherhood of the Rosary, crossed national boundaries. This confraternity, founded in Cologne, Germany, by Jacob Sprenger, reached a membership of 1 million, with members in Germany, Italy, France, Portugal, Spain, and the Low Countries.

Confraternities established hospitals and homes for orphans, the destitute, and the victims of epidemics. They collected alms for the poor, and in times of plague or natural disaster they organized relief for stricken families who had lost their breadwinners. A confraternity of Tuscany founded an ambulance service to transport the sick and wounded, an institution that has survived into the twenty-first century. Some confraternities had a more religious purpose, organized to build or maintain a local parish church, a function more common in northern Europe.

In Italy confraternities were organized in certain quarters of the cities and among certain communities. The structure and administration paralleled that of the merchant guilds by holding elections for their leaders and appointing secretaries and other functionaries. Members had to pass a review of their history and character, and had to be approved by a majority vote of the established members. Strict codes of behavior were set down for members, who were expected to contribute regular dues as well as labor and time; dues in some confraternities helped fund an early form of insurance, for the payment of medical, funeral, and other costs that members would have to bear in old age.

The confraternities held regular religious services, Masses, confession, and communion. Some penitential confraternities made their goal the expulsion of community sin by selling indulgences on behalf of the church, through acts such as flagellation in public, fasting and solemn religious processions. Confraternities staged mystery plays and musical works such as hymns and Masses that were commissioned from local composers.

The Protestant Reformation put an end to the traditional Catholic confraternities in many parts of northern Europe. In the doctrine of Martin Luther—who initiated the Reformation—salvation was secured by an individual's faith alone, which clashed with the Catholic emphasis on works and public piety. Many confraternities evolved into secular organizations, or limited their activities to church functions, a fate that was followed in later centuries by Catholic confraternities of southern Europe.

SEE ALSO: Catholicism; Reformation, Protestant

Copernicus, Nicolaus (1473–1543)

Polish astronomer who proposed a heliocentric (sun-centered) universe, an important foundation of modern scientific thought. Born in the town of Thorn (or Torun), then ruled by Poland, Copernicus was a member of a well-to-do merchant family. After the death of his father, he

A page from Nicolaus Copernicus's 1543 volume "De Revolutionbus Orbium Coelestium" that displays the relative positions of the planets around the sun. HULTON ARCHIVE/ GETTY IMAGES.

joined the household of his uncle, a local bishop, who saw to Nicolaus's upbringing and education. Nicolaus attended the university in Krakow, Poland, and then studied at Bologna and Padua in Italy, taking up law and mathematics. At the insistence of his uncle, he also became a trained physician. His true interest, however, lay in astronomy. While a student in Ferrara, Italy, he attended lectures given by the astronomer Domenico Maria Novara de Ferrara, who accepted Copernicus for a time as his assistant. Copernicus also traveled to Rome, where he held lectures on astronomy and made observations of a lunar eclipse.

When he returned to Poland, Copernicus was appointed as a canon of the cathedral at Frauenberg, where he earned a steady income as a church administrator. From his house, he observed the stars and planets and worked out a theory contrary to the notion of the ancient Greeks. Aristotle and Ptolemy believed the earth was the center of the universe; Ptolemy proposed the idea that the stars and planets move about the earth in a series of concentric shells. The Ptolemaic system became the accepted dogma of the Catholic Church, which during the Renaissance was still condemning new scientific ideas as impious heresies.

In the Copernican system, the universe is heliocentric, with the earth, stars, moon, and planets all revolving around the sun. The Copernican system explained the mysterious retrograde motion of the planets, which occasionally seem to move backward in their nightly tracks through the sky. Astronomers of ancient and medieval times had to explain retrograde motion with a series of complex schemes and mathematical calculations, while the heliocentric system solved it by pointing out that the position of planets in different orbits about the sun can have irregular positions to an observer on earth.

Copernicus summarized these ideas in a treatise, *Brief Commentary*, that he passed among friends and colleagues starting in about 1512. He kept a more detailed work that he entitled *On the Revolutions*, in manuscript form. In the meantime, he served in his professional capacities as a church canon, a doctor, and a tax collector. He produced a useful essay on the problem of monetary inflation in which he astutely observed that money will lose its value as more of it circulates. Copernicus's opinions and remedies on this subject, although effective, have been completely overlooked by his astronomy.

Copernicus's ideas were spreading throughout Europe despite his desire to keep them secret. He feared the harsh opinions of scientists, who were sure to ridicule his notion, as well as the judgment of the church, which he believed might find him to be a heretic. He was roundly criticized by the Protestant reformers at the same time Pope Clement VII and his cardinals were learning of the heliocentric theory through reports and lectures in Rome. In 1539 George Rheticus, a scholar attending the University of Wittenberg, met Copernicus, who agreed to tutor the younger man in mathematics and astronomy. Rheticus enthusiastically accepted the heliocentric theory and wrote his own treatise detailing it, entitled *First Account*. This emboldened Copernicus to bring out his own book, *On the Revolutions*, which was finally published in 1543, just a few weeks before its author died.

The Copernican system began a scientific and philosophical revolution in Europe. By moving the earth from its symbolic position at the center of the universe, it forced astronomers to consider the possibility that the known world was but a small and insignificant part of all creation. It also suggested that human observation and perception often led to false or misleading conclusions about the true state of the natural world. Scientific skepticism began with this questioning of a phenomenon obvious to everyone: that the sun moves through the sky every day.

The heliocentric theory was gradually accepted and modified by the leading astronomers and scientists in Europe, including Johannes Kepler and Galileo Galilei (who was among the first to make astronomical observations with a telescope).

The Catholic Church, however, found the Copernican system to be contrary to accepted Christian doctrine, and placed *On the Revolutions* on its Index of prohibited books in 1616. The Enlightenment, a movement of natural philosophy that rejected religious doctrine as a basis for scientific observation altogether, accepted the heliocentric system in the eighteenth century. But it wasn't until 1835 that the book of Copernicus detailing this system was taken off the list of books banned by the Vatican.

SEE ALSO: astronomy; Brahe, Tycho; Galilei, Galileo; Kepler, Johannes

Correggio
(1494–1534)

Italian artist, born Antonio Allegri in the town of Correggio in Lombardy. He was the son of a merchant and apprenticed as a painter in the city of Modena with Francesco Ferrara. He returned to Correggio in 1506 and began working on religious paintings for wealthy patrons and on commission from the city fathers of Mantua. He was influenced by Leonardo da Vinci and Andrea Mantegna in his early works, including *Madonna of St. Francis* and *Adoration of the Child with St. Elizabeth and John*. In about 1518 he went to Rome, where he studied the works of Michelangelo and Raphael, then returned to Parma, where he was commissioned to create frescoes for the convent of San Paolo. These paintings were done on the walls and ceiling of the Camera di San Paolo, the drawing room of Giovanna da Piacenza, the abbess of the convent. Depicted is the mythical figure of Diana, goddess of the hunt, and a scene of cherubs set in an arbor overgrown with fruits and vines. Correggio also painted the apse, nave, and interior dome of the church of

San Giovanni Evangelista. The dome painting—known as *The Vision of St. John the Evangelist on Patmos*—shows Christ and other figures in perspective, looking directly down on the view and worshippers. In the cathedral of Parma the painter created an even more elaborate cupola ceiling, depicting the assumption of the Virgin Mary among a crowded scene of saints and angels. In this work Correggio drew on his study of Michelangelo's Sistine Chapel ceiling, and his own great skill at perspective, to draw the viewer directly into the complex action of the painting.

Correggio executed several majestic, elaborate altarpieces, including the *Madonna of St. Sebastian, Adoration of the Shepherds*, and the *Madonna of St. George*. One of his most famous small paintings, *Christ on the Mount of Olives*, shows the figure of Christ kneeling and gesturing in a setting of darkness illuminated by a holy light from the heavens. Other renowned paintings of Correggio are the *Madonna of the Baske* and *Madonna Adoring the Christ Child*. Federigo Gonzaga, the duke of Mantua, commissioned from Correggio a series of six paintings of mythological scenes, inspired by the work of the ancient Roman poet Ovid. These paintings broke new ground in their eroticism and depiction of the human form, such as in *Leda and the Swan, Ganymede Abducted by the Eagle*, and *The Education of Cupid*, which shows a nude Venus looking directly at the viewer. Correggio remained in the town of Parma for most of his life, far from the mainstreams of Renaissance art and thought in Rome and Florence. But his work was admired by painters in the years to come, who adopted his depiction of figures in motion, foreshortening, and lush scenery to create new traditions in the Baroque and Rococo periods.

SEE ALSO: Michelangelo Buonarroti; painting; Raphael

Cortes, Hernán (1485–1547)

Spanish conquistador (conqueror), who subdued the Aztecs of Mexico and founded the colony of New Spain precursor to the modern Republic of Mexico. Born in the town of Medellin in the Estremadura region of Castile, Cortes was the son of a soldier and the cousin of Francisco Pizarro, the conqueror of the Inca Empire of Peru. Cortes attended the University of Salamanca but, in search of a more adventurous life, dropped his studies in law after two years. By this time, the discovery of a new continent was inspiring dreams of riches and glory among many young Spaniards.

Cortes first enlisted with the fleet of Nicolas de Ovando, the newly appointed governor of Hispaniola, but an accident while climbing out of his mistress's window in Medellin prevented him from sailing. He finally reached the West Indies in 1503, arriving with a Spanish expedition to Hispaniola and Cuba. He was granted an *encomienda* (estate) on Hispaniola by the governor, Diego Velazquez de Curellar, as well as a number of Indian slaves. In 1511 he set out with Velazquez to conquer the island of Cuba. For his service he was appointed treasurer of the new colony, responsible for directing 20 percent of all income from it to the Spanish crown, and an appointment as mayor of the town of Santiago, the island's capital city.

In 1519 he was appointed to lead an expedition to the mainland of North America. By this time, he was at odds with Velazquez, who recalled him at the last minute from the expedition. Cortes defied these orders and sailed with 508 men and sixteen horses for the Mexican coast. On reaching land, he promptly burned his ships to end any idea among his men of retreating from his intended conquest of establishing a new colony on the mainland. Cortes organized a *cabildo*, or town government, at Veracruz, then had the town appoint him as captain of an expedition to the interior, in this way escaping the authority of Velazquez.

At this time a powerful Aztec empire was ruling from a populous and wealthy capital, Tenochtitlán, built on a series of lakes and islands in the highlands of what is now central Mexico. To defeat the Aztecs, Cortez allied with their enemies, the Totonac and Nahua people, and gathered more allies in Tlaxcala, where he reinforced his small force of Spanish infantry and horsemen. On reaching Tenochtitlán, Cortes and his men were received as guests at the palace of the Aztec king, Montezuma, who believed Cortes to be a legendary god Quetzalcoatl. Cortes soon took the king prisoner, a hostage for the good behavior of the Aztecs.

On hearing of a second expedition arriving to relieve him of his command, Cortes left Tenochtitlán in the hands of one of his captains, Pedro Arias de Avila, and returned to the coast. There he defeated his opponents and persuaded many of their company to join his army. On returning to Tenochtitlán, Cortes found the city in revolt against de Avila, who was ruling the Aztecs as a tyrant. In the fighting Montezuma was killed and Cortes was forced to flee in what became known as *La Noche Triste*, or "The Unhappy Night." Cortes waited two years in the hills near the city and finally gathered his men for a siege. Eventually the Spanish horses and artillery overcame the city's defenders;

Cortes made the new emperor Cuauhtémoc a prisoner.

King Charles I of Spain appointed Cortes governor of the colony of New Spain. Under Cortes's rule, the ancient Aztec city was destroyed and a new colonial capital was raised. The Aztecs were converted to Catholicism and served their conquerors as peasant laborers; Cortes also imported slaves from Africa to work on the plantations of New Spain. But his defiance of Velazquez's orders in sailing to Mexico also made the king of Spain suspicious of Cortes's motivations and loyalty, and observers were sent to keep an eye on the colony and its governor.

Ever defiant, Cortes suspected Diego Velazquez of trying to undermine him, and issued an order for Velazquez's arrest. The king of Spain then sent an investigator to uncover the facts of the case. When the investigator died under mysterious circumstances, his successor appointed a replacement for Cortes, who was exiled from New Spain by his replacement. Cortes returned to Spain to answer the charges against him in 1528. He was received by Charles V, rewarded for his success with a title, Marquis of the Valley of Oaxaca, but stripped of his authority of governor.

Cortes returned to Mexico in 1530 and disputed his right to explore northern Mexico with the new governors and administrators of the colony. He set out in 1536 and reached Baja California and the Pacific coast of Mexico. Returning to Spain in 1541, he joined an expedition against the Barbary pirates of North Africa, then found himself back in Spain with heavy debts and disregarded by the Spanish court. Unable to make his case in the Spanish court, he felt himself the victim of injustice and neglect. Without prospects in Spain, he decided to return to the colony he had conquered, but came down with dysentery and died in Seville before his ship set sail.

SEE ALSO: Columbus, Christopher; exploration

Corvinus, Matthias (1440–1490)

King of Hungary, crusader against the Muslim Turks, and celebrated Hungarian patron of the arts and humanities. The son of Janos Hunyadi, himself a widely renowned military leader, Matthias Corvinus was born in Cluj, Transylvania. The nickname "Corvinus," comes from the Latin *corvusa*, or crow, a bird depicted on the Hunyadi coat of arms. Matthias was given a thorough education by an Italian scholar who fired him with enthusiasm for the classics of Latin literature.

He was betrothed to the daughter of Count Ulrich Czilley, a rival of Janos Hunyadi, but this girl died before the marriage. On the death of Hunyadi, a bitter struggle over the crown of Hungary broke out, with Czilley denouncing Matthias and his brother Laszlo as plotting the downfall of King Ladislas V. In 1457 Laszlo and Matthias were captured; Laszlo was executed. A few months later Ladislas V died, while Matthias became a prisoner of the king of Bohemia, George Podebrady. In 1458 a faction of Hungarian nobles elected Matthias as the next king, believing as a young and educated man he would be easy to control.

Opponents of Matthias proclaimed as king the Habsburg emperor Frederick III, who accepted his election and seized the crown jewels of Hungary as symbol of his authority. Matthias proved an able leader, however, and crushed opposition, taking as prisoners many of his rivals as well as Vlad Dracula, the prince of Wallachia. In 1463, Frederick gave up his claim, accepted Matthias as the king of Hungary, and returned the crown. Matthias raised a powerful army of mercenaries to expand the borders of Hungary to Moravia and Silesia in the north and Austria in the west. He campaigned against the Turks in the Balkan Peninsula, defeating them in several battles in Serbia and Transylvania.

At home he established a new judicial system, improved education, and patronized several Italian artists, whom he invited to work at his court. He also built a prestigious library of books and manuscripts, the second largest in Europe after the papal library in Rome.

Council of Basele

A church council held in 1431 in the town of Basele, Switzerland. Its members, including monks, bishops, and scholars, sought to discuss pressing church matters such as the challenge of the Hussites, the Czech reformers who defied the authority of the church. The council was officially convened by Pope Martin V, who died soon after it began meeting. Its members asserted their authority in matters of doctrine, even presuming to give direction to the pope himself in such concerns. They also guided the church in the matter of taxation, in the celebration of the Mass, and in the pope's authority over local church institutions. As the nations of Europe gradually emerged from medieval feudalism, the Council of Basele and others served to express their growing sense of independence from the authority of the Vatican, the papal headquarters in Rome. Greatly weakened by the Great Schism that divided the church among several factions, Pope Eugene IV agreed to recognize the council as legitimate. By a papal decree of

1437 the council was moved to Ferrara, Italy, where it began meeting again in 1438.

SEE ALSO: Council of Constance

Council of Constance

A church council that took place from 1414 until 1418 in Constance (present-day Baden, Germany), called by the Holy Roman Emperor Sigismund to resolve the schism in the church. Since 1378, the Catholic Church had been divided in two, with separate popes supported by different factions of church leaders and the kings and princes of Europe. When the Council of Constance began, an "antipope," John XXIII, was presiding over a rival court in Avignon, France, while Pope Gregory XII was head of the church in Rome and a third pope, Benedict XIII, was also claiming authority over the church.

The Council of Constance took place when the turmoil in the church was prompting an outcry for reform. With Sigismund presiding, the delegates asked all three rival popes to resign their titles, so that a single pope could be elected. In 1415, its delegates passed an important decree known as *Haec Sancta*. This document stated that a general church council took its authority directly from Christ, and that all members of the church, including the pope, were bound to obey its decisions. The Catholic Church has always considered this decree invalid, as the council had not yet been officially convened by the pope of Rome.

When Gregory XII made it known that he would be willing to resign, the delegates at the Council of Constance agreed to receive his representatives in Constance. After their arrival, the pope's representatives officially convened the council in Gregory's name. They then read out his resignation. The council deposed Benedict XII, while Gregory XII also gave up his title. Two years later, the council elected Cardinal Oddone Colonna, who took the name of Martin V. Although the council resolved the papal schism, it did not address important issues that were driving a protest movement led by such men as John Wyclif of England and Jan Hus of Bohemia. Instead, the council invited Jan Hus under a promise of safe passage, then arrested him and ordered him burned at the stake. The protest movement would gather force throughout the fifteenth century and bring about the Protestant Reformation.

SEE ALSO: Catholicism; Hus, Jan; Reformation, Protestant

Council of Ferrara/Florence

This council of bishops, scholars, monks, and church officials began in Basel, Switzerland, and moved to Ferrara, Italy, in 1438, and in the next year to Florence. The council sought to deal with a growing movement of protest and heresy against the corruption of the church. It also had to contend with the papal administration, which resisted its pronouncements and decrees. In the end Pope Eugene IV was forced to recognize the authority of the council, which limited many of the pope's privileges and even set down rules guiding papal elections. In 1439, the council deposed Eugene IV from his throne and elected an "antipope," Felix V, leading to a schism in the church that lasted for ten years. The many bitter controversies over doctrine and the struggle for power between the pope and the councils provided further impetus for the Reformation movement, which would gain strength in the early sixteenth century.

Council of Trent

The Council of Trent was an important church council, attended by cardinals, bishops, archbishops, and papal legates (representatives), who convened to make decisions on church doctrine and ceremony and to oppose the spread of the Protestant Reformation. The council met at the northern Italian city of Trent between 1545 and 1563. It refuted Martin Luther's ideas on the importance of certain books of the Bible, condemned the idea of grace by faith alone, and affirmed the traditional nature of the seven church sacraments. The council set down the liturgy of a standard Catholic Mass, known as the Tridentine Mass, and held that Christ was actually present in the bread and wine of the ceremony. It affirmed the rule of celibacy for priests, the need for infant baptism (which some Protestant sects considered optional), upheld the doctrine of purgatory and the veneration of relics, created an Index of forbidden books, and set down strict guidelines for marriage and divorce. The decrees of the council were ratified by Pope Pius IV in a papal bull of 1564. The council condemned the ideas of the Reformation and reserved to the church the right to punish Protestant heresy as it saw fit; many of its proclamations and decrees have been affirmed by the modern Catholic Church.

courtesan

A courtesan was a professional mistress, a prostitute of the highest rank who provided her services and companionship to wealthy nobles or rulers. Courtesans were popular among Renaissance aristocrats and royalty, whose marriages were often arranged for the political or financial gain of their families. With love an emotion that often remained outside of a legal marriage, the use of courtesans by husbands was often accepted by their wives, who were much more restricted in their actions, their

living conditions, and their ability to circulate in society.

Many women who became courtesans began as common streetwalkers or brothel workers, who welcomed members of the middle class, artisans, and travelers (some brothels were disguised as convents). Prostitutes in most Italian cities were registered, taxed, and regulated by law. Through intelligence, manners, and a good appearance, they gained a safer and more prestigious place in a court through the sponsorship of a man of high rank. Such courtesans were valued for their ability to converse with powerful and intelligent men and put them at ease. In some cases a highly valued courtesan was shared among a group of men, each of whom reserved her company on a certain night of the week. The life of a courtesan was always tenuous, however, as her career depended on gaining the trust and support of patrons. The alliance between a nobleman and a courtesan could end suddenly on the gentleman's whim, leaving the courtesan again with no place of business but the streets.

There were two kinds of courtesans in Italy: the higher rank belonged to the "honest courtesan," a partner for entertainment and intellectual discussion, who was educated and often talented as a writer, singer, or musician. The *cortigiana di lume* was a lower-class courtesan, one who took on all manner of customers, showed no special talent or intellectual ability, and who were generally looked at as prostitutes.

The honest courtesan was supported with gifts of money and other valuables, and sometimes property. In the drive to improve their circumstances, some married women engaged in the profession with the full knowledge and support of their husbands. If they were single, their careers sometimes ended when their customers arranged their marriage—or took them as wives themselves. The courtesan was an ornament, as well as a fashion trend setter and status symbol. She reflected the good taste and wealth of her patron. The most successful courtesans attained complete independence and lived out their lives in comfort and high regard. One such was the famous Roman courtesan Imperia, who lived like a princess in a magnificent suite of rooms.

Veronica Franco, one of the most famous Renaissance courtesans, plied her trade in Venice, a city where the profession of courtesan carried great prestige. The daughter of a courtesan, she was trained in the profession by her mother from a young age (mothers of courtesans often acted as managers for their daughters). She took part in Venice's vital new printing industry and published several books of her own poetry and letters. Under Franco's patronage, a charity for courtesans and their children was established in Venice.

SEE ALSO: Franco, Veronica; Venice

Cranach, Lucas
(1472–1553)

A German painter and engraver, known for his expressive religious paintings, his portraits of the German nobility, and his association with Martin Luther. His name comes from the town of his birth, Kronach, in central Germany. He may have trained with his father as a painter, and as a young man lived and worked in Vienna, the capital of the Habsburg dynasty. His reputation soon reached the elector of Saxony, who hired him as a court painter in 1504, the date of his first known painting, *Rest During the Flight into Egypt*. He was skilled in realistic still lifes and nature paintings, and his religious paintings often set his subjects in a gloomy and realistic wilderness. While in Saxony, he won commissions from the Saxon nobility to decorate the walls of their homes with hunting scenes; these same nobles also requested him to do pictures intended for private viewing that depict scantily clad or nude mythological figures. One of the most famous of these erotic paintings is *The Judgment of Paris*, which he completed in 1530.

In 1509 he journeyed to the Netherlands, where he painted portraits of the Habsburg royal family, including the boy who would later became Charles V. When he returned to Wittenberg, the capital of Saxony, he mastered the arts of engraving and printing, and managed an apothecary shop as well as a press that produced Bibles and tracts written by Luther. Cranach and Luther became friends, with Luther sitting for several famous portraits and Cranach printing woodcuts and tracts meant to spread Luther's message of redemption through faith. The elector Johann Frederick I appointed Cranach as the burgomaster (mayor) of Wittenberg in 1531 and again in 1540. Cranach returned this favor by interceding with Charles V on behalf of the elector when Johann Frederick was captured at the Battle of Mühlberg.

Cranach painted scenes of classical mythology as well as Christian religious subjects. He showed his greatest skill in portraits, and depicted himself as well as Martin Luther in a famous *Crucifixion*. He was one of the first Renaissance painters to depict his subjects as they sat and posed alone. In the eyes of many art historians Cranach was a more original draftsman than painter, with many seeing his engravings, including *St. Christopher* and *Elector*

Frederick Praying Before the Madonna, as among his best work. He produced woodcut engravings for the first German edition of the New Testament in 1522. He worked for both Catholic and Protestant patrons, however; and his workshop in Wittenberg became a productive center that attracted artists and patrons from throughout northern Germany.

SEE ALSO: Dürer, Albrecht; Luther, Martin

Cromwell, Thomas
(1485–1540)

Chief minister to King Henry VIII of England and a key figure in the Protestant Reformation that established the Church of England. Thomas Cromwell was born in Putney, the son of a humble artisan. He traveled to the continent as a young man and was employed by a merchant bank of Italy as a broker in the Netherlands. He also served in Rome as an agent for an English cardinal, Reginald Bainbridge. In about 1512 Cromwell returned to England, where his abilities as a lawyer brought him to the attention of Cardinal Thomas Wolsey, who hired him as a secretary. Cromwell was elected a member of the English Parliament in 1523; he was favored by Henry for his support of the king's efforts to obtain a divorce from Catherine of Aragon. He became a counselor to the king in 1530 and was named chief minister in 1532.

Cromwell played a key role in the Reformation of England. Under his guidance, the English government threw off papal authority and placed church property under the control of the king, church courts answerable only to the pope were dissolved and replaced by royal courts, and the Church of England was founded. Cromwell wrote an important law known as the Act in Restraint of Appeals that denied anyone convicted of the right of appeal to the pope. He also guided important legislation known as the Act of Supremacy that recognized Henry as the head of the Church of England. The king appointed Cromwell as "viceregent in spirituals," giving Cromwell the authority to investigate the religious orders and seize and distribute their property. For his role in directing the English Reformation he was rewarded with the noble title of Earl of Essex.

Cromwell ran afoul of many powerful nobles in England, however, and was also despised by many commoners for his ruthless methods in seizing church property. He incurred the anger of the king after the death of Jane Seymour, Henry's third wife. He advised the king to marry a German princess, Anne of Cleves, in order to tie England more closely to Protestant princes of northern Germany in an alliance against the Catholic emperor, Charles V. Unhappy with his German bride, however, Henry abandoned her and allowed Cromwell to be arrested and imprisoned in the Tower of London at the instigation of Cromwell's sworn enemy, the Duke of Norfolk. Soon afterward Cromwell was convicted of treason and heresy and beheaded.

SEE ALSO: Henry VIII; More, Sir Thomas

da Gama, Vasco
(ca. 1469–1524)

A Portuguese explorer, da Gama lived at a time when this small kingdom at the southwestern edge of Europe was building one of the largest colonial realms in history. Trained in the school of Henry the Navigator, Portuguese ship captains were braving unknown seas and building small trading stations along the west African coast. A sea route between Africa and Asia would, in theory, allow merchants to easily reach the Spice Islands, in what is now Indonesia, and the markets of South Asia. Da Gama first served his king as an officer in west Africa, where the Portuguese ports were under frequent assault by rival European nations. After proving his ability as a sailor as well as a soldier, he won a commission from Manuel I to discover a route to India, which could only be reached at that time by a long and dangerous land route through countries held by hostile Turks and Arabs. In the late fourteenth century, the more northerly Silk Route to Asia was also disrupted by unrest and war after the fall of the Mongol Empire.

In 1497 da Gama set out with four ships from Lisbon, Portugal, reaching the Cape of Good Hope and then continuing up the eastern coast of Africa. The fleet called at Madagascar, Mombasa (in present-day Kenya), and Malindi, and then crossed the Indian Ocean to Calicut, on the southwestern coast of India, reached in May 1498. Da Gama returned to Lisbon in September 1949 in triumph and with a fortune in trade goods, for which he was rewarded with a noble title. His journey had established the Portuguese claim to important trading posts in Africa and India. Da Gama returned to India on a second voyage in 1502, conquering the now-hostile port of Calicut and forcing further trade concessions. A third voyage in 1524 ended with da Gama's death from malaria in the small Indian realm of Cochin.

da Sangallo, Antonio (the Younger)
(1484–1546)

This renowned architect was the nephew of two well-known men, Giuliano da Sangallo and Antonio da Sangallo the Elder, also an architect. He was born in Florence and studied as a young man in Rome under Donato Bramante, the architect of Saint Peter's Basilica. One of his early commissions was a palace for Cardinal Alessandro Farnese (later Pope Paul III). This imposing structure, now known as the Farnese Palace, would be completed by Michelangelo Buonarroti and become one of the great Renaissance monuments of Rome. After 1520 Sangallo succeeded Bramante as the chief architect of Saint Peter's. His busy workshop in Rome produced designs for churches, monuments, and villas throughout Italy, and influenced Italian architecture for the next two centuries. Sangallo's most notable works are the church of Santa Maria di Loreto; the church of San Giovanni dei Fiorentini, built along the Tiber River; and the Paolina Chapel in the Vatican. After Rome was occupied and sacked by the forces of the Holy Roman Emperor in 1527, Sangallo left the city and was hired as a military architect. He designed fortifications for Florence, Perugia, Rome, and the city of Ancona, on the Adriatic coast, and Saint Patrick's well at Orvieto. He also helped to complete the Villa Madama, commissioned by Giulio de' Medici in Rome from the artist Raphael. In 1539 he began work on a large and detailed wooden model of Saint Peter's Basilica, a work that survived as one of the most famous possessions of the Vatican Museum.

de Gournay, Marie le Jars (1565–1645)

A writer and social critic, Marie de Gournay is also known as the lifelong friend and editor of the French essayist Michel de Montaigne. She was born in Paris and raised in the Picardy region north of the city. She developed a literary career of her own upon editing Montaigne's works for publication after his death in 1592. She gained a reputation in literary circles for her combative stance in favor of the intellectual equality of women. To underline her point, she produced a wide range of works and managed to earn an independent living from her poems, a novel (*Le Proumenoir de Monsieur de Montaigne*), stories, political tracts, and essays on education, poetry, and language. Her works *The Equality of Men and Women* and *The Ladies' Grievance* treated the moral strength and intelligence of women, as expounded by ancient and contemporary authors as well as the earliest leaders of the church. In her essays de Gournay explains that physical differences between the genders are irrelevant, and that a lack of education and society's restrictions on women lead to the impression of inferior intelligence and judgment on their part. She criticizes men who lack the ability to take women seriously, and believes their attitude arises from their own fears and insecurity.

de Pisan, Christine (1364–1430)

Writer and social critic, and one of the first women to make a profession from her literary pursuits, Christine de Pisan was born in Venice, the daughter of a physician and Venetian official. She moved to France when her father was appointed physician and astrologer to King Charles V. With her father's encouragement, she made an extensive study of the scientific, philosophical, and literary books available at the French court. She emerged as a writer after the death of her husband Etienne du Castel in 1390, an event that entangled her in a series of lawsuits over her husband's estate and forced her to seek out aristocratic patrons in order to support her family. She began writing lyric poetry on commission for nobles at court. In her work *Letters to the God of Love*, she objected to the chivalric ideals of knighthood and its attitude toward women and their role in society. This work brought her into a famous public debate over the depiction of women in the *Roman de la Rose* of Jean de Meun, one of the well-known chivalric ballads. An intense study of the classical techniques of rhetoric and debate allowed her to give a good account of herself in a male-dominated world of literary debate. She followed her early successes with *The Book of the City of Ladies*, an allegory that considers the world and social conventions from a woman's perspective. She also wrote *Song in Honor of Joan of Arc, The Book of Three Virtues*, as well as books of history, biography, religion, and politics.

de Poitiers, Diane
(1499–1566)

A famous consort of the French king Henri II, Diane de Poitiers was born of aristocratic parents in the castle of Saint-Vallier, in the French Alps. She married Louis de Breze, a courtier and grandson of King Charles VII, at the age of fifteen. On the death of her husband in 1531, she arranged to have his titles of seneschal (king's representative) of Normandy pass into her own hands, instead of allowing that office to return to the king, which was the traditional practice. After Francis I took the throne, Diane became a companion to his sons. When Francis was captured at the Battle of Pavia in 1525, he offered his sons Francois and Henri as hostages in exchange for his freedom. When Henri returned to France, at the age of twelve, Diane became his tutor and guide. The two grew close and as he matured Henri fell in love with his mentor.

Well before Henri became king of France in 1547, Diane became his favorite mistress, adviser, and companion. As king, Henri entrusted important correspondence and documents to her, and relied on her advice in important matters of state. Diane came to wield more authority in the French court than Henri's queen, Catherine de Médicis, and despite the fact that Catherine was a distant cousin of Diane, their rivalry for Henri's affections made them bitter enemies. Henri favored Diane by ordering the castle of Anet built for her, bestowing on her the title of Duchess of Etampes, and allowing her the custody of the crown jewels and the castle of Chenonceau, one of the most magnificent royal residences in Europe. In 1559, however, Henri died of injuries suffered in a duel, and soon afterward his jealous queen, Catherine, took possession of the crown jewels and permanently banished Diane from Chenonceau.

de Soto, Hernando
(1496–1542)

A Spanish explorer who led the first European expedition into the southeastern United States. De Soto was born into a poor family in the Estremadura region of western Spain. He joined the expedition of Pedro Arias de Avila to Panama in 1514, and successfully fought for de Avila against his rival Gil David Gonzales. De Soto accompanied Francisco Pizarro to Peru in 1528 but had a falling out with Pizarro after the Spanish defeated the Incas under their emperor Atahualpa. The Peru expedition had greatly enriched him, however, and de Soto returned to Spain in 1536 a hero for his part in the conquest of the Incas.

De Soto married and settled down in Spain. But when King Charles V honored him with the title of *adelantado* (colonial governor) of Florida, a place the Spanish still had not fully explored, his ambitions in the New World returned. He set out in 1539 with six hundred men and nine ships, landing at a bay he called Espiritu Santu (Holy Spirit), on the western coast of Florida. De Soto's mission was to establish a permanent settlement, make a claim for Florida in the name of the king of Spain, and to find legendary cities of gold. The expedition, however, spent three fruitless years in Florida, suffering hunger, disease, and the attacks of hostile Native American tribes. With his men dying at an alarming rate, de Soto attempted to return overland to New Spain (Mexico), and led the expedition across the southeastern United States, passing through Mississippi, Arkansas, Oklahoma, and Texas. Running out of provisions in the dry plains of

Texas, the expedition returned to the Mississippi River valley, where de Soto died of a fever in 1542. His body was wrapped in a blanket, weighted with stones, and sunk in the river by his men in order to avoid a clash with Native Americans, to whom he had claimed to be an immortal god.

SEE ALSO: Cortes, Hernán; exploration; Pizarro, Francisco

de Vega, Lope
(1562–1635)

A prolific Spanish playwright, Félix Lope de Vega y Carpi was born and raised in Madrid, the son of a common tailor. He wrote poetry and learned Latin at a young age, and began writing plays at the age of twelve. He joined the Spanish Armada during a campaign against the Portuguese in the Azores. After returning to civilian life, he became a professional playwright. His sharp tongue and hot temper, however, got him banished from the capital for slandering his former mistress, Elena Osorio. In 1588 he volunteered for the Spanish naval expedition against England; while the powerful Armada was wrecked in the turbulent seas of the English Channel, de Vega survived and returned home. Penniless, he became a secretary to the Duke of Alba. In 1595 he left the duke's estate near Toledo to return to Madrid. After a series of misfortunes, including the loss of his wife and son, he became a priest in 1614, and was soon appointed an officer of the Spanish Inquisition. In the meantime, he wrote an astonishing number of stage works: histories, romances, dramas, and comedies, as well as ballads, sonnets, verse histories and biographies, and other poetic works. He drew on material from ancient myths to current history, as well as his own turbulent personal life, creating quick-moving, cloak-and-dagger plots based on the rivalries and adventures of Spain's kings and nobles. He turned out plays in a few days or a week, making them to order for certain actors and theaters that commissioned his work. Although none of his plays was printed during his lifetime, about 450 of them, about one-quarter of all those he wrote, have survived to this day.

SEE ALSO: Cervantes, Miguel de

del Sartro, Andrea
(1486–1531)

Painter of Florence, Italy, born in the village of Gualfonda. His name "del Sartro" means the "son of a tailor;" his real name was Andrea d'Agnolo. He apprenticed to a goldsmith before taking up painting in the studio of Piero di Cosimo. After finishing his training he opened his own studio in Florence. His works were influenced by Leonardo da Vinci, Raphael, and Fra Bartolommeo. He had great skill in drawing and in imitating the works of his better-known rivals, and his art was in high demand in Florence after Leonardo, Raphael, and Michelangelo Buonarroti left the city in the early sixteenth century. Del Sartro's first major work was a series of five frescoes for the brotherhood of the Servites, who sought him out to decorate their Basilica della Santissimia Annunziata. The frescoes, depicting the life of a thirteenth-century saint named Filippo Benizzi, were so carefully drawn and executed that they earned del Sartro the nickname of "Andrea the Perfect." He later completed the *Birth of the Virgin*, his best-known fresco, influenced by the works of Leonardo da Vinci. For the convent of San Francesco he painted an altarpiece, the *Madonna of the Harpies*.

When two of his paintings were sent to the royal court of the king of France at

Fontainebleu, del Sartro was invited by Francis I to reside there permanently as court painter. He left in 1518 but soon was feeling homesick and missing his wife Lucrezia. In the next year he returned to Florence, where he remained for the rest of his life. Although Francis had lent del Sartro money in order to purchase works of art, del Sartro instead used it to build a house. He completed a series of mono-chromatic (single-color) frescoes for the cloister of the Scalzo in Florence. His major works from this period are *Dance of the Daughter of Herodias, Beheading of the Baptist, Apparition of the Angel to Zacharias,* and *Visitation.* His *Madonna del Sacco,* or "Madonna of the Sacks," was painted for the cloister of Santissima Annunziata and is considered by many art historians his best work.

One of del Sartro's most famous works is a copy of a portrait of Pope Leo X, done by Raphael. The painting was much admired by Duke Federigo Gonzaga of Milan, who requested it from the Florentine aristocrat Ottaviano de' Medici. As Medici did not want to give up the painting, he asked del Sartro to make the copy, which he then sent to Gonzaga as the original. The painting was so well done that it fooled art experts for many years afterward. Del Sartro was also an excellent portraitist. In 1527 he painted a *Last Supper* in the refectory (dining hall) of the San Salvi convent. This was his last major work before del Sartro contracted the plague during a siege of Florence in 1529; his wife Lucrezia, terrified of the illness, fled the house. Del Sartro died two years later.

d'Este, House of

An aristocratic family that ruled the cities of Ferrara and Modena and who were leading patrons of Renaissance writers,

musicians, and artists in Italy. The family came from the northern region of Lombardy and originally were lords of Este, a domain near Padua. In the Middle Ages the Este dynasty supported the popes and the Guelph faction in the struggles between the papacy and the Holy Roman emperors. Azzo VI d'Este reigned as the *podesta,* or magistrate, of Mantua and Verona; his son Azzo VII succeeded to that title in Ferrara. In 1264, Obizzo d'Este became the lord of Ferrara. The Este family held Ferrara as a fief granted by the pope, and served as the pope's vicars (representatives) from 1332.

Ferrara became a flourishing cultural center under Niccolo d'Este, who ruled from 1384 until his death in 1441. The court of the d'Este patronized artists, musicians, and writers. Niccolo's son Borso increased the family's lands and power through winning the title of duke of Modena and Reggio d'Emilia from Frederick III, the Holy Roman Emperor, and duke of Ferrara from Pope Paul II. Ercole d'Este, another son, married his daughter Beatrice to Ludovico Sforza, the duke of Milan; his daughter Isabella married Francesco Gonzaga, the marquis of Mantua, and through her lavish patronage of the leading artists and writers of the day, including Leonardo da Vinci, Titian, and Ludovico Ariosto, won the title of "Queen of the Renaissance."

Alfonso d'Este, who ruled the d'Este domain until his death in 1534, took an active part in the wars and diplomacy of northern Italy. He joined with Milan, the kingdom of France, and the pope in the League of Cambrai against Venice. The pope and Alfonso fell out of favor, however, and in 1510 the duke was excommunicated from the church and forfeited his titles in Modena and Reggio. In 1526 Alfonso joined the campaign of Emperor Charles V against Pope Clement VII, and won back the lost duchies in 1530. Ercole d'Este, the son of Alfonso, married the daughter of King Louis XII, and allied with France against the kingdom of Spain. His brother Ippolito, a cardinal of the church, built the lavish Villa d'Este at Tivoli, the finest example of a Renaissance palace to survive to the present day.

The last of the d'Este line was Alfonso II, who died in 1597. Although he sought to pass the duchy to his cousin Cesare, Pope Clement VIII did not recognize the inheritance and declared Ferrara a part of the papal territories.

SEE ALSO: Ariosto, Ludovico; d'Este, Isabella; Ferrara

Diet of Augsburg

The Diet of the Holy Roman Empire was an assembly of princes and nobles who convened to decide important matters of state and religion. In 1530, as the Protestant Reformation gathered force in Germany, Emperor Charles V, a determined defender of the Catholic Church, summoned the Diet to meet at Augsburg and invited Protestants to present a summary of their beliefs. The members of the Diet promulgated the twenty-eight articles of the Augsburg Confession, written by the reformer Philipp Melanchthon, who based his work on the teachings of Martin Luther. The Augsburg Confession remains a central creed of Lutheranism. In 1547 the Diet met again after the defeat of Protestant forces by the emperor. Charles attempted to establish Catholicism as the supreme church, but many German princes ruled independently of the emperor and claimed the right to establish the church of their choice in their own territories. In 1555 the emperor and the Protestants arrived at the Peace of Augsburg, which recognized the rights demanded by the princes.

Diet of Worms

A gathering of princes and officials of the Holy Roman Empire, who met in the town of Worms, Germany, to deal with the revolutionary religious doctrines espoused by a monk and university scholar, Martin Luther, the Diet was convened in early 1521 by Emperor Charles V, who commanded Luther himself to appear in order to debate and defend his ideas. Elector Frederick of Saxony, who was sympathetic to Luther's writings, demanded and received a guarantee of safe passage.

Luther's teachings—including the doctrine of justification by faith alone—had been disputed by Pope Leo X in his bull (decree) Exsurge Domine. The pope demanded that Luther retract forty-one assertions he had made in his writings and in the Ninety-five Theses, a pronouncement he had composed in the town of Wittenberg. But when Johann Eck, speaking for the archbishop of Trier, challenged Luther, the monk refused to recant. He then left the Diet under a safe-conduct pass before its members could take any action against him. As the Diet concluded, the emperor issued the Edict of Worms, which banned Luther's writings and commanded his arrest. Returning to Saxony, Luther assumed a disguise and managed to survive the edict while his revolutionary teachings set off the Protestant Reformation in Germany.

Donatello
(1386–1466)

A sculptor who revolutionized the art in Florence during the early Renaissance. Born as Donato di Niccolo Bardi, he was an apprentice in the workshop of Lorenzo

Ghiberti, and assisted Ghiberti in creating the famous bronze doors of the Baptistry of Florence. Donatello's first known work is a marble sculpture of the biblical figure of David that was intended for display on the exterior of the cathedral of Florence. Impressed by the work, and seeing in it a symbol of the entire city, the leaders of the city ordered it to be placed in the front of the Palazzo Vecchio, the seat of government. His reputation secured by this work, Donatello was given commissions to complete a marble Saint Mark for the church of Orsanmichele and statue of Saint John for the cathedral. Both of these were large, realistic works that broke with medieval sculptural tradition, which elongated and idealized the human face and figure. A statue of Saint George completed in 1417 was raised over a smaller relief of Saint George slaying the dragon, the first sculpture to use perspective to create a realistic illusion of space.

Donatello gave his figures lifelike and vigorous poses. His sculpture surprised and impressed viewers with its mastery of small details, such as facial expression and drapery, and the way it used and commanded the surrounding space. He brought out the inner emotions and character of his subjects, subtly distorting figures for dramatic effect, and mastered several different sculptural media, including wood, bronze, and marble. His reputation spread throughout Italy and he traveled often at the invitation of wealthy patrons. In the 1420s he completed a bronze *Feast of St. Herod* for the Baptistery of Siena. In this work he created a new sculptural technique, *schiacciato*, or shallow relief, which creates an illusion of depth through distortion of the figures.

Donatello spent several years in Rome, investigating ancient ruins with his friend and mentor Filippo Brunelleschi. In 1443 Donatello moved to Padua, a city near Venice, where he was commissioned to raise an equestrian statue of Erasmo da Narni, a famous condottiere (mercenary soldier) known better by his nickname Gattamelata. This was an imitation of a well-known statue of the emperor Marcus Aurelius. It was placed in a central square of Padua and began a craze for equestrian statues that continued throughout Europe well after the time of the Renaissance. Also in Padua he decorated the high altar of the church of San Antonio with an impressive series of reliefs representing the life of Saint Anthony.

In 1432 Donatello created his most famous work, a bronze statue of David, the first freestanding nude statue created since the time of ancient Rome. The statue, a symbol of Renaissance virtue triumphing over the superstition and violence of the past, was meant to stand independently and be seen from all sides. Later in life he continued experimenting in the form and expression of his subjects. He completed a dramatic series of bronze pulpits for the church of San Lorenzo. For the Baptistery of Florence he carved a striking portrait of Mary Magdalene in wood that represents her as thin, ugly, and a pathetic woman lost in the wilderness. A group of figures in bronze illustrates the biblical tale of Judith slaying Holofernes, a work originally intended for a courtyard in the palace of the Medici rulers.

SEE ALSO: Florence; Ghiberti, Lorenzo; sculpture

Donne, John (1572–1631)

English poet, essayist, and Anglican priest, Donne was born in London to a well-to-do ironmonger. His mother was the daughter of playwright John Heywood and a great niece of Sir Thomas More. Donne was educated by members of the Catholic Jesuit order and began attending the University of Oxford in England at the age of eleven. After three years, he entered the University of Cambridge. He failed to attain a university degree, as he refused to take the required Oath of Supremacy that recognized the monarch of England as supreme head of the Anglican church. After his university career, Donne entered Lincoln's Inn in London to train as a lawyer. He was often tormented by questions of religious faith and dogma, and his religious doubt intensified when his brother Henry died in 1593 while in prison, where he had been sent for harboring a priest. In this period he was also writing poetry that explored the physical and emotional intensity of love.

Donne took part in an expedition led by the Earl of Essex in 1596 against the Spanish at Cadiz and the Azores. After this adventure he was appointed secretary to Sir Thomas Egerton, the Queen's Lord Keeper of the Seal. However, Donne's public career was ended by his secret marriage in 1601 to Ann More, the niece of Egerton's wife. For this Donne was sacked from his position, arrested, and briefly imprisoned. After his release he moved to Surrey, where he eked out a bare living as a lawyer and depended on friends and family to support his growing family.

Donne wrote satires of English manners and also meditations on suicide (*Biathanatos*) and religion, including *Pseudo-Martyr*, a criticism of the Catholic tradition of martyrdom. A series of "Holy Sonnets" expressed his views on death and sin. In 1601 Donne was elected a member of parliament. He had gained a wealthy patron in Sir Robert Drury, for whom he wrote *Anniversaries, An Anatomy of the World*, a work that memorialized Sir Drury's daughter, Elizabeth, and *Of the Progress of the Soul* in 1612. Another satire of Catholicism, *Ignatius His Conclave*, reflected the new astronomy of Galileo Galilei and proposed sending a colony of settlers to the moon. Although he petitioned the king to return to public service, he was refused. On the king's recommendation, however, he was ordained a priest in the Church of England in 1615. By this time Donne had become a deeply religious man, attaining the post of reader in divinity at Lincoln's Inn, and was changing his focus to religion. Donne became the royal chaplain in 1615, and finally earned a doctor of divinity degree from Cambridge in 1618. His rising status in the Church of England did not relieve a deep grief felt at the death of his wife in childbirth in 1617. In 1621 he was appointed the dean of Saint Paul's, where his eloquent sermons drew large audiences to the cathedral. After falling ill in 1623, he wrote the *Devotions*, essays on death and salvation. His most famous speech, the "Death's Duel" sermon, was delivered before King Charles I in 1631, at a time when Donne was already on his own deathbed.

Donne's poetry is inventive, eloquent, often paradoxical, and filled with surprising, vivid metaphors and "conceits," which combine radically different ideas and imagery. His poetic rhythms discarded the measured, traditional style in favor of abrupt and jarring rhythms that were meant to remind the reader of everyday speech. His elegies, epigrams, and letters in verse were published after his death in *Songs and Sonnets.*

Dowland, John (1563–1626)

English composer and lutenist known for the expressively moody, downcast style of his music. Dowland was born in London and studied musical composition at the University of Oxford. He became a lute player for the English ambassador to France, where Dowland converted to the Catholic faith. Later he performed at the court of Queen Elizabeth I but failed to win an appointment from the queen because of his loyalty to Catholicism, a snub that in the opinion of some historians brought about his embittered and melancholy musical style. He journeyed later to Denmark, where he became court lutenist to the Danish king Christian IV. He won an appointment as official court lutenist by King James I. He began publishing collections of pieces for voice and lute in 1597, eventually publishing four books of more than eighty songs. His most famous works are melancholy songs that set the subjects of death and loss to beautifully flowing and balanced melodies, and accenting these melodies with strikingly dissonant notes and chords. Dowland's personal motto was "Dowland, Semper Dolens," a pun in Latin that means "Dowland, Always Doleful," taken from the name of one of his songs. *Flow My Tears*, his best-known piece, became one of the most commonly performed works of Renaissance music in modern times. He also wrote complex polyphonic suites, dance music, and sets of variations for the solo lute, as well as *Seaven Teares Figured in Seaven Passionate Pavans*, a piece based on *Flow My Tears* written for lute and five viols.

SEE ALSO: Byrd, William; music

Drake, Sir Francis (1540–1596)

English navigator and privateer. The son of a yeoman farmer and devout Protestant, Drake was born near the town of Tavistock in Devonshire. He was a relation of the well-to-do Hawkins clan, a family of local shipowners, and through his connection to John Hawkins Drake was taken on as captain of the *Judith* in 1567 during one of Hawkins's profitable slaving expeditions. Although the fleet managed to capture and sell its human cargo, the voyage ended in disaster when it was attacked by hostile Spanish ships in the harbor of San Juan de Ulua. Only two vessels made it back to England, including Drake's own *Judith*. After this encounter, Drake made it his life's work to exact revenge on Spanish men, treasure, and ships, wherever he might find them.

Queen Elizabeth, unwilling to allow Hawkins to counterattack yet still in favor of naval operations against Spain, allowed Drake to return to the Spanish Main in 1570. Aboard the *Susan*, Drake explored the coasts of Panama and discovered the route followed by the Spanish treasure caravans from Peru, across the isthmus of Panama, to the Caribbean Sea. He intercepted and captured a large train of silver and brought the treasure safely back to England, making him a wealthy man. Not happy with this act of open warfare against Spain, Elizabeth banished him to Ireland for a time, where Drake served under the Earl of Essex to put down one in a long series of rebellions against English rule.

In 1577, Drake was commissioned by Elizabeth to lead a raiding fleet against Spanish ports on the Pacific coasts of the Americas. The navigator set sail with a fleet of five ships, but mutiny and poor weather hampered the voyage and only his flagship, the *Golden Hind*, made it through the Straits of Magellan and as far as the Pacific Ocean. Searching for a northerly passage back to the Atlantic Ocean, Drake's vessel landed somewhere near Drake's Bay, now in the state of California, and named the surroundings "New Albion" in the name of the queen and England. Instead of retracing his route, Drake then sailed west, across the vast Pacific to the Philippines, the East Indies, and the Indian Ocean and then around the Cape of Good Hope. Having collected a considerable fortune from Spanish treasure ships, he returned to England in September 1580. The voyage had made him the second European to circumnavigate the globe after Ferdinand Magellan had died accomplishing the same feat in 1519. On his return Drake was rewarded with a knighthood by the queen on the decks of the *Golden Hind*.

In 1581 Drake settled in Plymouth, where his renown as an adventurer and privateer earned him election as the town's mayor. Still yearning for the sea, in 1585 Drake accepted orders to disrupt Spanish preparations for an expedition against England. Drake and his crew attacked the Spaniards on the coast of Spain as well as at the Cape Verde Islands. The fleet then crossed the Atlantic Ocean, captured Spanish towns in South America, plundered the Spanish colony of Saint Augustine in what is now northeastern Florida, and reached the English colony at Roanoke, where he took on survivors and returned them to England. This voyage provoked open warfare between England and Spain, and King Philip II was soon ordering preparations for a naval assault. Elizabeth allowed Drake to strike the first blow, and in 1587 he reappeared in the port of Cadiz, where he destroyed about thirty Spanish vessels.

In 1588, as the Spanish Armada was gathering, Drake was appointed a vice admiral of the English fleet. Drake disrupted the expedition by raiding supply ships, delaying and weakening the Spanish fleet. The Armada then set out for the English Channel, but turned back after losing several skirmishes with Drake and other English commanders as well as very poor weather. In 1595 Drake was again in command, along with John Hawkins, of an expedition to Panama ordered by the queen. This time, the Spanish were warned ahead of time and were waiting for the English privateers. Off the port of San Juan, Puerto Rico, Hawkins died and Drake was beaten back from the harbor. On reaching Panama, Drake was ambushed by Spanish troops and forced out to sea, where he soon died of a fever.

SEE ALSO: Elizabeth I; Magellan, Ferdinand; Spanish Armada

d'Aragona, Tullia (ca. 1510–1556)

A celebrated courtesan, musician, and author, Tullia d'Aragona was known to nobles, artists, philosophers, and princes as one of Renaissance Italy's most fascinating women. She was the daughter of Giulia Ferrarese, herself a courtesan of great beauty, and was educated by Cardinal Luigi d'Aragona, who may have been her father. She left her birthplace of Rome for Siena in 1519, and returned to Rome in 1526 to enlist as a professional courtesan, a woman engaged by wealthy men for entertainment, witty conversation, and physical pleasure. Among her clients were the banker Filippo Strozzi of Florence; Emilio Orsini, scion of a powerful Roman family; and the poet Bernardo Tasso. She married Silvestro Guiccardi in 1543 and several years later joined the Florentine court of

Duke Cosimo de' Medici. She was denounced for defying the dress code for courtesans in Siena, and in Florence, but escaped trial both times through her connections to influential men. Forty-nine of her poems were collected in the book *Rime della Signora Tullia d' Aragona*. She wrote *Dialogues on the Infinity of Love* in 1547 and found a publisher for the book almost immediately in Venice. This work boldly gave a woman's perspective on love, and relations between the sexes, a viewpoint extremely rare in the literature of Europe before the modern age. She also composed sonnets and an epic poem, *Il Meschino, Detto Il Guerrino*. Gathered poets and philosophers to her side at the Medici court, she prevailed over the intellectual life of Florence at a time when women were held as morally and intellectually inferior to men.

d'Este, Isabella (1474–1539)

A patron of the arts and writers during the Renaissance, whose brilliant court in Ferrara became a leading city of the new humanistic outlook, and who is known by historians as the "Queen of the Renaissance." The daughter of Duke Ercole I of Ferrara and of Duchess Leonora, the daughter of King Ferdinand I of Naples, Isabelle d'Este traveled extensively with her mother, visiting the various courts of Italy and educating herself in the language and literature of the ancient Greeks and Romans. In her travels and studies she gained a deep appreciation for the achievements of the ancient Romans in literature, sculpture, and architecture. She was engaged as a young girl to Francesco Gonzaga, finally marrying him at the age of sixteen. In Mantua the couple led a brilliant court that boasted the presence of Ludovico Ariosto, who wrote his epic poem *Orlando Furioso* while residing there. Baldassare Castiglione, who wrote *The Courtier*, an important book of courtly manners, also lived in Mantua and was given free reign by Isabella d'Este to make her court a model of good taste and proper decorum. The d'Este court served as a model for Renaissance princes all over Europe, who were leaving behind the rustic medieval manners of their forebears and striving to match each other in their patronage of men—and women—of learning and talent. Isabella boasted the presence of the painters Titian (who painted her portrait twice), Andrea Mantegna, Raphael, and Leonardo da Vinci, who drew a famous portrait of her. A musician and devoted patroness of composers, she also organized a court orchestra and had her palace composers set poetry she favored to music—an important first step on the path to the full flowering of Italian opera in the centuries to come.

As captain-general of the forces of Venice, Francesco Gonzaga was frequently away from the court in Mantua. While campaigning against the French he was taken prisoner in 1509. Isabella d'Este then ruled Mantua as Francesco's regent. She skillfully directed the defense of Mantua against its enemies until Francesco was released in 1512. The couple found themselves at odds afterward, however, and Isabella retreated to the court of Pope Leo X in Rome. She soon became one of the most popular figures in Rome and participated in the spirited defense of the city against the forces of the Holy Roman Emperor in the 1520s. After the death of Francesco Gonzaga, Isabella served as the regent for their son Frederico, the heir to the city who had been born in 1500.

SEE ALSO: Ferdinand I of Naples; Ferrara; Gonzaga, House of; Mantua

In "Ecce Homo," from Albrecht Dürer's "Great Passion" series of woodcuts, Christ is presented to the mob by Pontius Pilate and sentenced to death. Durer's monogram can be seen in the center bottom.

Dürer, Albrecht
(1471–1528)

A German painter and draftsman, a leading figure of the Renaissance in northern Europe, Albrecht Dürer was born in Nuremberg as the son and grandson of goldsmiths. His early training took place in the metalworking shop of his father, where he showed great talent in drawing. In 1486 he joined the workshop of Michael Wolgemut, a painter and illustrator. Dürer traveled as a young man to the Low Countries, the Rhine River valley, and Basel, Switzerland, where he worked as an illustrator for books and studied the work of masters of silverpoint engraving and woodcut block prints. His earliest known painting was a portrait of his father, completed in 1490. In 1494, he returned to Nuremberg, which became his permanent home, but after his marriage there he was soon voyaging again, this time to Italy. The ruins and literature of ancient Rome impressed him, as did the works of Italian painters of Venice, Milan, and Padua—foremost among them Giovanni Bellini and Andrea Mantegna. Their paintings in a new style had a strong influence on Dürer, who would synthesize in his works the Italian ideas of classicism, human proportion, and compositional balance with the northern European taste for detailed and naturalistic draftsmanship.

After returning to Nuremberg, Dürer published *The Apocalypse*, a series of woodcuts that illustrate events in the Bible's book of Revelation. Dürer also used biblical themes in later series known as *The Great Passion, The Small Passion*, and *The Life of the Virgin*. His famous *Self-Portrait* of 1498 is one of the renowned images of the Renaissance, showing Dürer as an idealistic humanist scholar, a type of person he had encountered often during his journey to Italy.

The Italian Renaissance had taught Dürer that certain principles of arranging scenes and rendering figures allowed the skilled artist to convey a sense of spirituality and reverence for religious subject matter. He put this principle to use in his altarpieces, paintings done for prominent display inside a church. One of the most famous of these works is the *Paumgartner Altarpiece*, which was completed by 1504. Dürer also adopted myth and allegory in his engravings, such as *Nemesis* and *The Prodigal Son*. Along with his watercolor painting of *The Wild Hare*, still one of the most common art reproductions, these works were reproduced as prints by the thousands and circulated throughout Europe.

Dürer returned to Italy in 1505; he visited Venice and Bologna and may have traveled as far as Rome. During this trip he wrote a series of engaging and observant letters to his friend, Willibald Pirckheimer, one of the leading humanist scholars of Germany. In Venice, where he lived for two years, Dürer struck up a friendship with Giovanni Bellini and other artists, and was hired to create a painting for the church of San Bartolomeo. He developed great skill at rendering the natural world of landscapes, plants and animals in his engravings, a skill he refined during his crossing of the Alps from Germany to Italy.

After his return to Germany, he completed two major altarpieces, *The Adoration of the Trinity* and *Martyrdom of the Ten Thousand*, and created a series of masterful engravings reflecting ideals of humanistic thought Dürer had encountered in Italy. These works include *Knight, Death, and the Devil; St. Jerome in His Study*; and *Melancolia*. They represented the new ideal of philosophy: the contemplative life of study in Neoplatonism and observations in science that countered medieval religious doctrines. On commission from the emperor Maximilian I, Dürer also completed two monumental engravings, *The Triumphal Arch of Maximilian I* and *The Triumphal Procession of Maximilian I*. In 1520 the new emperor, Charles V, continued the salary and privileges that Maxi-

milian had extended to Dürer, recognizing the artist's talent and importance. But the Catholic emperor was a powerful opponent of the Protestant Reformation of Martin Luther, a movement that Dürer wholeheartedly supported and celebrated in engravings such as *The Last Supper* and *Praying Hands*. One of his last works was *The Four Apostles*, a painting of the four apostles of the New Testament: John, Peter, Mark, and Paul. In his last years he wrote extensively on art theory and history. He published a work on fortifications and another on the science of perspective, *Instruction in Measurement*, and wrote *The Four Books on Proportions*, which was published a few months after his death.

Dürer's reputation spread throughout Europe, and particularly in Germany, in the years after his death. He ushered an entire nation of German artists from the medieval period into the Renaissance, and brought graphic art of printmaking and woodcuts to a higher level, where they began competing with painting and sculpture for the attention of art historians and patrons. His detailed, well-crafted allegorical works fit well with notions of the Romantic movement that emerged in northern Europe in the eighteenth century, and which adopted Dürer as an artistic forefather.

SEE ALSO: Maximilian I; Pirckheimer, Willibald; printing

Edict of Nantes

A decree passed by King Henri IV in 1598 that granted full religious liberty to the Huguenots (Protestants) of France. The decree allowed the Huguenots freedom to worship in private and public as they chose; it also granted them control of certain towns in France and set up courts of Catholic and Protestant judges that would hear cases involving Protestants. The edict was an attempt to end the decades of religious conflict in France that had resulted in thousands of deaths and decline in order throughout the kingdom. After the death of Henri IV, however, his successor King Louis XIV sought to consolidate royal control over the Protestant towns, including the strategic port of La Rochelle on the western coast. The armies of the king attacked and defeated La Rochelle in 1628, and by the Peace of Alais the Protestant towns lost their independence. In later decades Louis gradually ended the privileges granted to the Huguenots and in 1685 revoked the Edict of Nantes. This action resulted in the flight of thousands of Huguenot families to the Low Countries and to French colonies in North America, which drained France of a population vital to its growing manufacturing economy. The revocation also increased political tensions with France's Protestant neighbors.

education

Education in the medieval era was generally reserved for the wealthy and young members of ruling families. Most schooling took place in monastic and cathedral schools, or at the desk of a private tutor. In the fourteenth century, education became more widely available to an expanding urban middle class. Literacy increased, a few years of schooling were available to the young, and new universities were established to train scholars for religious, legal, or teaching professions. By the fifteenth century, a thorough education in grammar, rhetoric, history, and philosophy was considered essential for the well-rounded individual.

The *Institutio Oratoria* of the ancient Roman author Quintilian, discovered in the fourteenth century by the Italian poet Petrarch, was a guide to the training of a Roman orator. This book inspired a new, humanistic outlook on education. In his book Quintilian advocates a broad educational training suited to the abilities of the individual student. It encourages students to analyze the function and components of rhetoric in order to provide a sound basis for one's skill as a speaker and writer. This guidebook for the education of the young was a foundation of Renaissance learning.

Cicero's speeches, uncovered by Petrarch and others, also provided an important text for Renaissance-era students. Pietro Paolo Vergerio wrote *On Noble Customs*, a book that advocates training in the seven liberal arts of grammar, dialectic, rhetoric, music, arithmetic, geometry, and astronomy. Vergerio presents a detailed program for the teacher, emphasizing a method in which students take gradual steps in their lessons, and are also given rigorous physical training to achieve a balance of mind and body.

Humanism emphasized the study of the classic Latin and Greek writers in forming a valuable citizen, one who could read, write, and speak effectively and make a contribution to civic life. The most popular Latin authors for teaching purposes were Virgil, Ovid, Cicero, Terence, Livy, Sallust, and Horace. Students studied Latin spelling, grammar, and syntax, and translated classical authors. One common exercise was to write in the style of a certain author, or to translate a passage of Latin into everyday language, and then back into Latin. Students memorized important passages from the speeches of Cicero and others, and were encouraged to use Latin in the classroom and in their everyday conversation.

Humanist teaching first took place at private academies established in noble courts, where children of the aristocracy trained for careers as public servants and leaders. There were notable academies at the courts of Ferrara and Mantua, where the classical virtues of endurance, stoicism, morality, and valor were stressed, and the student was required to take part in physical activity as well as regular Mass and confession. Many of the Italian city-states, notably Florence, Verona, Venice, and Milan, adopted this program in their public schools in the middle of the fifteenth century. By the sixteenth century, humanist education was spreading from Italy to the rest of Europe.

Printed grammar books became commonplace after the printing press was invented in the 1450s. The use of paper, pens, and notebooks expanded at the same time. One of the most important school-

books was the *Institutiones Grammaticae Latinae*, or Principles of Latin Grammar, published by Aldus Manutius. In the 1520s, a Dutch printer, Johannes Despauterius, began printing the *Grammatica*, which was more popular in northern Europe and the British Isles. Those opposed to rote study of grammatical rules had students compose their own works in imitation of worthy authors such as Cicero, Tacitus, and Livy. Desiderius Erasmus, the Dutch humanist and scholar, collected several of these ancient authors in his book *De Copia Verborum*, which became the most popular schoolbook throughout northern Europe in the sixteenth century. He was also the author of the *Colloquia*, a collection of fictional dialogues used as models for conversation in Latin.

SEE ALSO: humanism

Edward VI
(1537–1553)

King of England from 1547 until his death of pneumonia at the age fifteen in 1553. Edward was the son of King Henry VIII and Jane Seymour, but at the time the throne passed to him he was only nine years old. England was ruled by regents, at first the Duke of Somerset and then, from 1549, the Duke of Northumberland. During his brief reign, the Protestant Church of England prevailed over the Catholic Church, expelled from England by Henry VIII. At the time of his death, the Duke of Northumberland promoted the accession of Lady Jane Grey, who was soon deposed from the throne and replaced by the Catholic queen Mary.

Elizabeth I
(1533–1603)

Tudor dynasty queen of England from 1558 until her death in 1603. The daugh-

In 1558, on the death of Mary, Elizabeth became the queen of England. The nation was militarily weak, struggling with debt, and the scene of violent conflict between Catholics and the supporters of the Church of England, the Protestant sect established by Henry VIII. Elizabeth also faced a threat from her cousin Mary, a Catholic grand-niece of Henry VIII and the queen of Scotland. The wife of King Francis II (Francois) of France, Mary was supported in her claims to the English throne by several wealthy English nobles and a French army stationed in Scotland. Her claims were supported by the fact that Elizabeth refused all offers of marriage, throwing the succession into doubt. In 1568 Mary abdicated her throne during a rebellion and fled to England. Elizabeth held her prisoner for the next nineteen years, and finally in 1587, fearing Mary's plots against her, allowed her execution.

Elizabeth's enforcement of laws against Catholics inspired several plots against her life; in 1570 the pope officially declared her deposed from the English throne by a bull (proclamation) that sanctioned open rebellion among Catholics in England. The queen responded by enforcing harsh laws against Catholics and having several prominent clergy executed. In 1588, the Catholic king Philip II sought to bring England to heel and counter English support of Protestant rebels in the Spanish-held Low Countries. Philip sent a massive naval fleet, known as the Spanish Armada, against England. The fleet arrived in the English Channel but was soon at the mercy of stormy weather and the skillful assaults of the English captains. As the Armada fled, Elizabeth's prestige in Europe soared.

With Elizabeth's encouragement, the English settled new colonies in the Caribbean and North America and English cap-

Queen Elizabeth I of England, in full court regalia, from an engraving by Crispin van da Passe.

ter of King Henry VIII and his second wife Anne Boleyn, she was educated at court and showed a talent for languages, learning several as a young girl. She lost her place in the succession when the king had Anne Boleyn executed on false charges in 1536. In 1544, however, she was restored to the succession by an act of the English Parliament. Her half brother Edward became king after Henry's death in 1547; the sickly Edward's reign was short-lived, however, and in 1553 Mary Tudor became the first reigning queen of England. A devout Catholic, Mary suspected the Protestant Elizabeth of harboring ill intentions toward her. In 1554, when a revolt led by Sir Thomas Wyatt challenged the queen, Mary had her sister thrown into the Tower of London, then held under house arrest at the royal palace of Hatfield, where Elizabeth continued her study with the scholar Roger Ascham.

tains, including Sir Francis Drake and Sir John Hawkins, carried out raids and piracy against Spanish ports and ships. At home, Elizabeth held a lively court, engaging musicians and playwrights to entertain her and holding processions in towns throughout the realm. Elizabethan poetry and drama brought the English language to a peak of its expressive intensity. The end of Elizabeth's reign in 1603 also brought about the end of the Tudor dynasty, as Elizabeth had remained unmarried throughout her life and left no heirs. James I, the first of the Stuart dynasty, ascended the throne.

SEE ALSO: Henry VIII; Spanish Armada; Tudor dynasty

England

While new scholarship and art were flowering in fifteenth-century Italy, England was recovering from defeat in the Hundred Years' War, and English claimants to the throne from the houses of York and Lancaster were fighting a long and bloody civil war. In 1485, when Henry Tudor defeated his rival Richard III at the Battle of Bosworth Field, the Tudor dynasty was established. Returning to political and social stability, England began absorbing humanist ideas from the continent. English schools followed the new humanism, instructing their students in Latin, Greek, and the classical authors. The first printed books spread literacy, while scholars from the continent, notably Desiderius Erasmus, arrived seeking patronage. In 1509, with the start of the reign of Henry VIII, England's Renaissance took its first steps at the king's royal court, where the painter Hans Holbein worked and the renowned scholar Sir Thomas More served the king as lord chancellor. The classical languages were taught at Saint Paul's school, founded by John Colet; William Lily wrote a Latin

grammar in the 1520s and Thomas Elyot a dictionary of Latin and English words.

The pivotal year in English Renaissance history was 1536, when Henry established the Church of England. The king became the supreme head of the church, which adopted many of the doctrines of Martin Luther and Protestant Reformation. Catholic property was seized and members of the church were arrested or driven into exile. Monasteries were closed and nuns and monks forced to renounce their vows. As monastic property was confiscated, large collections of books, including manuscripts of ancient Greek and Latin authors, spread to the universities. During the Tudor dynasty, religion played an important role in English foreign policy.

Henry's reign was followed by those of his son Edward and daughter Mary. Edward supported the cause of reform. During his reign the English *Book of Common Prayer* was published, advancing Protestant doctrine. Mary, however, was a fervently devout Catholic. She restored the traditional faith and had many Protestant leaders and nobles executed. After a short reign, she died without an heir, passing the throne to her Protestant half sister Elizabeth. Tutored by Roger Ascham, one of the foremost scholars of Latin and ancient literature, Elizabeth had an open mind to new ideas and encouraged humanist education. The queen was a lively and intelligent leader who enthusiastically patronized scholars and artists. English literature, art, architecture, and music flourished in the Elizabethan age of the late sixteenth century.

Music, drama, and pageantry were hallmarks of Elizabeth's royal court. Italian forms, such as the sonnet and the madrigal, were taken up in English poetry and music. The composer Thomas Morley set

Shakespeare's poetry to music in the Italian style; Thomas Tallis and William Byrd also experimented in musical form and style. Edmund Spenser glorified the Tudor dynasty in his epic poem *The Faerie Queene*. The theater was brought to new heights by William Shakespeare, Christopher Marlowe, Ben Jonson, and many others. The thorough knowledge of history and classical literature reflected in their plays demonstrated the broad humanistic education that was now widely available to English students. In the field of natural philosophy, Sir Francis Bacon made an important contribution with his concepts of the scientific method.

England still faced serious threats from the continent. England's support of Protestant rebels in the Netherlands prompted the Spanish king, Philip II, to send a powerful armada of warships to invade and conquer England. The Spanish Armada was turned away in 1588 by storms and outmaneuvered by skilled English navigators. In the meantime, England was joining the era of exploration, sending ships to North America to search for a northwest passage to Asia and establishing American colonies after the turn of the seventeenth century. These voyages expanded the kingdom's trade and stimulated its economy, as chartered companies such as the East India Company, the Hudson Bay Company, and the Muscovy Company set up operations in Asia, North America, and Russia.

SEE ALSO: Bacon, Francis; Elizabeth I; Henry VIII; Marlowe, Christopher; Milton, John; Shakespeare, William

Erasmus, Desiderius (ca. 1466–1536)

A scholar, theologian, and linguist of the Netherlands, whose ideas on the Bible and the Catholic Church attempted to reconcile the skepticism of humanists, the rebellion of Protestants, and the doctrines of the Catholic Church. Born in Rotterdam, he was the illegitimate son of Roger Gerard, a priest, and the daughter of a physician. He was educated in a religious community known as the Brethren of the Common Life. After the death of his parents during a plague epidemic in 1483 he entered a monastery, but found the strict vows and poverty of a monk's life not to his liking. His ability as a scholar and linguist spread his name in the Low Countries, and he won an appointment as a secretary to the bishop of Cambrai, who sent Erasmus to study at the College de Montague in Paris. Erasmus was ordained as a priest in 1492 but spent the rest of his life writing, publishing, and in intellectual debate with hundreds of scholars, humanists, and princes throughout Europe.

After completing his studies, Erasmus traveled to England in 1499 to gain the friendship of scholars such as Sir Thomas More and churchmen such as the archbishop of Canterbury. His book *Adages*, published in 1500, collected classical writings and proverbs, while he also published translations from ancient Greek sources including the plays of Euripides and the short biographies of Plutarch. Under the influence of English humanists, Erasmus wrote *Handbook of the Militant Christian* in 1503, calling for Christian believers to return to the simple piety of the apostles and followers of Christ.

As a young man Erasmus also made several voyages to Italy, where he was awarded an honorary doctorate from the University of Turin and where he worked as an editor for a Venetian printing house. Dismayed by the wars Pope Julius II was carrying out to conquer cities for the Papacy in northern Italy, Erasmus also wrote (anonymously) *Julius Exclusus*, in which the pope, greedy for treasure and worldly renown, is barred from the gates of heaven.

Erasmus returned to England in 1509, taking a position as a lecturer in divinity at the University of Cambridge. Hoping for an invitation to the court of King Henry VIII, who had just come to power, he was to be disappointed in his ambition and soon returned to the continent. In 1511 Erasmus published *In Praise of Folly*, a book that soon had an audience throughout Europe. In this work, which he dedicated to Sir Thomas More, Erasmus uses satire to hold the Catholic Church at fault for its worldliness and corruption, and offered his support to the gathering movement for reform of the church and a return to its roots. Instead of a hierarchy of bishops, cardinals, popes, and other privileged officials, Erasmus saw true Christianity as lying in the simple faith of the believer.

His fame as a writer assured, Erasmus was appointed as an adviser for Prince Charles, heir to the Holy Roman Empire, and for the prince wrote *The Education of a Christian Prince* in 1516, advising Charles that the best way to rule was to win the trust and respect of his subjects. Erasmus counseled the prince to find peaceful solutions to the religious and civil conflicts then brewing in Europe, and repeated these opinions in two works, *War Is Sweet to Inexperienced Men* and *The Complaint of Peace*.

In his study of the Bible and of the classical authors, Erasmus strove to reconcile the humanist movement with the traditional doctrines of the church. He translated long sections of the Bible as well as the writings of the early church fathers, including Saint Augustine, Origen, and Saint Jerome. In his translations he attempted to convey the original meaning of the texts, but in doing so offended church leaders who held his scholarship to be blasphemous and heretical. Undeterred, he brought out an edition of the New Testament, in which Greek text and Latin translation was printed side by side. First published in 1516, this *Novum Instrumentum* contained annotations, or explanations of the original meaning of the text. He changed and expanded his work in five more editions, one of which would later be used as the basis for the King James version of the Bible. In his preface to the work, Erasmus urged Pope Leo X to undertake a sweeping reform of the church and to disseminate the Bible among the common people. His work, however, ran counter to the idea that a single, fundamental meaning must be given to the words of the Bible, which as the original word of God could not be amended or annotated by scholars or other ordinary believers. In effect, Erasmus was proposing an alternative view of Christianity, and the wide popularity of his works and translations reflected the flowering of new doctrines brought about by the Protestant Reformation.

Erasmus favored reform of the church, however, not the establishment of an entirely new one, and accepted the final authority of the pope on matters of doctrine. He fled the city of Basel after it joined the ranks of the Protestants, and he debated with Martin Luther in his essay *On the Freedom of the Will*, which countered Luther's ideas on salvation and justification by personal faith. The church, however, saw him as an opponent, and after his death placed his books on its Index, a list of books that were prohibited to its members.

See Also: humanism; Luther, Martin; More, Sir Thomas; Reformation, Protestant

Eugenius IV
(1383–1447)

Pope from 1431 until his death in 1447, Eugenius was born Gabriele Condulmer, the son of a Venetian merchant. At the age of twenty-four, Pope Gregory XII, his uncle, appointed him as bishop of Siena. When the people of Siena opposed him as an outsider, Condulmer resigned to become the Vatican treasurer. He won election as pope after the death of Martin V in 1431. This event took place soon after the opening of the Council of Basel, a meeting of bishops, monks, and religious scholars who sought to reform the church and represented a serious challenge to the pope's authority. Eugenius issued a papal bull (decree) dissolving the council in December 1431, but the council members responded by demanding that he appear before the council and recognize its authority over him. In 1433, faced with rising opposition in northern Europe and a budding Protestant movement in Bohemia, the pope withdrew his bull and acknowledged the council as valid.

Eugenius took an active role in the wars and rivalries of northern Italy. He supported Florence and Venice in their struggle with Milan; to counter this, Milanese troops attacked papal territory in central Italy. The defeat of the pope's army set off a violent uprising in Rome, which Eugenius escaped by disguising himself as a monk and having himself rowed to safety down the Tiber River to the port of Ostia. The pope settled in the town of Bologna while, over the next few years, his armies reconquered the Papal States. In 1438 Eugenius convened another council at Ferrara, where he placed a ban of excommunication on the authorities meeting at Basel. They then accused the pope of heresy, announced him deposed from his throne, and elected the antipope Felix V. The rival popes made peace in 1442, after which Eugenius returned to Rome and persuaded the princes of Germany to support him. After many years of bitter struggle, he had prevailed over the conciliar movement that presumed to be the final authority in church matters.

exploration

The people of medieval times knew little of the world outside their towns and villages. The most knowledgeable people were unaware of distant continents and had no idea of the true size of the earth. Sailors had no maps to guide them beyond the familiar coasts. Navigational tools were of very limited use in long-distance voyages, especially in uncharted waters. Only a few merchants traveled any distance. Their reports from the coasts of Africa and Arabia, and the overland caravan route known as the Silk Road, made up the limits of exploration.

In the fifteenth century, Portugal began an important era of long-distance exploration. Portuguese navigators began maneuvering a lighter, more nimble craft known as the caravel down the western coasts of Africa. They sailed beyond the capes, which experienced mariners believed lay at the edge of the world. The craft of shipbuilding improved the caravels, making them larger and rigging them to handle the varying wind conditions of long sea voyages. With their larger holds and ability to support crews for months at a time, carracks came into use around the turn of the sixteenth century and allowed even longer voyages.

Henry the Navigator, a prince of Portugal, began sponsoring voyages of exploration after the conquest of Ceuta in North Africa. Henry sought to expand Portugal's trade with Africa and to convert that continent's pagan souls to Christianity. His officers touched at the island of Madeira, the Canary Islands, and the Azores. Gil Eanes passed Cape Bojador, the traditional limit of southern navigation, in 1434. Diogo Gomes reached the Cape Verde Islands in 1455. The Portuguese built fortified trading posts at the river mouths and obtained gold, slaves, and ivory. After figuring a method for determining latitude in the southern hemisphere, Portuguese sailors were able to navigate to the Cape of Good Hope, at the southern tip of Africa. After the death of Henry the Navigator, King Joao II continued royal patronage of exploration. The superior navy of the Portuguese limited the expeditions of their main rival, Castile. By a treaty signed in 1479, Castilian ships were barred from sailing past Cape Bojador. In 1487, Bartolomeo Dias became the first to round the Cape and explore the Indian Ocean coasts of Africa.

Vasco da Gama followed Dias in 1497, sailing up the east African coast and then across the Indian Ocean to India. This important voyage opened up trade in the valuable spices of the Moluccas and the East Indies. After da Gama returned, King Manuel I commissioned a second journey to the Indian Ocean in 1500 by Pedro Alvares de Cabral. Blown off course, Cabral was brought by wind and current to the coast of Brazil.

In the meantime, Spain was exploring west to the Americas, beginning with the first voyage of Christopher Columbus in 1492. Columbus had failed to interest the Portuguese king Joao II in a westward voyage that Columbus believed would reveal a faster route to the East Indies. Despite skepticism on the part of court scientists and astronomers, Ferdinand and Isabella agreed to back him in 1492. After Columbus returned with reports of unknown islands to the west, Spain claimed the new lands with the support of the Spanish pope Alexander VI. Columbus returned to the Caribbean three times, each time bringing home further knowledge of what European geographers now realized was an entirely new hemisphere.

Spain and Portugal were building rival commercial empires, and racing to establish hegemony over previously unknown parts of the world. The Portuguese established forts in India, Malaysia, and the Moluccas and prevented Spain from exploiting the rich trade in spices. By the Treaty of Tordesillas in 1494, a line drawn in the western hemisphere granted Africa, India, and Brazil trade to Portugal and all lands to the west to Spain.

At the same time, the English were sending expeditions across the North Atlantic. In 1497 Giovanni Caboto, known in English as John Cabot, reached Newfoundland. Cabot was lost on a second voyage with four of his ships, but the English did not give up their search for a northwest passage to Asia.

The Spanish explored the New World, the coast of Venezuela and the mouth of the Orinoco River. Goncalo Coelho led an expedition of 1501 that roamed the northern coasts of Brazil. A member of his company, Amerigo Vespucci, coined the term New World in his account of this voyage, which was the first to speculate that Europeans had found an entirely new continent. To honor Vespucci, the German mapmaker Martin Waldseemüller named this part of the world America.

In 1519, Ferdinand Magellan set out to reach the Spice Islands by a westerly route. Magellan navigated the straits at the southern tip of South America. After his death in battle in the Philippines, Sebastian del Cano led one ship back to Spain, becoming the first navigator to make a circumnavigation of the earth. The voyage brought the Philippines into Spain's possession and gave navigators a clear idea of the distances involved in transoceanic travel.

In the sixteenth century geographical knowledge of the Americas expanded as new voyages of exploration returned to Europe. Giovanni da Verrazano explored the Atlantic Coast of North America, from Maine to Florida, in 1524. Jacques Cartier made two voyages to Canada in the 1530s, attempting to colonize the banks of the Saint Lawrence River. Martin Frobisher and John Davis explored Greenland, Baffin Island, and the Arctic Ocean straits. Henry Hudson reached a great arctic bay in 1610, believing he had reached the Pacific Ocean. Hudson was cast adrift by his mutinous crew, but his discovery of Hudson Bay led to England's control of a new and lucrative fur trade.

Exploration in the Spanish Americas led to conquest and colonization. Spanish explorer Francisco de Orellana navigated the entire Amazon River in 1541–1542. Francisco Pizarro conquered the Incas of Peru and Hernán Cortes, the Aztecs. Francisco Coronado explored the American southwest in 1540. Spain now had claim to the largest colonial empire on earth. Spain also established a cross-Pacific trade route between Mexico and China. European exploration had led to the colonization of much of the world and control of trade. In turn this expanding trade brought about Europe's economic expansion and industrialization, allowing Europeans to dominate the global economy for centuries to come.

SEE ALSO: Cartier, Jacques; Columbus, Christopher; Cortes, Hernán; da Gama, Vasco; Henry the Navigator; Magellan, Ferdinand

Fall of Constantinople

Taking place on May 29, 1453, this turning point in European history marked the final conquest of the Eastern Roman or Byzantine Empire by the Ottoman Turkish Empire, a domain that covered territory in southeastern Europe, Asia Minor, the Middle East, and North Africa. Since the capture of Constantinople, the ancient capital of the Byzantine Empire, by members of the Fourth Crusade in 1204, the city and the realm had suffered a slow decline as the Ottoman Turks stepped up their attacks on Byzantine cities and ports in the Levant and Asia Minor. By the turn of the fifteenth century the Turks had built a stronghold on the southern side of the Bosporus, the strait dividing Constantinople from Asia Minor proper. The Ottoman sultan, Mehmed II, established another fortress on the European side of the Bosporus to prevent reinforcements from reaching the city from allied Black Sea ports.

As the Turkish siege began, Constantine sent for help to the nations of western Europe. But the division between the Latin and Greek (eastern) Christian churches, dating to the Eastern Schism of 1054, persuaded the pope and many Christian kings to ignore the urgent pleas. Europe had also been weakened by centuries of fighting and civil war, with the Hundred Years' War between England and France still burning in its final years.

Constantinople was protected by a ring of walls on both the land and the seacoast, but its defenders numbered only about ten thousand in the face of an enemy that, by some accounts, had as many as three hundred thousand men as well as a fleet of several hundred ships attacking from the waters of the Bosporus. Mehmed drew up his forces in early April and began a heavy cannonade of the walls on the western side of the city. A large boom placed by the Byzantines across the entrance to the Golden Horn, a waterway on the northern side of Constantinople, prevented Turkish ships from attacking on this front; to counter this Mehmed ordered a row of logs set down on which his ships could be rolled forward to block resupply of the city from the north. Meanwhile, Turkish sappers dug tunnels underneath the walls in order to penetrate and sabotage the city defenses; the Greeks counterattacked by digging their own tunnels and sending troops into them to fight hand to hand.

The final assault took place on May 29 in several waves of troops that attacked the western wall at its weakest points. The Turks found an unlocked gate and rushed into the city, and in the melee that followed Constantine XI died. The Turks renamed the city Istanbul and converted the Hagia Sophia, the great cathedral built under the Byantine emperor Justinian, into the mosque. The last Byzantine strongholds in Greece were conquered in 1460. Istanbul remained the capital of the Ottoman Empire until this state was dissolved after World War I.

SEE ALSO: Mehmed II

Farnese, Alessandro
(1545–1592)

Alessandro Farnese was the son of the Duke of Parma and grandson of Emperor Charles V of the Holy Roman Empire. He was a soldier and diplomat who fought ably in the service of Philip II, the king of Spain. In 1571, serving under his uncle, John of Austria, he fought the Ottoman Turks at the naval Battle of Lepanto. A few years later he accompanied his uncle to the Netherlands, at this time a possession of Spain that was in full-scale rebellion. Farnese defeated the Protestant opponents of Catholic Spain at Tournai, Bruges, Ghent, and other important cities. After winning a crucial victory at the Battle of Gembloux, he was appointed governor of the territory. In 1579 he persuaded the Catholic nobles of the southern provinces to form the Union of Arras, which banished all non-Catholic sects and supported Philip and his local ruler, Don Juan of Austria. This agreement inspired the formation of the Union of Utrecht, a union of seven northern provinces that renounced their allegiance to Spain. Farnese set out with his army to reconquer the rebellious provinces, finally besieging the wealthy port of Antwerp and starving the citizens into submission in 1585. Farnese was unable to conquer the rest of the rebellious territory, however, and eventually Spain was compelled to recognize their independence.

Farnese invaded France at the head of a Catholic army in 1589, after the assassination of King Henry III. His army fought in support of Catholic opponents to Henry IV, and in 1590 lifted a Protestant siege of Paris. Wounded at a siege of Rouen in 1592, he died a few months later, having lost his title of governor through the machinations of his rivals in Spain.

Fedele, Cassandra
(1465–1558)

A renowned scholar, born in Venice and educated in classical literature, rhetoric, science, philosophy, and the new humanistic tradition. While still a young girl, she learned to speak Greek and Latin and started to gain a reputation as a skilled, persuasive public speaker. She won notice throughout Italy with a stirring speech she gave at the University of Padua, on the graduation of her cousin, praising the study of the arts and sciences. This speech, the *Oratio pro Bertucio Lambert*, was printed in Italy and Germany. She corresponded with the leading scholars of Europe as well as the nobility. In 1488, she was invited by Isabella, the future queen of Spain, to join her court. She refused this invitation—some historians believe the Doge of Venice deliberately wished to keep her as an ornament of his city and prevented her from moving to Spain. After her marriage to Giammaria Mapelli in 1499 she traveled to Crete—then a possession of Venice—with her husband, a physician. On returning to Venice in 1520, the couple lost their possessions in a storm. Soon afterward, her husband died and she was thrown on hard times. She had ceased giving public orations and she gradually fell away from her studies and her correspondence. After writing to Pope Paul III for help, he appointed her as the prioress of an orphanage in the church of San Domenico di Castello. In 1556 she delivered her last public speech, to honor a distinguished visitor, Bona Sforza, the queen of Poland. Eighty years after her death, three of her speeches and 123 letters were published.

Ferdinand I of Naples (1423–1494)

King of Naples. Also known as Ferrante, Ferdinand was born in Valencia, Spain, as the illegitimate son of Alfonso V the Magnanimous, the king of Aragon who also ruled in Naples. As a youth Ferdinand was recognized as the Duke of Calabria, the customary title for the successor to the throne of Naples. On the death of Alfonso in 1458, Ferdinand succeeded his father, despite the determined opposition of Pope Calixtus III, who sought to place a member of his own family on the throne of Naples. The opposition ended when Calixtus III died and was succeeded by Pope Pius II, who supported Ferdinand's rights as king. Ferdinand was challenged by nobles who chafed under his strict limitation of their rights in his kingdom. To oppose him, these nobles allied with the Angevins, a French dynasty that had an ancient claim to the throne of Naples. Jean of Anjou, heir to the Angevin dynasty, rode into Italy to press his claim, but his army was defeated in 1462 at the Battle of Troja, an event that confirmed Ferdinand's authority and legitimacy.

Ferdinand had a reputation as a treacherous and utterly ruthless intriguer. Contrary to custom, he took vengeance on Jacopo Piccinino, a mercenary captain who had served against him; after promising him safe conduct to his court, Ferdinand had Piccinino thrown out of a high window to his death. Ferdinand ordered many of his other opponents imprisoned; after their deaths, it was whispered, he had their bodies embalmed and collected into a dungeon for his personal viewing. In the early 1490s, the newly enthroned King Charles VIII of France used this reputation for evil as an excuse to begin planning a campaign to conquer Naples for

the Angevin dynasty and make himself master of one of the wealthiest merchant cities in Europe. By the time the French forces arrived at the walls of Naples in early 1495, however, Ferdinand was dead; although his son Alfonso II capitulated, the French were eventually driven out of Italy and the Aragonese dynasty survived.

SEE ALSO: Charles VIII; Ferdinand II of Aragon; Naples

Ferdinand II of Aragon (Ferdinand V of Castile) (1452–1516)

King of Aragon who, by marriage to Queen Isabella of Castile, established the kingdom of Spain. Ferdinand was also the king of Sicily and Naples. The son of John II of Aragon, he was born in Sos. John granted Ferdinand the kingdom of Sicily in 1468 and the kingdom of Naples in 1503. Following his marriage to Isabella in 1469, the couple agreed to consolidate their authority in Castile in 1474, an act that brought all of Spain outside of the Moorish kingdom of Granada under a single monarchy. Ferdinand and Isabella sought to establish Catholicism as a dominating force in the new kingdom, establishing the Spanish Inquisition to root out heresy and false conversion on the part of the Jews and Moors. In 1492, Spain expelled all Jews who would not convert. In the same year, Granada was conquered, bringing the *Reconquista*, or Christian reconquest of Moorish Spain, to a successful conclusion.

The conquest of Granada allowed Ferdinand and Isabella to support the voyage of Christopher Columbus in the fall of 1492. Seeking a westerly route to the East Indies, Columbus instead discovered an entirely new hemisphere, where Spain was soon sending voyages of conquest and colonization. In 1494, Spain and Portugal agreed to the Treaty of Tordesillas, which set a boundary to their respective spheres of colonization. In the following years, Spanish explorers and *conquistadores* would establish colonies in the Caribbean, Mexico, Central America, and Peru; immense sums of silver and gold were brought to Spain from these colonies and much of the western hemisphere became a Spanish-speaking dominion.

Ferdinand disputed control of northern Italy with France, after coming to the defense of his cousin Alfonso II, the king of Naples who was expelled by the French in 1494. Spain allied with the emperor Maximilian I and ejected the French from Italy in 1496, after which Alfonso's son, Ferdinand, became the king of Naples. After this king's death in 1501, Ferdinand of Spain agreed with King Louis XII of France to divide Italy between them. The treaty failed, however, and gradually the powerful Spanish armies took control of Naples and ended French claims to that kingdom. Ferdinand later signed the Treaty of Westminster with King Henry VIII of England, allying the two countries against the rising power of France. In the same year, Ferdinand added the kingdom of Navarre, a frontier territory between Spain and France, to the kingdom of Spain.

After the death of Isabella in 1504, Ferdinand kept control of Castile by acting as regent for their daughter Joanna. Also known as *la loca* (the insane) or Joan the Mad, Joanna proved herself incapable of ruling, which left Castile under Ferdinand's control until his death in 1516. On this event, his grandson Charles became king of Spain, Naples, Sicily, and Sardinia, and later the Holy Roman Emperor as Charles V, concentrating more power in his hands than any European ruler since the time of Charlemagne.

SEE ALSO: Charles V; Columbus, Christopher; Isabella of Castile; Spain

Fernando Alvarez de Toledo (1507–1582)

The hereditary Duke of Alba, a skilled military commander and a Spanish governor of the Low Countries, whose reign over the Dutch was known for its cruelty. In 1525, he took part in the Battle of Pavia, a key event in the Italian Wars in which the king of France was taken prisoner. Showing skill and daring in the field, he was appointed by Emperor Charles V to lead the siege of Tunis, a city on the North African coast, in 1535. In 1547, he also took part in the Battle of Mühlberg, where the emperor defeated an alliance of German Protestant princes. When Charles V abdicated the throne, his successor Philip II kept Alvarez in his service, giving Alba appointments as military commander and sending the duke abroad at the head of an important embassy to the king of France.

Pleased with Alvarez's service, Philip sent Alba to the Netherlands in 1567, with his mission being to put down Dutch rebels who were fighting for their Protestant faith and for independence from Spain. Alba marched an army of ten thousand Spanish troops into the city of Brussels and set up a court, commonly known as the Council of Blood, that tried and executed thousands of Philip's opponents, including members of the nobility who had supported the rebellion. His most unpopular measure, however, was the imposition of a heavy tax, known as the *alcabala*, on the sale of any and all goods.

Alba's enemies organized a large fleet, known as the Sea Beggars, to oppose the

Spanish at sea, where the skill of the Dutch and the environment favored the rebels. The Sea Beggars harassed Spanish coastal forts and shipping. In the meantime, a parliament, known as the States-General, then gathered at the town of Dordrecht and declared war on the Spanish. The effort was taken up by the Prince of Orange, while Alba organized a powerful army to crush this revolt. The Spanish laid siege to several Dutch cities, eventually breaching their defenses and committing atrocities against their civilian populations. In 1573, Alba resigned from Philip's service and returned to Spain. In 1580, he was appointed as commander in Portugal, which he subdued in Philip's name and brought under the Spanish crown. Spanish troops pillaged the Portuguese capital of Lisbon, where Alba died in 1582.

Ferrara

City of northern Italy that was an important center of art patronage under the d'Este family during the Renaissance. The d'Este dynasty began in the thirteenth century with the victory of Azzo VII, who was named podesta of the city in 1242. The d'Este court was renowned for its opulence, and in 1402 with the opening of the University of Ferrara the city became a center of learning and scholarship. The dynasty grew even more powerful when Boros d'Este was granted the cities of Reggio and Modena from Emperor Frederick III in 1452, and was named Duke of Ferrara by the pope in 1471. Under Ercole I, Ferrara began a long rivalry with the much larger and wealthier city of Venice, and became an important center of music, notably with the presence of the Flemish composer Josquin des Prez and several Italian composers who pioneered new styles of composition. Under later dukes

several of Italy's most notable poets, including Ludovico Ariosto and Torquato Tasso, found a home with the d'Este family, and scholarship flourished in the city in the work of men such as Giovanni Aurispa, who journeyed to eastern Europe and returned with many ancient manuscripts that were still unknown in Italy.

Ercole's daughter, Isabella d'Este, reigned over a court that became a model for the Renaissance princes and nobility for its splendor, patronage, and courtly manners. The best artists of Italy, including Titian, Raphael, Leonardo da Vinci, and Andrea Mategna, visited her court or lived within her palace as official painters. Alfonso d'Este, who succeeded his father in 1505, made Ferrara a pivotal city in the Italian Wars that had been touched off by an invasion of the French in the 1490s. Caught between the more powerful states of Venice, Milan, and the papacy, Alfonso carried on the war with Venice and a campaign against the ambitious popes, who sought to extend their authority in northern Italy. This resulted in Alfonso's excommunication by Pope Julius II in 1509. Alfonso patronized leading writers and artists, including Titian and Giovanni Bellini, who completed his final painting, *The Feast of the Gods*, while at Ferrara. Alfonso's son Ercole II, who reigned from 1534 to 1559, carried on the family tradition of patronage of artists and writers; Alfonso II, the next duke of Ferrara, died without a male heir in 1597, after which the d'Este court passed into history and Pope Clement VIII declared Ferrara to be a fief of the papacy.

See Also: Ariosto, Ludovico; d'Este, House of; d'Este, Isabella

Ficino, Marsilio
(1433–1499)

A philosopher, astrologer, and translator of the works of Plato, Ficino was best known for advancing the cause of classical education and humanism in Florence. The son of a physician, he showed great ability and was taken under the guidance of Cosimo de' Medici. He studied the classics and was appointed by Cosimo to tutor his grandson Lorenzo de' Medici, to translate the works of Plato into Latin, and to found a new Florentine academy, modeled on the famous academy of ancient Greece. His translation of unknown Greek works into Latin played a major role in spreading classical learning and philosophy throughout Renaissance Italy. Ficino was a leading thinker of the Neoplatonic school, and believed in reconciling the ideas of Plato and the classical pagan world's concept of the soul with the teachings of Christianity. He outlined his beliefs in his best-known work, *Plato's Theology of the Immortal Spirit*. Seeing no contradiction in classical science and Christian doctrine, he also advanced the cause of talismans and astrology, which he describes in *Three Books on Life*. For these ideas he was condemned by the church, which accused him of magic and nearly brought him to trial on a charge of heresy.

SEE ALSO: academies; Medici, Cosimo de'; Neoplatonism

flagellants

The flagellants were a sect of devout Christians who whipped and otherwise abused themselves as a public demonstration of their faith. Their practice was common in the medieval era, when pilgrimages to holy shrines and sites were undertaken by all Christians who were able. The flagellants took the concept of pilgrimage to an extreme, demonstrating not only their ability to withstand wearying journeys but also physical pain, inflicted in memory of the pain suffered by Christ himself during his trial and crucifixion in ancient Jerusalem. The first flagellants were monks, who appeared in market squares and city streets to do public penance for their sins. Gradually the processions of flagellants grew in size, reaching several thousands in Italy and Germany. The movement reached a peak around the time of the Black Death—the bubonic plague that killed some one-third of Europe's population and which to many represented the wrath of God for the common people's immoral and unholy way of life. In some places, flagellants sparked violent public demonstrations that threatened disobedience toward civil and religious authorities. For this reason, the church condemned the flagellants and on many occasions they were tried and executed for heresy. The Inquisition—a Catholic tribunal that punished heresy—conducted several mass trials of flagellants in the fifteenth century, although it did accept flagellation as a form of penance under guidance. The movement survived among small and secret brotherhoods such as the Penitential Brothers of Spain, who brought their practices to the New World.

Florence

Florence emerged in the medieval era as an important banking center and the home of a bustling textile industry. Florentine banks established branches in London, Geneva, and other European cities, and the city's gold coin, the florin, circulated widely throughout the continent. By the fifteenth century, the city had a population of more than fifty thousand and was an independent city-state, governing itself through councils of the wealthiest citizens.

A print that shows the city of Florence, its major landmarks, and the surrounding country-side in the year 1580. HULTON/ARCHIVE. REPRODUCED BY PERMISSION.

This oligarchy based its power on control of the city's guilds, which were associations of civic leaders, merchants, industrial workers, artists, and artisans. Members of the guilds had the vote, making the rulers somewhat answerable to the public will; the oligarchy in turn ruled the city with a view to protecting trade, and increasing the city's prosperity and influence. Florence had a keen spirit of competition among its leaders and industries that extended to the commissions of public artwork. In 1401, a contest decided the best design for the doors of the Baptistery among Lorenzo Ghiberti, Filippo Brunelleschi, and Donatello. Spurred on by the desire to provide the most striking and innovative design, these artists made important innovations in the presentation of traditional biblical scenes.

The patronage of the leading Florentine family, the Medici, was a spur to Re-

naissance art and scholarship. The Medici ruled the city from their fortified palace in the center of Florence, controlling affairs and dispensing favors through ownership of one of the largest banks in Europe. They sponsored artists and writers, commissioning works of art for their private homes and for display in the city's churches, to serve as an example of their power and benevolence. Despite the wealth and the sure hand of the Medici at governance, the city remained turbulent, always riven by social and political factions and contending with the other powerful city-states of Italy, such as Milan and Venice, for territory in northern Italy. The Medici were expelled during a revolt in 1494, after which a Dominican monk, Girolamo Savonarola, ruled the city in a fanatical reaction to what he saw as the city's vain luxuries. Books and art work were publicly burned, and the city lived in fear of Savonarola until he was overthrown and publicly executed in 1498.

At the prompting of brilliant writers, including Petrarch and Giovanni Boccaccio, Florentine scholars were rediscovering classical authors and adopted the principles of humanism, a view of the world that ignored religious doctrines and medieval metaphysics, and advocated a scientific and realistic investigation of the world. Cosimo de' Medici provided a gathering place for humanists who held discussions and debate in the Medici palaces and country villas, often subjecting their patron to criticism of his antidemocratic methods of rule. Florence was home to Poggio Bracciolini, Marsilio Ficino, Angelo Poliziano, and Giovanni Pico della Mirandola, the leading humanist scholars of the fifteenth century. The city also established itself as a leader in public education, with schooling available to most of the city's families and literacy reaching a high rate.

Florentine painters and sculptors, including Fra Angelico, Donatello, Lorenzo Ghiberti, Alessandro Botticelli, Fra Filippo Lippi, and Masaccio, developed a new style that more realistically depicted human form and emotion, while its architects adapted classical motifs in the design of churches, palaces, and civic buildings. The most important monument to this new era was the Duomo, the city's cathedral, which was surmounted by the largest dome raised since antiquity. The dome was designed by Brunelleschi and endures to this day as a symbol of the capabilities of Renaissance science and art. Other important architectural landmarks, including the Medici palace, the Pitti palace, the church of San Lorenzo, the Strozzi palace, and the baptistry, were raised as monuments to the city's wealth and culture.

The Medici returned to Florence in 1512, were exiled again in 1527, and finally returned in 1530 after a long siege of the city. In 1532 they named themselves as the dukes of the city. Under the rule of Cosimo de' Medici Florence regained its position as the wealthiest and most influential city-state of northern Italy. In 1557 the Florentine army conquered the rival town of Siena and in 1569, Cosimo de' Medici named himself the Grand Duke of Tuscany. By the late sixteenth century, patronage of major artists had passed to Rome and the popes, who engaged Michelangelo and other former Florentines to work in their city and create works of art that would reinforce the ongoing Catholic Counter-Reformation.

SEE ALSO: Brunelleschi, Filippo; Ghiberti, Lorenzo; Masaccio; Medici, Cosimo de'; Michelangelo Buonarroti; Pazzi Conspiracy

Fontana, Lavinia (1552–1614)

Italian painter of the late Renaissance. Born in Bologna, Lavinia was the daughter of Prospero Fontana, a Bolognese artist who trained her in the Mannerist style. She was renowned in Italy as a portrait painter, with her famous works being a *Portrait of a Woman* and *The Gozzadini Family*. She is also known for a famous *Self-Portrait at the Harpsichord*. She was skilled at depicting clothing, jewelry, and interiors in fine detail and vivid colors. Her largest and most famous work was an altarpiece, *The Martyrdom of St. Stephen*, which she painted in 1604 for the Church of Saint Paul Outside the Walls in Rome. This work was destroyed in a fire in 1823. Fontana was one of a very few female artists to be elected to the Academy of Rome.

SEE ALSO: Anguissola, Sofonisba

Fonte, Moderata
(1555–1592)

Born Modesta Pozzo, Moderata Fonte was an author whose work *The Worth of Women* posed an early feminist challenge to the male domination of society, education, and the sciences. She was raised in Venice by relatives after the death of her parents; her first work was a chivalric romance entitled *Thirteen Cantos of the Floridoro*. Her most famous work is *The Worth of Women: Wherein Is Clearly Revealed Their Nobility and Their Superiority to Men*. This book in a popular literary form, the dialogue/debate, presents the view of seven women who discuss the worth of men and marriage and who demonstrate that women can hold their own in intellectual argument. The characters include women of different classes and ages, who are divided into two main groups: those in support of marriage, and those resolutely opposed. The group sets up for itself the difficult challenge of explaining the many defects in men's characters and their undying hostility toward women. Fonte completed her work shortly before dying in childbirth at the age of thirty-seven.

fortifications

Medieval fortifications made siege warfare a costly business during the Middle Ages. Thick vertical walls of stone, raised on high ground and defended by armies of archers and infantry, could protect a city indefinitely while an army had to forage in the surrounding countryside. The innovation of gunpowder and cannon in the fourteenth century turned the tide, however. Although defenders could return fire through gun ports, in time heavy artillery would always crumble high stone walls. A new strategy and design was needed.

To absorb cannon fire, military engineers of the Renaissance tore down the medieval fortifications and rebuilt them with lower walls, protected behind high ramparts of earth. They redesigned forts in a star-shaped pattern, with triangular bastions and ravelins allowing defenders to rake attacking positions from several points at once. Batteries were some distance from the main citadel, in order for cannon within the fort to fire from a forward position and make it more difficult for an attacker to reach the main walls.

Smaller cities surrounded themselves with walls and bastions, and allowed limited access to their streets through heavily defended gates. Larger cities had a series of defensive works, sometimes ranged as far as neighboring towns in the countryside that served as a first line of defense. In the Renaissance, fortifications became so effective that outright military conquest was made nearly impossible for all but the largest armies. Especially in Italy, the Netherlands, and Spain, where heavy fortification was commonplace, war became a tool of last resort, employed only after the failure of negotiation and diplomacy.

Foscari, Francesco
(1373–1457)

A famous Doge of Venice, who led the republic in its expensive and futile wars against Milan. Foscari held many important positions in the Venetian Republic, including ambassador, procurator of the Cathedral of Saint Mark, and member of the Council of Ten. Foscari was elected doge in 1423 after the death of Tommaso Mocenigo. He allied Venice with the city of Florence, a rival of Milan. The war dragged on for several years, draining the treasury of Venice and, at one point, inspiring Foscari to ask permission to resign his office. The Council refused.

Foscari's reign was tainted by the trial of his son Jacopo Foscari on charges of corruption by the Council of Ten, the governing council of Venice. The charges were first made in 1444; Jacopo was finally banished to the island of Crete, a Venetian possession. There he negotiated with Milan and the sultan of the Ottoman Empire; accused of treason, he was brought back to Venice and made to face another trial. Foscari refused to pardon his son, and Jacopo was shipped back to Crete, where he died in 1457. The Council of Ten forced Foscari out of office, soon after which he died. The story of Francesco and Jacopo Foscari inspired poetry, plays, and an opera by the nineteenth-century Italian composer Giuseppe Verdi.

Fouquet, Jean
(1420–1481)

French painter born in Tours, known best for his miniatures and his manuscript illuminations (illustrations). As a young man Fouquet trained in Paris and traveled in Italy, where he studied the works of Masaccio and Fra Angelico and completed a portrait of Pope Eugenius IV in 1437. The new science of perspective in Italian art influenced his work. On his return he created a new painting style that combined elements of monumental Italian and extremely detailed and precise Flemish painting. Fouquet left the idealized poses and stock expressions of medieval painting behind; he depicted his subjects in bold poses and with very individualistic features that remind the viewer of monumental, three-dimensional sculpture. About 1447 Fouquet completed a magnificent portrait of King Charles VII, a work that has become one of the most famous

French paintings of the Renaissance. His patron Etienne de Chevalier, a secretary to the king, commissioned Fouquet to paint a series of miniatures for *The Book of Hours*. These famous illustrations exhibit precise lines and astonishing detail. Fouquet rewarded his patron's support by painting him in the company of Saint Stephen, one half of the Melun Diptych, in which the other panel depicts Agnes Sorel, a mistress of the king, as the Virgin Mary. His illustrations for a French translation of the ancient Roman writer Josephus made ingenious use of perspective to unify the figures and structures in a clearly defined space. In 1475 Fouquet was appointed as the royal painter to King Louis XI. In this influential position, he had a lasting effect on French painting of the Renaissance.

Fra Angelico
(1395–1455)

Painter of Florence whose works depict a simple, fervent religious devotion. Born as Guido di Pietro in the town of Vicchio, near Florence, he lived in monasteries all his life and devoted himself to the decoration of churches, monastic chapels, cloisters, and the simple cells inhabited by his brother monks. After his death, he was given the nickname of Fra Angelico ("Angelic Brother").

Early in his life Fra Angelico lived in San Domenico, a monastery in the town of Fiesole, where he took the monastic name of Fra Giovanni da Fiesole. At the age of thirty, in 1425, he took his vows as a full member of the Dominican order. His earliest works were illuminated manuscripts and altarpieces, in which his painting style was influenced by Masaccio and the new science of visual perspective. As his fame spread outside the walls of the monastery, he won commissions to paint church interiors and altarpieces. The *Annunciation* and the *Linaiuoli Altarpiece*, painted between 1433 and 1436, were done for the guild of linen merchants in Florence. In these works, Fra Angelico made a startling advance over traditional Gothic painting by accurately depicting interior space, by using bright, vivid colors, and by a more sculptural and realistic treatment of human figures.

At this time he was operating a workshop that produced altarpieces and tabernacles for wealthy Florentine patrons. He also worked as a manuscript illuminator, whose paintings decorated the pages of Bibles created by monastic scribes. From 1438 to 1445 Fra Angelico completed a series of frescoes and an altarpiece for the monastery of San Marco in Florence. Cosimo de' Medici, the ruler of Florence, had ordered the reconstruction of the monastery and may have personally engaged Fra Angelico for its decoration. The painter and his assistants completed frescoes in the cloister (including the *Crucifixion with St. Dominic*), corridors, and chapter house. He also completed forty-five small frescoes in the cells of the convent. These simple but skillfully rendered devotional paintings were meant for a lifetime of study and contemplation by the monks who lived in the cells. The painter included some architectural details of the monastery in the paintings, giving them a startling immediacy to their surroundings.

His work in the convent gained widespread renown, The Strozzi family, rivals of the Medici, commissioned an altarpiece for the church of Santa Trinita. In this famous work, the landscape of Tuscany serves as a backdrop for scenes of the crucifixion. Pope Eugenius IV later brought Fra Angelico to Rome to paint frescoes in a chapel of Saint Peter's cathedral, where the artist worked in the last years of his life. In the private chapel of Pope Nicholas V, he completed a famous series of frescoes of the lives of Saint Lawrence and Saint Stephen.

In 1447 Fra Angelico completed paintings in the cathedral of Orvieto, including *Christ as Judge* and *The Prophets*, assisted by his student Benozzo Gozzoli. He returned to Fiesole in 1449, when he was elected prior (head) of San Domenico. A master of fresco painting, Fra Angelico had a long-lasting influence on the painters of the Renaissance.

SEE ALSO: Masaccio; Medici, Cosimo de'; painting

France

The kingdom of France emerged from the medieval era weakened from the Hundred Years' War and many years of poverty, stagnation, and plague in its cities and countryside. Economically weak and splintered into several semi-independent principalities, the realm managed under the Valois kings to slowly consolidate its authority in the capital of Paris. By the last decade of the fifteenth century, France was taking an aggressive role in the civil wars that were then occurring in northern Italy. King Charles VIII invaded Italy in 1494, capturing for a time the powerful duchy of Milan and threatening Rome and Naples. Although this campaign turned out badly for the king, it did expose France to the new ideas originating among Italian scholars and artists.

Gothic traditions dominated French art and architecture through the fifteenth century. Soaring cathedrals built in the Gothic style were the work of generations of skilled masons and carpenters. Artists,

The Chateau de Chambord in central France melds the traditional French castles of the medeival period with the new styles emerging during the Renaissance. FRANS LEMMENS/ICONICA/ GETTY IMAGES.

including Jean Fouquet, illustrated biblical scenes and created portraits and illuminated books. By the turn of the sixteenth century, France had become a unified kingdom, and its increasing wealth allowed royal patronage of writers and scholars. The reign of Francis I, from 1515 to 1547, marks the high point of the French Renaissance in art, music, and literature. Francis took a keen interest in Italian painting and architecture, and brought to his court several prominent artists, including Leonardo da Vinci. His attempt to conquer Italy, however, led to his defeat in the Battle of Pavia in 1525 and his capture. Although he eventually won his freedom, Francis did not forget the many examples of Italian art and craftsmanship he had discovered while on campaign. He brought Italian artists to France and sent men

south to collect antique and contemporary art, sculpture, and books.

King Henry II ruled from 1547 until his death in a contest of swords in 1559. He was followed in power by his widow, Catherine de Médicis, and by her sons Francis II, Charles IX, and Henry III. At this time, France was torn by religious strife. The Protestant movement had taken hold in northern France, where the kingdom's prospering industries were located. The realm remained tied to the Catholic Church, however, and open warfare between Catholics and Protestants disrupted French society for much of the late sixteenth century.

The Bourbon dynasty that rose to power adopted the trappings of imperial power. Magnificent palaces and chateaus, including Chambord, Chenonceau, Amboise, and the Louvre, were raised by the country's best architects, who married classical style to the decorative Gothic manner of the Middle Ages. The palace of the Tuileries, built just west of the Louvre in the center of Paris, held gardens, grottoes, and other trappings of Italian architecture that was directly influenced by the villas of the Roman emperors. These monuments symbolized France as an imperial power, the strongest unified kingdom in Europe. To reinforce this ambition, which began in the time of Francis I, explorers were sent across the oceans to compete with colonizers from Spain, England, and Portugal. While the Spanish and Portuguese claimed the Caribbean and South America, France sent its navigators on a more northerly route. Jacques Cartier sailed up the Saint Lawrence River, establishing France's claim to Canada, and Giovanni Verrazano, serving the French king, explored the Atlantic coast of North America.

Henry IV, who reigned in the late sixteenth century, helped to transform Paris from an overgrown medieval village to a Renaissance capital, decorating the city with the Pont Neuf and the Place des Vosges, a central square of uniform facades and balanced proportions. Architects who designed the Chateau of Fontainebleau, including Toussaint Dubreuil, Martin Freminet, and Ambroise Dubois, established the School of Fontainebleau, which imported Italian Renaissance style and served as an example for French architects for the next two centuries. French composers, including Josquin des Prez, made France a musical rival of Italy; the French chansons were a popular form of music that was widely imitated all over Europe. Artists of the late Renaissance in Italy created a new style that was meant to break

the heavy traditions of Italian painting and sculpture; Jean Clouet and his son Francois Clouet mastered the genre of portrait painting, giving it a particular elegance and intimacy that would become a hallmark of French art style in the centuries to come.

SEE ALSO: Charles VIII; Clouet, Jean; de Poitiers, Diane; Fouquet, Jean; Francis I; Henry IV

Francis I (Francois) (1494–1547)

Valois dynasty king of France from 1515 until his death in 1547. Francis (Francois in French) was born in the chateau of Cognac. He was the son of Charles, Count of Angouleme and Louise of Savoy. He became the heir and favorite of King Louis XII, who had failed to produce male heirs of his own and arranged Francois's marriage to his own daughter Claudia. In the first year of his reign, Francois scored an important victory against an army of Swiss mercenaries at the Battle of Marignano, after which France took control of the northern Italian city of Milan. To secure his authority in northern Italy, Francois signed pacts with the pope, the Swiss Confederation, Emperor Maximilian I, and Archduke Charles, the heir to the Holy Roman Empire.

After Maximilian died, Francois declared his candidacy for the title of emperor. He was thwarted when the electors chose instead Archduke Charles, now Emperor Charles V. This defeat resulted in France being surrounded by a string of territories, including the Low Countries, Spain, and Burgundy, which were ruled by the emperor, his rival. To achieve a balance of power in Europe, Francois allied himself with German Protestant princes who opposed the rule of the Catholic emperor in their domains. At a famous meeting known as the Field of the Cloth of Gold, Francois also tried to create an alliance with King Henry VIII of England.

Francois declared war against Charles in 1521. At the battle of Pavia, in 1525, he suffered a crushing defeat and was taken prisoner. In exchange for his freedom he agreed to the Treaty of Madrid in 1526, in which France gave up its claims to Italy as well as Burgundy, which became a territory of the Holy Roman Empire. After returning to France, the king renounced the treaty and formed the League of Cognac, which included France, England, Venice, Florence, and the pope. A second war against Charles V ended in the Treaty of Cambrai, which returned Burgundy to France. In the meantime, Francois supported several expeditions to the New World, including that of Jacques Cartier, which established French claims to Canada.

In 1535, when Duke Francesco Sforza of Milan died without an heir, Francois invaded Italy again. Charles responded by attacking Provence, the southeastern region of France. A truce was made in 1538 and then broken in 1542 when Francois allied with Sultan Suleiman I of the Ottoman Empire. Charles then allied with Henry VIII of England and attacked France, a war that, in the Treaty of Crepy, ended French claims to Naples as well as Flanders and Artois, but allowed France to keep mountains in Savoy and the Piedmont region of northern Italy.

Francois presided over military setbacks but one of the most brilliant Renaissance courts of Europe. Leading scholars, authors, and poets were given the king's patronage and protection. Francois invited to his courts Leonardo da Vinci, Andrea del Sartro, and Benvenuto Cellini, who brought with them the ideas and artistic styles of the Italian Renaissance. Under the king's patronage, a library of all French and Italian books was gathered and the College de France was founded. The king also decorated his realm with splendid royal chateaus at Chambord, Amboise, and Fontainebleau, hiring Italian architects to renovate and decorate many medieval chateaus that had fallen into disrepair. An avid buyer of art, he began gathering the Italian Renaissance paintings, including the *Mona Lisa* of Leonardo da Vinci, that would form the heart of the collections of the Louvre, a medieval fortress that he transformed into a Renaissance palace and the national museum of France. The overburdening expenses of this patronage and other building projects, as well as the costs of the many wars he had declared, however, emptied the royal treasury and nearly bankrupted the kingdom.

SEE ALSO: Charles V; France; Henry VIII; Leonardo da Vinci

Franco, Veronica (1546–1591)

A famous courtesan and poet of Venice. Trained in her profession by her mother, she married a physician while still a teenager, but on the breakup of her marriage she became a courtesan, highly regarded among the nobility of Venice and renowned throughout Europe for her intelligence, witty conversation, and gift as a writer. She walked in the city's literary circles and wrote *Terza Rime* and *Lettere Familiari a Diversi*, two books of poetry, as well as anthologies of the works of other writers and poets. She also founded a charity for courtesans. Franco survived an outbreak of plague that struck Venice in 1575, although her house was ransacked and she lost nearly all of her possessions. In 1577 she was accused and tried for witchcraft, but won an acquittal through an impassioned defense. Her books have survived as eloquent witness to the social life of Venice and her personal battles in support of women and the poor.

Fugger, Jakob
(1459–1525)

Born in Augsburg, Germany, the son of Jakob Fugger the Elder, Jakob Fugger the Younger was an investor, speculator and banker who built the most profitable commercial enterprise in Europe. His elder brother Ulrich had provided money and goods to members of the Habsburg dynasty, who came to rely on the House of Fugger for substantial loans in times of need. As a young man Jakob traded in valuable spices, which arrived from Asia at great cost and were readily sold at a large markup to Europe's wealthy families. He also took advantage of his family's control of mines in central Europe to monopolize the copper market. With the profits from these and other operations he began loaning money to kings, to hard-pressed members of the nobility, and to the church. Although usury was banned by law in many places and condemned by the church, authorities in need of money to finance military campaigns and grandiose construction projects managed to overlook Fugger's high rates of interest. He built a conglomeration of banks, mines, factories, and trading companies, earning enormous profits through the consolidation of his far-flung ventures. His true cash cow, however, was the banking business. In 1519, he raised nearly a million florins (more than five hundred thousand florins from his own bank) to help Charles V bribe the electors of the Holy Roman Empire and defeat his rival for the imperial title, Francis I of France. In 1514 he funded a complex of houses for the poor of Augsburg. These "Fuggerei" are still in existence and run by the Fugger family, who still collect from tenants the original Renaissance-era sum of one gulden (translated into .88 euros) a year for rent. Historians estimate that on his death Jakob Fugger was worth several million gold florins, making him by far the richest man in Europe, and one of the richest in history.

Galilei, Galileo
(1564–1642)

Italian physicist and astronomer, the first scientist to rigorously apply mathematical calculation to observation of the physical world, thus inventing a revolutionary scientific method that is still in use. Born in Pisa, Galileo was the son of Vincenzo Galilei, a musician and amateur mathematician. His father's calculations of musical intervals and tonality inspired Galileo's interest in mathematics. Although he entered a medical school at the University of Pisa, Galileo did not complete the course of study, turning instead to the field of mathematics and becoming head of the university's mathematics faculty at the age of twenty-five, a reward for a paper he wrote on the center of gravity in solid objects. While at Pisa he studied magnetism, optics, and the phenomenon of the tides. His invention of the hydrostatic balance won him even wider renown in 1586, but his innovative idea that the velocity of a falling body was independent of its weight—contradicting the classical teachings of Aristotle—aroused a storm of opposition. In 1592 he joined the faculty of the University of Padua, where he taught mathematics, astronomy, and physics; he remained in this post until 1610.

In 1608, news of the invention of the telescope in the Netherlands reached Italy. Galileo soon fashioned one of his own that allowed him to make important observations of the moon and the solar system. In 1610, he discovered Io, Europa, and Callisto, three of the moons of Jupiter; four days later he discovered the moon of Ganymede. As these moons occasionally disappeared, Galileo surmised that they were regularly orbiting and disappearing behind Jupiter; from this he concluded that the traditional Ptolemaic, earth-centered view of the universe was incorrect, as not all heavenly bodies revolved around the earth. These observations made Galileo a committed believer in the theory of Nicolaus Copernicus, who placed the sun at the center of the universe. To prove his point, Galileo traveled to Rome, where he demonstrated the telescope and allowed church leaders and distinguished scholars to view the satellites of Jupiter for themselves.

Galileo Galilei. AP IMAGES.

With the telescope Galileo also observed the phases of Venus, the mountains and craters of the moon, the individual stars that make up the Milky Way galaxy, and the rings of Saturn (although the limited power of his telescope prevented him from recognizing their true nature). He was regarded throughout Italy as a leading scientist and philosopher of astronomy, and was appointed as official mathematician and philosopher to Cosimo de' Medici, the Duke of Tuscany. His support of the Copernican system, however, aroused strong opposition within the church. Although Copernican astronomy was widely accepted in Protestant northern Europe, in Catholic Italy a different philosophy still held sway, one that did not allow for alternate systems that contradicted the accepted wisdom of the Bible or of the ancient thinkers Aristotle and Ptolemy.

From their pulpits, Catholic clergymen denounced Galileo's opinions as heresy, and in 1616 Galileo was officially admonished to cease and desist from advocating the Copernican system. He held to his beliefs, however, and found himself unable to deny the plain fact of observation and the confirmation of the Copernican system through the use of mathematics. In 1632 he published *Dialogue Concerning the Two Chief World Systems*. In this book, he disguised the opinions of an ally, Pope Urban VIII, in support of geocentrism, an idea that he then discredits with his own heliocentric views. Although Galileo was given formal permission to publish the book, his instructions were not to advocate heliocentrism; worse, the pope was offended by his thinly disguised portrayal in the *Dialogue* as a simplistic fool. Galileo was summoned before the Roman Inquisition, tried for heresy in 1633, and found guilty. The Inquisition banned the *Dialogue*, required Galileo to give up his heliocentric teachings, sentenced him to house arrest, and banned him from any future publication.

While living in a country villa near Florence, he wrote *Two New Sciences*, a work about basic physical properties of various materials and the nature of motion. Galileo's other important works are *Dialogues Concerning Two New Sciences*, written toward the end of his life; *Starry Messenger*, a book written in 1610 that describes his many discoveries made through the telescope; and *The Assayer*, in which he grapples with the strange phenomenon of comets.

Galileo's innovations include the use of the microscope and the refracting telescope, the invention of the thermometer, an early attempt to calculate the speed of light, and studies on the phenomenon of mass, inertia, and the properties of falling objects, which three centuries later formed a basis for Einstein's theory of relativity. Many of his theories, reached through extensive and ingenious experimentation, were later proven by scientists such as Isaac Newton. Galileo disagreed, however, with the astronomer Johannes Kepler, who maintained that the planets moved in elliptical orbits and that the gravitational pull of the moon caused the tides.

SEE ALSO: astronomy; Copernicus, Nicolaus; Kepler, Johannes

Galindo, Beatriz (1465–1534)

A Renaissance humanist and professor at the University of Salamanca, by many accounts the first woman in history to attain a university chair. She was born in Salamanca, Spain, and, under the guidance of a tutor, showed a talent for writing and reading in Latin. Formal education was reserved for boys, however, and her parents intended for her to enter a convent. As her fame spread beyond her home town, and all the way to the royal court of Spain, Queen Isabella summoned her for Latin lessons and to tutor Princess Juana. Historians believe Galindo may have served the queen as an adviser. She founded a hospital for the poor in the capital of Madrid, whose leaders commemorated her by naming a district of the city La Latina. Her appointment as tutor to the queen led to another as a professor at Salamanca, where for many years she suffered the jibes and condescension of scholars and fellow lecturers at the all-male institution. She authored volumes of Latin poetry and also wrote commentaries on the works of Aristotle; at the university she lectured in rhetoric, philosophy, and medicine, while advocating equal educational opportunity for girls and women.

Gentileschi, Artemisia
(1593–1652)

Painter of the Italian Baroque period whose masterful religious works reflected a turbulent life. Born in Rome as the daughter of Orazio Gentileschi, a leading artist of Rome, she may have collaborated with her father on his works from a young age. Her first picture to be signed is *Susanna and the Elders*, which she completed in 1610. About the time she was working on this painting, at age seventeen, she was raped by Agostino Tassi, a landscape painter and colleague of her father, who had hired Tassi to tutor her. When Tassi refused to marry her despite his promises, Orazio Gentileschi brought him to court. During the trial, in which Tassi was found guilty and sentenced to a year in prison, Artemisia was forced to recount her assault while under torture.

In 1612 Gentileschi moved to Florence, where she became the first woman accepted into the prestigious Florentine Academy of Design. She had married the Florentine artist Antonio di Vicenzo Stiattesi in 1612 but separated from her husband after a short time and lived the rest of her life as an independent woman and painter. In Florence she enjoyed the patronage of Duke Cosimo II and gained a reputation as a woman artist unafraid of rendering powerful and violent scenes from biblical and classical traditions, subjects that many believed were beyond the abilities of a female artist. Michelangelo Buonarroti, the nephew of the Renaissance artist, commissioned her to paint the ceiling of a picture gallery in the Casa Buonarroti, his uncle's home.

Despite her growing fame in Florence, well-paying commissions were given to other artists, and with poverty threatening Gentileschi settled again in Rome in 1620. She received few commissions for major works, but found herself in greater demand as a portraitist, a genre thought more suitable for a woman. In about 1627 she moved to Venice, where she absorbed the Venetian painters' taste for subtle effects of light, shown in her paintings *The Sleeping Venus* and *Esther and Ahasuerus*. In about 1630 she moved to Naples, where she spent the rest of her life. In the late 1630s she also spent time in England, where she worked as a painter at the court of King Charles I and helped her father create ceiling paintings for the queen's royal palace in Greenwich.

Gentileschi's pictures express her fascination with the theme of women struggling and eventually triumphing over adversity. An early work, *Judith and Her*

Maidservant with the Head of Holfernes, also shows the influence of Michelangelo da Caravaggio, who brought a stark realism and drama to religious paintings with his use of chiaroscuro, or contrasting light and shadow. Gentileschi transferred this sense of drama and her keen perception of human emotion to her other major works: *Judith Slaying Holofernes*, *The Penitent Magdalen*, and *Lucretia*. After moving to Naples, Gentileschi completed several late masterpieces, including *Bathsheba*, *The Discovery of Moses*, and *The Annunciation*. She had a strong influence on painters of Naples in the Baroque period, while in later centuries her life inspired plays, novels, and several historical works that painted her as one of the original feminist artists.

SEE ALSO: Caravaggio, Michelangelo da; Naples

Gesualdo, Carlo (ca. 1560–1613)

A musician and composer, Gesualdo was born into a noble, wealthy family and in 1584 inherited the title of Prince of Venosa, a small domain in southern Italy. He studied composition from an early age and devoted himself to music for the rest of his life. His work and life were strongly affected by a sensational crime he committed on October 16, 1590, when on discovering his wife Donna Maria d'Avalos with her lover, the Duke of Andria, Gesualdo brutally stabbed the pair in the Palazzo San Severo in Naples and dragged the bodies into the street for public viewing. As a nobleman, he was safe from prosecution; he also managed to escape informal justice from the family of his wife and her lover. In 1594 Gesualdo moved to Ferrara, a cultural capital of Italy under the rule and patronage of the d'Este family. The six

books of madrigals Gesualdo began composing in Ferrara are his most famous works, in which he experimented with new techniques of composition that are startling precursors of the impressionistic music of the early twentieth century. He moved back to his family estate in 1595 and assembled a company of musicians and performers, but his solitary nature prevented him from developing a musical school of his own. Gesualdo suffered from depression and remorse over the murders he committed in Naples; his troubled nature is expressed in the strange and jarring dissonances, chromatic melodies, and surprising chord combinations of his madrigals and other vocal works.

ghetto

Originally a district in Venice reserved for Jewish inhabitants of the city, and a name applied to any neighborhood that, either by law or custom, holds a majority of any single national, ethnic, or religious group. There were Jewish inhabitants of Venice early in its history, with most earning their livings from certain trades permitted to them: moneylending, tailoring, and medicine. After Jews were expelled from Spain in 1492, however, the arrival of several thousand foreign Jews prompted the Venetian Republic to take action restricting their movements in the city. One law allowed them to live in the city for no more than fifteen days every year. In 1516 Venice designated the ghetto as the restricted area where Jews could live. The city also had designated areas of residence for other groups, including German merchants, who were limited to a single building known as the Fondaco dei Tedeschi, and the Turks, in the Fondaco dei Turchi.

The Venetian ghetto was linked to the rest of the city by two small bridges that were patrolled after sundown in order to prevent any of the inhabitants from mingling with Gentiles (non-Jews) in the rest of the city. As the Jewish population increased, and the neighborhood grew dangerously overcrowded, the ghetto was expanded into neighboring quarters. The ghetto came to an end with the Republic of Venice, which was overthrown in 1797 by the armies of Napoléon Bonaparte. The neighborhood has remained a center of the Jewish religion and culture up to the present day.

The idea of a ghetto for Jewish residents spread to other cities in Italy and Europe. In Rome, Pope Paul IV established a small Jewish ghetto of four city blocks in 1555. As in Venice, the neighborhood was surrounded by a wall and not allowed to expand even as its population grew. The pope enforced the requirement that Jews live there by a papal bull (decree), *Cum Nimis Absurdum*. The ghetto of Rome was opened in 1870 and its walls torn down in 1888.

SEE ALSO: Jews; Venice

Ghirlandaio, Domenico (1449–1494)

A painter and renowned fresco artist of Florence, Domenico Ghirlandaio was born in the city as the son of a goldsmith, Tomasso Bigordi. At a young age he helped in the workshop of his father, who earned the nickname "Ghirlandaio" from the golden garlands he created for wealthy young women of the city. Domenico later studied painting and mosaic with the artist Alesso Baldovinetti, in whose workshop he developed great skill at the art of fresco painting, in which paint is applied to wet plaster and allowed to combine and dry with the plaster on a wall. About 1475, he was commissioned by the family of Amerigo Vespucci to paint the *Madonna of Mercy* and the *Lamentation over Christ in the Church of Ognissanti*. Vespucci himself appears in this work in a small portrait. In the same church the artist painted a *Last Supper*, which some historians believed influenced Leonardo da Vinci in his fresco of the same scene in Milan. In the town of San Gimignano, Ghirlandaio completed a series of frescoes in the chapel of Santa Fina, ingeniously incorporating elements of the building into his picture. He was also hired to paint fresco scenes in the Palazzo Vecchio, the city hall of Florence.

In 1483 Ghirlandaio traveled to Rome, where he painted the *Calling of Peter and Andrew* on a commission of Pope Sixtus IV for the Sistine Chapel. He returned to Florence and in 1486 completed frescoes in the Sassetti Chapel of the church of Santa Trinita, showing the life of Saint Francis. The frescoes were set in Florence and contain many portraits of the artists' acquaintances, including Lorenzo de' Medici and the writer Angelo Poliziano. After this work Ghirlandaio completed his most famous fresco cycle in the church of Santa Maria Novella, describing the life of Saint John the Baptist and Mary, in fourteen separate pictures along the side walls of the church choir. In this work, he had the help of a young apprentice, Michelangelo Buonarroti. The details and the many portraits of this cycle have provided historians with a rich source of information on the clothing, interior architecture, and personalities of Renaissance Florence.

Ghirlandaio's most famous panel paintings include the *Adoration of the Shepherds*, the *Adoration of the Magi*, and several famous portraits, including *Francesco Sassetti and His Son* and *Grandfather with His Grandson*, the artist's most familiar single work. The tender moment between an old man and a young boy captures the essential humanist element of the Renaissance, when heartfelt and familiar emotions became a worthy subject for painters besides the loftier sentiments of biblical scenes and stories. Still in the prime of his creative powers, Ghirlandaio died as an epidemic of plague swept the city of Florence in 1494.

SEE ALSO: Florence; painting

Giorgione
(1477–1510)

Venetian painter of the High Renaissance, known as a master for the handful of his paintings that have survived. Born as Giorgio Barbarelli da Castelfranco in the small town of Castelfranco Veneto, he apprenticed in the workshop of Giovanni Bellini, who was at that time one of the most respected painters in Venice. His talent was recognized from an early age; he was commissioned to paint a portrait of Doge Agostino Barberigo and, in 1504, an altarpiece commemorating Matteo Constanzo for a church in Castelfranco. He also worked on frescoes for the walls of the Fondaco dei Tedeschi, the Hall of German Merchants that served as a warehouse. These frescoes were painted in collaboration with Titian, another major Venetian painter, but were later destroyed. Giorgione specialized in paintings commissioned from private individuals, with whom he had a much greater range of possible subject matter and style than he would have in works commissioned by the church or public officials.

Historians have disagreed on works attributed to Giorgione, with only about six definitely by his hand. Only one of his paintings, a portrait entitled *Laura*, was signed. Others include the *Three Philosophers, Portrait of a Young Man*, the *Pastoral Concert*, and *Sleeping Venus*, in which a nude figure is placed in a natural background, and which directly inspired the *Venus of Urbino* of Titian. The most famous Giorgione painting, *The Tempest*, is a startling landscape that shows a seated woman, who is breast-feeding an infant, near the figure of a standing soldier. In the background a storm approaches over the ruins of a city. *The Tempest* challenges the viewer to decipher the meaning of the figures, the storm, and other symbols, which originate completely in the artist's imagination.

In this and other works Giorgione was the first to place figures in a landscape setting. Possibly under the influence of Leonardo da Vinci, Giorgione also adopted the sfumato technique of soft, shaded contours, a sharp break from the clear lines and brighter colors of early Renaissance paintings. In several of his works, he ignored traditional subjects of the Christian religion or classical mythology, and created personal allegories, set in symbol-rich landscapes that give his works an air of mystery and poetic charm. By the time of his death of the plague at the age of thirty-three, his works had a strong influence on many Venetian painters, including Bellini and Titian, and Venetian painting of the next two centuries, notably in the Baroque works of Palma Vecchio and Dosso Dossi, who borrowed many of the techniques that Giorgione pioneered.

SEE ALSO: painting; Titian; Venice

Giotto di Bondone
(1267–1337)

Painter of Florence who made an important break with the medieval Byzantine style of painting, and whose works helped bring about the more intensely personal and humanistic outlook of Renaissance artists. Historians are unsure of his birthplace, although by some accounts he was born in Colle di Vespignano, in rural Tuscany. The son of a peasant, he spent his youth as a shepherd. By one tradition, while walking in the countryside the painter Cimabue came across one of Giotto's drawings, rendered in chalk on the rough surface of a stone, and was so impressed by the simple power of the work that he invited the boy to join his workshop.

In the late thirteenth century, the Byzantine style of painting had reached the height of its expressive power but was in the process of being replaced by new techniques of the more realistic Gothic style. As a pupil of Cimabue, Giotto became a leading figure of this transition. Early in his career he was commissioned to direct the painting of a series of frescoes for the church of San Francesco in Assisi, a church dedicated to the founder of the Franciscan order. The series illustrates the life of Saint Francis and dozens of stories from the Bible, including the Resurrection, the Lamentation of Christ, and the stories of Isaac and Joseph. The humble life and heartfelt devotion of Saint Francis called for a new style, in which the severe, ethereal figures of Byzantine paintings were replaced by figures with earthy, simple emotions that ordinary Christians could understand.

In 1302 Giotto traveled to Padua, where over the next four years he painted a series of frescoes in the Arena Chapel for a local nobleman, Enrico Scrovegni. Raised on the site of an ancient Roman arena, the chapel was meant to atone for the sins of Scrovegni's father, a usurer made famous by his appearance in the works of Dante. Considered to be among the finest works of Italian art of any period, the Arena Chapel frescoes cover the interior walls of the chapel and include the *Life of Christ, Flight into Egypt, The Betrayal of Judas, Adoration of the Magi, Lamentation* and many other scenes. The frescoes are startlingly lifelike; the figures convey emotion through simple gestures and expression, while the painter guides the viewer's eye through the stories by the use of architectural elements and the deep perspective provided by the background of a dark blue sky. The Arena Chapel had a major influence on Masaccio, a later master of perspective, as well as Michelangelo, who imitated Giotto's painted architectural framework for his frescoes on the ceiling of the Sistine Chapel.

Giotto is also credited as the painter of the *Madonna Enthroned*, a painting of the Virgin Mary and Jesus seated on a throne, surrounded by angels and gazing at the viewer with simple, direct expressions. For the Peruzzi Chapel of the church of Santa Croce, in Florence, he painted a fresco series of the lives of Saint John the Baptist and Saint John the Evangelist. An adjacent chapel, known as the Bardi Chapel, contains the story of Saint Francis in a series of six scenes. The complex design and use of perspective in Santa Croce took Giotto even further beyond his work in the Arena Chapel.

In 1328 Giotto began working as a court painter for Duke Robert of Anjou, the ruler of Naples. None of his work from this period survived, however, and he returned to Florence in 1334; his wide acclaim as a painter had convinced the town fathers to appoint him as chief architect and engineer of the city and its cathedral. Giotto executed designs for the campanile (bell tower) of the cathedral, which still stands and is commonly known as Giotto's Tower. The two lower stories carry sculptural reliefs designed by Giotto and later carved by Andrea Pisano. The rest of the structure was completed well after Giotto's death and its design was altered by the architects who succeeded him.

Inspired by Saint Francis and the Fransican order, which was relatively new in Giotto's lifetime, the artist made of traditional Christian parables a powerful drama, and related the fear, hope, desire, betrayal, and inspiration contained in the biblical passages that were familiar as their own names to the original viewers of his works. He had a major impact on several generations of artists who followed him and was also renowned among the greatest writers of his day, including Dante, Petrarch, and Boccaccio.

SEE ALSO: Florence; Masaccio; Michelangelo Buonarroti; painting

Gonzaga, Gianfrancesco (1394–1444)

Ruler of Mantua from the year 1407, when he inherited the title at the age of twelve. Gianfrancesco ruled through his uncle Carlo Malatesta. Two years after attaining his title, he married Paola Malatesta, daughter of the ruler of Pesaro. In alliance with the Malatesta family, he led Mantua into a military alliance. In 1433 the Holy Roman Emperor Sigismund bestowed the title of Marquis on him. In 1432 he became the commander of the Venetian army. Afterward he allied with the Visconti family of Milan, rivals of the pope. Under his patronage, several important Renaissance artists flourished at the Mantuan court.

Gonzaga, House of

Ruling dynasty of the northern Italian city of Mantua from the early fourteenth century until 1708, under which the city be-

came a center of art, literature, and Renaissance humanism. The Gonzaga reign began with Ludovico I Gonzaga, who warred his way to control of Mantua in 1328, and his son Guido, who defeated a rival clan in the nearby town of Reggio. Under Gianfrancesco II, who ruled in the early fifteenth century, the Gonzaga allied themselves with Holy Roman Emperor Sigismund. In gratitude the emperor bestowed the title of marquess on Gianfrancesco and his heirs in 1432. This ruler invited the scholar Vittorino de Feltre to establish a school of learning in one of the Gonzaga castles, and invited some of the finest artists of the time, including Andrea Mantegna and Leon Battista Alberti, to Mantua. His heirs Federigo I and then Gianfrancesco III brought Mantua to the height of its prestige in the arts as well as its military power. The city allied with Emperor Charles V against the French and sent a powerful detachment to fight the French king Charles VIII at the Battle of Fornovo. Gianfrancesco served Naples as a captain of mercenaries but was captured by Venice in 1509. After he won his freedom he returned to Mantua, and with his wife Isabella d'Este presided over a court renowned throughout Europe for its promotion of Renaissance ideals. Federigo II, who succeeded Gianfrancesco in 1519, fought with the armies of the pope and was named Duke of Mantua by Charles V in 1530. Federigo commissioned new palaces and public buildings in Mantua and invited Raphael, Titian, Leonardo da Vinci, Claudio Monteverdi, and Ludovico Ariosto to his court. After Federigo the Gonzaga dynasty went into decline under the rule of greedy and incompetent dukes; the city was invaded in the seventeenth century and the dynasty was overthrown by the Habsburg rulers of Austria in 1708, the year of death of Ferdinand Charles, the last of the line.

SEE ALSO: d'Este, Isabella; Gonzaga, Gianfrancesco; Gonzaga, Ludovico

Gonzaga, Ludovico (1412–1478)

Duke of Mantua, the son of Gianfrancesco Gonzaga. He inherited the throne of Mantua in 1444 and allied his forces with that of Milan in 1446. In the next year he joined an alliance with Florence and Venice against Milan. In 1450 he fought for King Alfonso of Naples in northern Italy, but was bribed by Francesco Sforza of Milan with territories belonging to Venice. Ludovico scored an important victory against his brother Carlo, who was fighting for Venice, at the Battle of Goito in 1453. In 1454 the Peace of Lodi returned cities Gonzaga had conquered to Venice. When Carlo died without an heir in 1487, Ludovico inherited his lands. In 1459 Ludovico presided at an important council convened by Pope Pius II, who was intent on turning back the Ottoman Turks from Europe after their conquest of Constantinople.

Ludovico was a patron of the arts and appointed Andrea Mantegna as his court painter. He died of the plague in 1478.

Granada (Sultanate)

A Moorish realm established in what is now southern Spain, the Granada Sultanate was the last remnant of the Moorish invasion of Europe from northern Africa in the early eighth century. Granada originated as a provincial capital of the caliphate of Cordoba. In the eleventh century, the Zirid dynasty was founded and Granada became an independent sultanate. In 1228, the leader Mohammad Ibn al-Ahmar established a new dynasty, known as the Nasrids, that later began paying tribute to the Christian kingdom of Castile and helped the Castilian kings put down Moorish revolts in their own realm. In Granada, the sultan Muhammed V built an elaborate palace, the Alhambra, that still stands as the most important work of Moorish architecture in Europe.

Granada became a center of Moorish scholarship and learning with the establishment of a university, known as the Madraza, under the sultan Yusuf I in 1349. The city also provided Spain and the rest of Europe with an important link to markets in North Africa. Through Granada, European goods were traded for gold, ivory, and other items brought north across the Sahara Desert in long caravans. The kingdom's economic importance declined, however, as the Portuguese opened up new sea routes to western and southern Africa. In the fifteenth century, with the unification of Castile and Aragon, the Catholic monarchs Ferdinand and Isabella resolved to conquest the remaining Moorish states in the Iberian peninsula, and the territory of Granada gradually shrank under repeated assaults by the Christian armies. In 1492, Muhammad XII, also known to the Christians as Boabdil, surrendered Granada after a siege, and the Reconquista was complete. By the Alhambra Decree, the rulers of Spain demanded the sincere conversion of the Moors from Islam (as well as Jews) to Christianity. Those who resisted or falsely converted were tried by the Inquisition and executed, while others fled to Africa. The city's mosques were converted to Christian churches, and the Madraza was rededicated as the University of Granada by Emperor Charles V in 1526.

Granada's art and architecture had a lasting effect in Spain. The Moorish artists and builders, known as the Mudejars, had developed an intricate geometrical style, inspired by the Islamic strictures against depicting the human form. Skilled Mudejars worked in stone, brick, wood, and tile, and their motifs and designs were later incorporated into many public buildings in Granada and the surrounding region.

SEE ALSO: Ferdinand II of Aragon; Isabella of Castile; Spain

Great Schism

A divide in the Catholic Church that brought an institution that dominated medieval Europe to the lowest point of its reputation, and became a key impetus for the Protestant Reformation. In 1377, the papal court, which had resided in the southern French town of Avignon, was returned to Rome on the orders of Pope Gregory XI. In the next year, Gregory's death was followed by the election of Urban VI who, much to the chagrin of the cardinals who had elected him, soon took steps to reform the corrupt bureaucracy of the church. A faction of French cardinals met in the town of Agnani and declared the election of Urban as null. They elected Robert of Geneva as Clement VII, a French-speaking rival pope who returned to Avignon. Urban's papal court in Rome survived, and Christians throughout Europe found their loyalties demanded by two separate and hostile factions of Italian and French prelates. Urban VI was followed in Rome by Boniface IX (1389–1404), Innocent VII (1404–1406), and Gregory XII (1406–1415). Clement was succeeded in Avignon by Benedict XIII (1394–1417). To resolve the schism, the cardinals gathered in the Tuscan city of Pisa, on the advice of religious scholars that the pope was subject to the decisions of a holy council. The Council of Pisa then

elected a third pope, Alexander V, who was not recognized by either of the popes in Rome and Avignon. The Holy Roman Emperor summoned church officials to the Council of Constance in 1414. The council declared the two rival popes deposed and elected Martin V. This pope managed to return the Papacy permanently to Rome, but not before the church suffered a serious loss in its reputation as the supreme religious authority, paving the way for the dissidents and Protestants whose movement would sweep northern Europe in the sixteenth century.

SEE ALSO: Hus, Jan; Luther, Martin; Reformation, Protestant

Greco, El
(1541–1614)

A painter born as Domenikos Theotocopoulos on the island of Crete, and who made his home and career in Spain (thus the Spanish nickname El Greco, "the Greek"). At a young age he painted icons in the Byzantine style, and much of his later work reflects this training. He left Crete for Venice (of which Crete was then a colony), and after a few years moved to Rome, where he was influenced by the works of Titian, with whom he studied, as well as Tintoretto and Michelangelo Buonarroti. Some time in the 1570s he moved to the city of Toledo, Spain, where he had won a commission to paint an altarpiece for the church of Santo Domingo. *The Assumption of the Virgin*, a canvas 4 meters (13 feet) high, formed the central part of this work. This work gained him renown throughout Spain, and he was commissioned to create altarpieces for the Toledo cathedral and the church of San Tome. He created sculpture for church altars and painted portraits of nobles and church officials as well as a famous landscape, known as *View of Toledo*, that remains one of the best known paintings of his time. His elongated and rapturous figures are cast in a pale, luminous light. This unique and personal style was startlingly advanced for its day and had few imitators until the Expressionist school of painting developed in the twentieth century.

Grey, Lady Jane (1537–1554)

The reigning queen of England for nine days, Lady Jane Grey was the great-granddaughter of King Henry VII and the grandniece of King Henry VIII. She was born in Leicester, the daughter of the Marquess of Dorset, who sent her to the royal court when she was nine to tend to Catherine Parr, the sixth wife of Henry VIII. In July 1553, she was proclaimed as queen—although never officially crowned—after the death of Edward VI, the young Protestant son of Henry who had passed the monarchy to Jane in his will. Under the protection of the Duke of Northumberland, she was supported by English Protestants who opposed the Catholic princess Mary, a daughter of Henry who was threatening to return property seized by the Church of England to the Catholics. When her accession was found unlawful, Grey was deposed from the throne. In 1554, a rebellion against Queen Mary broke out. Suspecting Grey of taking part in the plot against her, Mary had her young cousin arrested, imprisoned, and beheaded.

Gritti, Andrea (1455–1538)

The Doge of Venice from 1523 to 1538, Gritti was born in Bardolino, a town near Verona, and traveled widely in Europe as part of his education. He lived for a time in Istanbul, the capital of the Ottoman Empire, where he made his living as a merchant and served as a representative of the merchants and traders from western Europe who were doing business with the Turks. He first served the Venetian Republic as an envoy to Sultan Beyezid. At this time the Ottoman Empire and Venice were vying for control of ports and trade in the eastern Mediterranean. The conflict worsened in 1499, when Gritti was arrested on charges of spying. He was imprisoned for several years and, thanks to his acquaintance with the sultan, narrowly escaped execution. After returning to Italy, he became the podesta (mayor and governor) of the city of Padua. In 1509, shortly after Venice lost the Battle of Agnadello against the armies of the pope and the League of Cambrai, Gritti was given command of the Venetian army.

Gritti's great skill both as diplomat and military strategist earned him election to the post of doge in 1523. A forceful personality, who ruled Venice much as a feudal lord rules his private domains, he was determined to make the republic influential and indispensable in the political affairs of Europe. He also embellished Venice with skilled musicians, artists, and architects, and hired renowned scholars and humanists, including Pietro Bembo, to serve the city. Venice and Emperor Charles V concluded an important peace agreement during Gritti's term, but Gritti failed in his efforts to unite Charles, the king of France, and Venice against the Ottoman Empire, which would soon eclipse Venice in Greece and the Mediterranean.

Grotius, Hugo (1583–1645)

A Dutch jurist and historian, Hugo Grotius (born Huig de Groot) was the first to set out important concepts of international law. He was born in the town of Delft and was a precocious student of Latin, writing his first poems in that language at the age of eight. Schooled by his father and his tutors in classical humanism, he entered the University of Leiden at the age of eleven. He graduated four years later, his reputation as a brilliant scholar rapidly spreading after an appearance at the court of King Henry IV of France. In 1599 he earned his doctorate in law at the University of Orléans. Under the patronage of Johan van Oldenbarnevelt, Land's Advocate of Holland, he advanced in the ranks of public officials, and was named by the Dutch government as an official historian in 1601.

At this time Holland was at war with Portugal; the battle was taking place far from the European continent, in the distant seas of East Asia and the Spice Islands. In 1603, when a ship of the Dutch East India Company seized a Portuguese merchant ship, the *Santa Catarina*, in the Straits of Singapore, the arrival of the seized goods in Holland touched off a legal controversy. Grotius was called on by the Dutch East India Company to defend their actions and the seizure of foreign property at sea. Grotius wrote *De Indus*, also known as *The Law of Prizes*, a treatise that set out first principles of natural law. A single chapter, "The Free Seas," was published in book form in 1609. Because the trading company won its case, the full treatise was never published and remained unknown until 1864, when it was rediscovered and appeared as *On the Right of Capture*.

Grotius defended the rights of free movement and trade in *The Free Seas*. The concept of "freedom of the sea" in effect meant that nations could harass rivals and seize their property at will, and that no court could claim jurisdiction over the claims of a wronged party. Grotius was called on to defend the Dutch East India Company in its disputes with the East India Company of England; much later England would pioneer the concept of territorial seas by declaring its sovereignty to extend 3 miles (4.8km) from its shoreline.

Grotius attained the post of pensionary, or representative, of the city of Rotterdam in 1613. He was soon involved in a religious dispute involving Jacobus Arminius, a professor at the University of Leiden, and those following a strict interpretation of the teachings of John Calvin. Grotius was asked by the States of Holland to support Arminius's position that Calvinist doctrine was incorrect, and that religious belief should be left up to the conscience of the individual. The dispute flared into outright rebellion, with Grotius and his patron Oldenbarnevelt defying the authority of the Prince of Orange, Holland's head of state.

For his part in inspiring these events, Grotius was arrested in 1618 and sentenced to life in prison (Oldenbarnevelt was executed). Hiding himself in a chest of books, he escaped in 1621 and fled to Paris, where King Louis XIII rewarded him with a pension that allowed him to research and write his most famous works, including *On the Truth of the Christian Religion* (1627), which was translated into many languages and brought to Asia by missionaries. Grotius also addressed the issue of a common law among nations in *On the Laws of War and Peace*, published in 1625. This treatise explains a just war as based on universal principles of "natural law," which follow from the natural order of the world and which should be binding on all nations. *On the Laws of War and*

Peace also deals with legal conduct during war time, the "rules of warfare," a revolutionary concept in a Europe torn apart by endless wars undertaken by princes and kings for purely personal gain.

Grotius's legal and religious opinions made the powerful Cardinal Richelieu of France one of his most dangerous enemies. Fearing trouble in Catholic France, he returned to Holland in 1631, but his refusal to admit his guilt and the error of his opinions forced him again into exile. He moved to Germany and then to Sweden, where in 1634 he won an appointment as the ambassador to France. In 1645, while sailing from Sweden, he was shipwrecked and forced to swim to shore, dying two days later of exhaustion.

Grünewald, Matthias
(ca. 1475–1528)

A German painter of expressive religious works, Grünewald is a mysterious figure whose real name—Matthias Gothart Neithart—wasn't generally known until the seventeenth century. Very little is known about his life, and only about ten of his paintings have been identified. He was born in Würzburg and spent his life in the upper Rhine River region of Germany. He worked as a painter and as a hydraulic engineer; his patrons included two archbishops of Mainz. His first known painting, *Mocking of Christ*, dates to about 1503. He began his masterpiece, the *Isenheim Altarpiece*, in 1510 on commission from the Church of the Anthonites in Isenheim. The altarpiece is an elaborate construction of movable panels that can be revealed and concealed according to the proper religious observance. Grünewald is known for his expressive use of color and his skillful placement of figures in per-

spective. He served as court painter to Cardinal Albrecht of Brandenburg from 1516. In the cardinal's service he painted altarpieces for the Church of Saint Moritz at Halle and *Meeting of the Saints Erasmus and Maurice*, in which his patron is shown as Saint Erasmus. He earned the cardinal's enmity, however, for his interest in Martin Luther and the Protestant movement. After the Peasants' War of 1525 he was dismissed from service. A solitary figure, he had no following outside of his homeland and was little known even to art historians and experts until the twentieth century, when the Expressionist movement found inspiration in his somber and atmospheric religious scenes.

SEE ALSO: Dürer, Albrecht

Guicciardini, Francesco
(1483–1540)

Italian writer of Florence whose methods in research have given him the title of the "first modern historian." He studied at the universities of Ferrara and Padua and at first sought a career in the church. His father disapproved of his choice and he turned to the law and a political career in Florence. The government of Florence appointed him as an ambassador to King Ferdinand of Spain. In 1515, he entered the service of Leo X, the son of Lorenzo the Magnificent of Florence. Guicciardini became the papal governor of Reggio and Modena, towns of northern Italy then under the control of the pope. As governor of Parma, he defended the town against an assault by the French, an action that was rewarded by Pope Clement VII with an appointment as vice regent of Romagna and then as lieutenant-general of the army of the pope.

In 1531 Guicciardini became the governor of Bologna, but in 1534 resigned his post. By this time he was disillusioned with the ambition and greed of the popes and decided to seek his fortune by allying with the Medici clan. For this the city of Florence, which had expelled the Medici, declared him an outlaw. After Alessandro de' Medici, his patron and protector, was murdered in 1573, Guicciardini allied himself with Cosimo de' Medici, a boy whom Guicciardini believed he could manipulate and through whom he hoped to rule Florence as a regent. Seeing through his machinations, however, Medici dismissed Guicciardini and exiled him to his country home.

With his hopes of power and influence in Florence ended, Guicciardini began to write *The History of Italy*, the work for which he is best known. In great detail, this work describes events in Italy in the late fifteenth and early sixteenth centuries. He also set down his thoughts on politics and religion in the *Ricordi Politici*, a commentary on the works of Machiavelli, and essays collected under the title of *Political Discourses*.

SEE ALSO: Machiavelli, Niccolo; Medici, Cosimo de'

Gutenberg, Johannes (ca. 1398–1468)

German inventor whose new system of movable type pioneered the craft of book printing in Europe. Gutenberg was born in Mainz into a successful merchant family that fled the city during an uprising against its patricians in 1411. His whereabouts after this event are unknown until he moved to Strasbourg, now in France, in the early 1430s. A skilled goldsmith and craftsman, Gutenberg was inspired by the idea of a system of cast-metal type that would allow an easier and more efficient production of manuscripts.

Johannes Gutenberg. THE LIBRARY OF CONGRESS.

Although wood-block printing had existed for centuries in China, the medieval manuscripts of Europe were painstakingly created by hand, with scribes carefully drawing letters and illustration into sheets of vellum that were then bound together. Gutenberg mechanized this process by creating a system of movable type—small pieces of metal with matrices punched into the face in the form of individual letters. The type, for which Gutenberg invented a method of mass production, could then be set into a large wooden matrix, or frame. Paper or vellum could then be placed over the frame, where the inked type created the image of a letter by being pressed against it. Gutenberg adapted the wine press to serve as a printing press, and also developed new varieties of paper and printing inks that were more useful for his process than the traditional materials used by scribes.

Not a wealthy man, Gutenberg was forced to borrow money and accept partners in order to purchase materials necessary for his enterprise. While he refined his system he made every effort to keep it a secret from his partners and the world at large. Through the 1440s he improved his invention, borrowing money from a relative in order to buy needed materials and signing another partnership with the wealthy Johann Fust, who advanced Gutenberg the hefty sum of eight hundred guilders. Impatient to see a return on his investment, Fust sued Gutenberg after making another investment of eight hundred guilders, accusing Gutenberg of embezzling the money, and won his case in the court of the archbishop. The court proceedings refer to works already printed by Gutenberg, which included a "42-line Bible," today known as the Gutenberg Bible, which was created sometime before 1455, as well as a *Psalter* (a volume of the Book of Psalms), books of Latin grammar, and printed indulgences issued by the church. The Gutenberg Bibles were printed on paper and vellum; while the letters were printed by the type, the book was illustrated by hand. About sixty Gutenberg Bibles are known, with eleven of them printed on vellum (calf skin) and the rest on paper.

With Gutenberg's type and printing press in his possession, Fust began printing his own versions of these works, employing Gutenberg's assistant Peter Schoeffer, a skilled manuscript scribe who had helped Gutenberg design his type. In Mainz, Fust and Schoeffer produced the first European book to carry the name of its printers, a *Psalter*, in 1457. Historians believe that the multicolored letters and intricate decorations of the book were Gutenberg's work.

In the meantime, Gutenberg established another workshop and created another Bible in around 1460. In 1462 he left Mainz and moved to Eltville, where he built a new press. During the next generation, civic violence in Mainz drove many printers out of the city; the capital of the industry moved to Italy and the city of Venice, which became an important book-publishing center during the Renaissance.

In 1465 Gutenberg was granted a pension of grain, wine, and clothing from the archbishop of Mainz. By the time of his death, his printing technology was spreading throughout Europe. The use of the printing press allowed publishers to create large numbers of identical books, which effectively spread classical literature, religious tracts, political pamphlets, and other works to the general population. With this knowledge and information becoming more widespread, a rebirth of learning and debate was kindled throughout Europe, ending the monopoly on intellectual pursuits by the nobility and a privileged class of scholars, monks, and scribes. Historians credit printing as an impetus to the Protestant Reformation; Martin Luther's writings and important Protestant treatises were printed in the form of broadsheets in the early sixteenth century.

Habsburg dynasty

A royal dynasty whose members became the hereditary rulers of the Holy Roman Empire, and held authority over the largest realm in Europe during the Renaissance. The Habsburgs originated in Swabia, a duchy of southwestern Germany. In 1246 they took control of the duchy of Austria. In the late thirteenth century, Rudolf I became the first of the line to be elected as Holy Roman Emperor; he passed this title on to his son Albert I. In 1438, Albert II succeeded to the title, followed by Frederick III. A capable ruler with a wide education, Frederick consolidated Habsburg rule in Germany, expanded the domain to the east, and signed the Concordat of Vienna with Pope Nicholas V, an agreement that allowed the Habsburgs some independence from the control of the church. At this time, the ideas of the Italian humanists were starting to arrive in northern Europe. Frederick named an Italian scholar, Enea Silvio Piccolomini, as his secretary and then as official poet laureate.

The Habsburg rulers were skilled in enlarging their domains through marriage agreements. Frederick engaged his son Maximilian to Mary of Burgundy, heir to the prospering duchy of Burgundy. A well-educated man and skillful diplomat, Maximilian was a patron of the arts, literature, and scholarship at his court in Vienna. He defended Burgundy against the French and founded the Holy League, an alliance of the Holy Roman Empire with the pope, Venice, Milan, and Spain to fight the attempted French conquest of Italy. He expelled a Hungarian army from Vienna and brought Bohemia within the Habsburg lands through marriage arrangements.

Maximilian's grandson Charles inherited the throne of Spain as well as the title of Holy Roman Emperor. A devout Catholic, Charles fought against the Protestant Reformation, which was supported by German princes who sought independence from Habsburg control. In 1527, when rebellious troops sacked Rome and took Pope Clement VII as a prisoner, Charles soon restored the pope to his throne. Charles defeated a French army and King Francis I at the Battle of Pavia in 1525, and fought off an assault by the Ottoman Turks on Vienna in 1529. In 1549, he defeated the Protestant Schmalkaldic League at the Battle of Mühlberg. Unable to return the German territories to Catholicism, however, he agreed to the Peace of Augsburg in 1555, allowing the German princes to establish the religion of their choice in their own domains.

The immense empire ruled by Charles V—the largest since the time of Charlemagne—posed a serious problem regarding succession. Rivalries for land and authority within the Habsburg family were intense. Charles finally arranged for his brother Ferdinand to inherit the imperial throne, which would then pass to Philip, Charles's son. Weary of his heavy responsibilities, Charles abdicated in 1555; three years later Ferdinand was crowned emperor. Philip inherited the Netherlands,

Spain (as King Philip II), the Habsburg territories in Italy, and the Spanish colonies in the Americas. On the death of Ferdinand I in 1564, the Habsburg domains were divided among his three sons: Maximilian II became Holy Roman Emperor, and also ruled Bohemia and Austria. Charles and Ferdinand shared Austria.

With an enormous sum in silver and gold arriving from the Spanish colonies, Philip set out on an ambitious campaign to expand and defend his empire. He defeated the Ottoman navy at the Battle of Lepanto in 1571, and mounted assaults on the lairs of Mediterranean corsairs in North Africa. Seeking to end English support for a revolt in the Netherlands, and return England to the Catholic fold, he sent a huge armada north in 1588. The armada was turned away, however, and this defeat dealt a severe blow to Philip's power and prestige as a defender of the faith in Europe.

Philip established new academies in Spain, patronized leading artists, and built the Escorial palace, the finest example of Renaissance architecture in Spain. From the time of his reign, the Habsburg dynasty remained divided between an Austrian and a Spanish branch, with each having its own lines of succession. Philip was succeeded by his son Philip III, and Ferdinand by his son Maximilian II. Rudolf II, Maximilian's successor as Holy Roman Emperor, made Prague a center of the new astronomy, bringing Tycho Brahe and Johannes Kepler to his court in the capital of Bohemia. His cousin Ferdinand II, who succeeded him, was a staunch Catholic whose attempts to enforce Habsburg authority in Bohemia touched off the Thirty Years' War.

SEE ALSO: Charles V; Holy Roman Empire; Philip II; Reformation, Protestant

Hakluyt, Richard
(1552–1616)

English explorer and author of two famous volumes on the voyages of English navigators. Born in Hereford, Hakluyt was the son of a skinner who showed promise as a scholar and was admitted to Oxford University, where he took a deep interest in geography and the history of exploration. He became a lecturer on the subject and in 1582 printed *Divers Voyages Touching the Discovery of America* that inspired several English voyages to the New World. His work brought him to the attention of Sir Edward Stafford, Queen Elizabeth's ambassador to France, who asked Hakluyt to accompany him to Paris as his chaplain and secretary; in France Hakluyt also worked as well as a spy whose task was to discover the efforts of French companies and explorers to claim land and resources in Canada. Hakluyt's pamphlet known as *A Particular Discourse Concerning Western Discoveries* was read by the queen and her ministers, who took to heart Hakluyt's recommendation of setting English farmers and artisans in new colonies along the coasts of North America.

Hakluyt secured appointments as a clergyman in the Church of England, while he continued his work as a geographer and historian. He met and interviewed navigators and sailors, and compiled hundreds of diaries, letters, histories, and eyewitness accounts. In 1589, he published this massive collection as *The Principal Navigations, Voyages and Discoveries of the English Nation*. He translated works of French and Spanish historians of exploration in North America and, after the turn of the seventeenth century, took part in organizing the colony of Virginia, which he promoted with an account of the voyages of Hernando de Soto in *Virginia Richly Valued,* which appeared in 1609. He was a member of the East India Company and also joined the Northwest Passage Company, meant to discover a northern route to Asia that would avoid the seas controlled by Spain.

SEE ALSO: exploration; Raleigh, Sir Walter

Henri III
(1551–1589)

The last king of the Valois dynasty of France was born in the chateau of Fontainebleau, the son of King Henri II and Catherine de Médicis, and the grandson of Francis I. At the age of nine he was named as the duke of Angouleme and Orléans, and six years later became the Duke of Anjou. A dedicated Catholic, Henri led the French army against the kingdom's Protestants (known as Huguenots) and scored important victories at the battles of Jarnac and Moncontou. He presided over the bloody event known as the Saint Bartholomew's Day Massacre, when Catholics murdered Protestants throughout the kingdom by the thousands. He ascended to the throne in 1575; in the same year he married Louise de Lorraine, who doomed the Valois dynasty by failing to produce an heir. When in 1576 Henri signed the Edict of Beaulieu that temporarily resolved the religious conflict in France, he made an enemy of Duke Henry of Guise, who formed the Catholic League to oppose the agreement. Unwilling to lead the kingdom into all-out civil war, Henri rescinded the Edict of Beaulieu in the face of the duke's challenge.

The death of Henri's younger brother Francis (Francois) left the succession to the throne of France to Henri of Navarre, a Protestant. The king issued an edict banning Protestantism and denying Henri of Navarre's rights. The Duke of Guise invaded Paris in 1588, driving Henri from the city. Determined to rid himself of Guise, Henri invited the duke to a council at the chateau of Blois. The duke was seized and murdered by three of Henri's guards, after which the duke's son was thrown in prison. The murder caused an uproar in France. Citizens mobbed the streets while the king was charged with crimes by the Parlement, which forced him to again flee Paris. While in camp with his army at Saint-Cloud, Henry was stabbed by a Dominican friar, who had entered the camp claiming to have a secret message for the king. Henri soon died of his wounds. He was succeeded by Henri of Navarre, who reigned as Henri IV, the first ruler of the Bourbon dynasty.

SEE ALSO: Médicis, Catherine de; Henri IV

Henri IV
(1553–1610)

The first monarch of the Bourbon dynasty of France, Henri IV was king from 1589 until his assassination in 1610. He was born in the town of Pau, the son of Antoine de Bourbon, the Duke of Vendome, and Jeanne d'Albret, the Queen of Navarre, a committed Calvinist Protestant.

He fought for the Huguenots (Protestants) during the Wars of Religion. In 1572, he became Henri III, king of Navarre. His marriage in 1572 to Marguerite de Valois, the sister of King Charles IX, inspired the Saint Bartholomew's Day Massacre of August 24, in which Protestants throughout the kingdom were murdered by the thousands. Henri claimed to convert to Catholicism, the faith of his new bride, but he was held under arrest for several years. He escaped his confinement in 1576 and took the field at the head of the Huguenot forces.

In France, according to the Salic law, women could not reign as monarchs. Without a male heir, King Henri III recognized Henri of Navarre as legitimate heir to the throne through the latter's descent from King Louis IX. As a Huguenot (Protestant) in Catholic France, however, Henri was strongly opposed by the French church as well as a powerful faction of nobles, led by Henri, Duke of Guise. In 1588, Henri of Guise was murdered on the orders of Henri III, who was in turn assassinated by a monk. As a result of these events, Henri of Navarre became Henri IV, king of France, at the age of thirty-six in 1589. The allies of the Catholic Church forced him out of Paris, however, and named Henri's uncle Charles as King Charles X. Henri held Charles in his custody but was forced to rally an army and fight for the kingdom that was legitimately his to rule.

Stymied in his efforts to capture Paris, Henri publicly declared his conversion to Catholicism in 1593. The announcement ended the wars of religion, and Henri was crowned in 1594. Determined to end the generation of violence between Catholics and Protestants, in 1598 he passed the Edict of Nantes, which allowed Protestants freedom of religion throughout the kingdom. With the Duke de Sully, his able minister, Henri was an active king, working in support of important reforms. The French economy was improved through reclamation of marshland and other measures to promote agriculture. The state's finances were put on sound footing, and Paris became the sight of important public works projects, including the Grand Gallery of the Louvre, a residential square known as the Place Royale, and the famous Pont Neuf, a wide, paved bridge across the Seine River. Henri also promoted explorations to

North America that allowed France to establish its claims to Canada. Although he was a popular monarch, known best for his proclamation that the French would enjoy "a chicken in every pot," the bitter resentment against his Protestantism still burned in France, and in 1610 he was assassinated by a devout Catholic believer, Francois Ravaillac. His nine-year-old son Louis, the daughter of his third wife Marie de Médicis, inherited the throne of France as Louis XIII.

SEE ALSO: Bourbon dynasty; France; Henri III

Henry the Navigator (1394–1460)

Prince of the ruling Aviz dynasty of Portugal, the third son of King John I, and leader of Portuguese exploration of the African coasts. In the early fifteenth century, Portugal and the Iberian Peninsula were the scene of frequent attacks by pirates based in North African ports. To thwart these attacks, in 1415, Henry planned and took part in the conquest of Ceuta, on the North African coast. There the Portuguese encountered the lucrative trade in gold and slaves across the Sahara Desert. Inspired by the possibilities of joining this trade, and by the legend of a Christian king known as Prester John, said to rule somewhere in Africa, Henry sponsored voyages of exploration down the Atlantic coast of Africa.

In 1419, Henry was named as the governor of Algarve, the southernmost province of Portugal. From his headquarters on the Sagres Peninsula, at the southwestern limit of Europe, Henry planned explorations into unknown reaches of the Atlantic Ocean and helped develop a new kind of ship, known as the caravel, that was lighter and nimbler than the heavy ships used as freighters by the Portuguese in the Mediterranean. Henry paid for the explorations he sponsored through his appointment as governor of the Order of Christ, a religious order holding estates and benefices throughout the kingdom, and through his right to one-fifth of all the trading profits from lands he discovered.

Leaving from the port of Lagos, the Portuguese fleets set out to rescue and ransom Portuguese prisoners of the Barbary Coast pirates. The small caravels sailed down the coast of Mauretania and returned with slaves, thus beginning the era of European slave trading. Henry's fleets discovered Madeira and, in 1427, the Azores Islands, which were soon colonized by Portugal. In 1434 Gil Eannes rounded Cape Bojador, up to that time the southernmost limit of European exploration. An expedition led in 1437 by Henry to Tangier, however, ended in failure when the Portuguese were defeated by the Moors and Henry's brother Fernando was made a prisoner.

Portuguese ships later reached Cape Blanco, the mouth of the Senegal River, and Cape Vert, eventually reaching the sub-Saharan coasts that lay beyond the limits of Muslim-held Africa. The trade in African gold greatly enriched the kingdom of Portugal, which began minting the famous gold coins known as cruzeiros in 1457. In addition, the establishment of bases closer to the prevailing westerly trade winds greatly eased the task of navigating across the Atlantic to the Americas. Eventually Portuguese navigators would push well beyond Africa—to Brazil in South America as well as the Indian Ocean and the Spice Islands.

SEE ALSO: Aviz, House of; Camoes, Luis Vaz de; exploration

Henry VIII
(1491–1547)

Tudor dynasty king of England from 1509 until his death, best known for his defiance of the Catholic pope in the matter of his divorce from Catherine of Aragon and his establishment of the Church of England. Born in a royal palace in Greenwich, he was the son of King Henry VII and Elizabeth of York and became heir apparent on the death of his elder brother Arthur in 1502.

Henry's marriage to Catherine of Aragon, daughter of Ferdinand II of Aragon, was arranged by his father in order to make a useful alliance with the kingdom of Spain, recently united by the marriage of Ferdinand and Isabella of Castile. The younger Henry, although opposed to the marriage, went through with it after the death of his father and just before his own coronation as the king of England.

A patron of the arts, and himself a competent musician and poet, Henry invited scholars, musicians, and humanists to his court. He ambitiously sought a place for England in the political affairs and wars of the European continent, and to this end joined the Holy League with Spain and Venice against France in 1512. He contested control of Italy with Francis I, who became king of France in 1515; after Francis was captured at the Battle of Pavia in 1525, Henry joined the League of Cognac with Pope Clement VII to prevent Emperor Charles V from dominating the Italian peninsula.

Early in his reign Henry was a staunch Catholic, and through his writings against the teachings of Protestant reformer Martin Luther earned the honorary title of Defender of the Faith. But when it became apparent that Catherine of Aragon would not provide him with a male heir, Henry petitioned Clement for a dissolution of his marriage, which Clement adamantly refused to grant. On the suggestion of his adviser Thomas Cromwell, Henry declared an end to the supremacy of the pope and the establishment of an English church with himself as its leader. His break with the church was sealed by his secret marriage to Anne Boleyn in 1533.

When the pope excommunicated the king for this act, the English parliament passed measures to ban appeals from English religious courts to the pope, to force the English clergy to elect bishops that Henry nominated and, by the Act of Supremacy, to recognize Henry as the supreme head of the Church of England. English citizens had to acknowledge this Act by swearing an oath; punishment for defiance was imprisonment or execution; a measure that was taken against Henry's own Lord Chancellor and trusted adviser Sir Thomas More. Uprisings against the new church were put down without mercy; Catholic shrines were destroyed, and the property of the church was seized by the crown and redistributed to loyal ministers, nobles, and courtiers.

Anne Boleyn, mother of the future Elizabeth I, was unable to produce a male heir; for this Henry blithely arranged charges of witchcraft, incest, and adultery against her, for which she was executed. Henry's third wife, Jane Seymour, gave birth to Prince Edward in 1537 but died shortly afterward. A marriage to a German princess, Anne of Cleves, ended swiftly in divorce, after which Henry married Catherine Howard. This fifth wife was executed in 1542; Henry's sixth and last wife, Catherine Parr, survived him.

Henry's reign saw an important transformation in England to Protestantism, an event that would have violent repercussions in the kingdom for the next century. He annexed Wales, defeated the rebellious Scots at the Battle of Solway Moss, and captured the port of Boulogne from the French, who regained the city through the payment of a ransom. The more prominent role of England in the affairs of Europe would be affirmed by political and military victories achieved by Henry's daughter Elizabeth in the last half of the sixteenth century.

SEE ALSO: Boleyn, Anne; Cromwell, Thomas; Elizabeth I; More, Sir Thomas; Tudor dynasty

Holbein, Hans (the Younger) (1497–1543)

A German artist, a leader of the Renaissance in northern Europe, who achieved his most famous works at the court of King Henry VIII of England. Born in Augsburg, a town of southern Germany, he was a student of his father, Hans Holbein the Elder, a noted painter of the late Gothic style in Germany. Holbein the Younger journeyed to Switzerland, where he apprenticed with the painter Hans Herbster and where he joined the painters guild. He also encountered the humanist scholar Desiderius Erasmus, who engaged him to create illustrations for his book *In Praise of Folly*. Holbein ran a busy workshop in Basel that turned out portraits on commission from the city's leading families, as well as altarpieces and stained glass for local churches. Well-known works from this time are the paintings *Dead Christ* and *Madonna and Child Enthroned with Two Saints*, and a series of forty woodcut prints known as the *Dance of Death*. In 1524, he visited France, where he discovered the technique of drawing in chalk, a method employed by the French portraitist Jean Clouet. Holbein left Basel in 1526 to seek better opportunities in England. Through a letter of introduction written by Erasmus, Holbein met Sir Thomas More, who was serving as a chancellor for Henry VIII. Holbein returned to Basel in 1528, completing several more woodcut series for books as well as *The Artist's Family*, a picture of his wife and two children. Although he planned to settle in Basel, Holbein found that the Protestant Reformation under the leadership of Huldrych Zweingli was hostile to patronage of artists by the church. In 1532 he returned to England and became a citizen of London.

At the royal court, Holbein painted a series of royal portraits, and also served as a designer of ceremonial clothing, monuments, and palace decor. Holbein painted the king, the king's wives and courtiers, and notables such as More, Thomas Cromwell, Desiderius Erasmus, Sir Henry Guildford, the astronomer Nicholas Kratzer, and William Warham, the archbishop of Canterbury. Holbein also earned many portrait commissions from the German merchants living in London. His portraits—carefully prepared pencil or chalk sketches that were transferred directly to oak panels—are masterpieces of color, strong outline, and realistic detail, especially in the depiction of the emotions and character of their subjects. Holbein was among the first portrait painters to gain renown; before his time, portraitists were simply artisans who prepared a work of art much as a carpenter creates a piece of furniture.

SEE ALSO: Erasmus, Desiderius; Henry VIII; More, Sir Thomas

humanism

The culture of the Renaissance was modeled on a new doctrine of art and philosophy known as humanism. Based on the revival of classical scholarship in medieval Italy, humanism took man as the new measure of things, and ignored the Christian traditions of miracles, sin and repentance, and ultimate salvation. Humanism lay outside the doctrines of the church, the dominant social and cultural institution of the Middle Ages. It broke with the past in elevating individual talent and inspiration above spirituality and faith. Humanism was the aspect of the Renaissance that had the most drastic and lasting impact on European culture, one that remains significant in modern times.

The study of ancient Latin and Greek authors revived the field of natural philosophy—the investigation of the surrounding world, without considering mythology or religious faith, and how that world is organized and functions. The Christian emphasis on humility and faith took a secondary position, replaced by the contemplation of beauty and how a sense of balance, proportion, and seriousness reflects inner virtue. To reach these ideals, education and study of the liberal arts—and the classical texts—were held as a basic requirement of the well-rounded Renaisssance individual, and absolutely necessary to the ability of a prince to rule justly and wisely.

Humanism was first displayed in the work of Petrarch, the Italian scholar and poet who was the first to offer a critical analysis of classical authors. Petrarch represented thinking contrary to that of the medieval scholastics, who founded their philosophies on interpretations of the Bible and the early church fathers, and on medieval scholars who concentrated on dry, lifeless, logical theories to explain the workings of the divine. Petrarch studied original texts, ignoring interpretations of medieval commentators and striving to reach the original meaning as revealed in the language used by classical authors. He began the craze for manuscript hunting, in which scholars fanned out to monasteries and cathedral libraries to uncover long-forgotten manuscripts and bring the works of Greek and Roman authors to light. In some cases, these newly discovered works had a direct effect on the work of artists and architects; a first-century work by the Roman architect Vitruvius, for example, discovered by Poggio Bracciolini, influenced the design of the dome of the cathedral of Florence, a work completed by the architect Filippo Brunelleschi in the fifteenth century.

Following in Petrarch's footsteps were several generations of scholars, who were invited to Renaissance courts of Italy and offered positions as teachers, tutors, and advisers to aristocrats and princes. Their principle subjects were rhetoric, grammar, music, history, philosophy, and poetry. To have a humanist scholar in one's household was the mark of breeding and good taste; the leading families, such as the Medici of Florence, set up academies within their palaces for an education that would stamp young people with the new outlook and make them loyal to new ideals. Leading humanists of the Renaissance include Desiderius Erasmus, who attempted to combine classical philosophy with Christian outlook, as well as Sir Thomas More, Marsilio Ficino, and Giovanni Pico della Mirandola, whose *Oration on the Dignity of Man* was an important humanist manifesto. In this work, Pico della Mirandola held man to be an essential intermediary between the Divine and the natural world, and unique in his ability to choose his own nature and develop his natural abilities. Writers such as Francois Rabelais adopted the humanist outlook, as did painters such as Leonardo da Vinci, whose wide-ranging genius allowed him to master painting, military engineering, anatomy, and the science of flight. One notable Renaissance humanist, Silvius Piccolomini, also was a scholar of ancient pagan and Christian values and attained the highest position in the church as Pope Pius II.

The trial of the Italian scientist Galileo Galilei represented the climax of the struggle between faith and reason. Having discovered the moons of Jupiter with a telescope, Galileo was forced to explain his observation by a contradiction to accepted doctrine of the Christian faith—that the earth was the center of the universe, around which all other observed celestial phenomena revolved. Galileo escaped with his life, but his works were banned and humanist learning was, temporarily, suppressed. But humanism in the way of scientific investigation eventually triumphed over the church's attempts to suppress it, and went hand in hand with the dawning of a new age of reason in Europe.

Hungary

A kingdom of central Europe, established by the eastern nomads known as the Magyars in the tenth century. In the fourteenth century, Hungary was ruled by the foreign Anjou dynasty, whose kings presided over a time of peace and general prosperity. Silver and gold mines enriched the treasury, while the Anjou kings asserted effective control over Hungary's landowning nobles and allied Hungary with Naples and Poland through marriage. Under King Louis I, who ruled from 1342 until 1382, trade with the rest of Europe increased and the kingdom's artisans began forming craft guilds to standardize their production of goods and limit competition. Louis founded the first university in Hungary and also encouraged the work of scholars and manuscript copyists. The reign of Louis's son-in-law, Sigismund, turned out badly for the kingdom, however. Sigismund was opposed by many Hungarian nobles, who were angered by the king's arbitrary cruelty, his heavy taxes, his costly foreign wars, and his many absences from the kingdom after he was elected as the Holy Roman Emperor in 1410 and king of Bohemia in 1419.

In the meantime, Hungary was threatened from the east by the expansion of the Ottoman Empire. The Ottoman Turks had conquered Bulgaria and Serbia in the late fourteenth century. Determined to stop their advance, Sigismund led an army against them and was routed at the Battle of Nicopolis, barely escaping the field with his life. The two kings who followed Sigismund, Albrecht V and Vladislav III, both died while campaigning in the Balkans. The nobles then elected Laszlo V, an infant, and selected Janos Hunyadi to rule the kingdom as regent. A brilliant military leader, Hunyadi defeated the Turks in Serbia and in 1456 lifted the siege of Belgrade, but soon died of the plague. Hunyadi's son, Matthias Corvinus, succeeded as the king in 1458. Seeking the title of Holy Roman Emperor, Matthias campaigned in Bohemia and Austria, and proclaimed his intention to forge a Christian alliance to oppose the Turks.

Matthias was a capable and enlightened ruler who reformed the old legal system of Hungary and established one of Europe's finest libraries, known as the Corvina, for which he hired a small army of copyists and illuminators to create original manuscripts. He promoted scholarship and book publishing, and established Hungary's second university. Latin translations of Hungarian writings circulated, and Latin remained an important language of administration, law courts, and education. Matthias hired an Italian architect, Chimenti de Leonardo Camicia, to rebuild the royal palace of Buda.

The reign of Matthias represented a brief golden age in Hungary's turbulent Renaissance history. His successor, Vladislav II, was a Polish heir who was incapable of standing up to the demands of the Hungarian nobles. Abolishing the taxes opposed by the nobles, Vladislav also disbanded Hungary's large mercenary army as the Ottoman Empire was threatening. His son Louis II succeeded to the throne in 1516, at a time when the treasury was empty and border defenses abandoned, with the king unable to maintain fortresses or pay his soldiers. At the Battle of Mohacs in 1526 the Hungarians were defeated by an Ottoman army and Louis himself died after being thrown from his horse. After several years of conflict over the succession, the Turks seized the capital of Buda and occupied much of the kingdom.

Hungary's political turmoil and military conquest by the Turks limited the spread of Renaissance art and ideas. The library of the Corvina was closed, and its books sent to his own capital by the Ottoman sultan Suleiman. Many Hungarian scholars fled the occupied provinces, while others joined the courts of the Habsburg dynasty, which under Ferdinand I came to control the parts of Hungary free of Turkish control. Hungarian writers began creating a new national literature in the vernacular language, and translating the works of ancient authors. Balint Balassi was renowned for his poetry, and Faustus Verantius, an author and inventor, created a dictionary of eleven languages.

SEE ALSO: Corvinus, Matthias; Habsburg dynasty; Ottoman Empire

Jan Hus was branded a heretic and burned at the stake for his attempts to reform the Catholic Church. © BETTMANN/CORBIS.

Hus, Jan
(1371–1415)

Religious reformer and scholar of Bohemia who led one of the first movements for independence from the established Christian church. Hus was born in Husinec, a town in southern Bohemia. He excelled as a student and earned an appointment as dean of the University of Prague. At the university he soon gathered support for his outspoken views on the corruption and imperialism of the Papacy. Hus believed in a personal faith, one based on the original scriptures and not practiced through the medium of a bureaucratic and corrupt church hierarchy. These ideas made up the foundation of the Protestant Reformation that would take place in the next century.

Hus arrived on the scene at a timely moment. In 1408 the university was embroiled in a debate over the papal schism, in which two rival popes competed for followers throughout Europe. Hus led a neutral faction, the only one at the university that favored neither Gregory XII nor Benedict XIII. At the same time, he was inspiring followers by preaching in the Czech language, an important break from the traditional Latin of church ceremony and university scholarship.

His writings and sermons came at a time of rising Czech nationalism and opposition to domination by German scholars. Hus gained widespread support throughout Bohemia and the support of the Czech king Wenceslaus. In 1408, however, the synod of Prague placed a ban on his preaching for his criticism of the church.

In the next year, when the Council of Pisa elected Alexander V as the new pope, Hus gave his support to Alexander. At this time, the writings and teachings of the English reformer John Wyclif were gaining an audience in Bohemia. When Alexander issued a papal bull against Wyclif, Hus directly appeared to the new pope, who responded by ordering Wyclif's books burned. Alexander also excommunicated Hus and his followers—officially banning them from the church and its sacraments. This action touched off riots among followers of Hus called Hussites in Bohemia. When Hus continued his defiance, the pope initiated a religious ban against the entire city of Prague, the capital of Bohemia, that did nothing but increase the bitterness and violence in the city.

In 1412, Hus defied church representatives who had come to Prague to sell indulgences (remissions of sin). The indulgences were meant to finance a military crusade by Pope John XXIII against the king of Naples, who supported Gregory XII as pope. Hus's sermons against the indulgences lost him the support of King Wenceslaus. In 1414 the Holy Roman Emperor Sigismund promised him safe passage to the Council of Constance, where he was to debate his views with church officials. Instead of hearing him out, however, the council ordered his arrest and had him burned at the stake on July 6, 1415. The career of Jan Hus greatly influenced the German reformer Martin Luther, who also brought about the rise of a national independent church that broke away from the control of the pope. The modern Czech Republic still celebrates the anniversary of Hus's execution as a national holiday.

SEE ALSO: Luther, Martin; Reformation, Protestant

Hutten, Ulrich von (1488–1523)

German author, humanist, and militant defender of Martin Luther's Protestant Reformation. Born near Fulda, Hutten was sent as a boy to a Benedictine monastery, where he was prepared to join the order. Unwilling to submit to monastic discipline, however, he escaped and wandered from town to town, eventually arriving in Italy, where he became a student at the universities of Pavia and Bologna. On his return to Germany in 1512, he joined the armies of the Habsburg emperor Maximilian I. His essays and poetry gained him acclaim from the emperor, who named him poet laureate of the realm in 1517.

In 1519, he was converted by Protestant Reformation leader Martin Luther's doctrine of "justification by faith" and his stand against the corrupt and tyrannical practices of the Catholic hierarchy. Hutten wrote *Vadiscus*, a bitter denunciation of the Papacy, in 1520, and in the same year published a work in German, *Arouser of the German Nation*, which called on his countrymen to rally to Martin Luther's side. Hutten took the Reformation one step further by organizing an anti-Catholic militia with Franz von Sickingen. The two men led the Knight's Revolt, mounting an attack on the estates of the Archbishop of Trier. They were defeated, however, and Hutten was forced to flee Germany. Arriving in Basel, he failed to enlist the widely respected humanist Desiderius Erasmus to his side. By this time he had made an enemy of the emperor Charles V, and the knights he had enlisted had degenerated into a rabble of highwaymen and thieves. Still a rallying figure for Protestants, Hutten was given shelter by Huldrych Zwingli on an island in Lake Zurich. There he died of an illness in 1523.

SEE ALSO: Luther, Martin; Reformation, Protestant; Zwingli, Huldrych

Index

A list of books that the Catholic Church held to be contrary to church doctrine, and thus forbidden to its members. The official name of the list was the *Index Librorum Prohibitorum*, or List of Forbidden Books. The first edition of the Index was published in the Netherlands in 1529, while the first to be published in Rome appeared during the Papacy of Paul IV in 1557.

The Index contained rules concerning the publication, selling, and reading of prohibited books. Those works placed on the Index were believed to endanger the faith of Christians, and be damaging to their moral and spiritual life. The works of Copernicus, for example, were placed on the Index and held to be contrary to the traditional idea that the earth lay at the center of the universe. Other authors whose works were condemned by the Index were Giordano Bruno, Desiderius Erasmus, Francis Bacon, John Calvin, Francois Rabelais, Martin Luther, and Niccolo Machiavelli. Authors could submit their works to the church for review, and were granted an opportunity to correct those passages that the authorities found to be in error. Anyone found publishing, reading or possessing the books on the Index were subject to excommunication, which meant separation from the church and a ban on attending the Mass.

In 1571 the church organized the Sacred Congregation of the Index, which dealt with books accused of errors, and published a list of corrections, the *Index Expurgatorius*, for books that were not deemed worthy of a complete ban. Some books were classified as forbidden, without any hope of being admitted by the church, while others were labeled "forbidden if not corrected" according to the list created by the Sacred Congregation.

The latest edition of the Index was published in 1948, and the church ended the authority of the list in 1966. The modern Curia, the administration of the Papacy, still includes an important department, known as the Congregation for the Doctrine of the Faith, meant to uphold sound moral doctrine and suppress heretical or immoral teachings among its members.

SEE ALSO: Inquisition; Reformation, Catholic

Inquisition

Although there were many violent controversies over Christian doctrine, until the Middle Ages, the church had no organized courts to try religious crimes, such as impiety, blasphemy, and heresy. In the thirteenth century, however, the rise of the new sect of Cathars seemed to pose a mortal danger to the organized church. The Cathars defied the authority of the pope and the entire Catholic church hierarchy, and were gaining followers throughout southern France. The church responded by establishing its first courts of Inquisition to try and then punish its opponents and those who strayed by preaching false doctrine. Most of these medieval Inquisitions were operated by members of the religious orders, particularly the Dominicans.

The first Inquisition of Renaissance times was established by Ferdinand and Isabella, the king and queen of Spain, in 1478 on the authorization of Pope Sixtus IV. These courts were created to find and punish *conversos*, or Jews that had falsely professed to have converted to Christianity. In the years that followed, many Jews fled Spain to the neighboring kingdom of Portugal; the Spanish monarchs then ordered all Jews to convert sincerely or leave Spain. The Spanish Inquisition would eventually found new courts in Mexico, Peru, and the Philippines. In 1536, King John III would establish the Inquisition in Portugal. Six years later, Pope Paul III decreed the founding of the Holy Office of the Inquisition in lands controlled by the Papacy in Italy. The papal Inquisition was established to seek out and eradicate Protestantism, the new branch of Christianity that was spreading across northern Europe and dividing the Christian church. A supreme court of appeals, known as the Congregation of the Holy Office, was organized by the Papacy in 1588.

The Inquisitions had a strict hierarchy and rules of procedure. The inquisitors were experts in canon law, or the law of the church, and presided over large staffs of theological experts, bailiffs, clerks, lawyers for the defendants, and jailers. Inquisitors made regular visits to the cities in their districts. They issued an Edict of Grace that listed the heresies they were seeking out, and invited those with any information to come forward. They offered a short grace period, in which those accused could repent of their crimes and be rewarded with light sentences. The Edict of Faith, that followed, threatened more severe punishment for those who would not confess. The tribunal then made arrests, jailing their prisoners and offering them no chance to defend themselves or face their accusers. Secret trials then examined the confessions and any evidence, decreed torture if necessary to gain more information, and then passed sentence in public in an elaborate ceremony known as the auto-da-fé (act of faith). Those found guilty had to publicly repent and humiliate themselves by wearing a distinctive garment that marked them as penitents. The most serious offenses were punished by execution; the Inquisition would hand over the prisoners to the public authorities, who would ceremoniously burn them at the stake. All property of condemned prisoners was forfeited to the church.

The Inquisition arrested and tried a great range of people, from commoners to nobles to church leaders with suspect opinions, including Saint Ignatius of Loyola and Saint Theresa of Avila. Its most famous defendant was the Italian scientist Galileo Galilei, who was condemned to renounce his ideas on astronomy and cease publishing his writings.

The institution gradually died out in the eighteenth century, an age of rising skepticism toward religious doctrine and greater tolerance of competing religious ideologies. The Spanish Inquisition was officially abolished in 1834. The Congregation for the Doctrine of the Faith, however, survives to this day as one of the largest departments of the Vatican, with its mission the rooting out of incorrect doctrine and religious heresy among members of the church.

SEE ALSO: Index; Reformation, Catholic; Reformation, Protestant; Torquemada, Tomás de

Queen Isabella I of Castile. THE LIBRARY OF CONGRESS.

Isabella of Castile
(1451–1504)

Queen of Castile whose marriage to Ferdinand of Aragon was the foundation of a united Spanish kingdom. Born in Madrigal, in the kingdom of Castile, she was the daughter of King John II of Castile and Queen Isabella of Portugal. In 1454, her half brother Henry IV became the Castilian king. When Henry sought to deny the succession to his brother, Afonso, supporters of Afonso rebelled, fighting with Henry's army at the Battle of Olmedo in 1467. In the next year, Afonso died, and the rebels then supported Isabella as their candidate for the throne. In 1469, Isabella married Ferdinand, prince of the kingdom of Aragon. Henry conferred the succession on his daughter Juana, a candidate supported by the monarch of Afonso V of Portugal.

In 1474, on the death of Henry IV, Isabella was crowned Queen of Castile, but she was challenged by Afonso and Joan. Ferdinand's army defeated the Portuguese at the Battle of Toro in 1476, after which Afonso gave up his opposition to Isabella. Three years later, Ferdinand became the king of Aragon. Ferdinand and Isabella united the courts of Castile and Aragon. A new parliament, the Cortes, began meeting, and a new system of laws and administration laid the groundwork for a united kingdom of Spain.

Determined to establish her legitimacy as queen, which had been so forcefully challenged, Isabella set out to enlarge and enhance the kingdom and her own authority. She led the campaign to recapture the kingdom of Granada, the last vestige of Moorish control of the Iberian Peninsula. Over ten years, the Spanish armies laid siege to a series of fortified towns while the Moors laid waste to the countryside. This campaign ended with final victory at Granada in 1492, ending the centuries-long campaign against the Moors known as the Reconquista.

In the meantime, Isabella had been rejecting the request of an Italian navigator, Christopher Columbus, to support a voyage of discovery to the west, where Columbus believed he would find an easy route to the spices and other riches of the East Indies. Such a route, Columbus promised, would allow Spain to bypass the Indian Ocean, which was under the control of the Portuguese, and build its own trading empire in Asia. In August 1492, she finally gave in, and Columbus's voyage to the New World that fall began Spain's conquest of colonies in the Western Hemisphere. The rivalry between Spain and Portugal was partially resolved by the Treaty of Tordesillas in 1494, by which the two nations divided the world into two spheres of colonization.

At home, Isabella was transforming Spain into a purely Christian state. Ferdinand and Isabella had established the Inquisition in 1478 to investigate charges of false conversion and heresy. The 1492 Decree of Alhambra called for all Jews to either convert to Christianity or leave the kingdom. In 1502, after a revolt, Muslims were subject to forced baptism or exile. Isabella also vigorously pursued a policy of strengthening Spain's ties to other European realms through marriage. She allied Spain with the Habsburg monarchy by arranging the marriage of her son Juan and daughter Joanna into the Habsburg dynasty. She also engaged her daughter Isabel to the king of Portugal, Manuel, and after the death of Isabel engaged her second daughter Maria to the same king. Her grandson Charles became king of Spain as Charles I and Holy Roman Emperor as Charles V. Her astute marital diplomacy raised Spain's importance in European affairs, while her sponsorship of Columbus established a realm of overseas colonies that would enrich the Spanish treasury for the next two centuries.

SEE ALSO: Charles V; Columbus, Christopher; Ferdinand II of Aragon; Inquisition

Italy

Italy was no more than a peninsula at the time of the Renaissance. It had no central authority or king, and no national identity, either cultural or political. As in the rest of Europe, the fall of the Western Roman Empire in the fifth century had left it fragmented into a patchwork of small, independent states. In the Middle Ages, three major regions had emerged in the penin-

sula. Northern Italy, the most prosperous region, was dominated by a few wealthy city-states, including Milan, Florence, and Venice. Smaller cities, such as Lucca, Pisa, and Siena, fought for any independence they could win from their more powerful neighbors. In the center of Italy lay the Papal States, cities and principalities nominally ruled by the pope. In the south were the kingdoms of Sicily and Naples, which were united under the Spanish rulers of Aragon in the mid-fifteenth century.

Through the Middle Ages, Italy had been open to many different influences through the invasion and assimilation of foreigners, including Normans in the South, Lombards and later Germans in the north, and the Byzantine Empire, which fought for control of the Adriatic coast. As secular heads of Christendom, the Holy Roman Emperors claimed sovereignty in Italy, and contended with the popes for the loyalty of city governments. Throughout Italy two political factions, the Guelphs and Ghibellines, supported the cause of the pope and the emperor, respectively. The prosperity of the later medieval period allowed the cities some independence from foreign rule in northern Italy. Florence became a center of banking, while Venice established a Mediterranean maritime empire. These cities expanded their control to the surrounding regions, becoming powerful states in their own right, fighting for control of trade and territory, and using mercenary armies recruited from the poor regions of the Appenines.

During the Renaissance, leading families emerged to take control of the cities. The Medici dynasty ruled Florence, the Visconti and later the Sforza in Milan, and the Bentivoglio in Bologna. Throughout the period, Venice kept its status as a republic, governed by a doge and a council of nobles. There remained little consciousness of Italy as a united nation at the time of the Renaissance. Italians thought of themselves as coming from Florence, or Siena, or Padua, and looked on their cities as their homeland. The cities competed fiercely for trade, for land, and for the presence of scholars and artists who gave the dynasties an appearance of taste, wealth, and advanced thinking. Scholars and artists wandered from one place to another, seeking the best situation at a ducal court or university. The frequent travel between Rome and the outlying cities spread classical styles, architecture, literature, and ideas.

In large part, the innovations and discoveries of the Renaissance were the achievement of Italians. It began with the study of ancient manuscripts newly discovered in monasteries and libraries throughout Europe, giving rise to a new study of the Latin language in its original form. Painters made important breakthroughs in the techniques of their art, discovering the use of perspective, using a larger palette of colors, and allowing a greater range of naturalistic appearance and human emotion in their works. Drawing on the work of Vitruvius, and the ancient buildings that had survived the fall of Rome, architects strived to achieve the harmony, balance, and proportions of classical temples and monuments. A new philosophy of humanism ran through all of these works, in which human talent and ingenuity became a new ideal, a new path to God and divinity that took no account of the doctrines and traditions of the medieval church.

With the revived study of classical authors, ancient Rome served as the source of a national identity. The ideals of the ancient past took hold first in Italy, and endured there longest. But the divisions within Italy also invited foreign interference, and national rulers such as the kings of France and Spain schemed to assert their authority in the peninsula. This came disastrously with the invasion of the French in 1494, when Charles VIII brought his army to back up French claims to Milan and Naples. Although the French were eventually routed from Italy, the Italian cities proved unable to unite their forces for a common cause of asserting a national independence from outside interference. The rivalry of the popes and the emperors continued. In 1527 came a devastating pillaging of Rome by the rebellious armies of Emperor Charles V.

SEE ALSO: architecture; Florence; humanism; Lucca; Naples; painting; Venice

James I of England (James VI of Scotland) (1566–1625)

King of Scotland who succeeded the last Tudor monarch, Queen Elizabeth in 1603 as King James I. The first monarch of the Stuart dynasty, he was the son of Mary, Queen of Scots, and the Duke of Albany. When Mary abdicated her throne in 1567, James became by right of inheritance the king of Scotland, although he was only one year old at the time. Royal power in Scotland was in the hands of several regents, while the country was divided between Catholics, who sought an alliance with France, and Protestants, who wanted closer relations with England. James assumed authority over Scotland in 1583 and proved a skilled diplomat, especially in his dealings with England and Elizabeth. When Elizabeth permitted the execution of his mother Mary, James did nothing in order to prove his loyalty. This action, and descent from the sister of King Henry VIII, earned James the throne of England on Elizabeth's death in 1603.

After succeeding Elizabeth, however, James ruled with a heavy hand over the English Parliament, toward which he showed hostility and indifference. At the Hampton Court Conference, he refused to allow religious tolerance for English Puritans, a stand that eventually drove many of the Puritans to exile and settlement in North America. There were several plots against his life and reign, with the most famous being the Gunpowder Plot of 1605, when Guy Fawkes was arrested while caught with dozens of barrels of gunpowder underneath the House of Lords. Two years later, Parliament prevented the union of Scotland and England, which James supported. The king indulged himself with expensive luxuries and reigned over a court of incompetent and corrupt ministers, giving rise to an anti-Stuart rebellion that finally flared into civil war in the 1640s, during the reign of his son Charles I.

Under James, England began establishing colonies in North America in Massachusetts and Virginia. James was the author of several works on politics and government, including *The True Law of Free Monarchy*, in which he explained his belief in the divine right of kings to rule by their own will. He is also known for commissioning a translation of the Bible into English. This King James Version, first published in 1611, has remained the standard text of the Bible for the Protestant, English-speaking world to the present day.

SEE ALSO: Elizabeth I; England; Scotland

Jews

Jews had been a persecuted minority throughout the Middle Ages, and the humanism and questioning of Christian doctrine during the Renaissance did little to improve their status. Many European cities forbade them to pass through their gates at all; most others severely restricted their movements, their professions, and the neighborhoods in which they lived. From time to time, Jews were completely expelled by decree of a prince or city council. Their property was confiscated and the debts owed to them were cancelled—in this way, expulsion was often a convenient way for a prince or monarch to relieve a debt from his treasury. Expulsions occurred in France in 1394, in Portugal in 1497, in the southern French duchy of Provence in 1502, and from southern Italy in 1541. Jews were completely forbidden to live in England throughout the Renaissance, a restriction that dated to the year 1290 and did not end until the middle of the seventeenth century. The most important expulsion of this period occurred in Spain in 1492, when Ferdinand and Isabella expelled Jews as well as Muslims from their united kingdoms of Castile and Aragon. Jews who claimed to convert to Christianity in order to keep their homes and property were known as *marranos* or *conversos*. Such converts were under constant suspicion and often prohibited from leaving the confines of the cities where they lived. They were often brought to trial for heresy; the Spanish Inquisition was established in the late fifteenth century for the express purpose of testing the sincerity of *conversos* and rooting out the insincere.

Jews were often restricted in the clothing they could wear and in their general appearance; in fifteenth-century Spain Jewish men were forced to grow their beards long. In some cities they were forced to wear a circle of yellow felt to identify themselves as Jews; other places required wide-brimmed hats or a long dark cloak. The professions available to them were also limited. Jews were banned from traditional artisanal guilds, but permitted to work as moneylenders and as dealers in second-hand goods. Many Italian communes granted charters allowing Jews to settle for a limited time, for the purpose of serving as lenders to the poor of the city.

In the literature of the time, including works of Christopher Marlowe and Sir Francis Bacon, Jews were often depicted as greedy and villainous. Shakespeare's *The Merchant of Venice* presents one of the most memorable Jewish villains, the moneylender Shylock. European Christians branded Jews with sinister libels, such as claiming that they made their ceremonial food with the blood of Christians. These libels could sometimes lead to violence and massacre, occasionally with the approval of the city authorities. In 1475 the city of Trent arrested every Jewish male on the suspicion of carrying out the ritual murder of Christian children, and put the captives to death.

At the same time, however, Hebrew, the language of the Jews, became a respected subject of interest to many scholars, including the Protestant scholar Johannes Buxtorf, who taught at the University of Basel in Switzerland and published Hebrew dictionaries and grammars. Jewish texts were translated into Latin, and several universities established departments of Hebraica, or Jewish studies. The study of the Jewish kabbalah, a medieval system of symbols and esoteric knowledge, was undertaken by humanist scholar Giordano Bruno, Giovanni Pico della Mirandola, and others interested in systems of thought that lay outside traditional Christian teachings.

In 1516, the first Jewish ghetto was established in Venice, in a quarter known as the Ghetto Nuovo. The Jewish ghetto became a neighborhood cordoned off from the Christian population, often with a system of walls and gates. In 1555 the Catholic Church began enforcing a twelfth-century law that prohibited Jews from living in the same neighborhoods as Christians. This law was strictly enforced within the Papal States, the cities and territories under the control of the papal administration in central Italy. The ghetto spread to Germany and then the rest of Europe. Jews were commonly confined to the ghettos permanently, and were only allowed to leave in order to transact necessary business in other parts of the city. The gates were locked and no traffic permitted at night; Jews caught out after curfew were subject to arrest and a term in prison. The ghetto walls prevented Jewish communities from expanding, and as a result they became the most crowded and least healthful neighborhoods, with families raising tenements ever higher in order to accommodate the growing population.

SEE ALSO: ghetto

Joan I of Naples
(1326–1382)

Queen of Naples, the daughter of Duke Charles of Calabria and the niece of King Philip VI of France. She was engaged to Prince Andrew of Anjou, but when Prince Andrew inherited the throne of Hungary on the death of Robert, the king of Naples (Joan's grandfather) she claimed the title of sole monarch. Pope Clement VI took advantage of the struggle over the succession to make his own claim as the lord of Naples. Clement's envoy Cardinal Americ crowned Joan Queen of Naples in 1344; in the next year Prince Andrew died at the hands of an assassin, who may have been acting on Joan's orders. The death of Andrew prompted Louis I, the king of Hungary, to invade. When the western Christian church split into French and Italian factions, Joan allied with the king of France and supported the French popes who resided at Avignon. Angered by this

alliance, which countered his power in Italy, Pope Urban VI denounced Joan's title to Naples and donated the kingdom to Charles of Durazzo. Charles marched on Naples at the head of a Hungarian army and took Joan a prisoner in 1381. In the next year, while imprisoned at the Castle of San Fele, she was strangled by her prison guards. Charles then succeeded to the throne of Naples.

Joan of Arc
(1412–1431)

A patron saint of the French nation, Joan of Arc was born in the village of Domremy, in the Vosges region of eastern France. Her father owned a small estate and served as a village official. At the time of her birth and childhood, much of France lay in ruins from the conflict with England that had begun more than seventy years earlier. The war had started over English claims to the French throne, claims supported by the powerful dukes of Burgundy. While the English controlled Paris, the capital, the Burgundians held Reims, the traditional site of French coronations. For this reason, the heir to the French throne, the son of King Charles VI, remained an uncrowned dauphin (eldest son of a king) while the English fought for the claim of Henry VI, an infant who ruled through the regent John of Lancaster.

Inspired by visions of the saints to defend France from its powerful enemies, the sixteen-year-old Joan rode to the French camp at Vaucouleurs to demand an audience with the dauphin. At first mocked and refused, she persisted and eventually won over the garrison commander. Arriving in the dauphin's presence at the chateau of Chinon, she asked Charles permission to lead an army to the relief of Orléans, a French city then holding out against an English siege. In a desperate situation, and with little realistic hope of success, the dauphin agreed. In just nine days, however, Joan led the French to victory at Orléans. She was rewarded with co-command of an army, with which she defeated the English at the Battle of Patay. She then marched to Reims, where she witnessed the coronation of the dauphin as Charles VII of France on July 17, 1429.

After the coronation, Joan continued to lead the French against the scattered enemy troops in northern France. At the town of Compiègne, she was captured by a company of Burgundians and then sold to the English. The English governor in France, Duke Henry of Bedford, put her on trial for religious heresy. Her impassioned defense proved futile, as the English and Bishop Cauchon of Beauvais, an ally of England who presided at the trial, were determined to see her dead. She was convicted and burned at the stake in Rouen on May 30, 1431.

Joan's inspired leadership of the demoralized French army proved a turning point in the Hundred Years' War. By the Treaty of Arras in 1435, the Burgundians ended their alliance with the English, who lost Rouen in 1449 and their last stronghold at Calais in 1558. Under the successors of Charles VII, a unified French kingdom emerged that would develop by the end of the Renaissance into the largest and wealthiest realm in Europe.

Joanna of Castile
(1479–1555)

Queen of Castile and Leon whose life was troubled by the recurring bouts of insanity and extreme behavior that earned her the nickname of "Joan the Mad." She was born in Toledo, the daughter of Ferdinand II of Aragon and Isabella of Castile, who united these two kingdoms to establish the monarchy of Spain. In 1496 Joanna married Philip the Handsome, son of Emperor Maximilian I. After the death of her brother John, her elder sister Queen Isabella of Portugal, and nephew Miguel of Asturias, she was the eldest surviving daughter of Ferdinand and Isabella, and as such was officially recognized by the Spanish Cortes (parliament) as the heir to the throne of Castile in 1502. The death of Queen Isabella in 1504 brought Joanna the formal right to this title, but her claim was clouded by the ambitions of her husband and of her father Ferdinand, who maintained that she had been made a prisoner by Philip. Her husband's death of typhoid fever in 1506 left her in a deranged state of mind, under which she allowed Ferdinand to rule with her as co-regent. Ferdinand took advantage of the situation to imprison Joanna in the castle of Tordesillas, where she remained. In 1516, on Ferdinand's death, her son Charles became co-regent. The nobles of Spain did not take to Charles, however, and revolted against the foreign governors he sent to rule over them in the Revolt of the Comuneros in 1520. Kept prisoner at Tordesillas, Joanna was unable to summon the rebels to her side, and after the revolt was put down she was confined to an isolated room, where she remained until her death in 1555.

Jones, Inigo
(1573–1652)

English architect who introduced the building styles of the Italian Renaissance to his native country. Jones was born in London, the son of a Catholic clothworker. Sometime in the late sixteenth century, he traveled to Italy, and lived for a time in Venice. He also spent time at the court of King Christian IV of Denmark. In Italy he studied the designs of Andrea Palladio, whose villas and monuments were inspired by the classical architecture of ancient Greece and Rome. Jones absorbed the ideals of classical architecture through Palladio and the writings of Vitruvius, an ancient Roman author on architecture who set out in his book *De Architectura* the ideals of harmonious proportions and balanced elements.

Jones returned to England in 1601. His talents were noticed by King James I, and he was appointed official court surveyor to Henry, the son of James and heir apparent. Jones won commissions to design several important London buildings, including the New Exchange in the London quarter known as the Strand. Jones also designed scenery for court masques, short allegorical dramas that combined theater, music, and dance. He returned to Italy in 1614, in the company of the Earl of Arundel. On his return to England, James appointed him as the Surveyor of the King's Works. In this position Jones designed the Banqueting House at the palace of Whitehall. As a Catholic, however, Jones came under general suspicion from those fearing a Catholic attempt to return England to the authority of the pope.

Jones's most famous buildings include several country mansions, including Lindsey House, Shaftesbury House, the Queen's House at Greenwich, and the Grange. He also designed public places, including the London square known as Lincoln's Inn and the district known as Covent Garden that Jones developed on the model of ancient Roman market towns known as *bastides*. On commission of King Charles I, Jones also became the first to survey the prehistoric monument known as Stonehenge, in southern England. Jones opined in his book *Stone-Heng Restored* that the towering pillars of Stonehenge represented the remains of a Roman temple.

On the outbreak of the English Civil War in 1642 Jones fled London. The conflict ended with the execution of his patron Charles I; Jones's property was seized and he lost his position as the royal surveyor. He was officially pardoned in 1646 and lived out his days in obscurity and poverty. His reputation grew after his death, however, as his buildings and his classical ideals became an important model for future generations of English builders.

SEE ALSO: architecture; Palladio, Andrea; Vitruvius

Julius II
(1443–1513)

Pope from 1503 until his death in 1513. Born in the village of Albissola as Giuliano della Rovere, he was the member of a noble but poor family. He was educated in the city of Perugia by his uncle, Francesco della Rovere, a member of the Franciscan order. When Francesco was elected as Pope Sixtus IV in 1471, Giuliano's prospects in the church improved dramatically. He was immediately made bishop of Carpentras, a diocese in France, and named cardinal-priest of San Pietro in Vincula (Saint Peter in Chains), an important Roman church. He won several more appointments as bishop, in Lausanne, Coutances, Catania, Mende, Viviers, Sabina, Bologna, Ostia, Lodeve, Savona, and Vercelli. In 1476, he was named archbishop of Avignon, and in 1480 became the papal legate (ambassador) to the king of France.

Della Rovere's ambition reached all the way to the papal throne, and through skillful diplomacy and bribery attained a powerful position within the College of Cardi-

Pope Julius II, in a portrait by master painter Raphael. © NATIONAL GALLERY COLLECTION; BY KIND PERMISSION OF THE TRUSTEES OF THE NATIONAL GALLERY, LONDON/CORBIS. REPRODUCED BY PERMISSION.

nals, the body responsible for electing the pope. In 1492, on the death of Sixtus IV, he was thwarted in his goal by Cardinal Rodrigo Borgia, his rival, who attained the Papacy as Alexander VI. Angrily denouncing the election, Della Rovere fled Italy in fear for his life and journeyed back to Paris, where he convinced King Charles VIII to attempt an invasion of Italy and the conquest of Naples. Della Rovere's aim was to depose Alexander, but when he reached Rome in the company of the king, the pope outmaneuvered him by bribing one of Charles's key ministers.

In 1503 Alexander became gravely sick after a banquet and soon died. His successor, Pius III, reigned for only a few days after his election. Della Rovere then con-

vened the College of Cardinals and through bribery managed to have himself raised to the Papacy through the shortest conclave in the history of the church.

Taking the name Julius II, he set out to regain control of the Romagna region of north central Italy, where many prosperous cities were being ruled by tyrants, including Cesare Borgia, and rival states, particularly the Republic of Venice, that had little allegiance to the Papacy. In 1506, marching northward at the head of a papal army, he defeated the Baglioni clan of Perugia and Giovanni Bentivoglio, the ruler of Bologna. In 1508 Julius formed the League of Cambrai with Louis XII of France, Maximilian I, and Ferdinand II of Aragon against Venice. The pope put the city under an interdict. At the Battle of Agnadello the League routed the mercenary army raised by Venice, and Julius brought the cities of Rimini and Faenza back under his own authority. Seeking to liberate Italy completely from foreign domination, Julius then turned against the French, forming the Holy League with Ferdinand II, Henry VIII of England, and his former enemy, Venice, to attack French troops in Italy.

Julius began the attack by excommunicating and deposing Alfonso, the duke of Ferrara, who at the time was allied with France. The pope's actions raised the ire of the French king Louis XII, who gathered his bishops into a synod at the city of Tours to declare themselves free of obedience to the pope, and who conspired with Emperor Maximilian to dethrone Julius. The French invaded Italy and seized Bologna in 1511, reinstating Giovanni Bentivoglio as the city's ruler. The French army was thrashed at the Battle of Ravenna in 1512 and driven out of Italy, Bologna as well as Param, Piacenza, and Reggio came under the pope's control, but Julius found to his chagrin that the cities of Italy, weakened by many years of warfare, remained an inviting prey to the armies of the Holy Roman Empire, which after the death of Julius in 1513 would invade the peninsula and devastate Julius's imperial city in the brutal Sack of Rome in 1527.

Julius is remembered by historians as the "Warrior Pope," determined to make the Papacy a political and military power that would be feared throughout Italy and in the rest of Europe. But he is more respected as a patron of the arts. Determined to turn Rome into an imposing symbol of the church's power, he brought artists and architects to the city and paid them generously to dedicate their lives and works to producing monumental works for the church. He commissioned Donato Bramante to rebuild Saint Peter's Basilica and Michelangelo Buonarroti to decorate the ceiling of the Sistine Chapel with a series of fresco paintings that would become the single most imposing work of Italian Renaissance art. He contributed a large portion of the income he earned from his estates and benefices to the raising of palaces and fortifications in the city, playing a key role in transforming Rome from a chaotic medieval town into the imposing and monumental city that it remains to this day.

SEE ALSO: Alexander VI; Bramante, Donato; Charles VIII; Michaelangelo Buonarroti

Kepler, Johannes (1571–1630)

German astronomer who was the first to develop accurate theories of planetary motion. Born in the town of Weil, the son of a mercenary soldier, Kepler was educated at seminaries and the University of Tubingen. He was named as a royal mathematician in 1594; in this position, the accurate predictions of political and weather events published in his almanacs gained him renown as a prognosticator. In 1595 he began a serious study of planetary motions that he published in his first book *The Secret of the Universe*. This book defended Nicolaus Copernicus's theory of a heliocentric universe, introducing the idea that the planetary orbits were based on different geometric shapes. In 1600 Kepler became an assistant to Tycho Brahe, court astronomer to Emperor Rudolf II, and who remained an adamant supporter of the geocentric (earth-centered) Ptolemaic system, Brahe's sudden death the next year allowed Kepler to take over as court astronomer. He published *Optics*, a treatise on the use of telescopes in observational astronomy, in 1604; in the meantime, while studying the exhaustive calculations and observations of Brahe, Kepler concluded that the planets moved in ellipses, rather than circles, a theory now known as Kepler's First Law of Planetary Motion. This law proved superior to the theories of Copernicus and Brahe in explaining the irregular motion of the planets. Kepler's First Law, and a second law

stating that the radius of a planet sweeps across equal areas in equal spans of time, were published in *New Astronomy*, which appeared in 1609. His *Conversation with the Starry Messenger*, published in 1610, supported the observations of Galileo Galilei, whose sighting of Jupiter's moons Kepler confirmed with his own instruments. In his writings Kepler also hit on the idea of an elemental force emanating from the sun and controlling the motion of the planets—an early notion of the phenomenon of gravity.

In 1611, as Rudolf II gave up his throne, Kepler moved from the imperial court at Prague to Linz, in Austria, where he became official mathematician. In his *Harmony of the World*, Kepler attempted a grand, unified theory of geometry, mathematics, and astronomy, and published his third law of planetary motion, in which the square of the sidereal period of a planet is proportional to the cube of its distance from the sun. Kepler summarized his laws in *Epitome of Copernican Astronomy*, written between 1618 and 1621, which built on the heliocentric model of the universe proposed by Copernicus but also introduced Kepler's own theory of elliptical orbits. His book *Rudolfine Tables* set out charts of planetary positions. Its accurate prediction of a transit of the sun by the planet Mercury proved Kepler to be the most capable astronomer of his time, and the book remained in use for several generations after his death in 1630.

John Knox. © ARCHIVE PHOTOS, 530 W. 25TH STREET, NEW YORK, NY 10001.

SEE ALSO: Brahe, Tycho; Copernicus, Nicolaus; Galilei, Galileo

Knox, John
(1514–1572)

Church reformer, preacher, author, and founder of the Presbyterian Church of Scotland. Born in Haddington, Knox was ordained a priest in the Catholic Church in 1536, and worked as a notary and tutor to the noble families of Lothian. By 1545 he had converted to the cause of the reformed church under the influence of George Wishart. Despite the founding of the Protestant Church of England, Scotland's rulers remained resolutely Catholic, and in 1546, Wishart was arrested for his teachings and burned at the stake. When his Protestant followers avenged themselves by killing a Catholic cardinal, Knox joined them at Saint Andrews Castle, where he rallied the besieged reformers with his fiery sermons and his polemics against the evils of the Catholic Church. The group took refuge from Scottish and French soldiers but was finally overwhelmed in 1547. Knox was sentenced to a term of service in the French navy as a galley slave.

In 1549, after his release, Knox returned to England, where he served as one of the king's chaplains. Unwilling to accept an appointment as a bishop in the Church of England, Knox was unwilling to temper his scathing denunciations of his religious enemies. His stand made him a wanted man on the accession of the very Catholic queen Mary in 1553. He escaped to Europe, joining John Calvin in Geneva and preaching Calvinist reforms and government in the German city of Frankfurt, which expelled him in 1555. Knox did not improve his standing with the queen of England with his pamphlet *First Blast of the Trumpet Against the Monstrous Regiment of Women*, which denounced Queen Mary as well as the Catholic Mary of Guise, who ruled Scotland as a regent. The pamphlet ridiculed the notion of women holding political power, and so enraged Mary's Protestant successor Elizabeth I that she prohibited him from ever setting foot in England.

In 1559 Knox was invited back to Scotland to lead Protestants rebelling against the authority of Mary of Guise. Knox and his allies forced French troops out of Scotland and defeated the Catholic Church. The new Presbyterian Church was established, in which each congregation elected its parish leaders, and by an act of the Scottish parliament in 1560 Scotland officially threw off the authority of the Catholic pope. Knox was also author of *History of the Reformation in Scotland*, an important history of this period.

SEE ALSO: Calvin, John; Elizabeth I; Reformation, Protestant; Tudor, Mary

Labe, Louise
(1520–1566)

French poet born as Louise Charly in Lyon. The daughter of a rope maker, and later the wife of one, she was given the nickname *La Belle Cordiere*. She was educated in music and languages, and as a writer joined a prominent literary circle in Lyon. In 1555, the Lyon printer Jean de Tournes published her *Euvres* (Works), a volume of twenty-four love sonnets, an allegory entitled *Debate Between Love and Madness*, three elegies, and twenty-four poems written by others in her own praise. The book went through several editions, while the sonnets made her name among the School of Lyons and have survived as her best-known works. Labe fervently encouraged other women to exercise their new found freedoms to write, speak, study, and debate in the male-dominated world of letters. Her erotic love poetry, however, inspired scandal, as did a rumored penchant for dressing as a man. She was accused of being a courtesan and was condemned by reformers such as John Calvin.

Las Casas, Bartolomée de
(1474–1566)

Spanish missionary and historian, known today as an advocate for the rights and liberty of Native Americans. Born in Seville, he was the son of a middle-class merchant who had little traditional schooling. His father and uncle joined the second expedition of Christopher Columbus. In 1502, Bartolomée voyaged to the New World in the expedition of Nicolas de Ovando, the new governor of Hispaniola, in order to manage lands granted to his father by Columbus. In 1510 he became the first priest to be ordained in Spain's American colonies. He served as a missionary in Cuba, Mexico, Central America, and Peru, and was appointed as the priest-procurator of the Indies in 1516, with his duties being to investigate fraud and abuse of the Indians by the Spanish colonists. He eventually came to oppose the system by which the Spanish were destroying the culture of Native Americans, forcibly converting them to Christianity, and using them as slaves. Las Casas advocated a new system in which Europeans and Indians would cooperatively work rural plantations, but when one such experiment failed on the coast of Venezuela, he gave up his livelihood as a landowner and retired to a Dominican monastery in Santo Domingo.

Las Casas' stand on Native Americans was based on the idea that the grant of the right to colonize this part of the New World by the pope was for the purpose of converting Indians to Christianity, and not for economic benefit. This aroused strong opposition among the Spanish landowners, who absolutely depended on forced labor in order to make their plantations profitable. He pled his case before King Ferdinand II and the officials of Spain, and won an important success with a code of New Laws promulgated by Emperor Charles V in 1542 that banned slavery in Spain's colonies, as well as the right of the colonists to pass their lands to their heirs. In 1544, he was appointed as the bishop of Chiapas, where his primary task was to see the New Laws enforced. In 1547, when the ban on inheritance was rescinded, he resigned this office. In 1550 Las Casas returned to Valladolid, Spain, to take part in a famous debate with the scholar Juan Gines de Sepulveda on the future of the *encomienda* system of slave-worked plantations. Speaking for five days, Las Casas succeeded in having Sepulveda's book, which advocated outright war against the Indians, suppressed. In 1552 Las Casas chronicled the cruelty of the *encomienda* system in his most famous work, *Brief Account of the Destruction of the Indians*. He also wrote a comprehensive history of the Spanish conquest, *History of the Indies*, as well as a book detailing the lives and culture of Native Americans, *History of the Indians*, in which work he showed that the Native American subjects of Spain should enjoy the same rights and freedoms as their European conquerors.

SEE ALSO: Columbus, Christopher; Cortes, Hernán; exploration

Lasso, Orlando di (1532–1595)

Composer born in Mons, in the county of Hainaut, a city of the Low Countries then under the rule of Spain. A tradition says that Lasso was kidnapped several times as a boy for his beautiful singing voice. At the age of twelve, he traveled to Italy, where he worked at the Gonzaga court in Mantua and also studied composition in Milan and Naples. In the 1550s he worked in Rome, first in the service of Cosimo de' Medici and then as choirmaster of the Basilica of San Giovanni di Laterano. He returned to the Low Countries after this engagement and was hired by Albrecht V, the duke of Bavaria. By this time his compositions were known throughout Europe, and he was considered the finest musician and composer to come from the Low Countries. Lasso was appointed *kapellmeister* by Albrecht V, and he would serve in this post at the ducal court in Munich, Bavaria, for the rest of his life. His fame attracted many young musicians to Bavaria to study with him; Pope Gregory XIII knighted him and Emperor Maximilian II rewarded him with a title of nobility. Although many kings invited him to their courts, he preferred the Bavarian court, where he remained the unquestioned master of a dedicated group of singers and instrumentalists. He was expected to write music for special occasions and ceremonies, train young singers for performance in the choir, and compose settings of the Mass. The duke granted Lasso a lifetime appointment, as well as a generous budget for performances, instruments, and musicians, and the Bavarian court became a bustling center of music during the late Renaissance.

Lasso was a master of many different musical forms, including sacred masses, hymns, and motets, as well as secular madrigals and *chansons* (songs) written in Latin, Italian, French, and German. He set the poetry of the Italian writers Petrarch and Ludovico Ariosto to music, as well as a verse from the ancient Roman author Virgil. One of his songs was included by William Shakespeare in the play *Henry IV, Part II*. Lasso wrote four passions—*a capella* (voice only) settings of the four evangelical books of the New Testament—that combine plainsong chant (single-line melodies) with passages of multivoiced polyphony, of which Lasso is still considered the absolute master of all Renaissance composers. He wrote in the many different musical styles and forms that he encountered on his extensive travels. Some of his music includes daring harmonies and strange chromatic melodies that were unknown among other Renaissance composers (with the exception of Carlo Gesualdo). All of his music was written for voice and, as far as music historians know, he wrote no purely instrumental music at all. He published hundreds of his own compositions during his lifetime, a rare achievement for any Renaissance composer. Many of his sixty masses were based on secular compositions, including bawdy popular songs, that he adapted for the traditional Latin text of the Catholic Mass. His last work, the *Tears of St. Peter*, was a group of twenty-one madrigals, and remains his most famous work.

SEE ALSO: Gesualdo, Carlo; music; Palestrina, Giovanni

Leo X
(1475–1521)

Pope and patron of the Italian Renaissance, Leo X was born as Giovanni de' Medici, the son of Lorenzo the Magnificent of Florence. His powerful and wealthy family secured important posts for him at a young age: head of rich abbeys in France and Italy and appointment as a cardinal of the church in 1489, at the age of thirteen. He was educated by the leading humanists of the Italian Renaissance, including Pico della Mirandola and Marcilio Ficino, and studied at the prestigious University of Pisa.

After the election of Alexander VI, a member of the rival Borgia family of Spain, he left Rome for Florence. When a rebellion expelled the Medici rulers from Florence in 1494, he escaped the city disguised as a monk. He returned in 1512 when the family returned to power. In the next year, on the death of Julius II, he was elected pope.

Leo was a generous patron of the arts and literature, and made his papal court a center of learning and amusement. The pope hosted lavish banquets staged elaborate plays and pageants, and hired musicians and entertainers for the pleasure of himself and his guests. He supported charitable institutions in Rome and gave alms to the poor and crippled. He invited poets to Rome and lavished them with official titles and generous salaries. He founded the Medicean Academy in Rome to pursue the study of the Greek classics and sent collectors to the four corners of Europe to find and return unknown volumes of ancient Greek and Roman writers, who were collected in the Vatican Library.

Leo also took the painter Raphael under his wing, keeping the artist at the Vatican until Raphael's death in 1520. Raphael became the dean of artists at the Vatican, and completed his most famous works under Leo's patronage, including the decoration of the Vatican *stanze*, or halls, the *Sistine Madonna*, and cartoons for the tapestries of the Sistine Chapel. The great expenses, however, quickly drained the treasury, and to raise money Leo ordered the sale of church offices and indulgences, in which people simply paid money to have their sins officially forgiven.

Under Leo's reign the Papacy was embroiled in political and military conflict with France, which Leo pursued by making and breaking alliances all over Europe and running up a huge debt for the Vatican treasury. In the end, the pope and King Francis I signed a Concordat in 1516, in which the pope conceded the authority of the king over church property in France. These events helped to keep France a Catholic nation even as Germany and other countries of northern Europe were breaking away from the church.

Leo also provided for his family, working to secure them leadership of wealthy cities in Italy. He named his cousin Giulio as the archbishop of Florence and fought an all-out war against the city of Urbino in order to replace the Duke of Urbino with Leo's nephew Lorenzo. His actions angered many Roman cardinals, and even inspired a failed plot to assassinate him. Leo responded by having several cardinals poisoned and by blackmailing others. In 1517, he made a clean sweep of the college of cardinals, appointing thirty-one new members, many of whom he appointed simply to secure money or political influence.

At the same time, the greed and corruption of Leo's administration was inspiring a movement for reform in Germany. Martin Luther, a German monk and scholar, was denying the authority of the church and spreading his ideas rapidly and effectively through the new medium of printing. Leo excommunicated Luther in 1521 and had him summoned to the Diet of Worms, but Leo's orders and instructions to Luther to recant his writings met with defiance. Shortly after this, the pope died of a sudden attack of malaria. His term as pope is remembered for its generous patronage of the arts but also for disastrous management that allowed the Protestant Reformation to gain widespread support, permanently dividing the Christian community of Europe.

SEE ALSO: Alexander VI; Francis I; Raphael

Leonardo da Vinci
(1452–1519)

Painter, engineer, scientist, and inventor who mastered many fields of study and

Leonardo da Vinci's masterpiece the "Mona Lisa" is one of the world's most famous works of art. NEW YORK PUBLIC LIBRARY PICTURE COLLECTION.

has become a world-renowned figure of the Renaissance. Da Vinci's artworks had a profound influence on the painters of his time; his many inventions—including the helicopter, bicycle, and parachute—were inspired by a lifelong investigation into the properties of motion, force, and gravity. He is still regarded as the archetypal Renaissance Man, an individual of profound creative genius and wide-ranging scientific curiosity.

Born near the town of Vinci, west of Florence, Leonardo was the illegitimate son of a notary and a peasant woman. He showed a talent for drawing and composition very early in his life and, at the age of fifteen, was sent to Florence as an apprentice in the workshop of Andrea del Verrocchio. He met the leading painters of the

Sketches of war machines by Leonardo da Vinci. At the top is a chariot fitted with scythes for striking nearby enemies. At bottom are diagrams of an armored vehicle outfitted with firearms, hundreds of years before the first actual tank was built. DE AGOSOTINI/GETTY IMAGES.

city, including Sandro Botticelli and Domenico Ghirlandaio. From Verrocchio he learned the craft of painting, the science of perspective, and techniques of depicting the human form in motion. Da Vinci collaborated with Verrocchio on the *Baptism of Christ*, produced in about 1475, in which Leonardo painted the background landscape and an angel. By one tradition, Verrocchio was so astonished at the beauty and composition of these elements that he gave up painting for the rest of his life. During his time in Florence, Leonardo also painted the *Annunciation* and a portrait of Ginevra de Benci. In these works, he was striving for a new style of painting that went beyond the conventions of the early Renaissance. Leonardo gave the figures softer contours by the *sfumato* technique,

in which he blended colors and used light and shadow to give his works dramatic intensity.

Leonardo established his own studio in Florence, and in 1481 was commissioned to paint an altarpiece, the *Adoration of the Magi*. This work has become an important study for art historians, as it was left unfinished. In 1482 Leonardo accepted a position as a court painter and architect for Ludovico Sforza, the Duke of Milan. For the duke he designed artillery, fortifications, and military equipment; he collaborated with Donato Bramante on the design of churches, public buildings, and streets. While in Milan Leonardo was also commissioned to paint the *Madonna of the Rocks*, which sets the biblical family of Jesus in a scene of natural wilderness. The painting exists in two different versions, providing art historians with a source of endless debate over the authenticity of the works and Leonardo's methods of painting. In 1495 he began the *The Last Supper*, a fresco for the refectory of the convent of Santa Maria delle Grazie. For this work Leonardo made a change in the traditional formula of fresco paint, in order to more easily blend the colors on the hard stone surface of a wall. His experiment turned out a failure, as the paint soon began flaking from the wall and over many years the image deteriorated. Nevertheless, *The Last Supper* remains one of Leonardo's most famous works and the archetypal image of this biblical event.

While in Milan he also worked on the design of a bronze equestrian statue of Francesco Sforza, the Duke of Milan's father and predecessor. Despite years of study and preliminary sketches, he was unable to overcome the difficulty of raising a balanced sculpture of a horse in dynamic motion. When the French invaded Italy, the duke was overthrown and Leonardo left Milan, moving for short periods to Venice and Mantua, and then back to Florence. There he painted the *Virgin and Child with St. Anne*, a striking study in the balance and harmony of a group of figures, and the portrait known as the *Mona Lisa*, or *La Gioconda*—names that were given to the painting in the nineteenth century. The painting depicts Lisa Gherardini, the wife of a Florentine silk merchant, wearing a somber black dress and gazing at the viewer with a mysterious smile, and posing against a natural background. In these paintings Leonardo introduced new aspects of "perspective of color," in which distant objects lose their outline as well as their hue. This aspect of his works had a major influence on the painters of the later Renaissance, including

Piero de Cosimo, Raphael, and Michelangelo Buonarroti.

Through his many travels and projects Leonardo kept a series of notebooks, in which he used a backward script that was not deciphered until long after his death and which were not published until the late nineteenth century. The notebooks are filled with anatomical drawings, artistic studies, scientific observations and speculations, and inventive designs, including hundreds of new war engines, flying machines, canal locks, and vehicles, many of which were not produced until centuries after his death, when the fields of engineering and manufacturing caught up with the artist's genius.

In 1506, Leonardo was summoned back to Milan by Charles d'Amboise, the French governor of the city. In this period of his life he took up scientific research and observation. In his notebooks, he studied geology, botany, hydraulics, and human anatomy and produced a series of accurate drawings of the body and its internal organs. From 1513 until 1516, he lived in Rome at the invitation of Pope Leo X. He completed *St. John the Baptist*, worked on several architectural projects, and worked in his notebooks. By this time his fame had spread throughout Europe and in 1516 he was invited to the royal French court of Fontainebleau by King Francis I. He was named the court painter and architect and was given a handsome country home in which to live until he died in 1519.

SEE ALSO: Michelangelo Buonarroti; painting; Verrocchio, Andrea del

Lepanto, Battle of

A momentous naval battle that took place off the western coast of Greece on October 7, 1571, between the Holy League—

allied Christian forces of Spain, Venice, Genoa, the Papacy, and other states—and the fleet of the Ottoman Empire. Members of the Holy League were determined to end Ottoman dominance of the eastern Mediterranean, and Turkish interference with merchant shipping of Spain, France, and Italy. To that end, the Christians assembled at Messina, Sicily, a fleet of about two hundred ships, most of them large rowed galleys, placing them under the command of John of Austria, the illegitimate son of Emperor Charles V. Aboard the ships was a powerful force of thirty thousand infantry, a number that approximated a Turkish war fleet commanded by Ali Pasha.

The two fleets engaged for several hours before the Turks fled the scene with about forty of their ships intact. Several thousand Christian galley slaves were liberated, and the Turks lost eighty ships and about fifteen thousand killed or captured sailors. About seven thousand members of the Holy League were casualties, including the Spanish writer Miguel de Cervantes, who suffered a grievous wound to his arm. Although their navy was severely weakened by the defeat, the Turks remained in control of the eastern Mediterranean and soon afterward seized the island of Cyprus from control by Venice.

SEE ALSO: Cervantes, Miguel de; Ottoman Empire; Venice

Lovati, Lovato dei (1240–1309)

A leading civic official of Padua, a noted poet and scholar, and one of the first European humanists. The scion of a wealthy family, Lovati was devoted to recovering classical Latin authors, in editing their works, and in developing a new style of writing influenced by the ancients, who were dismissed as unworthy pagans by the scholastic schoolmen and philosophers of his day. Lovati edited a manuscript edition of the tragedies of Seneca, and introduced works of the Roman poet Ovid and the Greek poet Horace. He sparked widespread interest in these and other ancient authors, and inspired further research by Petrarch and Giovanni Boccaccio, men of a later generation that were once credited as pioneers of the humanist movement.

Lovati saw the medieval fashion for French troubadours and their ballads of romantic love and chivalry a throwback to an age of ignorance. In the plays and histories of ancient Roman authors he admired a sense of dignity, balance, and clarity, and a source of cultural pride for the authors and scholars of Italy. His Latin poems written in 1267 emulated the forms and style of ancient authors, and pioneered a humanist strain in poetry that would continue in the works of Dante and much later extend to prose writings.

Lovati also was one of the first scholars to make a close inspection of ancient ruins in the search for the truth about the classical past. In the cathedral of Padua, he uncovered a tomb he believed to be that of the Trojan founder of the city, a discovery that gave strength to the city's claim for status as an independent commune.

SEE ALSO: Boccaccio, Giovanni; humanism; Petrarch

Loyola, Saint Ignatius (1491–1556)

Founder of the Society of Jesus, a religious order also known as the Jesuits, and dedicated opponent of the Protestant Reformation. Born in Loyola, near San Sebastian in the Basque region of northwestern Spain, he entered the service of the treasurer of Castile as a teenager. He joined the Spanish army in its fight against the kingdom of Navarre and was severely wounded while defending the city of Pamplona against a siege in 1517. While recovering from his injuries, he dedicated himself to the church and became a solitary devotee of the Virgin Mary. He resolved to establish a religious order that would be organized much like an army, and fight to defend the authority of the pope. He wrote the *Spiritual Exercises*, a book of meditations, and used this work to proselytize for his new order. Attending the University of Paris, he earned a master's degree in theology and gathered a small group of followers who together proclaimed the founding of the Society of Jesus in the Church of Saint Mary in Paris in 1534. The order won the approval of Pope Paul III and was soon sending its members to build new schools and seminaries throughout Catholic Europe. The Society's goal was to educate the young, carry out missionary activities, and stamp out Protestantism; it was organized according to Loyola's *Jesuit Constitution*, which commanded complete obedience to the pope.

SEE ALSO: Reformation, Catholic

Lucca

An independent city of Tuscany that produced many renowned Renaissance artists, scholars, and musicians. The Roman town of Lucca became the capital of a duchy in the sixth century, and then in 1162 an independent commune. Lucca prospered as a center of textile industries, the silk trade, and banking. It enjoyed the privilege of coining its own money and remained independent of Florence, the strongest power of Tuscany, although it also experienced periods of rule by tyrants. A condotierre named Castruccio Castracani took power in Lucca in 1316 and made the city a wor-

thy rival to the military and economic power of Florence (later Niccolo Macchiavelli would commemorate Castracani's rule in his writings on able political leaders). The city was seized by kings of Bavaria and Bohemia, and sold to and from aristocrats of Genoa, Parma, and Verona. In 1628 an oligarchy took power, which managed to keep the city independent until its conquest by Napoléon Bonaparte in the early nineteenth century.

The Cathedral of San Martino served as the center of religious life in Lucca since it was first constructed in the sixth century. The building underwent construction throughout the medieval period. Its interior chapels hold several significant works of Renaissance art, including paintings by Domenico Ghirlandaio and Tintoretto, and a carved sarcophagus by Jacopo della Quercia. The latter artist also created an altarpiece for the Basilica of San Frediano.

Lucca is also known for an impressive set of walls that have survived intact to the present day. The city was surrounded by strong walls since its time as a Roman colony. High towers were also raised throughout the city to serve as defensive strongholds for aristocratic families. In 1544, with Florence menacing Lucca with conquest, the walls were strengthened with a series of bastions, ditches, underground rooms, and ramparts—a project that took more than a century.

SEE ALSO: Florence

Luther, Martin
(1483–1546)

A German monk, scholar, and writer, and leader of the Reformation that brought about a new Protestant church. Luther was born in Eisleben, in the kingdom of Saxony. His father was a mine operator who

Martin Luther defends his views on Christianity at the Diet of Worms in 1521, before Holy Roman Emperor Charles V and the members of the Reichstag. © HULTON/ARCHIVE. REPRODUCED BY PERMISSION.

sought to make a lawyer of his son. Luther's days at the University of Erfurt, however, were shadowed by doubt and guilt over his sinfulness and his worthiness in the eyes of God. On passing through a forest in a thunderstorm, Luther vowed to follow a life of devotion should he survive. He decided to drop his study of the law to become a monk, much to his father's dismay, and entered the Augustinian monastery of Erfurt. He led a strict life of confession, fasting, and prayer, which did little to relieve his self-doubt and uncertainty.

Luther was ordained as a priest in 1507 and studied for a doctorate in theology at the University of Wittenberg. After winning his doctorate in 1512, he was appointed to a teaching position at the university that he held throughout his life. In the meantime, the questions of worthiness plagued him; he came to the conclusion that only a relationship with God based on personal faith could bring redemption and grace. This idea provided the foundation of his revolution against the Catholic Church hierarchy that had long been plagued by greed, corruption, and bureaucratic struggles for power. The church judged Christians by their charitable works, their obedience to the pope, and their purchase of indulgences—a system that Luther saw as the artificial and unholy creation of unworthy men.

In 1517, a monk named Johann Tetzel arrived in Wittenberg on a mission to sell indulgences for the archbishop of Mainz, who would use the money to pay off loans he had used to pay bribes. This inspired Luther to write the founding document of the Reformation, known as the Ninety-five Theses. By tradition, he posted this bold challenge to the papacy on the door of the castle church in Wittenberg. Only God could grant remission of sin, in Luther's opinion, and only God can judge souls worthy of release from purgatory and salvation from hell. The Ninety-five Theses were soon printed and circulated throughout Europe, touching off a controversy that permanently divided the Christian community.

Over the next few years, Luther debated his ideas with leading religious men in Germany. He denied the infallibility and primacy of the pope; he defied the pronouncements of the Papacy and of the church councils; he condemned the sale of indulgences; he appealed for a return to the scriptures in all questions of faith and doctrine. Luther set out his ideas in two important books, *The Babylonian Captivity of the Church* and *The Freedom of a Christian Man.*

His stand earned him excommunication from the church by Pope Leo X in 1521; Luther had defied the papal bull challenging him by publicly burning it. He was now at risk for arrest and execution on a charge of heresy. Emperor Charles V, who reigned supreme in the Holy Roman Empire, ordered Luther to appear before the Diet of Worms and state his case. Guaranteed safe passage, Luther arrived at Worms and refused to recant his writings. He then rode in disguise to Wartburg Castle, where he lived under the protection of Frederick the Wise, the elector of Saxony. Luther grew a beard and took the name of Knight George while Charles V declared him an outlaw subject to immediate arrest.

At Wartburg Luther completed a German translation of the New Testament, which was published in 1522 and which helped to spread his ideas and influence among the common people of Germany. In 1524, however, a bloody Peasants' Revolt broke out in Germany, in which the old social order was threatened by mobs proclaiming adherence to Luther's ideas. Appalled by the violence, Luther condemned the revolt in his pamphlet *Against the Murdering, Thieving Hordes of Peasants*, in which he urged that revolting peasants be struck down like dogs.

After the Peasant's Revolt, Luther found himself embroiled in controversy within the Reformation movement. He broke with Desiderius Erasmus, the leading humanist of his time; but Lutheranism was enthusiastically taken up by German princes who saw it as a way to escape the authority of the emperor and his ally, the pope. In the meantime, Luther completed a German translation of the Old Testament in 1534; he wrote many treatises on the Bible as well as instruction on the Mass, several hymns, and pamphlets and essays on matters of personal faith. In 1543 he completed *On the Jews and Their Lies*, in which he condemned in the strongest terms the freedom of Jews to follow their faith and advocated their homes and places of work be burned to the ground. In the meantime, the Protestant Reformation was taken up in Scandinavia, England, the Low Countries, and in France, where the struggle between Catholic and Protestant would turn into a virtual civil war.

SEE ALSO: Diet of Augsburg; Hus, Jan; Reformation, Protestant

Machiavelli, Niccolo (1469–1527)

Diplomat and author, and a central figure of the Italian Renaissance whose short work *The Prince* has remained a classic of political philosophy. Born in Florence, Machiavelli was schooled in classical Latin literature. He began his career as a government clerk in 1494, the year in which the Medici dynasty fell from power and republican government in Florence was restored. He rose in the ranks of public servant and was appointed a diplomat. He traveled on diplomatic missions to the courts of King Louis XII of France and King Ferdinand II of Aragon, and to the headquarters of the Papacy in Rome.

In 1503 Machiavelli became an officer of the Florence city militia. He observed with great interest the career of Cesare Borgia, the ruthless and ambitious son of Pope Alexander VI. Borgia never hesitated in using deceit, violence, and all-out war to further his own goals, which was the conquest of territory in the name of the Papacy that he would rule personally.

In 1512, the Medici regained power and the Florentine Republic came to an end. Machiavelli was forced out of office, arrested, and charged with conspiracy. Subject to torture, he refused to confess to his crime. He survived this ordeal and retired to his estate in the nearby countryside, where he took up study of the classics and setting down his experiences and his philosophy of government.

In *The Prince*, he drew on the works of ancient authors as well as his own experience of government and of political leaders, giving his opinion that a ruler must be prepared to act unscrupulously, and inspire fear in his rivals, in order to ensure his authority and the well-being of his nation. Machiavelli's rather dark view of human character and the nature of politics is tempered by his opinion that the ultimate goal of the actions of a prince should be the stability of the state he rules. The ends do not necessarily justify the means, and power alone does not excuse violence, dishonesty, and criminality. In the case that a ruler must act with violence or cruelty, in his view, he must act quickly and effectively, strike balance between idealism and reality, and mitigate harsh actions as soon as possible.

Machiavelli believed *The Prince* might place him in the good graces of the returning Medici; instead it earned him condemnation by the church, which placed the book on its Index of banned works. His contemporaries among the Renaissance humanists saw the author as an opportunistic and cynical politician, a reputation that survived into modern times in the term "Machiavellian," meaning to act unscrupulously in the quest for power.

Machiavelli's interests led him well beyond politics; he was also a poet, musician, and a scholar of the classics. In this field he produced *Discourse on the First Ten Books of Livy*, a book describing the history of the Roman republic. The *Dis-*

course is a guidebook to republican government, holding up the early Romans as an ideal to be followed by his Italian contemporaries and all others to follow. He most admired the balanced, three-part nature of the early Roman government, divided as it was into rulers, aristocrats, and common citizens. Two centuries later this opinion would be reflected in the United States Constitution.

SEE ALSO: Borgia, Cesare; Medici, Cosimo de'

Magellan, Ferdinand (1480–1521)

A Portuguese explorer whose ill-fated expedition, sponsored by the king of Spain, was the first to circle the globe. Born in Saborosa, Portugal, he was the son of the town's mayor, who sent him to be educated at the court of the king of Portugal. Magellan studied navigation and astronomy at a time when nautical exploration was opening up new continents for Portuguese captains. A key event in this history was the signing of the Treaty of Tordesillas by Spain and Portugal in 1494. The two kingdoms divided the globe between them: lands west of a meridian drawn about 1,500 miles (2,414km) west of the Cape Verde Islands were the property of Spain, to explore and colonize, and lands to the east were Portuguese. The treaty shaped the history of exploration over the next generation as well as Magellan's career.

Magellan first went to sea in 1505, when he accompanied the Portuguese governor Francisco de Almeida to his post in India. He became a captain in 1510 but was relieved of his rank in the next year as punishment for sailing into the East Indies without formal permission. He returned to Portugal in 1512. In the next year he traveled with a Spanish army to Morocco, where he was severely wounded in the Battle of Azamor. Accused by his commander of insubordination in Africa, he fell out of favor with King Manuel I, who refused him any further commissions. As a result, Magellan resigned his commission and offered his services to the king of Spain.

Magellan had come to believe that the Spice Islands might be within the Portuguese domain according to the Treaty of Tordesillas. He was determined to find a westward-sailing route to the Spice Islands of East Asia, which promised fabulous wealth to any individual or company that could find easier access to them. The Spanish monarchs, realizing that the voyages of Columbus had not reached Asia, needed to forge a new westward route in order to avoid the Portuguese who, after the pioneering voyages of Vasco da Gama, had established well-defended trading stations in India and the Spice Islands.

King Charles V agreed to sponsor Magellan, who assembled a fleet of five ships and set out in September 1519. The ships reached the coast of Brazil in December, then sailed south in search of the route that would lead them to the Pacific Ocean. Fearing that Magellan was leading them on a futile mission, several of his officers mutinied. The uprising was put down and Magellan had two of his captains executed and two others marooned. One of his ships was wrecked in a storm, and another would abandon the fleet. In August 1520, Magellan found a long and narrow channel across the southern tip of South America that now is known as the Strait of Magellan.

The three remaining ships made the crossing of the Pacific Ocean, reaching the island of Guam on March 6, 1521, and soon thereafter the Philippine Islands.

Here Magellan delayed in order to make an alliance with the ruler of Cebu and intercede in a conflict between that tribe and the ruler of the nearby island of Mactan. On April 27, the Mactans attacked a party Magellan was leading ashore and killed the commander.

After Magellan's death, the survivors abandoned another ship and fled the Philippines. Juan Sebastian Elcano took command of the company. The expedition reached the Spice Islands in November and took on their hard-won cargo of cloves and cinnamon. Another ship was captured by the Portuguese and the sole remaining ship, the *Victoria*, set out for the return to Spain. Suffering from disease and malnutrition, the crew struggled into port on September 6, 1522, with only 18 members of the original 270-man expedition alive.

Magellan's expedition was the first to circumnavigate the globe and the first to navigate the strait in South America connecting the Atlantic and Pacific oceans. Magellan's crew made numerous, valuable discoveries. They observed several animals that were entirely new to European science. These included the "camel without humps" (possibly the llama, guanaco, vicuña, or alpaca) and a black "goose" that had to be skinned instead of plucked (the penguin).

Two of the closest galaxies, the Magellanic Clouds, were discovered by crew members in the southern hemisphere. The full extent of the earth was also realized, since their voyage was 14,460 leagues (69,800 km or 43,400 miles).

Finally, an international date line was established. Upon their return they observed a mismatch of one day between their calendars and those who did not travel, even though they faithfully maintained their ship's log. However, they did not have clocks accurate enough to observe the variation in the length of the day during the journey. This phenomenon caused great excitement at the time, to the extent that a special delegation was sent to the pope to explain this oddity to him.

Malatesta, Sigismondo Pandolfo (1417–1468)

The lord of the Italian city of Rimini, Sigismondo Malatesta was a tyrant, a ruthless commander of mercenary armies, and a significant patron of Renaissance artists and architects. He was born in Brescia, the son of Pandolfo Malatesta, whose ancestral home of Rimini was violently contested by the armies of the pope. At the age of thirteen, Sigismondo began his military career, taking up arms against Carlo Malatesta, the lord of Pesaro, who had allied with Pope Martin V in hopes of conquering Rimini. After defeating Carlo, Sigismondo was appointed vicar of the towns of Rimini, Cesena, and Fano by the pope; in 1432, at the age of fifteen, he became the lord of Rimini by succeeding his half brother Galeotto Roberto, who resigned the title to escape the many conspiracies and violence surrounding his family's court.

His renown as a military leader spreading throughout Italy, Sigismondo joined forces with the pope while still in his teens to defeat a campaign by the Spanish mercenary Sante Cirillo. In 1437 he occupied the city of Cervia; although the pope excommunicated him for this action, he was soon restored to the good graces of the church and made a commander. He allied with Francesco Sforza of Milan and in 1442 married Sforza's daughter, Polissena. He became Sforza's rival when the latter obtained Pesaro from Carlo Malatesta. He entered the service of King Alfonso V of Naples but turned against his patron by fighting with Florence, defeating Alfonso's siege of Piombino.

Malatesta had a reputation as an unscrupulous and violent tyrant, but he also sought a brilliant legacy as an art patron. He invited Leon Battista Alberti to design the Temple of San Francesco, also known as the Tempio Malatestiano, in Rimini. This structure is known for Alberti's use of the Roman arch, the first Renaissance building to adopt this ancient pagan motif. Malatesta himself was a skilled poet who dedicated his verses to Isotta degli Atti, his third wife and the woman who may have inspired the death of Polissena Sforza, who succumbed to a sudden illness possibly brought on by poisoning.

After the Peace of Lodi, an alliance of Italian forces joined against Malatesta and attacked his territory. His skill as a military leader made him a serious threat to the pope and the princes of Italy; in order to thwart his ambition Pope Pius II accused him of heresy and sodomy in 1460. Pius sent his armies against Rimini and in 1462 Malatesta's army was smashed near the town of Senigallia. His conquered territories lost, Malatesta had only the ancestral seat of Rimini remaining in his possession. With Italy united against him, he enlisted in the service of Venice and fought against the Ottoman Turks in Greece in 1465. When he returned to Italy he plotted a return to dominance through the murder of Paul II, the successor of Pius. When he arrived in Rome, intending to carry out the deed himself, he lost courage and returned to Rimini, where he died.

SEE ALSO: Alberti, Leon Battista; Pius II

Mantegna, Andrea
(1434–1506)

Italian painter whose new techniques in the composition of his pictures had a long-lasting effect on later Renaissance painters. The son of a woodworker, he was adopted at a young age by Francesco Squarcione, a painter and collector who ran an art studio in the city of Padua. Mantegna struck out on his own at the age of seventeen, and soon afterward won important commissions, to paint an altarpiece for the Church of Santa Sophia and several large frescoes in the Church of the Eremitani. In these works Mantegna developed the new technique of perspective, which gives the illusion of three-dimensional subjects on a two-dimensional surface.

Mantegna was strongly influenced by the sculpture of Donatello, and the paintings of Paolo Uccello and Andrea del Castagno. He allied himself with the humanist movement that was flourishing in Padua, where university professors and scholars from all over Europe arrived to study the works of ancient Greek and Roman authors. He studied Roman ruins and literature, and consciously incorporated elements of the classical world into his works, one of the first Renaissance painters to do so.

In 1453 Mantegna married Nicolosia Bellini, the daughter of Jacopo Bellini and the sister of Giovanni and Gentile Bellini. Six years later he was invited by Ludovico Gonzaga, the marquess of Mantua, to become a court painter. He was commissioned to paint in the ducal palace of the city, where he completed two important works, the *Wedding Chamber* and the *Painted Chamber*. In these works Mantegna created an entirely new environment, covering all surfaces with striking, illusionistic pictures that place the viewer in another world, well outside the walls of the palace and the city. An *oculus*, or circular opening on the ceiling, gives way to a brightly painted sky, surrounded by a se-

Andrea Mantegna's "Crucifixion" from the San Zeno Altarpiece. Christ is crucified among thieves, while soldiers stand and watch and the Madonna and the apostles mourn. © COR-BIS. REPRODUCED BY PERMISSION.

ries of foreshortened figures. These striking paintings established an entirely new technique of ceiling paintings done for private homes and churches that flourished in the late Renaissance and the Baroque eras. In the 1480s, while still in Mantua, Mantegna also completed *The Triumph of Caesar*, a series of nine paintings that showed a triumphal procession in ancient Rome. Soon after this work, Mantegna was commissioned to paint the private chapel of Pope Innocent VIII at the Belvedere Palace in Rome.

Mantegna's late paintings celebrate the accomplishments of the Gonzaga dynasty. He painted *Lady of Victory* to commemorate the success of Francesco Gonzaga at the Battle of Fornovo, and *Parnassus*, to mark the wedding of Francesco to Isabella d'Este. After his death Mantegna was hon-

ored by Mantua with an imposing funerary monument, a rare honor for an artist even at the height of the Italian Renaissance.

SEE ALSO: Bellini, Giovanni; d'Este, Isabella; Gonzaga, House of; Mantua

Mantua

An influential city in the Renaissance that came under the control of the Gonzaga family, among Italy's leading patrons of writers, artists, and scholars. Mantua dates to well before the time of Rome, and was best known in the Middle Ages as the birthplace of the Roman poet Virgil. The city was an independent commune from the eleventh century but was seized by a member of the Bonacolsi family in 1273. The reign of this dynasty brought the city prosperity until a revolt occurred in 1328, led by Luigi Gonzaga, a city official, and his three sons. Mantua went through a century of turmoil until Ludovico Gonzaga seized power and his descendant, Gianfresco Gonzaga, was named as the marquess of Mantua by the Holy Roman Emperor through his marriage to the emperor's daughter Barbara of Brandenburg. In 1530, Federigo Gonzaga was given the title of Duke by Emperor Charles V, and it was under Federigo's reign that Mantua reached its full glory as a center of art, architecture, and music. Federigo commissioned the lavish Palazzo Te and improved the city with new gardens, roads, and monuments. The Gonzaga dynasty came to an end in 1627, after which it came under the control of a related French clan, the Nevers. A war soon broke out over the contested duchy, and a siege of the city by the emperor's forces in 1630 brought hunger, destruction, and the plague. Prominent citizens and artists fled the city and Mantua entered a long period of neglect and decline. The dukes were overthrown and the city finally seized by the Habsburg dynasty in 1708.

SEE ALSO: Gonzaga, House of; Tasso, Torquato

Manuel I
(1469–1521)

King of Portugal during whose reign the Portuguese extended their overseas empire and made it the largest among all European nations. Born in Alcochete, he was the grandson of King John I and the cousin and brother-in-law of John II, whom he succeeded as king in 1495. Although he was raised in a court of dangerous intrigue and violence, he was favored by John II as his heir after John's legitimate son died in an accident and his illegitimate son was denied the throne. For this reason Manuel is also known as "the Fortunate."

Manuel was an enthusiastic supporter of Portugal's explorations in Asia and South America. During his reign, Vasco da Gama found a sea route to the Indian port of Calicut, Pedro Alvares Cabral discovered Brazil, and Portugal won a monopoly over the trade of the entire Indian Ocean. Portuguese merchants were settled in the Indian port of Goa, which served as a central base for Portugal's commercial empire in the east. These merchants brought home a fortune in trade goods from the East Indies, allowing the king the money to raise many important palaces and religious buildings designed in a uniquely national style known as Manueline. The king signed important trade treaties with China and Persia, and also was an energetic ruler at home, reforming the tax and justice systems and making the nobility more subservient to the king. He took two daughters of King Ferdinand and Queen Isabella as wives, but failed in his ambition to unite the monarchies of Spain and Portugal and pass the throne on to his descendants. Although the Spanish monarchs demanded that Manuel expel all the Jews from his kingdom as a condition of these marriages, he instead allowed them to remain for a period of twenty years and banned any official inquiry into their religious beliefs.

SEE ALSO: Aviz, House of; da Gama, Vasco; exploration; Portugal

Margaret of Austria
(1480–1530)

The daughter of Emperor Maximilian I and Mary of Burgundy, Margaret of Austria became known as a wise and just ruler of the Spanish Netherlands, then part of the Holy Roman Empire. She was born in Brussels and betrothed at the age of three to Prince Charles, later King Charles VIII. She moved to the royal court of France but returned to her family when Charles repudiated her and married Anne of Brittany. In 1497 she married Prince Juan of Asturias, the heir of Ferdinand and Isabella of Spain, but the marriage ended with Juan's death six months after the wedding ceremony. In 1501 she married Philibert II, the Duke of Savoy, who died in 1504. She became regent of the Netherlands in 1507, and played an important role in the troubled and rebellious lands that were under the nominal rule of her father, the emperor. A talented musician and composer, she welcomed many of Europe's leading musicians to her court. In 1529, representing her young nephew Charles V, she settled the Treaty of Cambrai with Louise Savoy, mother of Francis I. This "Ladies' Peace" confirmed Habsburg control of contested territory in northern Italy.

SEE ALSO: Charles V

Margaret of Parma
(1522–1586)

Duchess of Parma and regent of the Netherlands. Margaret was the illegitimate daughter of Emperor Charles V and Johanna van der Gheynst, the servant of a Flemish noble. Her great aunt was Margaret of Austria, who was regent of the Netherlands from 1507 until her death in 1530. In 1533, Charles recognized her as his legitimate daughter. She was engaged to Alexander de' Medici, the son of the pope, and married him in 1536. After her husband was assassinated in the next year, she married the Duke of Parma. She was an able and intelligent woman who was appointed regent of the Netherlands by Philip II in 1559. Her reign was marked

by a general revolt against Habsburg rule by the Protestant Netherlanders. In 1567, Margaret resigned her regency and fled the troubled Netherlands for Italy. Her son Alexander Farnese succeeded her as governor-general.

Marguerite of Navarre
(1492–1549)

A French author, religious reformer, and noble, the sister of King Francis I (Francois I) who played a major role in the cultural flowering and religious conflicts of Renaissance France. The daughter of Charles, Count of Angouleme, and Louise of Savoy, she was raised in Angouleme and Cognac and was offered an education in Latin and letters. Through her marriage to King Henry II of Navarre, she became the queen of Navarre, a realm lying just beyond the borders of France and Spain. She held a salon that attracted the most renowned writers and poets of France, including Francois Rabelais, Pierre de Ronsard, and Desiderius Erasmus. An able diplomat, in 1525 she negotiated with Emperor Charles V for the release of her brother after his capture at the Battle of Pavia. The king allowed her to sit on his council of ministers and negotiate treaties with England.

The queen took a strong interest in reform of the Catholic Church, in order to counter the radical Protestant movement that was sweeping away traditional church institutions in Germany, Switzerland, and the Netherlands. She defended French "Evangelicals," or reformers, including Gerard Roussel, from charges of heresy, and allowed many of them to take refuge in Navarre. In 1534, she helped John Calvin to escape France under threat of persecution for heresy. She also established charities and a system of public education for the needy, a unique institution in Renaissance Europe.

Marguerite authored poetry and stories. On the death of her infant son in 1530 she wrote *Miroir de l'Ame Pecheresse*, which Catholic theologians labeled a heretical work. After her death, her stories were collected in a volume known as the *Heptameron*. These tales took as their model the *Decameron* of Giovanni Boccaccio but took the woman's side in the conflicts and misunderstandings between the sexes.

SEE ALSO: Calvin, John; Francis I; Rabelais, Francois

Marlowe, Christopher
(1564–1593)

English playwright and contemporary of William Shakespeare who wrote moving, tragic plays in the new medium of blank verse. Born in Canterbury, he prepared for the ministry at the University of Cambridge. Some historical documents indicate that Marlowe was engaged by the minister Sir Francis Walsingham, Queen Elizabeth's secretary of state, to serve as a spy in France. After earning a master's degree at Cambridge, he moved to London, where he joined the Lord Admiral's Company and soon ran into trouble with the law. He was arrested and jailed in 1589 for taking part in a deadly brawl. In 1593, he was arrested again under the charge of atheism.

Historians are still piecing together the obscure details of Marlowe's life and writing career. In the course of his short life, he wrote only one extended poem and six plays. His earliest work, *Tamburlaine the Great*, was written in two parts and printed in 1590. The play describes the career of a cruel Mongol tyrant. This play was followed by *Dido, Queen of Carthage; The Massacre at Paris; Edward, II*; and *The Jew of Malta*, which presents a deviously ambitious central character presented quite sympathetically among a hostile milieu of Christians. All of Marlowe's works involves a powerful man who is laid low by his own outlandish personality and ambition. His best-known play is *Doctor Faustus*, which recounts the familiar story of a brilliant scholar who sells his soul to the devil.

Marlowe died in the town of Deptford on May 30, 1593, during a brawl in a private home. The circumstances of his murder are shrouded in mystery, and some historians believe it is connected to his shadowy double life as a spy and government agent. According to some accounts, his killer, Ingram Frizer, was working on instructions of a more powerful man or on the government's wishes for Marlowe's death. Others believe Marlowe's own fiery temperament and penchant for physical assault brought about his death at the hands of Frizer, who was judged by the authorities to have acted in self-defense.

SEE ALSO: drama; England; Shakespeare, William

Masaccio
(1401–1428)

Tommaso Cassai, nicknamed "Masaccio" or "Thomas the Absent-Minded," was an artist of the early Renaissance who broke new ground in the technique of painting. Born in San Giovanni Valdarno, a small town near Arezzo in Tuscany, Italy, Masaccio traveled to Florence, where he joined the city's painters guild as well as a circle of artists, including Filippo Brunelleschi and Donatello, who were developing new ways of depicting the human form and setting it in three-dimensional space. His first major work was a fresco painting, *Sagra del Carmine*, done for the cloister of Santa Maria del Carmine in Florence. This work, one of the first large paintings to render a contemporary event, was completed by 1425 but since that time has been destroyed.

Very few other works of Masaccio's have survived into modern times, but on these paintings rests his reputation as a highly skilled and original painter. He collaborated with Tommaso Masolino on a polyptych, or multipaneled altarpiece, for the church of Santa Maria del Carmine in Pisa. This work was broken apart and found its way to several museums. The central panel, the *Madonna and Child Enthroned*, was flanked by portraits of Saint Paul and Saint Andrew.

Masaccio also completed an important series of frescoes in the Brancacci chapel of the Church of Santa Maria del Carmine in Florence, as well as a fresco of the Trinity in the church of Santa Maria Novella. The Brancacci chapel fresco was commissioned by Felice Brancacci to Masaccio and his collaborator Masolino da Panicale. The paintings include depictions of biblical events, set in a classical world: the *Expulsion from the Garden of Eden, Tribute Money, St. Peter Baptizing, Miracle of the Shadow*, and *St. Peter and St. John Distributing Alms*. Inspired by the new sculpture of Donatello's, Masaccio composed powerfully expressive and monumental figures, an important change from the slender, ethereal figures of the saints that were a tradition in European Gothic art. He depicted a wide range of emotional expression and more realistic human emotion, skillfully used light to sharpen and define contours, and incorporated classical architecture to reflect the new respect artists were showing for the works of the ancient Romans. The invention of artificial perspective by Brunelleschi also had an important impact on Masaccio. The painter used foreshortening of the figures and perspective as a means of guiding the specta-

tor of the paintings to certain elements of the work, and of setting the figures in a more dramatic, natural world. This approach revolutionized painting and set the stage for the monumental and powerfully realistic paintings of the Renaissance.

The Brancacci chapel frescoes became a place of pilgrimage and study for many major Italian artists, including Michelangelo Buonarroti, Leonardo da Vinci, Sandro Botticelli, Andrea del Verrocchio, Andrea del Sartro, and many others. Before completing this work, however, Masaccio left for Rome, where he died at the young age of twenty-six.

SEE ALSO: Brunelleschi, Filippo; Donatello; Florence; painting

mathematics

Mathematical knowledge in medieval Europe was strongly influenced by treatises of Arabic scholars that were imported to the continent from Sicily and Moorish-controlled Iberia (modern Spain and Portugal), and by the works of ancient Greeks such as Ptolemy, Erastothenes, and Euclid that had survived in Arabic versions and were later translated into Latin. The Italian scientist Leonardo Fibonacci had revived original research in the thirteenth century. The calculation of speed and uniform motion were problems tackled by a school of mathematicians known as the Oxford Calculators of the fourteenth century. Everyday calculation, however, was still a difficult process. It involved the use of cumbersome Roman numerals and complex methods of doing division and multiplication—without the use of algebraic symbols and mathematical signs.

The study of mathematics was spurred by growing trade and international banking, which followed an earlier period of localized trade and the barter system. The expanding economy demanded a better ability to calculate sums, percentages, foreign exchange, and rates of interest. The new double-entry method of bookkeeping allowed merchants to carefully track income and expenses. Abacists were math teachers who imparted the needed mathematical skills to the sons of traders, bankers, and long-distance merchants. The invention of printing in the middle of the fifteenth century allowed mathematical texts to circulate widely, beginning with *Theoricae Nova Planetarum* of Georg von Peuerbach in 1472 and a guide to arithmetic, known as the *Treviso Arithmetic*, in 1478. The *Elements*, a study by the ancient mathematician Euclid, first appeared in printed form in 1482. The Arabic numerals, decimal places, and mathematical signs and symbols borrowed from India came into common use in Europe at about the same time.

Sixteenth-century mathematicians began solving many thorny problems, such as cubic and quartic equations. The German philosopher Johann Müller, known as Regiomontanus, wrote commentaries on Ptolemy's *Almagest* and published his own book of calculations, *Detriangulus*. Another German, Johann Widman, was the first to use the plus and minus signs in a published work. Other significant German mathematicians were Adam Riese, Christoph Rudolff (who pioneered the use of root symbols), and Michael Stifel, who wrote an algebra text, the *Arithmetica Integra*, dealing with powers, radicals, and negative numbers. In Italy, Geronimo Cardano wrote *Ars Magna*, the first algebra treatise written in Latin. Cardano's followers included Niccolo Tartaglia, who drew up the first "firing tables" for use by artillery, and was the first to discover a formula for solving cubic equations.

At the same time, astronomy was becoming a sophisticated mathematical method of predicting planetary orbits, the path of the stars, and the occurrence of eclipses and other celestial phenomena. The precise observation of the skies and the measuring technique of trigonometry were spurred by the demands of navigators, who needed accurate charts of newly explored areas that lay thousands of miles distant from familiar home shores. The first textbook in this subject was the *Trigonometria*, written by Bartholomaeus Pitiscus and published in 1595. The investigation of the heavens by telescope enabled more precise astronomical calculations, undertaken by Galileo Galilei, Tycho Brahe, and Johannes Kepler, who devised a systematic mathematical system for determining planetary orbits. The French philosopher René Descartes developed a new method of depicting calculations on charts and a system of analytic geometry. The culmination of Renaissance study of mathematics was the system of calculus, a method of solving complex problems that was first developed by Sir Isaac Newton and the German scholar Gottfried Wilhelm Leibniz.

SEE ALSO: Brahe, Tycho; Kepler, Johannes

Maximilian I
(1459–1519)

Holy Roman Emperor who greatly expanded the realm under the control of the powerful Habsburg dynasty. He was born in Wiener Neustadt, a suburb of Vienna, the son of Emperor Frederick III and Eleanor of Portugal. In 1477, he married Mary of Burgundy, who brought the Low Countries and Burgundy under Habsburg control. In 1482, on the death of Mary, Burgundy became a part of France while the Netherlands, which had always resisted

Habsburg control, signed a treaty with King Louis XI of France. On the death of his father Frederick in 1493 he ascended to the Habsburg throne; in the next year he married Maria Sforza, daughter of the Duke of Milan. In 1493 Maximilian signed the Treaty of Senlis that surrendered Burgundy and Picardy (in northern France) in exchange for the Netherlands and the territory of Franche-Comte. He later appointed his daughter Margaret of Austria as the regent of the Netherlands.

His marriage to Maria Sforza fired Maximilian's ambitions to contest control of the wealthy cities of northern Italy. This touched off the Italian Wars with France that dragged on for a generation and embroiled nearly every major city of Italy as well as the Papacy. After the Battle of Dornach, Maximilian signed the Treaty of Basel, which granted independence to the Swiss Confederation. He arranged a marriage for his granddaughter Mary with Louis, the son of the king of Hungary and Bohemia, and his grandson Ferdinand to marry Louis' sister Anne. These betrothals eventually brought Hungary and Bohemia under Habsburg control.

SEE ALSO: Charles V; Margaret of Austria

Medici, Cosimo de'
(1389–1464)

Ruler of Florence and founder of the Medici dynasty, one of the wealthiest and most influential clans of Europe. The son of Giovanni de' Medici, a *gonfalero* (high official) of Florence, Cosimo inherited a fortune made by his father in the new industry of international banking. The Medici profited from expanded trade and business contacts among the nations, which called for more sophisticated methods of exchanging and investing money. On inheriting the family's bank in 1429,

Cosimo set out to increase business by lending money to European rulers and investing in trading expeditions to Africa and Asia.

Cosimo rankled the aristocrats of Florence by enlisting the artisans and guilds of the city to his side. He was arrested in 1433 at the instigation of his most powerful rivals, the wealthy Albizzi clan. Threatened with a trial and execution, he was eventually exiled from the city after paying a bribe to the head of the city's justice department. In the next year, a new Florentine government overturned his sentence, the Albizzi were banished, and Cosimo returned to the city. He soon held the reigns of power firmly in his hands, by appointing his own supporters to the high offices known as magistracies. Although he held no formal title, Cosimo enjoyed fervent support among common people and ordinary workers. With his popularity greater than ever, he reformed the tax system to favor the middle class and spent great amounts of money on important public works, including the restoration of the Church of San Lorenzo. He allied the city with Milan and Venice, in order to balance the power of Naples and the Papacy. This balance of power survived into the late fifteenth century under the skillful management of his grandson, Lorenzo de' Medici.

Cosimo also began a Medici tradition of patronage of the arts and letters. He invited artists and sculptors to contribute their works to his palace and local churches. He collected manuscripts from throughout Europe and had them copied and preserved. The books were gathered in local monasteries and made available to scholars and writers. Cosimo also founded the Academy of Plato, also known as the Neoplatonic Academy, to teach the philosophy and writings of this ancient Greek writer, under the leadership of Marsilio Ficino. These actions made Florence the center of an emerging new view of the world that placed the genius of human artists and philosophers on an equal footing with the inspiration of traditional religion.

SEE ALSO: Ficino, Marsilio; humanism; Medici, Lorenzo de'

Medici, Lorenzo de' (1449–1492)

Lorenzo il Magnifico, or Lorenzo the Magnificent, ruled the Italian city of Florence as a patron of artists, writers, and humanists. During his reign, the city saw a rebirth of the arts and scholarship that is known as the Renaissance.

The scion of a wealthy family of bankers, he was the grandson of Cosimo de' Medici, the first of the Medici to rule Florence. Lorenzo's father Piero de' Medici il Gottoso (the Gouty) was a collector of ancient works and contemporary art; his mother Lucrezi Tornabuoni was an amateur poet. His parents gave Lorenzo a thorough education in ancient Greek and Latin, and the classical authors. At the age of seventeen he married Clarice Orsini, a member of a wealthy and influential Roman family. On the death of Piero de' Medici in 1469, Lorenzo became head of the family and, with his brother Giuliano serving as his co ruler, the leading citizen of Florence.

One of Lorenzo's first achievements was to affirm the handling of the papal finances by the Medici bank. But the great wealth and influence of the Medici family were cause for grave alarm for Pope Sixtus IV, who sought to extend the papal territories northward to the frontier of Tuscany. Over the next few years, the pope formed an alliance with the Pazzi clan, rivals of the Medici. On April 26, 1478, a few of the Pazzi and their hangers-on attacked Lorenzo and his brother, Giuliano, during Mass in the cathedral of Florence. Although Lorenzo escaped his would-be assassins, Giuliano was stabbed to death. The pope then excommunicated Lorenzo and put the city of Florence under an interdict, forbidding the Florentines to celebrate Mass.

At the pope's urging, King Ferdinand I of Naples then ordered an assault on Florence. In response, Lorenzo courageously sailed to Naples and negotiated directly with the king. Persuaded by his adversary's bold actions, Ferdinand made a truce with Florence, and both Naples and Florence were spared a costly war. Eventually the pope also ended hostilities, and Lorenzo emerged as the most influential ruler in northern Italy.

Lorenzo passed a new constitution for the city in 1480, establishing a council of seventy leading citizens who would govern the city for life. He brought the leading artists of Italy, including Domenico Ghirlandaio, Fra Filippo Lippi, Andrea del Verrochio, Sandro Botticelli, and Michelangelo Buonarroti, as well as the scholars Marsilio Ficino and Giovanni Pico della Mirandola to his splendid court. He expanded his family's splendid library by sending agents through southern and eastern Europe in search of unknown ancient manuscripts, which became the foundation of Florence's famous Laurentian Library. As copies of these books traveled through Italy and Europe, they played a vital role in the spread of classical learning and humanism that was the foundation of the Renaissance.

Lorenzo staged great festivals, processions, and entertainments for the citizens of Florence. Early in his reign, he ensured the city's grain supply during a famine, an action that won over the population to enthusiastically support him. Nevertheless, he was careless with money, and his expensive tastes and desire for fine art and spectacle drained the treasuries of both his family and city. In addition, a backlash arrived with Girolamo Savonarola, a fiery Dominican monk who bitterly condemned the lavish and decadent tastes of the Florentines and conducted public burnings of art and books in the city's central square.

After the death of Lorenzo, the truce he had arranged among the city-states of northern Italy soon gave way. The peninsula again fell into violent squabbling and became prey to foreign rulers, including the king of France, who invaded Italy in 1494. His son Giovanni was elected Pope Leo X, and his nephew Giulio, the son of Giuliano, was Pope Clement VII.

SEE ALSO: Medici, Cosimo de'; Michelangelo Buonarroti; Pazzi Conspiracy

medicine

The practice of medicine in the early Renaissance was still bound by the study of the ancient Greek doctors and writers, in particular Hippocrates, Dioscorides, and the second-century physician Galen. The writings of Galen were the accepted teaching in universities and sanctioned by the Catholic Church, which held control through the universities over the training of professional doctors. Galen's own anatomical knowledge was limited, however, by a prohibition on human dissection, a practice still banned by the medieval church. Thus the limitations of Galen's knowledge persisted for a thousand years within Europe, even as the church held his teachings to be infallible.

A new approach to knowledge and investigation of science bloomed in the Renaissance. Old methods and treatments came under question. The German philosopher Paracelsus was the son of a physician, and one of the most important figures of Renaissance medicine. He believed that sickness resulted from imbalances of essential minerals and chemicals in the body, and prescribed medicines meant to correct these imbalances. He also investigated the action of poisons, and hit upon the idea that a toxic substance, when applied in a limited dose, can cure the body of illness. Paracelsus applied his theories to the treatment of miners, who seemed to have several dangerous illnesses in common that resulted from their occupation and not from the state of their bodily humors (fluids) or their souls.

In the generation of Paracelsus, new treatments for sickness and injuries were developed, which bypassed many of the old superstitions of the medieval age. The French surgeon Ambroise Pare developed the use of ligatures to close battlefield wounds, a method intended to deter infection and avoid the complications caused by sealing wounds with burning irons. Pare set down his findings in *Method of Treating Wounds Inflicted by Arquebuses and other Guns*, which after its publication in 1545 became a standard medical textbook for military doctors. For the majority of the population, however, medical practice still held to medieval traditions, and spiritual healing was still the most commonplace approach to sickness. Barber/surgeons set bones, pulled teeth, carried out bloodlettings, and performed amputations of infected limbs. Ordinary medical doctors still relied on the philosophy of the four humors of the body (blood, phlegm, yellow bile, and black bile) to diagnose illness and prescribe treatment. Apothecaries and herbalists offered a wide range of plant and animal products to apply or to ingest, mixtures designed to heal disease through their sheer repulsiveness.

The discovery of new land in the Western Hemisphere and Asia also had an important impact on Renaissance medicine, bringing new treatments and medicines to Europe. University professors and doctors put dissection and the new microscope to work to explore the human body, while artists such as Leonardo da Vinci undertook their own investigations in order to render the human body as realistically as possible. The first translation of Galen's work *On Anatomical Procedures* into Latin was accomplished in 1531 by Johannes Guinter. In this book Galen recommends human dissection, a stand that promoted the practice by doctors and scientists in the late Renaissance. A new age of investigation was opened up, led by anatomists such as Andreas Vesalius, a professor of surgery at the University of Padua, the academic center of medicine in the Renaissance. Vesalius was the first to practice public dissection before students on human corpses. His book *On the Structure of the Human Body*, first published in 1543, offered detailed and accurate anatomical drawings. These investigations culminated in the discovery of the circulation of the blood by William Harvey, an English doctor who published *On the Motion of the Heart and Blood in Animals* in 1628.

SEE ALSO: Paracelsus

Médicis, Catherine de (1519–1589)

Queen of France as the wife of King Henry II, and a woman who wielded a powerful influence on French politics and on the violent religious conflict that was dividing the realm into hostile camps of Protestants and Catholics. Born in Florence as the daughter of Lorenzo de' Medici and a French princess, Madeleine de la Tour d'Auvergne, she was orphaned soon after

Catherine de Medicis, queen and regent of France. THE LIBRARY OF CONGRESS.

her birth and then raised in the midst of stormy conflict between France, the Holy Roman Emperor, and the popes over control of Italy's wealthy cities and principalities. In 1527 the Medici dynasty in Florence was overthrown, and Catherine was taken hostage for the good behavior of her family. She was freed by her uncle, Pope Clement VII, who was temporarily dethroned before being restored by Emperor Charles V.

Clement arranged the marriage of his niece to Henry, the Duke of Orléans, in 1533. A member of the Valois dynasty, Henry became King Henry II in 1547. Although Catherine remained his wife, her influence over him was overshadowed by Diane de Poitiers, who became the king's confidante and mistress. As a foreigner, Catherine's loyalty to France came under suspicion, and she had little influence to match that of her rival Diane. At a festival to celebrate the betrothal of their daughter

Elizabeth, however, Henry was severely injured in a joust, and soon afterward died. Catherine had Diane banished from the court and then saw her son succeed to the throne as Francis II. At this time French Protestants were gaining strength and allying with the Protestant monarch of England, Elizabeth I, raising suspicion of treason among them by Catholic nobles and ministers. In 1560, after the death of Francis, Catherine served as regent for her son Charles IX. Catholics and Protestants were unable to reconcile their differences and in the 1560s their disagreements brewed into open warfare.

Catherine took the Catholic side in the Wars of Religion and conspired endlessly against the French Protestants, known as the Huguenots, as a way of strengthening her family's position at the royal court. In the countryside, Huguenot armies ravaged Catholic towns, raided convents and monasteries, and committed atrocities, while the Catholic forces staged bloody reprisals in northern France, a Huguenot heartland. By the Peace of Saint Germain in 1570, she arranged the marriage of her daughter Marguerite to Henry of Navarre, a Huguenot leader. In 1572, on the occasion of the wedding, Catherine plotted at a wholesale massacre of Protestants in the kingdom, known as the Saint Bartholomew's Day Massacre. Four years later she helped to form the Catholic League, an anti-Huguenot army, and worked tirelessly to garner support for her son, King Henry III. Shortly after her death, this king was assassinated by a Dominican monk, and Catherine's ambitious dreams for the Valois dynasty came to an end when the Protestant Henry of Navarre came to the throne (after converting to Catholicism) as King Henry IV.

SEE ALSO: Henry IV

Médicis, Marie de (1573–1642)

The queen consort of King Henry IV of France. The daughter of Francesco de' Medici, the Duke of Tuscany, and the Archduchess Joanna of Austria, she married Henry in 1600. When Henry was assassinated in 1610, she served as regent for their son and successor, Louis XIII. She made a truce with the Habsburg dynasty, the traditional enemies of France, and allied with Spain through the marriage of her son Louis to Anne, a princess of the Habsburg clan. In control of the royal treasury, she squandered vast sums on court festivities and on bribes to nobles hostile to the crown. She also ordered important building projects in the capital of Paris, gracing the city with imposing monuments and palaces, including the Luxembourg Palace on the city's formerly neglected Left Bank. This palace was decorated with an important series of paintings describing her life, by the Flemish artist Peter Paul Rubens.

Marie's regency saw trouble brewing among the French nobility, which was asserting ancient rights to balance the authority of the king. A general assembly known as the Estates General was convened in 1614; at the same time Marie promoted an Italian friend, Concino Concini, to a powerful position within the government over the capable Duc de Sully. Resentment at the meddling of this outsider hardened opposition to the monarchy. Louis came to the throne in 1617, three years after his age of majority. Concini was assassinated on Louis' orders in the same year and the young king soon exiled his mother to the castle of Blois, fearing conspiracies on her part against him. In 1619 Marie escaped her virtual captivity and raised an open revolt against her son, but her forces were defeated. The son and his mother were reconciled in 1622, with Marie advancing her ally Cardinal Richelieu to the position of the king's chief minister. Within a few years Richelieu and Marie de' Médicis were adversaries, with the king eventually siding with Richelieu and again banishing Marie. After she mounted a foiled coup against the king, she was exiled by the king, this time to the city of Compiegne and then out of the kingdom permanently. Marie fled to the Netherlands, where she continued to rally opponents of Richelieu in hopes of returning to Paris in control of the royal court. She failed, however, and lived a shadowy life as an exile until her death in 1642.

SEE ALSO: Bourbon dynasty

Mehmed II
(1432–1481)

Sultan of the Ottoman Empire, and conqueror of Constantinople and the Eastern Roman or Byzantine Empire. Born in the Ottoman capital of Edirne, Mehmed II was the son of Sultan Murad II. He was trained as a ruler in the province of Amasya, and at the age of twelve became the titular Ottoman ruler after his father abdicated his throne. Hard-pressed to rally troops behind him for an assault against Christians in the Balkans, Mehmed ordered his father out of retirement to lead the Turks in the Battle of Varna in 1444, a complete victory for the Ottoman forces. In 1451 Murad II died and Mehmed became the unquestioned leader of the empire. Over the next two years, he rallied his forces for an assault on Constantinople, defended by a stout ring of fortifications. The siege of Constantinople ended in May 1453, with the fall of the city and the death of the last Byzantine emperor, Constantine XI.

After this victory, Mehmed was able to extend his authority throughout Anatolia and use Constantinople as a base for further assaults against Christian states in the Balkan Peninsula. Mehmed besieged Belgrade in 1456 and in the following years battled an army led by Prince Vlad Dracula of Wallachia. Mehmed seized the last remnants of the Byzantine Empire in the Peloponnesus in 1460 and Trebizond, in Anatolia, in 1461.

Mehmed allowed Byzantine Christians to remain in Constantinople and freely practice their faith. He attempted to forge cultural links with European nations, inviting artists and scholars to work under his patronage. He improved roads and canals in his newly conquered capital and also raised important structures, including the Topkapi Palace, which remained the home of the sultans throughout Ottoman history. Mehmed's personal ambitions were unsatisfied by the fall of Constantinople, however. He attacked the Italian peninsula in 1480, intending to besiege Rome and become the ruler of a reunited Roman Empire. Although he captured the southern Italian port of Otranto, his lines of retreat were threatened by a rebellion in Albania and, under pressure from a Christian army gathered by Pope Sixtus IV, he retreated from Italy in 1481.

SEE ALSO: Fall of Constantinople

Melanchthon, Philipp

German theologian, ally of Martin Luther, and early leader of the Protestant Reformation in Germany. Born in the town of Bretten in the Palatine, Melanchthon studied the Latin and Greek classics and, at the age of thirteen, was admitted to the University of Heidelberg. Too young to earn a degree, he moved to the University of Tubingen in 1512, and took up the study of philosophy, astrology, and mathematics. He became a lecturer in rhetoric and poetry. He became a professor of Greek at the University of Wittenberg, where he inspired a large following and won the friendship of Martin Luther. He defended Luther's challenge to the Catholic hierarchy, at the risk of his own life, and helped to write the Augsburg Confession, which Luther presented at the Diet of Augsburg in 1530.

Memling, Hans
(1430–1494)

Flemish painter whose works continued the richly colored and precisely drawn style of Jan van Eyck and Rogier van der Weyden. Memling was born in the town of Seligenstadt, near Frankfurt, Germany, and as a young man moved to the city of Brussels, in Burgundy. He may have worked as an apprentice with van der Weyden, whose work had a strong influence. In 1466 he moved to the city of Bruges, a Flemish town that had grown wealthy from the wool trade and that offered many opportunities for a skilled painter to find patrons and commissions. Memling prospered by painting for churches, guilds, civic organizations, and private citizens, who commissioned the portraits that have become Memling's best-known works in modern times. His major works include an altarpiece known as the *Seven Griefs of Mary*, painted for the guild of booksellers of Bruges, and *The Last Judgment*, a work that Memling painted for a Bruges merchant that was stolen at sea by a pirate and brought to the cathedral of Gdansk, Poland. Memling's renown spread to Italy, where his works were in demand from wealthy collectors such as the Sforza rulers of Milan and the Medici of Florence. He painted a *Virgin and Child* for the English poet John Donne, for whom Memling also did a portrait with the poet's wife and children. Memling is also known for series pictures, including the *Seven Griefs of Mary* and the *Seven Joys of Mary*. His last great work was a series of six paintings done for a small shrine of Saint Ursula, commissioned by two nuns for the Hospital of Saint John in Bruges. He died a wealthy man and was regarded by many as one of the best painters in Europe.

SEE ALSO: van der Weyden, Rogier; van Eyck, Jan

Mercator, Gerardus
(1512–1594)

A Flemish cartographer who invented a system of setting lines of latitude and longitude on charts of the spherical earth, the "Mercator projection," which has become a standard for maps into modern times. Born in Rupelmonde, a small town in Flanders, he studied at the University of Louvain, where he achieved a master's degree in 1532. Troubled by the conflict of ancient Greek philosophy with Christian doctrine, Mercator studied mathematics, philosophy, geography and astronomy in order to reach some conclusions about the origins and true nature of the world. He was above all fascinated by the developing art of mapmaking, which in his day benefited from the discoveries of explorers and traveling merchants. He became a skilled maker of globes and instruments; under the training of Gemma Frisius and Gaspar Myrica, two men expert in the craft, he also mastered the difficult art of engraving. A workshop set up by the three men turned Louvain into an important center of globe making, cartography, and the production of sextants, telescopes, and other scientific instruments. His far-ranging exploration and questioning of accepted Christian doctrines, however, landed him in trouble with the religious authorities, and in 1544 he was arrested, tried, convicted, and briefly imprisoned on a charge of heresy.

In 1552 Mercator moved to Duisburg, in the Germany duchy of Cleves, where he was appointed a professor of mathematics and also became a land surveyor. In Duisburg, where he remained for the rest of his life, he helped to found a grammar school and continued his work in cartography. After publishing a map of Europe in 1554 and then several other local maps of Britain and the European continent, his reputation spread. He also developed a new method of producing globes, in which he pasted on the sphere printed maps that were cut to fit by tapering their edges toward the top and bottom.

Mercator was appointed by the Duke of Cleves as an official court cartographer. He perfected his system of marking parallel lines on a map to indicate degrees of longitude that could be applied to navigation charts and allow ship captains to more accurately follow their course at sea. He first used this system on a map of the world he completed in 1569. In the 1570s he began producing an atlas, a collection that included the maps of the ancient Greek astronomer Ptolemy as well as his own maps covering France, Germany, Italy, the Netherlands, eastern Europe, Greece, and the British Isles. This work, which he completed over the span of more than twenty years, was finally published by his son after his death.

mercenaries

Warfare went through an important change in the late Middle Ages. Once the domain of mounted knights who fought in the service of their feudal overlords, war became a matter for professional mercenary armies that fought for powerful kings. The mounted knight was no match for masses of archers and crossbowmen, who dominated the battlefield during the Hundred Years' War in France. This war, which dragged on for generations until the final defeat of the English in the 1450s, demanded permanent armies in the field. A permanent force was an impossibility under a feudal system that demanded only forty days of annual service from a king's vassals.

At the same time, the economy of Europe was expanding through better transportation and communications, and the new international banking system relied on credit, money, and bills of exchange. This made it possible for rulers to borrow and to hire mercenaries to fight their battles. Mercenaries could take the field for as long as they were paid, allowing kings and princes to mount long campaigns against their rivals and undertake sieges of enemy fortresses. The system had its roots in the practice of scutage, or payment by a vassal in lieu of military service. The payment of scutage allowed feudal lords to hire professional soldiers, who trained from a young age in the military arts and often proved more able than hereditary knights who simply fought out of traditional obligation.

Mercenaries came from all corners of Europe, but they were especially numerous in Switzerland, then a poor land where young men looked elsewhere for opportunity. The Swiss infantry enjoyed a reputation as skilled fighters, well disciplined and well armed with fearsome halberds, which could kill an armored knight at a single blow. Mercenary captains assembled small armies, drilling them relentlessly with formation and fighting tactics, in which infantry, archers, and cavalry were carefully coordinated.

The city-states of Italy favored mercenaries as an alternative to levies of the citizens. Bankers, industrialists, and merchants did not want to go to war, and disrupt the commerce that was essential to their prosperity. Instead, they hired condottieri (a word that means "contractors") to fight their battles. The best mercenary captains were well paid and in very high demand, and were honored by their patron cities with noble titles and monuments. Not everyone in Renaissance Italy appreciated the service of mercenaries, however. The diplomat and political philosopher Niccolo Machiavelli detested mercenaries as a symptom of a divided and weak Italian nation, one that was losing out while rival societies were organizing themselves into powerful, centralized kingdoms.

The French king Charles VII organized a standing army of mercenaries, organized into *compagnies d'ordonnance*. These permanent armies of France as well as the Holy Roman Empire invaded Italy in the late fifteenth and early sixteenth centuries, and eventually put an end to the independence of the Italian city-states. By the end of the Renaissance, mercenary armies that were hired for short campaigns were obsolete. They were replaced by standing national armies, which were raised by levies, and permanently garrisoned in strongholds.

SEE ALSO: Macchiavelli, Niccolo; Montefeltro, Federigo da

Michelangelo Buonarroti (1475–1564)

Italian sculptor, fresco painter, architect, and poet, whose works have become popular and world-renowned examples of Renaissance art. Born in the town of Caprese, near Florence, he was the son of Ludovico de Buonarroti, podesta of the town of Ca-

Michelangelo's "David." PHOTOGRAPH BY SUSAN D. ROCK. REPRODUCED BY PERMISSION.

prese, and Francesca Neri. His father sent him to study with Francesco Galeota, a scholar of Urbino. At a young age Michelangelo took an interest in painting, and at thirteen he joined the studio of Domenico Ghirlandaio. His ambition to be an artist, however, was opposed by his father, who saw painters and sculptors as lowly craftsmen and wanted his son to become a merchant and civic leader. Michelangelo's talent earned him an invitation from Lorenzo de' Medici, a distant cousin to his father, to join the Medici court, then a center of Renaissance learning and art. Medici had organized a school of sculpture in the Garden of San Marco, near the San Lorenzo church, where Michelangelo studied classical statues to create his first works, *Sleeping Cupid, The Madonna of the Stairs,* and *Battle of the Lapiths and Centaurs.*

In 1492 Lorenzo died and several factions began a violent struggle for control of Florence. The weakened state was defeated by the French army under Charles VIII. Girolamo Savonarola's campaign to rid the city of art and frivolity goaded Michelangelo into leaving Florence for Rome, where he made an intense study of classical ruins and created the sculpture *Bacchus,* a commission from a wealthy banker who next commissioned a Pietà, a sculpture of the Virgin Mary holding the body of a crucified Christ. This work, completed in 1498, still stands in the original place intended for it in Rome's Saint Peter's Basilica. After overhearing a bystander remark that the Pietà was the work of Christoforo Solari, a rival artist, Mich-

In "La Pietà," Michelangelo shows the Virgin Mary mourning as she holds the body of Christ in her arms.

elangelo flew into a rage and carved his name into the sash running across the figure of Mary, making the Pietà the only work of art that he signed. The Pietà, a vivid evocation in marble of death and resignation, displays both great strength and tender sadness.

After the overthrow of Savonarola and the proclamation of the Florentine republic, Michelangelo returned to what he always considered his home town. The city's Wool Guild, responsible for decorating and furnishing the Florence cathedral, commissioned a stone statue of David, which Michelangelo began in 1501. Over a period of three years, the statue emerged from a block of marble 19 feet (5.8m) long. The finished work stood 14 feet (4.2m) in height; the figure of David represents Florence itself, strong in youthful vigor and spirit and ready to defy any and all tyrants and foreigners seeking to challenge it. At Michelangelo's insistence, the sculpture was carefully moved to the large square in front of the Palazzo Vecchio, the town hall of Florence; later the statue was moved to the gallery of the Accademia, and replaced with a copy.

By the time of the completion of *David,* Michelangelo's reputation as an artist of genius had spread throughout Italy. In 1505 Pope Julius II invited Michelangelo and many other important artists to glorify the city of Rome and the papacy with original works of arts. From Michelangelo he commissioned sculptures for his own tomb, which was intended to display several dozen life-size statues. Michelangelo's painstaking work in the marble quarries of Carrara ended in a dispute with the pope over the costs of the project, and the artists fled Rome in disgust in 1506. Julius and Michelangelo soon reconciled, however, and the artist was then asked to suspend work on the tomb and take up the painting of twelve apostles on the ceiling and walls of the Sistine Chapel. The idea for this project was relayed to the pope by Michelangelo's own rivals, who believed him an inferior painter, incapable of carrying out the task, and likely to run into trouble with the pope and lose his commission for the papal tomb. In the meantime, the tomb project was proving so costly to Julius II that he ordered it stopped.

At first reluctant to undertake the Sistine Chapel ceiling, Michelangelo finally accepted the commission and began work in 1508. He introduced a new concept in fresco painting by rendering complete dramatic scenes on an overhead space, something no other artist had ever attempted. By the time he completed the ceiling, in 1512, he had rendered nine scenes from the Bible's book of Genesis, including the creation of man, the temptation of Adam and Eve, and the biblical flood, with more than four hundred larger-than-life figures, all while lying on his back on top of a wooden scaffold. The Sistine Chapel ceiling was a magnificent achievement that left the artist emotionally drained and physically weakened. He then completed the tomb for Julius II that included the dour figure of Moses, a sculpture created from a lump of marble so poorly proportioned and misshapen that several artists had already refused to work with it. Also as part of this tomb were to be two important sculptures, *Bound Slave* and *Dying Slave*, which he left unfinished at the death of the pope in 1513.

After completing the Sistine Chapel ceiling, Michelangelo returned to Florence. He took on architectural projects, including the design of the Laurentian Library. In 1526 the Medici were again driven out of Florence, while Pope Clement VII ordered German mercenaries to surround the city and prepare for an assault. The city of Florence asked Michelangelo to design a series of fortifications. He joined the army defending Florence but then fled the city for Venice when it appeared the mercenaries would actually invade. The artist was exiled for this act but later was allowed to return.

In 1519 the artist was commissioned to design two tombs for Lorenzo and Giuliano de' Medici, to be built in the sacristy of Florence's San Lorenzo Church. The tombs were designed with symbolic representations of dawn, dusk, day, and night. The figures are shown crying in grief at the passage of time and the inevitability of death. The artist left them incomplete when he returned to Rome in 1534. Pope Clement VII commissioned him to paint *The Last Judgment* fresco in the Sistine Chapel. A huge painting, the largest fresco painting of its time, *The Last Judgment* was completed in 1541. The painting caused a scandal because of its depiction of nude figures on the wall of a sacred chapel, and for a time after its completion the figures were covered with cloth drapery for the sake of modesty.

In the meantime, Michelangelo had met Vittoria Colonna, a poet dedicated to the reform of the church. The two became close friends, a relationship that inspired the artist to write fine lyric poetry, sonnets, and madrigals in her honor. At this time he was commissioned to design buildings on the Campidoglio, the ancient Capitoline Hill of Rome. The construction of the buildings was not begun until the late 1550s and not completed for another century. The bronze equestrian statue of Marcus Aurelius was placed in the center of the square.

In 1546, Michelangelo was appointed chief architect of Saint Peter's Basilica. Donato Bramante, who had died in 1514, had designed the structure but had left it unfinished; it was now left to Michelangelo to design the dome.

Late in life Michelangelo designed the *Rondanini Pietà* for his own tomb, but unsatisfied with the material or the design he constantly altered it and ultimately damaged it. At his death Michelangelo was honored by the citizens of Florence, who recognized him as the greatest artist their city had produced. He was known as "The Divine One" during his lifetime, and since that time his works have been widely regarded as the highest achievements of the Renaissance in Italy or any other country.

SEE ALSO: Julius II; Leonardo da Vinci; Medici, Lorenzo de'; painting; sculpture

Milton, John
(1608–1674)

Essayist and poet whose *Paradise Lost* is widely considered the greatest epic of the English language. The son of a prosperous scrivener, he was born in London and educated in the classics at Saint Paul's, one of the city's finest private schools. He was educated at Christ's College, Cambridge, where he began studies at the age of fifteen and prepared for a career as a minister in the Church of England. He wrote epigrams, eulogies, and poems in Latin, as well as short epics on English history. He first gained notice with his poem *On the Morning of Christ's Nativity*. He turned away from Latin and Italian and began writing English verse, which he used for his essay "On Shakespeare," written in 1632 for a book about the playwright, whose reputation was gaining in the generation after his death. In 1634 one of his masques—a combination of music, dance, and poetry—was performed on a stage at the castle of Ludlow. This work, *Comus*, deals with the themes of purity and temptation,

and was a precursor to subjects Milton would take up in his most famous work.

Milton lived on his family's country estate after leaving Cambridge. He spent a year in Italy and, in 1639, returned to England, where he wrote in support of reform of the Church of England. He became an ardent supporter of Oliver Cromwell during the English Civil War, which pitted Cromwell's anti-royalist forces against defenders of the monarchy. Milton wrote in support of the new English commonwealth that Cromwell established and in favor of the execution of King Charles I. His essay "Areopagitica" stoutly defended the principle of freedom of speech and debate, and the right to publish without censorship by the church or government. Historians believe this stance had a lasting effect in the American colonies, where its principle was officially adopted in the U.S. Constitution. "The Tenure of Kings and Magistrates," published in 1649, was a defense of controls on the power of kings, arguing that the people have a right to rise up and end the service of incompetent or corrupt monarchs. He was rewarded for his anti-royalist stance with an appointment in 1649 as a foreign secretary in Cromwell's government, a position in which he wrote in support of the government and translated its official documents into Latin. Although he was imprisoned at the restoration of the monarchy in 1660, and his books were publicly burned, he was eventually granted a pardon.

By this time he was blind, and forced to dictate his letters and poetry to a secretary. In this way he completed *Paradise Lost*, which describes the revolt of Satan and the story of Adam and Eve and their expulsion from the Garden of Eden. Milton wrote the epic in ten books of blank verse, describing Satan's war against God, the biblical stories of the creation of the world and the fall of man. Milton's vivid and powerful imagination was a strong match to the ancient, familiar themes of his subject; his poetry inspired generations of later English writers, who most admired his Satan as a complex, fascinating, and dramatic rebel—an icon for the age of Romantic poetry in the nineteenth century. Milton later published a sequel, *Paradise Regained*, about the temptation of Christ by Satan, and the way to ultimately triumph through humility and faith. Along with this work Milton published a drama entitled *Samson Agonistes*, telling a biblical story in the form of an ancient Greek tragedy.

Montaigne, Michel de (1533–1592)

French writer whose very personal thoughts and confessions—in the form of *essais* or "tries"—have remained influential in modern times. Born into a wealthy family that owned estates in the Aquitaine region of southern France, Montaigne was the son of Pierre Eyquem, a mercenary soldier and one-time mayor of Bordeaux. Montaigne was given a humanist education and a thorough training in the use of Latin as both written and spoken language. Trained as a lawyer in Toulouse, he became counselor to the Parlement court in Bordeaux in 1557. He entered the service of King Charles IX in 1561.

Montaigne took a much greater interest in letters and poetry than the study and practice of law. The politics and rivalries of the royal court, and the demands of public service, left him yearning for privacy, solitude, and enough time to read, study, and work out a personal philosophy of life and how it should be lived. In 1569 he published a translation of *Natural Theology*, a work of the Spanish monk Raymond Sebond. In 1570, he retired as a lawyer and moved to the family estate, known as the Chateau de Montaigne. There he began work on a series of short writings, in which he expressed his private views on politics, society, literature, family life, childhood, and many aspects of the common human experience that had never been considered suitable material for a serious writer. Working for ten years in isolation, he brought out his book of *Essais* in 1580, to widespread puzzlement and disdain on the part of serious writers, scholars, and philosophers. Gradually, as the writing of personal experience and confession grew in popularity, Montaigne's work won widespread acceptance.

Seeking a cure for poor health and painful kidney stones, Montaigne set out on a journey across Europe in 1580. From this experience he wrote a series of travel essays that were eventually published in the late eighteenth century as the *Travel Journal*. In the meantime, the citizens of Bordeaux elected him mayor, in honor of his capable statesmanship during the violent Wars of Religion between Protestants and Catholics. After his term as mayor ended in 1585, he returned to his country estate, where he died in 1592.

Montaigne's book of *Essays* is one of the most important and original literary works of the Renaissance. In these short works, all literary pretense and artificiality is dropped, and the author reveals his own thoughts and emotions directly to the reader. Montaigne's work created a foundation for the confessional literature that remains a popular literary genre to the present day.

Montefeltro, Federigo da (1422–1482)

The Duke of Urbino, a skilled condottiere, and a renowned patron of Renaissance art and scholarship. Born in the Umbrian hill town of Gubbio, an illegitimate son of Guidantonio da Montefeltro, the Duke of Spoleto and lord of Urbino, Federigo was raised in an aristocratic court and knighted by the Holy Roman Emperor at the age of fifteen. Soon afterward he became a condottiere, or captain of mercenaries. In 1444 he became the leader of Urbino after the assassination of his half brother, Oddantonio da Montefeltro. Federigo's great skill on the battlefield earned him a reputation all over Italy; he finally enlisted with the illustrious Sforza family, the rulers of Milan, and married a member of the Sforza clan. In the late 1450s he served Pope Pius II in the pope's campaign against Sigismondo Malatesta, defeating Malatesta at the Battle of Cesano in 1462. Montefeltro's loyalty was easily lost, however, as he soon turned against the pope to wrest control of the territory forfeited by Malatesta in the Marches region and the Adriatic port city of Rimini.

In Urbino, Montefeltro built a large library in his ducal palace and employed scribes and scholars. He created the finest collection of manuscripts in Italy, after that of the pope. Realizing that the duke made a much better ally than enemy, Pope Sixtus arranged the marriage of Giovanni della Rovere, his nephew, to Federigo's daughter, and bestowed the title of duke on Montefeltro. The pope hired him to captain the papal forces against the city of Florence, where Montefeltro allied with the Pazzi conspirators against the Medici. The failure of the plot to overthrow the Medici was a serious blow to the duke as well as the pope. In 1482, while besieging the city of Venice, Montefeltro died, leaving the duchy of Urbino to his son Guidobaldo, a sickly and ineffective ruler at whose death the duchy was seized by the Papacy.

SEE ALSO: Malatesta, Sigismondo Pandolfo

Monteverdi, Claudio (1567–1643)

Composer who pioneered the art of opera, born in Cremona, Italy. Monteverdi's first works were motets and madrigals, completed when he was still a teenager. He joined the court of Vincenzo I of Mantua as a singer and musician, and later was appointed conductor of the court orchestra. He pioneered many innovations in the writing of music, including the use of instrumental accompaniment known as continuo and the use of monody, a simpler and clearer melody that would be taken up by composers of the Baroque period that followed the Renaissance. Monteverdi combined vocal music with drama, and invented opera with the premier of L 'Orfeo in 1607. This work was the first to assign musical parts to specific instruments and to convey a dramatic plot with the use of musical devices and the singing voice. He wrote *The Vespers of the Blessed Virgin* in 1610, a work that began the practice of repeating melodies for dramatic effect and to unify the composition. Monteverdi became the conductor of San Marco Cathedral in Venice in 1613. There he wrote more books of madrigals and invented new techniques of playing string instruments, including the tremolo, in which a note is rapidly repeated or "shaken," and pizzicato, in which the musician plucks the string with his finger. Late in his life he completed *The Return of Ulysses* and *The Coronation of Poppea*, a work based on the life of the Roman emperor Nero.

More, Sir Thomas (1478–1535)

An English statesman, author, and renowned Renaissance humanist who ran afoul of King Henry VIII's break with the Catholic Church, Thomas More paid for his stand with his life. His father, Sir John More, was persecuted by Henry VII, the first Tudor king. He was Lord Chancellor of England from 1529 to 1532. In 1510 he became an undersheriff of London. He became a counselor to the king in 1517 and was sent as a diplomat to Emperor Charles V. His success in this mission earned him a knighthood, attaining the title of under-treasurer in 1521. More served the king as adviser and go-between with Cardinal Thomas Wolsey, the leading representative of the pope in England.

In 1516 More completed *Utopia*, a book describing an ideal political and economic system in which religious tolerance and the common ownership of property bring about a peaceful and orderly society. More was inspired by ideal societies described by classical Greek authors such as Plato and Aristotle; his name of Utopia is derived from the Greek phrase eutopos, or "no place."

In 1523 More was named speaker of the House of Commons and in 1525 chancellor of Lancaster, a key post in northern England. In the meantime he wrote several tracts against the Protestant reformers who were gaining a following on the continent of Europe. His *Defence of the Seven Sacraments*, written for Henry VIII, earned the king a commendation as "Defender of the Faith" from Pope Leo X. At the same time, however, Henry was growing strongly disenchanted with his wife of twenty years, Catherine of Aragon, who had failed to provide him with a male heir. In 1527 he asked Cardinal Wolsey to petition Pope Clement VII to have his marriage annulled. The pope refused to cooperate; Henry reacted by forcing Wolsey from his post and, in 1529, replacing him with More. Henry's argument that the pope had no authority in England was opposed by More, who saw the Protestant movement as a deadly threat to the survival of Christianity. He ordered the imprisonment and execution of many Protestants in England.

More did not support Henry's efforts to divorce Catherine of Aragon, however, and to protest the king's actions he asked to resign his post. Although the king granted this request in 1532, he was deeply angered by More's refusal to take an oath acknowledging Henry as the head of the Church of England. When Henry's second wife, Anne Boleyn, was crowned the new queen of England in 1533, More avoided the ceremony. This snub and his continuing friendship with Catherine of Aragon made him a marked man. In 1534 he was arrested for refusing to take another oath, one that would acknowledge an Act of Succession denying the ultimate authority of the pope in matters of religion. He was brought to trial; unwilling to recant his belief that a king could not replace a pope, he was found guilty and sentenced to be drawn and quartered—a severely cruel punishment. Henry spared him this ordeal, ordering him instead to be beheaded, which took place on July 6, 1535. More became a martyr for the Catholic Church in its efforts to halt the spread of Protestantism in Europe.

SEE ALSO: Boleyn, Anne; Erasmus, Desiderius; Henry VIII

Mühlberg, Battle of

A battle between the forces of the Holy Roman Emperor Charles V and the Schmalkaldic League, a band of Protestant German princes opposed to the emperor's authority in their domains. By the evening of April 23, 1547, the Schmalkaldic commander, John of Saxony, had gathered about eight thousand foot soldiers and three thousand cavalry on the eastern bank of the Elbe River, in what is now northeastern Germany. Charles and his commander, the Duke of Alba, had about thirteen thousand foot soldiers and five thousand cavalry. This force of Spanish, Flemish, and German soldiers took up their lines on the river's western bank. With the advantage in numbers, Charles decided to take the initiative and attack on the morning of April 24, 1547.

Early that morning, men of the imperial army armed with muskets and harquebuses forded the Elbe and created a strong bridgehead on the eastern shore. Maneuvering in a thick fog, and told of an easy ford of the river by a local peasant, a large squadron of Spanish cavalry followed, throwing the forward scouts of the Schmalkaldic League into a panic. Several hundred yards to the east, John of Saxony then drew up his forces, with infantry flanked by cavalry, to face the assault. Alba, forming a squadron of heavy cavalry, charged the left flanks of the Protestant position and threw its men into a panic. In the meantime, the harquebusiers and lancers were attacking the Saxon horses on the other wing, causing the horses to break and run into a nearby forest. The Protestant infantry remained to face flanking attacks on both sides. The battle continued for two hours before the Saxon foot soldiers finally broke and retreated from the field.

With the defeat at Mühlberg, the Schmalkaldic League lost two of its most important leaders, John of Saxony and the Duke of Brunswick, as prisoners. The league broke apart and submitted to Charles V, but the dispute between Protestant rulers and the emperor would continue for eight years before the Treaty of Augsburg would temporarily settle their differences.

SEE ALSO: Charles V

music

Composers of the Renaissance built on a centuries-long tradition of sacred music that had its roots in the plainsong chants and Masses of the early Middle Ages. But whereas a single line of unaccompanied melody, improvised or committed to memory, had once sufficed for the chanting of the Catholic Mass, the psalms, and other sacred music, the late Middle Ages had seen a flowering of polyphonic (multipart) music and written compositions, and the emergence of professional composers. Polyphonic music reached new heights of complexity in the late Middle Ages, as the range of voices was extended and new scales and melodic intervals were put to use.

Mass settings and motets remained the most popular musical forms, but many Renaissance composers began working in secular song forms such as the Italian madrigal and the French chanson, which grew out of the sung poems of the medieval troubadours. An important school of musical composition emerged in fifteenth-century Burgundy. Led by Guillaume Dufay, it bridged the medieval and Renaissance periods. Johannes Ockeghem was a master of counterpoint, able to set several complex lines of music in motion from a simple motif, a precursor to the elaborate fugues of Johann Sebastian Bach in a later century. Josquin des Prez, was the most significant composer of the Flemish school, whose musicians and composers were in high demand throughout Europe.

Purely instrumental music also emerged during the Renaissance in a variety of forms: The toccata ("touched" rather than sung) was a piece that showed off the musician's ability; the pavane was a slow lament for the dead; and the allemande, galliard, and courante were popular dance forms. Musicians were given wide latitude to improvise their parts; the best could play elaborate free cadenzas while staying within the limits of a strict system of harmony, counterpoint, and melodic progression. In England, many skilled composers took up the Italian madrigal, a sung form that relied on the texts of well-known sonnets and other poetry.

In the late Renaissance composers began to simplify complex melodies and emphasize a single pure line, accompanied by one or several lesser parts. Imitative counterpoint allowed the composer a wider range of melodic devices in order to show off his skill at combining different voices and instruments. This new freedom was applied to sacred music, which could change from polyphonic to homophonic (written in a single voice) and back again, as the composer wished. Dissonance and chromaticism—the use of notes not part of the key scale—was tolerated and in the work of some composers, notably Carlo Gesualdo, strongly emphasized, causing strange and surprising shifts in mood and tenor.

In Venice, sacred music was often composed for multiple choirs and groups of instruments, laying the groundwork for the classical symphony. Giovanni Palestrina, a Roman composer, mastered the difficult art of polyphony and wrote textbooks that instructed composers in this art up to the twentieth century. A new form of sung drama was taken up by many skilled composers, notably the Italian Claudio Monteverdi, whose *Orfeo* is considered by many to be the first opera. This new form combined music, singing, and dance in the presentation of a tragic or comic play. The Venetian School influenced music in the rest of Italy, as well as Germany and France, while opera emerged in the seventeenth century as a form that brought music into direct competition with the theater for the attention of a mass audience.

SEE ALSO: des Prez, Josquin; Gesualdo, Carlo

Muslims

The Islamic conquest that began in the early seventh century spread the new faith from its home in Arabia to the north, east, and west. At its height, the Muslim caliphs (rulers) held both secular and sacred authority over a realm stretching from northern India and central Asia west to Persia, Mesopotamia, the Levant, North Africa, and Iberia (modern Spain and Portugal). The campaigns between Christians and Muslims in the Levant, known as the Crusades, ended with the last Christian states destroyed by the armies of the Mamluks. The Mamluk dynasty, with its capital in Cairo, Egypt, originated in a caste of soldiers. The Mamluks turned back the Christians as well as the Mongols, who in the middle of the thirteenth century invaded and destroyed Baghdad, the center of the Abbasid caliphate. Cairo was the most prominent center of learning in the Islamic world, with the Tunisian scholar Ibn Khaldun who was the leading historian and philosopher of this period.

The Mongols ruling in Iran and Iraq were converted to Islam in the late thirteenth century. In the sixteenth century, a new Safavid dynasty emerged in what was ancient Persia. In India the Mughal Empire was established in 1526 by Babur, a Timurid prince of Kabul. The Mughal rulers built their capital at Delhi and collected tribute from Hindu states south of the Indian peninsula. In the meantime, the medieval Muslim societies of the Middle East developed a productive agricultural system, building new irrigation systems that put former desert land into production. New food and cash crops imported from India and Southeast Asia, including bananas, rice, cotton, citrus, eggplants, and many others, were propagated in the west. Many Muslim cities were surrounded by large rings of market gardens and small farms that supplied their harvests to a growing and prospering urban population.

Control of the spice trade between Asia and Europe contributed to the general wealth and security of the medieval Islamic world. The search for a route to bypass the Middle Eastern spice markets was the prime reason for Portuguese exploration of the African and the Indian ocean coasts in the fifteenth century. As Portugal and later Spain established overseas colonies, and began drawing on their newly discovered resources, the Muslim world entered a period of economic decline. In Spain a Reconquista (reconquest) eventually drove the Muslims out of al-Andalus. The kingdom in Granada, the last remnant of the Moorish conquest of the eighth century, paid a heavy tribute to the rulers of Castile, a Christian kingdom, until the united forces of Castile and Aragon captured Granada in 1492. Muslim farmers fled to North Africa or were absorbed into the newly united kingdom of Spain as converts to Christianity.

After the Mongol invasion the Ottoman tribe of Turks rose to prominence in Asia Minor. They crossed into Europe in the fourteenth century and in 1453 conquered Constantinople and the Byzantine Empire. The Ottoman domains extended into the Balkan Peninsula, and during the European Renaissance the Turkish armies posed a constant threat to Christian territory. The Ottoman Turks crushed a Hungarian army at the Battle of Mohacs in 1526 and eventually reached Vienna, the seat of power for the Habsburg dynasty. Although the sieges of Vienna failed, the Ottomans remained a force to be reckoned with by the Renaissance princes of Europe, who were unable to set aside their differences and unite their forces for the recapture of the eastern Mediterranean.

SEE ALSO: Mehmed II; Ottoman Empire

mythology

The mythology of the classical world entered the mainstream of Renaissance art and thought through the work of scholars, as well as the poetic works of medieval writers who adopted the themes of ancient writers such as the Roman poet Ovid. In Italy, translators and commentators on writers such as Plato and Virgil spread the knowledge of classical mythology to students and university scholars. The trend began in the works of Petrarch, who rendered ancient myths in his collection of poems entitled *Canzoniere*, and Giovanni Boccaccio, whose *Genealogy of the Gods* was the first serious study of the pagan deities and the myths associated with them. With the invention of printing in the middle of the fifteenth century, the works of Ovid were presented in new editions, in Latin and in vernacular languages, gradually spreading throughout the continent and to newly literate social classes. The study of pagan myths made them common knowledge, and with the religious significance long stripped away, the gods became symbols of purely human qualities, adopted by many poets and painters in their works.

Renaissance sculptors, woodworkers, jewelers, and painters depicted these deities, who replaced the biblical events and themes that dominated the art of the Middle Ages. At first, classical mythology served as diversion, entertainment, and simple decoration in the form of garden sculptures and ceiling frescoes for private salons and public halls. Serious art was Christian art in the early Renaissance until Sandro Botticelli—in works including *Primavera* and *The Birth of Venus*— put pagan gods at the center of his canvas, making paganism a visual reflection of the emerging humanism in literature. Mythology allowed artists freer reign in their choice of subject matter—they could treat lust, pride, avarice, and other sins by adopting an ancient myth and giving it a personal interpretation, and not one controlled by medieval pictorial traditions. Eventually, political leaders took up mythology as well, identifying themselves with the ancient gods and taking on their attributes (Emperor Charles V, for example, was often shown as the Roman god Jupiter, and the Tudor dynasty of England modeled itself on the ancient Trojans).

Eventually pagan mythology became popular subject matter for the most renowned of Renaissance artists, including Leonardo da Vinci, Michelangelo Buonarroti, Michelangelo da Caravaggio, and Titian, whose mythological paintings, including *Venus of Urbino, The Rape of Europea, Diana and Actaeon*, and *Bacchus and Ariadne*, are considered his masterpieces. Writers, including Francois Rabelais, Ludovico Ariosto, William Shakespeare, and Pierre de Ronsard, drew heavily on mythology, while Diane de Poitiers, the mistress of the French King Henri II, became the subject herself of a pagan cult, in poetry and art, in which she was given the attributes of Diana, Roman goddess of the hunt. In the meantime, the use of classical mythology had a subversive effect on Christianity and its institutions. Giving a prominent place in poetry and sculpture to the Greek gods, for example, implied that religious faith—whether that of the pagans or the Christians—was simply a reflection of the human imagination. At the end of the Renaissance, ancient myths began to prevail in public art and in serious poetry, accompanying an age of skepticism that eventually resulted in the Enlightenment, a movement that cast doubt on religious faith of any kind.

Naples

City of southern Italy that was the capital of a kingdom covering the southern regions of the peninsula and the island of Sicily. Naples had been a thriving port city from the time of the ancient Greeks, who founded the metropolis and called it Neapolis or "new city." After the fall of the western Roman Empire, the Byzantine Empire made Naples a key port. Trade from southern Europe to Greece and the Middle East brought great wealth to the city and made it a valuable prize for the Normans, who established a kingdom in southern Italy and the island of Sicily in 1039.

During the Renaissance, the kingdom of Naples was contested by the Angevin dynasty, which had its roots in northern France, and the rulers of the Spanish realm of Aragon. The Angevin dynasty was granted Naples by Pope Clement IV in 1266. Angevin kings brought important Italian artists, including Giotto and Simone Martini, to the city to decorate churches, palaces, and buildings belonging to the Franciscans, an order of monks established in the thirteenth century.

In 1373, when Queen Joan I renounced the Angevin claim to Naples, she named Duke Louis I of Anjou as her heir. The rival of Louis, the Prince of Durazzo, took his vengeance by murdering Joan and conquering Naples in 1382, when he was crowned as Charles III, king of Naples. Although Naples was seized by Alfonso V of Aragon in 1442, the Angevin dynasty did not give up its claim to the kingdom.

Alfonso celebrated his victory by raising one of the most famous monuments of Naples, the Arco di Trionfo di Constantio, a monumental arch inspired by the architecture of ancient Rome. Under the Aragonese dynasty Naples became an important center of painting, with a renowned school established in the city by Colantonio del Fiore. Neapolitan kings commissioned works by Pisanello, Donatello, and Michelozzo, all artists of Florence and Tuscany, while noble families of Naples hired these and other northern painters to decorate their private chapels in the city's leading churches. A unique Neapolitan style of painting and sculpture developed in the late fifteenth century; its leading artists were Diego de Siloé and Bartolomé Ordonez, both Spaniards.

In the meantime, the Angevin line died out in 1481, and the French claim to Naples was taken up by the Valois dynasty. The Valois was given support by Pope Innocent VIII, who saw the Aragonese as a serious threat to his own authority in central Italy. When Alfonso's son and heir Ferrante died in 1494, the pope invited King Charles VIII to invade Italy with the goal of seizing Naples and allying it with the Papacy. The French troops defeated the Aragonese but facing a much stronger army sent by Ferdinand II of Aragon, Charles soon retreated from Italy. The Aragonese remained in control of Naples while the kings of France made unsuccessful efforts to wrest it from their control. Finally Spain united Naples and Sicily under its own government in 1501 and sent viceroys to rule the city. By the Treaty of Cateau-Cambrésis of 1559 France officially ceded Naples to Spain. Under Spanish rule Naples grew to become the second-most populous city in Europe, after Paris, and attracted renowned painters, writers, scholars, and sculptors from throughout Italy.

In the sixteenth century Naples was visited by Raphael, who painted the *Madonna del Pesce* for a family chapel in San Domenico Maggiore, and Giorgio Vasari, who painted frescoes and paintings for the monastery of Monteoliveto. In the early seventeenth century, the wealthy religious orders were hiring Neapolitan and foreign artists to decorate the chapels, refectories, and halls of their monasteries in and around the city. Noble patrons also commissioned important works from Michelangelo da Caravaggio, who spent several years in Naples and left behind *The Seven Acts of Mercy* and the *Flagellation of Christ*. The sculptor Pietro Bernini was also working in Naples at this time as was the philosopher Giordano Bruno.

Under the Spanish viceroys Naples experienced the peak of its prestige and wealth, but it also suffered under oppressive tyranny. In 1647 a violent revolt led by a humble fisherman, Masaniello, broke out in the city. The revolt was put down but after an outbreak of plague killed half the population in 1656, Naples began to decline as an economic and artistic capital.

Neoplatonism

A philosophy that originated in the third century A.D., modeled on the ideas of the Greek thinker and teacher Plato, and which was revived by scholars, essayists,

and poets during the Renaissance. The Neoplatonist school began in the books of Plotinus and his student Porphyry, the author of the *Enneads*, an important early book of the Neoplatonist school. These scholars of Alexandria sought to explore and clarify Plato's original philosophy, and extend it into new doctrines using Platonism as a foundation. The central belief of Plotinus and his followers was that the universe emanated from a divine, all-pervading "Source" in the form of lesser beings, and that human spirituality and philosophy strived for a return to that Source. Later students of the Platonic tradition, including Iamblichus and Proclus, added to these writings an element of mysticism and magic, and the idea that semidivine beings such as angels and demons served as intermediaries between ordinary humans and the Source. Neoplatonism can be seen as a synthesis of ancient Greek mythology with the monotheism that was gaining followers throughout the Mediterranean, notably in the beliefs of the early Christians.

Important Neoplatonic philosophers lived in Alexandria, Asia Minor, and Greece; their ideas were a strong influence on Christian writers and church fathers, including Saint Augustine of Hippo, and the medieval philosophers Boethius and John Scotus, as well as medieval Islamic and Jewish philosophers. The Neoplatonist doctrines of the soul, the afterlife, and the divine source were incorporated into many aspects of Christian doctrine.

In the Renaissance, many scholars of ancient Greek philosophy studied Neoplatonism, reviving its beliefs as a counter to the strict and orthodox Christianity that had held sway throughout the Middle Ages. This Neoplatonic revival took place in the writings of Giovanni Pico della Mirandola, Marsilio Ficino, and Giordano Bruno, and was taken up by significant artists such as Sandro Botticelli and Michelangelo Buonarroti. Ficino was a scholar of Plato as well as Plotinus who sought to reconcile Neoplatonism and Christianity, and one of the first to translate the works of the ancient Greeks. His writings, in particular commentaries on Plato's dialogues, served as a foundation for new concepts of beauty and romantic love, and the idea that philosophy should be part of any serious work of art or literature. Neoplatonism found a wide following in France, and its adherents included renowned essayists and poets including Marguerite of Navarre, Pierre Ronsard, and Francois Rabelais.

SEE ALSO: Bruno, Giordano; Ficino, Marsilio; Pico della Mirandola, Giovanni

Netherlands

In the Middle Ages the Netherlands, or Low Countries, was a territory of the duchy of Burgundy, a wealthy realm that stretched from the English Channel south to the Alps. The major Flemish cities, including Brussels, Bruges, and Ghent, were among the most prosperous in all of Europe. The dukes of Burgundy were patrons of the arts and the Netherlands was home to the most innovative painters and composers of northern Europe. Musicians of the Flemish School were in high demand throughout Europe. Josquin des Prez, Guillaume Dufay, and Johannes Ockeghem developed a widely imitated style, written for selected groups of instruments and always with a mind to balanced melody and careful harmonic progressions. Local artists traveled to Italy and brought home new trends in art, while Italian artists and architects came north to enjoy the patronage

The 17th-century Vleeshall (meat market) in Haarlem, Netherlands. The Netherlands were a major trading center during the Renaissance, a fact reflected in the size and elaborate detail of this and other commercial buildings. LIPNITZKI/ROGER VIOLLET/GETTY IMAGES.

of Burgundian monarchs and aristocrats. While the ideals of classical Greece and Rome had less importance, the artists of the Netherlands made their own innovations. Jan van Eyck developed an astonishing realism in his pictures, while Pieter Brueghel turned to the natural world and the lives of ordinary townsmen and peasants for inspiration. Hieronymus Bosch used the startling imagery of fantasy and dreams to convey his deep religious convictions. Later painters of the Netherlands specialized in still-lifes, landscape paintings, and portraits.

In 1496, the marriage of Philip the Handsome with Joanna, a Habsburg princess of Spain and daughter of Ferdinand and Isabella of Castile, eventually brought the Netherlands under the rule of Emperor Charles V, their son and the ruler of Spain and the Holy Roman Empire. During the next century, the region suffered occupation by Spain and a destructive civil war. The Protestant Reformation took hold during the sixteenth century, when the Netherlands were in revolt against the rule by the Catholic Habsburgs. The emperor sent armies to put down the rebellion and enforce Catholicism. At the end of the period, the Habsburgs retained control of the Flemish provinces (now Belgium), while Holland won its independence and built a far-flung colonial empire, from the Americas to East Asia.

SEE ALSO: Bosch, Hieronymus; Brueghel family; Rubens, Peter Paul; van Eyck, Jan

Nicholas of Cusa
(1401–1464)

Humanist, papal legate, and scholar whose skeptical inquiries into the natural world broke new scientific and philosophical ground at the dawn of the Renaissance. Born Nicholas Krebs in the Moselle River valley, Nicholas of Cusa was schooled in a religious fraternity known as the Brothers of the Common Life. Although he trained in the law as a university student, Nicholas also attained a doctorate in the field of canon law from the University of Padua and finally decided on a career in the church. He attended the Council of Basel in 1432 and argued in favor of a general church council that would hold authority over the pope and the institution of the Papacy. To support his views, he wrote *De Concordantia Catholica*. The endless bickering and politics of church councils

changed his opinion, however, and he later became a proponent of a supreme pontiff. He entered the service of Pope Eugene IV in 1437 and became a wide-ranging papal diplomat, who mediated disputes within the church and attempted to resolve the long-standing schism between the eastern and western branches of the faith. He also attempted to raise an alliance against the Ottoman Turks, who were threatening an invasion of Europe from their base in the Balkans, but found his efforts thwarted by the rivalries among Christian princes of Europe.

In 1440 he completed *Of Learned Ignorance*, a book that propounds the idea that humans can only have limited knowledge of the true state of the universe, and that their experience of God must come through a sense of the divine that has no relation to ordinary, rational thought and observation of the senses. Nicholas was ahead of his time in the subjects of mathematics, medicine, and astronomy, and held that the earth revolved about the sun well before the observations of Nicolaus Copernicus. His writings were known to Copernicus as well as Isaac Newton, Galileo Galilei, and Johannes Kepler, and he was regarded as one of the true scientific geniuses of the fifteenth century. He also applied his knowledge in a practical way by inventing convex lenses to correct nearsightedness.

He was appointed a cardinal in 1448. Two years later he became the bishop of Brixen, in the Tyrol region of the Alps. Here his efforts to reform the church and its monasteries brought him into conflict with Sigismund, the Habsburg Duke of Austria, who had Nicholas briefly imprisoned, an act for which the pope excommunicated Sigismund. In 1458, Nicholas returned to Rome, where he joined the court of Pope Pius II.

Nicholas V
(1397–1455)

Pope from 1447 until 1455 who resolved the long-standing conflict between the conciliar movement and the Papacy and whose efforts to restore classical Rome made him in the view of many historians the first "Renaissance pope." Born as Tommaso Parentucelli, in Sarzana, a town near Genoa, he was the son of a physician and a talented scholar and linguist. He traveled to Florence, where he was hired as a tutor to the city's aristocratic families. After studying theology at the University of Bologna, he traveled throughout northern Europe as a scholar and book collector.

Nicholas was appointed as the bishop of Bologna in 1444. He was sent by Pope Eugene IV to the Holy Roman Empire in order to resolve the dispute between the pope and the emperor. His skillful diplomacy was rewarded with an appointment as cardinal and in 1446, as the successor to Eugene IV.

As pope, Nicholas's mission was to undo the work of the Council of Basel, whose delegates were asserting the primacy of church councils. He signed an important treaty known as the Concordat of Vienna with Frederick III, the king of Germany, who agreed that the council's decisions would have no effect in his lands. Nicholas made great efforts to resolve simony and other corrupt practices that were throwing the church into ill repute. Nicholas ended the long schism in the western church by convincing the last antipope, Felix V, to give up his claim to the Papacy in 1449. Nicholas crowned Frederick III as the Holy Roman Emperor in 1452, the last pope to carry out this service. In the same year, he wrote a papal decree, *Dum Diversas*, that allowed the king of Portugal to take non-Christians as slaves, thus giving the papal stamp of approval to the growing African slave trade.

Nicholas began the revival of culture and learning in the city of Rome. He rebuilt and repaired the city and aspired to make it a monument to the power and prestige of the popes. Rome's walls were fortified, its streets paved, its sewers and water systems repaired, and its ancient system of Roman aqueducts returned to service. He sponsored the work of scholars and copyists in bringing the works of ancient writers to light after centuries of neglect. Nicholas also established the Vatican Library, the largest repository of books in Europe.

SEE ALSO: Council of Basel; Fall of Constantinople; Papacy; slavery

Nogarola, Isotta
(1418–1466)

An Italian scholar, author, and feminist who was renowned, and notorious for her ambition to debate religion and philosophy with the men of the Renaissance. Born into a noble family of Verona, she was offered an extremely rare (for a young girl) private education. Her tutor, Martino Rizzoni, followed the new humanist philosophy and instructed her in Latin, moral philosophy, poetry, and history—leaving out rhetoric, considered to be the exclusive domain of young men preparing themselves for a public career. She wrote skillful essays and letters in classical Latin and sought a mentor in Guarino of Verona, then the leading humanist of northern Italy, who ignored her for a full year before deigning to reply to her letter with a scornful rejection.

In 1438 Nogarola fled plague-stricken Verona for Venice. She drew criticism in that city for presuming to debate male scholars, and was satirized in an anonymous play for her alleged decadence. In 1441 she returned with her family to Verona, where she studied the Bible and classical authors, lived with her family, avoided marriage, and wrote nothing that has survived to modern times.

Her letters were considered good enough to be copied and circulated, however, and reached a wide audience, from Venice to Rome, by the middle of the fifteenth century. Later in her life Nogarola aspired to a synthesis of Christian ethics with the emerging humanist philosophy. In 1451 she came out of isolation to debate Ludovico Foscarini of Venice, a diplomat then living in Verona. From their correspondence and argument she authored a dialogue, *Of the Equal or Unequal Sin of Adam and Eve*, over the fall of humanity into sinfulness and God's expulsion of Adam and Even from the Garden of Eden. In hundreds of letters, Nogarola defended Eve and maintained her sins and guilt to be less than those of Adam—contrary to the popular and traditional view that Eve's temptation of Adam was the cause of the expulsion. After her death the dialogue was published, along with her lone surviving poem, *Elegia de Laudibus Cyanei Ruris*, a eulogy praising the charms of the countryside.

Nostradamus
(1503–1566)

A French physician and prognosticator, whose fame as a Renaissance prophet has endured into modern times. "Nostradamus" is the Latin form of his given name, Michel de Nostredame. Born in the town of Saint Remy de Provence, the son of a grain dealer, he studied at the University of Avignon but left after a short time when a plague struck southern France and the university closed. He then studied medicine for a brief time at the University of Montpelier, which expelled him for engaging in the lowly craft of apothecary. Deciding on a career as a physician, he moved to Agen at the invitation of a celebrated Italian scholar and physician, Jules-Cesar Scaliger.

Nostradamus's brief training as a physician, his knowledge of medicines, and his assumed title of "Doctor" gained him a reputation as a healer. During an epidemic of plague in 1546–1547 he treated and cured many cases of the disease—so it was believed. In 1547, he settled in Salon de Provence, where his marriage to a wealthy widow provided him with the means to buy a comfortable house and write at his leisure. He made several voyages to Italy, a land that kindled his interest in the arts of magic and prophecy. In 1550, he began writing a yearly almanac, a calendar accompanied by prophecies written in the form of four-line verses known as quatrains. The almanacs found a large audience, and as his reputation spread people began calling on Nostradamus for his services as an astrologer and seer. He began collecting the quatrains separately and published them in *Le Propheties*, which first appeared in 1555 and in which the verses are grouped in sets of 100 known as a "century." With an ambition to publish 1,000 of his short and obscure poems, he published a second edition in 1557 and a third in 1558; all three surviving volumes of *Le Propheties* contain a grand total of 942 quatrains, all but one of them rhyming.

Nostradamus based his predictions on his own knowledge of the Bible, of historical events, of classical Latin authors such as Livy and Plutarch, on medieval historians such as Jean Froissart and seers such as Girolamo Savonarola, and on astrology. He sought to create a system of prediction based on the configuration of stars and planets as it would exist at some future point, and finding correspondences in that configuration to important events in the past.

In 1555, Nostradamus attracted the attention of Catherine de' Médicis, the queen of King Henri II. A prophecy concerning the royal family prompted her to summon him to Paris, where he cast the horoscopes of the king's children and where, in 1560, King Charles IX made him one of the royal physicians. Nostradamus's prophecies hinted at occult knowledge, but he was always careful to remain in the good graces of the church. One of the king's decrees demanded that he secure permission from the church before publishing his almanacs, and in 1561 he was tried, found guilty, and jailed for not heeding this order.

Nostradamus's legacy has endured through his own skill in predicting natural and man-made disasters in vague terms that are open to many interpretations. He has been credited with predicting the French Revolution, the campaigns of Napoléon, the rise of Adolf Hitler, the two world wars of the twentieth century, and the terrorist attacks of September 11, 2001. Believers unable to decipher his quatrains as corresponding to any specific event allow them to stand for an event that has not yet taken place. Many commentators view Nostradamus as a historian who wrote in verse rather than a "prophet"—a term he never used to describe himself—and believe he wrote in deliberately vague language in order to avoid persecution as a heretic or as an opponent of the French monarchy.

SEE ALSO: astrology

Ottoman Empire

The Ottoman Empire was established by Osman, a Turkish tribal leader who overthrew the Seljuk Turks in Anatolia in the late thirteenth century. The Ottoman armies crossed into the Balkan Peninsula in the middle of the fourteenth century and won crucial victories in the Battle of Kosovo in 1389 and the Battle of Nicopolis in 1396. In 1453, the Ottoman sultan Mehmed II extended Ottoman authority throughout Asia Minor and conquered Constantinople, the capital of the Byzantine Empire, thus destroying the last remnants of the Eastern Roman Empire.

Mehmed's successors, Selim I and Suleiman the Magnificent, who ruled from 1520 to 1566, brought the realm to the height of its power in southeastern Europe, the Levant, North Africa, and Mesopotamia. Suleiman reorganized the law and justice system of his realm and was a patron of the arts, literature, and Islamic scholarship, as well as a brilliant military leader. Under his leadership the Turks crushed a Hungarian army at the Battle of Mohacs in 1526, and then captured the capital of Buda in 1541, overthrowing the Hungarian ruling dynasty. Ottoman sultans ruled as caliph, or head of the entire

A map of the Ottoman Turkish empire in 1606, from the Mercator "Atlas." THE STAPLETON COLLECTION. REPRODUCED BY PERMISSION.

Islamic community. In the meantime, the Ottomans drove into Arabia and Persia, overthrew Mamluk dynasties in Syria and Egypt, and fielded the most powerful navy in the Mediterranean.

The Ottoman government controlled its far-flung domains through a system of vassalage, in which local rulers paid an annual tribute in gold or in goods in exchange for their limited independence. Ottoman's governors oversaw the administration of these territories, paying princely sums in bribery for their lucrative posts and exacting heavy taxes from the populace. During the Renaissance in Europe, the Ottoman Empire posed a most serious foreign threat to Europe's Christian states and rulers. The disunited Christian states, however, were unable to rally an effective striking force to counter Turkish control of the Balkans. The calls for further crusades to the east went unheeded, while in the 1530s the French king Francis I struck up an alliance with the sultan against the Habsburg dynasty. Ottoman armies arrived twice at the gates of Vienna, and Turkish corsairs raided European ports and shipping, taking treasure and slaves back to the Barbary Coast ports in North Africa. Piracy in the Mediterranean finally inspired a united effort on the part of the Habsburgs and Venetians, who gathered a powerful naval force and defeated the Ottoman navy at the Battle of Lepanto in 1571.

A decline began in the late seventeenth century. The succession to the throne, which was not limited to the eldest son of the sultan, brought about constant palace intrigue and frequent assassinations. Grand viziers governed the state and a military caste known as the Janissaries, who had originated as a company of Christian slaves converted to Islam and

trained as elite warriors, posed a constant threat to the sultan's authority, while the sultans themselves lived in luxury and indolence, completely cut off from their subjects and unable to exercise effective control over their domains. The last siege of Vienna was turned back in 1683, and in 1699 the Turks surrendered Hungary to the Habsburg dynasty. The empire grew weaker under a succession of corrupt and incapable rulers, and after long and expensive wars with Russia and the Habsburgs.

SEE ALSO: Fall of Constantinople; Mehmed II; Muslims

Ovid
(43 B.C.–178 A.D.)

Roman poet whose works were revived and widely admired during the Renaissance. Born Publius Ovidius Nao in the town of Sulmo, he was trained as a lawyer and educated by leading rhetoricians, who taught the craft of making persuasive and eloquent speeches. Ovid traveled widely as a young man but returned to Rome at the urging of his father. Finding the life of a public official not to his taste, Ovid began writing poetry and soon attracted notice and a circle of admirers. He collected his first short love poems into a volume called *Amores*, in which he wrote of an unattainable love by the name of Corinna, and some fictional letters into *Heroids*.

Metamorphoses is an epic written in fifteen books of hexameters, the same poetic form used by Virgil in his epic *The Aeneid*. Considered Ovid's masterpiece, *Metamorphoses* describes myths that have the common theme of physical transformation. The stories come from the Greeks as well as the Romans, from the time of the Creation down to Julius Caesar, the Roman general and statesman who was assassinated in the year before Ovid's birth. The poet skillfully revives the nearly forgotten mythologies of Greece and finds in them an endless source of beauty, cleverness, and profound philosophical truths.

Ovid's work *The Art of Love* was a parody of conventional love poems and a witty and biting portrayal of Roman aristocrats. The poem was widely admired in Rome but also criticized as a work of loose morality. It also brought him trouble with the emperor Augustus, who may have been infuriated by Ovid's revelation of misbehavior on the part of the emperor's granddaughter Julia. Augustus censored all of the poet's works and banished him to permanent exile in a distant Roman colony on the Black Sea in about A.D.8 (Julia was banished from Rome in the same year). Ovid spent the rest of his life writing complaints of his lonely exile in a boring frontier town, and sending petitions for a recall to Rome that were never granted.

The poetry of Ovid was held in high regard throughout the Middle Ages and the Renaissance. His elegant wit and sensuous writing, and his talent for storytelling, inspired writers as well as sculptors and painters, who illustrated many of his most famous themes and subjects. The leading writers of the Renaissance, including John Milton, Edmund Spenser, and William Shakespeare, freely borrowed Ovid's plots and incorporated Ovidian legends into their works.

SEE ALSO: classical literature; Virgil

painting

As the primary art associated with the Renaissance, painting reflects many of the most important discoveries, philosophies, and innovations of this historical period. The greatest artists of the period were painters, and their works have remained the most familiar Renaissance artifacts, especially in Italy. The most important aspect of Renaissance painting is the ideas the artworks expressed. It was seen as novel at the time for a scene on wood or canvas to carry the philosophy and personality of the artist. Artists emerged from obscurity and anonymity to become renowned individuals, and the works of the

The Renaissance saw major advances in the art of painting. Artists like Michelangelo Buonarroti used new techniques to produce masterpieces that are still familiar today, such as the "Creation of Adam" from his fresco on the ceiling of the Sistine Chapel in Rome.

best of them were sought after by collectors, monarchs, and nobles.

Painting in the Middle Ages was dominated by religion and familiar scenes from the Bible and Christian mythology. It was an art closely associated with architecture, as painting was a medium used most often for the decoration of church walls, ceilings, altars, doorways, and naves. In the early Renaissance, this tradition began to change, as artists began creating works intended to stand alone as works of art admired for the skill of the artist rather than for their function as an object of worship or religious instruction.

The humanism of the Renaissance left an important stamp on painting. Humanism passed over religious faith to seek out essential truths through rational investigation, deduction, and debate. Painters in the humanist tradition set pagan myths and philosophies on an equal footing with Christianity. They studied anatomy to arrive at a more accurate depiction of the human form, and developed the science of perspective to lend their painted scenes the illusion of three-dimensional reality. These new techniques were greatly helped by the invention of oil painting and the artist's easel, which enhanced the idea of the painting as a self-contained work of art. The greatest humanist monument of the Renaissance, however, was the immense frescoed ceiling of the Sistine Chapel, created by Michelangelo, which depicted biblical themes in the dramatic and monumental style of ancient classical sculpture.

Painters of the Renaissance usually trained as apprentices in the workshops of older, more experienced men. After serving their terms, many of them traveled in order to study, to discover classical architecture, or to view the works of their con-temporaries. An independent career as a painter, however, was still an impossibility for most, and painters eagerly sought the patronage of wealthy noblemen, kings, or popes in order to support themselves with well-paid commissions. Private citizens ordered portraits of themselves or their families; and had painters decorate the chambers of their homes. Prosperous cities asked artists to enhance their public buildings with frescoes and create interior murals celebrating their history.

The wealth earned through trade and banking made Florence a center of art patronage that had no rival in Europe. At the same time, ideas were spreading rapidly as communications improved and long-distance travel grew easier, and as printed books became available after the 1450s.

Leading Italian painters of the Renaissance include Masaccio, Paolo Uccello, Fra Angelico, Sandro Botticelli, Piero della Francesca, Leonardo da Vinci, Raphael, Michelangelo Buonarroti, Andrea Mantegna, Titian, Tintoretto, Paolo Veronese, the Bellini family, and Giorgione. Major painters of the Northern Renaissance, in England, the Low Countries, and Germany, included Albrecht Dürer, Lucas Cranach, Matthias Grünewald, Pieter Brueghel, and Hans Holbein. These painters were concerned with a precise rendering of natural detail, with the astonishing technique of the Dutch painter Jan van Eyck serving as their model. Religious imagery still played a strong role in art of the north.

In the late Renaissance, several Italian painters developed a new, "Mannerist" style in reaction to the naturalistic detail of leading painters such as Michelangelo, Raphael, and Leonardo. Mannerist paintings created crowded and elaborate scenes, exaggerated certain details of the human form, and tricked the observer's eye with techniques of perspective and optical illusions. Mannerism was meant not to convey a religious scene or classical myth, but to simply display the skill of the painter. It ended innovation in the Renaissance era and ushered in the new period of Baroque painting that would dominate European art for two centuries.

SEE ALSO: Bellini, Gentile; Bellini, Giovanni; Bellini, Jacopo; Botticelli, Sandro; Caravaggio, Michelangelo da; Fra Angelico; Giorgione; Grünewald, Matthias; Leonardo da Vinci; Masaccio; Michelangelo Buonarroti; Raphael; Titian

Palestrina, Giovanni Pierluigi da (1525–1594)

Italian composer born in the town of Palestrina, east of Rome. He began his musical career as a choirboy and organist, and in 1551 was appointed by Pope Julius II as director of the Julian Chapel at Saint Peter's in Rome. His reputation as a composer grew with Masses that he wrote for performance in Rome, where Dutch and French composers had once dominated the scene. He became musical director of the Roman Church of Santa Maria Maggiore from 1561 until 1566, and then served as a court musician for the d'Este family at their palace in Tivoli, in the hills north of Rome. He returned to Saint Peter's in 1571, and remained in the service of the popes for the rest of his life. Palestrina was commissioned by Pope Gregory XIII to return church music to the traditional style of plainchant, in which different voices sung melodies in unison. But he found himself poorly suited to this antique form of music and instead became one of the most skilled composers of polyphonic (multi part) music of the Renaissance. He wrote exclusively vocal music: Masses, motets, hymns, madrigals, and other sacred music that exhibited a complete mastery of the difficult craft of counterpoint (the balanced setting of two or more lines of music under very strict rules of harmony). He provided a model for Italian composers of sacred music for a century after his death and was also an important influence on the works of Johann Sebastian Bach. Palestrina remains a widely studied model for students of composition into the twenty-first century.

SEE ALSO: Byrd, William; Dowland, John; music

Palladio, Andrea (1508–1580)

Italian architect and writer who adopted classical motifs and style in his public and private buildings. Born in Padua as Andrea di Pietro della Gondola, he served as an apprentice to a stonecutter. He worked as a stone carver in Vicenza, where he was further trained by the scholar Giangiorgio Trissino, who gave him the nickname of "Palladio" after the Greek goddess Pallas Athena. Palladio began designing private homes in Vicenza and, in 1541 traveled to Rome, where he began studying the monuments of ancient Rome. When he returned to Vicenza, he began incorporating designs of Roman temples, baths, and monuments into the facades of buildings he designed.

In 1546 the city of Vicenza commissioned Palladio to renovate the Palazzo della Ragione, the city's law court. He surrounded the building with loggias, or walking passages covered by an arcade. With this work Palladio's reputation spread among the wealthy merchants and aristocrats of the Veneto region, which was prospering through trade within Venice's far-flung Mediterranean empire. In honor of its architect, the project, which was not completed until the early seventeenth century, came to be known as the Basilica Palladiana. Palladio wrote a guidebook to the antiquities of Rome, illustrated a Renaissance edition of the writings of the Roman architect Vitruvius, and founded an academy in Vicenza. His *Four Books on Architecture*, completed in 1570, is a complete account of techniques of architecture applied to private homes, religious buildings, and civic buildings.

Palladio is best known for private villas he designed in the Veneto, including the Villa Barbaro and the Villa Capra, an elegant symmetrical cube topped by a dome and displaying a temple front on each of its four sides. His elegant "Palladian" style combined ancient building elements and the Renaissance taste for the opulent display of wealth. Drawing on his discoveries in the ruins of ancient Rome, he employed classical columns, arches, pediments, atriums, and peristyles (courts), always careful to balance the different elements of a building and consider the structure's presence on its natural site. Palladian buildings exhibited the harmony and balance of the classical world. Palladio swept away the decorative Gothic style and set the standard for architecture for the next two centuries, when builders in Europe and the United States, including Thomas Jefferson, were imitating his style in structures large and small.

See Also: Alberti, Leon Battista; architecture; Bramante, Donato

Papacy

Since the time of the early Roman Empire, when the Christian faith was banned, the bishops of Rome exercised a wide-ranging authority over Christian believers, based on the establishment of the Roman church by the apostle Peter. After the fall of the western empire in the fifth century, the city of Constantinople became the seat of power of the eastern Roman (Byzantine) emperors, and the Christian bishops of that city challenged the authority of Rome. The popes of Rome sent missionaries to northern Europe to convert pagans to the new faith, a process that took five centuries through the early Middle Ages. In the meantime, the Eastern and Western Christian churches contended for centuries over doctrine and their respective authority in Europe, with a Great Schism occurring between the two in 1054. In the meantime, the popes of Rome were fighting the emperors of the Holy Roman Empire for control of Italy, with the popes wielding the power of excommunication over the emperors, who had large, multinational armies and allied Italian cities and states on their side.

The medieval Papacy was torn by its own inner conflicts and rivalries, leading to the "Babylonian Captivity" in which the popes moved from Rome to a palace in the city of Avignon in southern France. The schism within the Papacy, which at times was claimed to be led by three different men, and the worldliness of the church inspired a movement for reform and defiance of the pope's authority. Under the leadership of Jan Hus, Martin Luther, Huldrych Zwingli, and John Calvin, the Protestant Reformation sought a return to the early simplicity and purity of the Christian faith, and an end to the worldly power and wealth claimed by the popes and their representatives. In Rome, the papal court became a leading center for the patronage of artists, sculptors, scholars, and architects, and the Papacy grew wealthy from the system of tithing and the selling of indulgences—the pardoning of sins.

A Counter-Reformation began in the late Renaissance after several meetings of the Council of Trent, which set down new doctrine to be enforced by the members of the church. Making alliances with Catholic rulers, such as the Emperor Charles V, the popes sought to return Protestant lands to Catholicism, with mixed results. The popes claimed civic as well as religious authority in several principalities of central Italy, known as the Papal States. During the sixteenth century, the Papacy conquered many important cities of Italy and imposed direct rule over them. The power of the Papacy over even Catholic rulers declined after the Renaissance, until the Papal States were finally dissolved in the nineteenth century and the Papacy became a purely religious institution.

SEE ALSO: Alexander VI; Julius II; Papal States; Reformation, Protestant

Papal States

The states where the Catholic pope held direct "temporal" authority in central Italy, beginning in the middle of the eighth century, and where papal sovereignty ended with the unification of Italy in 1870. The fall of Rome in the fifth century left the popes as the strongest power in the city and its surrounding region. When Italy was under the threat of total conquest by the Lombards, Pope Stephen II sent for help from the Franks and their king Pepin the Short. The Franks invaded Italy despite the efforts by the eastern Roman (Byzantine) empire to establish rule over the peninsula and restore the empire. In 756, the Franks turned over territories under their control to the church, an event known as the Donation of Pepin. The domains of the popes expanded in the Middle Ages, to include Naples, Sicily, and Sardinia under Pope Sylvester I, and Tuscany in the early twelfth century. From 1305, the seat of the Papacy was in Avi-

gnon, France, and the Papal States fell under the authority of secular princes.

The restoration of the Papacy in Rome led to the expansion of papal authority in central Italy, beginning in the late fifteenth century. Pope Alexander VI sanctioned a campaign by his son Cesare Borgia to conquer these small principalities, which did not have effective defenses against Borgia's large and disciplined forces. Cities of the Romagna, a region centered in the valley of the Po River in northern Italy, and the Marches, along the central Adriatic coast, came directly under the pope's authority. The power of the Papacy was strengthened in the late Renaissance, after Pope Julius II and later popes abolished secular governments in several key cities, including Ferrara and Urbino. The Papal States remained independent of more powerful states that were emerging in the north (such as Venice and Tuscany) and the south (including Naples). In 1796 a French army under Napoléon Bonaparte, a determined opponent of the church's civic authority, invaded and disbanded the Papal States, which were restored for a last time in 1815. The last remnant of the Papal States is Vatican City, a small enclave in Rome that is the seat of the modern Catholic Church.

SEE ALSO: Italy; Julius II; Papacy

Paracelsus
(1493–1541)

Germany physician and alchemist who pioneered a new approach to treating illness, and helped usher medicine out of its medieval occultism and into the more rational scientific philosophies of the Renaissance. The son of a physician, his given name was Philippus Aureolus Theophrastus Bombast von Hohenheim. He was born and raised in the town of Einsiedeln in what is now Switzerland and spent several years wandering to the far corners of the known world to learn from philosophers, scientists, and doctors from Europe to Arabia and India. He studied in several universities, poring over the medical texts of the ancient writers and exploring the alchemical tracts of medieval writers. His studies and experiments led him to the conclusion that all matter derived from three basic substances—salt, sulfur, and mercury—that originated in a matter known as *mysterium arcanum*.

Paracelsus rejected the traditional practices of physicians, who in his day worked to rid the body of impurities through bleeding and purging. In his book *Archidoxis*, he explained his theory that certain essential qualities all derive from substances found in nature. He believed that philosophy, astronomy, alchemy, and virtue were all necessary to the work of a doctor, and that disease represented a malfunction of the body and not, as was traditional, the imbalance of the bodily humors. He elaborated his ideas in another major work, *Opus Paramirum*, or Work Beyond Wonder, which also explained the organs of the body as containing a guiding spirit that separated good qualities from bad. To cure disease, the physician needed to apply a substance manufactured from minerals, metals, or other compounds that was proper to the functioning of the diseased organ and could mimic the body's natural balancing action.

Paracelsus saw man as a microcosm of the universe, a being in which all the qualities found in nature had their counterparts on the human scale. The physical body, the soul, and an astral body were present, in which the latter spirit—which originated in the heavens—served as a blueprint for the form and function of all things and as an important link between the mind, the body, and the spiritual world. For this reason, the study of both human philosophy and scientific astronomy were needed for a physician to truly understand the workings and diseases of the body.

In 1524 Paracelsus became a lecturer and physician in the city of Basel, where his strange new ideas and his teaching in German instead of traditional Latin sparked bitter conflict with his physician rivals and quickly drove him from the city. In 1536 he published a handbook of surgery, *Der Grossen Wundartzney*. He died five years later under mysterious circumstances, with many historians believing that he was poisoned by rivals.

SEE ALSO: medicine

Parr, Catherine (1512–1548)

The sixth and last wife of King Henry VIII of England. She was born in Kendal, the daughter of Sir Thomas Parr, a court official. She married twice, the first time to Lord Edward of Borough. After his death, she married Baron John Neville, who died in 1543. Although she was drawing close to Thomas Seymour, the brother of the king's late wife Jane Seymour, Henry himself proposed marriage to her. His previous wife, Catherine Howard, had been executed on a charge of adultery, after which the enraged king's ministers and inner circle felt a great reluctance to propose any woman as his next consort. Parr was an acceptable candidate by the fact that she had been twice married already, and thus her chastity was not an issue as it would have been for an unmarried woman. She accepted the proposal despite her love for Thomas Seymour, and the sixth royal wedding of Henry's reign took place on July 12, 1543, at the palace of Hampton Court.

After his five marriages had ended in divorces or executions, Henry was growing stout, sickly, and extremely paranoid and fearful of cabals and conspiracies at court. In this troubled atmosphere Catherine helped tutor the king's two daughters, Mary and Elizabeth, who had grown estranged from their father. Catherine succeeded in softening Henry's intolerant attitude toward his daughters and possibly saving them from accusations of treason.

In the summer of 1544, Henry took the field for a campaign in France, appointing Parr as regent to rule England in his place. She carried out her duties with competence, attending to the finances of the realm and supplying Henry's armies with men, supplies, and provisions. The queen regent's ability greatly impressed the young Elizabeth, who looked to her stepmother as a model for her own management of England after she took the throne.

Parr's sympathies for the new reformed faith, however, made Catholic courtiers hostile to her, and their machinations with the king put her in danger. She was guilty of debating religious issues at court and encouraging commoners to read the Bible in an English version, an act that constituted defiance of the king as the supreme head of the church. An arrest warrant was issued but on the eve of being taken prisoner Catherine soothed the king's ego with submissive and penitent speeches; when palace guards arrived to take her prisoner the king angrily sent them away.

After the death of Henry in 1547, Catherine Parr carded the title of Dowager Queen of England and quickly married Thomas Seymour. She took a strong interest in the Reformation ideas then current on the continent, and commissioned an English translation of a work of Desiderius Erasmus. In the next year, however, she died of a fever shortly after giving birth to her first child, a daughter.

SEE ALSO: Elizabeth I; England; Henry VIII

Paul III
(1468–1549)

Pope of the Catholic Church from 1534 until his death in 1549. Born Alessandro Farnese in Canino, in the Latium region surrounding Rome, he was the scion of a wealthy family who was educated in Rome by humanist scholars and in Florence, where he was tutored at the court of Lorenzo de' Medici. He entered the service of the church but remained a devoted scholar of the classics and a friend to many of Europe's leading artists, writers, university professors, and collectors. In 1493, he was appointed a cardinal by Pope Alexander VI. He was ordained as a priest in 1519, but in the meantime had fathered four children, whose careers he was determined to advance through his position in the church. He became dean of the College of Cardinals and in 1534, after the death of Clement VII, was elected to the Papacy.

Paul III came to office at a time when the Catholic hierarchy was dealing with a spreading Protestant Reformation in northern Europe. To deal with the demands for reform of a church that many saw as corrupt and worldly, he appointed capable ministers and assembled a committee of nine church leaders to make recommendations for reform. One of his first important acts in office was to convene a general council at Mantua, but when German Protestants refused to attend, the pope canceled the council and waited nearly ten years to finally assemble the Council of Trent. He sent representatives to debate with Protestants in Regensburg, Germany, with the intention of reconciling

Protestant and Catholic branches of the Christian faith, with the eventual goal of bringing Protestants back under papal authority within the traditional church. To this end, he founded the Congregation of the Holy Office, also known as the Roman Inquisition, in order to try cases of heresy. During his tenure, the Society of Jesus, or Jesuits, was established in order to teach Catholic doctrine to students, carry out the Catholic Reformation in Europe, and enforce the church's missionary activities in the new colonies of Asia and the Americas. (For one, Paul decreed that Native Americans should not be taken as slaves.) Taking more direct action, Paul allied the Papacy with Emperor Charles V in his campaigns to smash the Schmalkaldic League of Protestant German princes.

Determined to return Rome to its role as a leading city of the arts and scholarship, Paul hired Michelangelo Buonarroti to paint the giant fresco known as *The Last Judgment* on a wall of the Sistine Chapel. Paul ordered the renovation of ancient monuments in Rome, such as the Castel Sant' Angelo and the Roman monuments of the Capitoline Hill. He was also responsible for the building of the massive Palazzo Farnese in central Rome, a magnificent Renaissance palace that currently houses the embassy of France. Like other Renaissance popes, however, Paul saw the Papacy as an opportunity to enrich and empower his close relatives, who received appointments in the church, land, and other property.

SEE ALSO: Paul IV; Reformation, Catholic; Reformation, Protestant

Paul IV (1476–1559)

Pope of the Catholic Church from 1555 until 1559. A zealous reformer of the church, Paul took the Papacy in a direction away from what he saw as the dangerous humanist secularism of the Renaissance. Born as Giovanni Carafa, in the town of Capriglio in the Campagna region, he belonged to a noble family that counted cardinals and high church officials among its members. He was trained in Latin and Greek but rejected the humanist teachings of the Renaissance, instead following the philosophies of medieval Scholasticism. He was ordained as a priest in 1505 and shortly afterward made bishop of the town of Chieti. He was appointed archbishop of Brindisi, a port town on the Adriatic Sea, in 1518, and in 1536 he was appointed as a cardinal. He became the archbishop of Naples in 1549 and in 1555 was elected pope as Paul IV.

Paul was a harsh disciplinarian who had poor relations with the Catholic rulers of Europe, including the Habsburg emperors and the king of Spain. He spared little effort in enforcing a strict and sweeping reform of the church. He had monks, priests, and cardinals tried for minor infractions and sentenced to prison and to slave galleys, and banished church officials from other towns who had taken up the easy court life in the city of Rome. He was fervently opposed to the presence of Jews in Rome and decreed in 1555 the building of the city's ghetto, a walled compound where Roman Jews were forced to live and work.

To prevent opposing opinion and heretical views from spreading to the public, he established in 1559 the *Index Librorum Prohibitorum*, or Index of Forbidden Books, a list of volumes (including all books and tracts written by Protestants) that were henceforth banned to Catholics. Paul had little regard for the work of general church councils, however, and failed to convene the Council of Trent, which still had unfinished business in the matter of reform and the reconciliation of Catholics and Protestants. When the Habsburg emperor Charles V agreed to the Peace of Augsburg that allowed Protestant princes to establish the faith of their choosing in their own domains, Paul threatened to depose the emperor and replace him with someone more loyal to the Catholic Church.

Paul carried out war against the Spanish king Philip II in 1556. The forces allied to the pope suffered a rout within a year, and the heavy burdens the war placed on the church, as well as his flagrant nepotism in appointing his relatives to high positions, made the pope widely unpopular. On his death in 1559, the people of Rome rioted to show their displeasure at his policies and burned the offices of the Roman Inquisition.

SEE ALSO: Index; Inquisition; Paul III; Reformation, Catholic

Pazzi Conspiracy

The Pazzi Conspiracy was an important event in the history of the city of Florence, a center of the Italian Renaissance. The name comes from a wealthy banking family of Tuscany who traced their lineage to a famous eleventh-century crusader, whose bold fighting style during a siege of Jerusalem earned him the nickname of "Pazzo" (the Madman). In honor of their illustrious ancestor, each year the Pazzi struck a light from a stone of the Basilica of the Holy Sepulchre on Holy Saturday, the day before Easter, to relight the altar candles in the Duomo, the cathedral of Florence.

At a time when the Medici family ruled Florence, the wealthy and ambitious Pazzi were striving to usurp the Medici and take control of the city for themselves. To this end, they allied with Pope Sixtus IV, who was at odds with the Medici over contested territory between the Papal States of central Italy and Tuscany, the region dominated by Florence. A loan from the Pazzi bank allowed the pope to purchase strategic land and cities in exchange for granting the Pazzi a monopoly on valuable mines. Furious by this arrangement, Lorenzo de' Medici took his revenge by thwarting the pope's efforts to appoint Francesco Salvati, an ally of the Pazzi, as an archbishop in Tuscany.

With the pope's connivance, the Pazzi then allied with Salvati and Girolamo Riario, the pope's nephew, to kill Lorenzo and his brother Giuliano de' Medici during Sunday services in the Duomo. Federigo da Montefeltro, the Duke of Urbino, was brought into the plot and promised to bring a company of six hundred men to Florence in support of the Pazzi. During the solemn singing of Mass on the appointed day, April 26, 1478, a group of men fell on Giuliano de' Medici and brutally stabbed him to death, while his brother escaped to the sacristy of the church. Unable to reach Lorenzo through a locked door, the conspirators left the Duomo and then attempted to capture the Signoria (town hall) of Florence. They were captured by an angry mob of Florentine citizens and immediately lynched. Salviati himself was hanged from the wall of the Signoria, an execution captured in a famous sketch by Leonardo da Vinci. In revenge for the killing of the archbishop, the pope forbade Mass to be held in Florence, and enlisted the king of Naples to attack the city. Lorenzo de' Medici, however, voyaged to Naples to surrender himself to the king and dissuade him from this plan. The conspiracy resulted in the exact opposite of what it intended, laying low the Pazzi dynasty in Florence and inspiring widespread support of Medici rule in Florence.

SEE ALSO: Medici, Lorenzo de'

Peasants War

A rebellion that lasted from 1524 to 1525 in German-speaking domains of the Holy Roman Empire. The revolt originated in opposition to the heavy burdens of taxes and duties on the German serfs, who had no legal rights and no opportunity to improve their lot. These conditions had sparked conflict in the fifteenth century, but these uprisings remained local and contained. A more widespread rebellion was finally sparked in the 1520s by the movement for reform in the Catholic Church, and the social and political upheavals that the Protestant Reformation caused. With the authority of church prelates challenged by Martin Luther and others, the peasants saw their cause supported by the Protestant emphasis on individual faith. Empowered in their religious views, and pressed by crop failures that threatened starvation, they saw an opportunity to overthrow the feudal system, in which they were bound to the estates of the nobles and forced to give up the produce of the fields in which they worked.

The revolt began in the summer of 1524 in the county of Stühlingen, in the region of Upper Swabia near the border of Germany and Switzerland. It spread quickly in southern and western Germany, and as far as Switzerland and Austria. In the spring of 1525, there were five large bands of peasants roaming the countryside, burning homes of nobles and princes, and bringing townspeople over to their side. The peasants sought relief from heavy taxes, an end to serfdom, fair trials, and an end to the taxes they owed on the death of a member of their families. They set down these demands in a document known as the Twelve Articles. The rebels seized the town of Heilbronn, where they formed a parliament, as well as Würtzburg, the seat of a Catholic bishop. In Thuringia, the rebels were led by Thomas Muntzer, a fiery Protestant leader.

Poor townspeople and urban artisans joined the rebellion, which also won the support of Huldrych Zwingli, a prominent Protestant leader, but was opposed by Martin Luther. In the meantime, an army of the Swabian League gathered and marched north into Franconia, in central Germany, defeating the peasants in battle at Frankenhausen and Königshofen. About one hundred thousand combatants and civilians were killed before the fighting died down in late 1525, while the armies of the opposition carried out deadly reprisals for the next two years. Small local rebellions continued into the next year in Austria, but the defeat of the peasants in Germany brought a complete repudiation of their demands for a more just economic system. The discontent of the peasants would continue through the sixteenth and early seventeenth century, adding to the bitter conflicts between Protestant and Catholic territories that would finally erupt into the Thirty Years' War in the early 1600s.

SEE ALSO: Reformation, Protestant; Thirty Years' War

perspective

Although the classical Greek and Roman world was widely admired and imitated in the Renaissance, the art of antiquity was surpassed in several technical aspects by later artists. One of the most important advances was made in the science of perspective. The artists of the classical world attempted in vain to accurately portray three-dimensional space on their wall paintings, while medieval artists had depicted scenes and figures on a flat plane, with no attempt to create an illusion of depth. The techniques of perspective were finally developed in Italy in the early Renaissance, in the work and the writings of several Italian artists. "Linear perspective" makes use of a single vanishing point, toward which objects appear to grow smaller and the lines of structures and surroundings appear to converge.

The basic principles of this system were discovered by the Florentine architect Filippo Brunelleschi in the early fifteenth century. While observing the Baptistery, an octagonal structure near the cathedral of Florence, Brunelleschi painted the structure directly onto a mirror, then held up a second blank mirror in order to verify that his painted version was an exact replica. He then carefully analyzed and measured his painting to discover the underlying mathematical principles that governed perspective. The Baptistery instructed Brunelleschi in the use of a vanishing point and the horizon line, where the lines of different planes and objects converged.

Brunelleschi published his findings to be used by other artists, and Renaissance painting took on the most important aspect of its naturalistic, lifelike quality. Paolo Uccello, another artist of Florence, used perspective with surprising effect on his mural *The Battle of San Romano*, where horses, weapons, and human figures all serve to emphasize lines of perspective and the vanishing point. The science of perspective was further explored in *Della Pittura*, a work by Leon Battista Alberti, who offered precise mathematical formulas for the use of artists. Later artists developed new systems of perspective, including aerial perspective, in which objects go out of focus and appear in a bluish light with

greater distance. Leonardo da Vinci put aerial perspective to use in *The Virgin of the Rocks*, in which a sense of great depth and mystery is achieved by the rendering of the natural landscape as well as the contours of the figures.

SEE ALSO: painting

Perugino
(1450–1523)

Italian painter whose style expressed classical ideals of balance and harmony, and whose works made him an important forerunner of the High Renaissance style of Italian art. Nicknamed for the town of Perugia, he was born in the Umbrian town of Citta della Pieve as Pietro di Cristoforo Vannucci. He studied painting as a boy with the leading masters of Perugia, then left for Florence, where he apprenticed with Piero della Francesca and, as a fellow pupil of Leonardo da Vinci, with Andrea del Verrocchio. Two of his early works are *The Miracle of St. Bernardino* and *The Adoration of the Magi*. He joined the confraternity of Saint Luke, a painters guild, in the early 1470s. In 1479 he was summoned to Rome by Pope Sixtus IV and in 1481 completed a commission to assist in the decoration of the Sistine Chapel in Rome. His work for the famous chapel included *The Baptism of Christ, Moses and Zipporah*, and *Christ Giving the Keys to St. Peter*, a painting noted for its expansive open spaces and idealized, symmetrical architecture. The careful composition and harmony of the poses give this and other works of Perugino a sense of philosophical dignity and calm, ideals to which artists of the later High Renaissance would strive. Unfortunately, the paintings covered the section of wall that would later carry *The Last Judgment* of Michelangelo Buonarroti, and would be destroyed in order for Michelangelo to carry out his design.

In 1486, after the Sistine Chapel commission ended, Perugino moved to Florence, where he completed several major works in which human figures are artfully placed in a setting of classical architecture to achieve a sense of symmetry and serenity. These works include *The Vision of St. Bernard* and a *tondo*, or circular painting, entitled *The Madonna Enthroned with Saints*, both painted in the mid-1490s, as well as a *Crucifixion* painted for the Santa Maria Maddalena dei Pazzi in Florence. Perugina established a thriving workshop in Florence but found his work coming under criticism in the city's highly charged and competitive atmosphere. Sometime around 1496 he moved back to Perugia, where he remained for the rest of his life. He completed an altarpiece, *The Ascension*, for the Church of San Pietro and in 1497 he began work on a fresco series in the Audience Hall of Perugia's Collegio del Cambio, the guild hall of the city's bankers. Historians consider two of Perugino's designs, *The Nativity* and *The Transfiguration*, to be among the finest examples of his work, showing a mastery of composition and architectural perspective. The walls also carry a variety of portraits of Greeks and Romans, depictions of the cardinal virtues, and a self-portrait; historians believe that the younger Raphael, at the time Perugino's apprentice, may have helped him complete the work.

Perugino won several commissions from the aristocratic patrons, including Isabella d'Este, for whom he painted *The Triumph of Chastity*. He was still unsuccessful in winning the respect of his peers, however, and on one occasion had his ability insulted by Michelangelo himself. Unsuccessfully suing Michelangelo for belittling his character, Perugino responded with *The Madonna and Saints*, a multi-paneled altarpiece completed in the Certosa of Pavia. He returned to Rome on the invitation of Pope Julius II in 1508 to paint sections of the Stanza dell'Incendio del Borgo in the Vatican, but found his own paintings overlooked for the masterpieces of his pupil, Raphael. Finally returning to Perugia in 1512, he completed frescoes for the Church of Madonna delle Lacrime in Trevi and for the monastery of Sant' Agnese in Perugia. He died during a plague epidemic in 1524.

SEE ALSO: painting; Raphael; Verrocchio, Andrea del

Petrarch
(1304–1374)

Italian poet and scholar who idealized the classical world and introduced a new, humanist sensibility to the secular literature of Italy. Born in Arezzo, in Tuscany, he was the son of a notary of Florence who had been exiled from the city. In 1312, the family moved to Avignon, the city of southern France that was serving as the seat of the Catholic popes. He studied at the University of Montpellier, also in France, and the University of Bologna, where he trained as a lawyer. His interest in poetry was strongly discouraged by his father, who on one occasion seized and burned several volumes of ancient Latin authors found in his son's possession.

After the death of his father Petrarch gave up the study of law and returned to Avignon. In 1330 he joined the household of Cardinal Giovanni Colonna, a member of an aristocratic Roman family. Granted the freedom to travel and study, Petrarch journeyed to France, Germany, and the Low Countries in 1333, searching in churches, libraries, and monasteries for forgotten classical manuscripts. He began writing poetry and in 1342 produced a set of sonnets and *canzoni* (songs) in a volume entitled *Canzoniere*, a collection that would grow to nearly four hundred poems in a variety of forms—sonnets, ballads, and madrigals—through several later revisions. In his early works Petrarch describes a mysterious and distant love, Laura, whom he had first seen in 1327 in Avignon's Church of Saint Clare. Although his love was unrequited, the figure of Laura would haunt Petrarch's poems and letters for the rest of his life.

As his family was not wealthy, and he had no interest in public life or a career in the law, Petrarch took the vow of Holy Orders as a young man. His work as a representative and diplomat for Cardinal Colonna allowed him the freedom and the income to pursue his true interest: classical scholarship. He was one of the first medieval writers to closely study the ancient Roman authors and take these pagan writers seriously as a model for his own works and philosophy. In the late 1330s he was living the life of a hermit in the mountainous region of Vaucluse, in the French Alps, where he began working on scholarly and historical works, including the epic poem *Africa* on the career of the Roman general Scipio Africanus. In the meantime, the poems of *Canzoniere* won renown throughout Europe. In 1341, Petrarch was crowned as a poet laureate in Rome, becoming the first writer to enjoy this honor since the time of the Roman Empire.

Still in the service of the cardinal, Petrarch was sent on a mission to Naples in 1343. On his return to France, he traveled through Verona, where he discovered unknown letters of Cicero in the library of the cathedral. Transcribing the manuscripts, he deliberated on a collection of his own letters as a personal testament to his life and philosophy. Returning to Vaucluse, he wrote a biographical work, *De Vita Solitaria* (Of the Solitary Life). In the late 1340s the Black Death struck Europe, eventually killing many of Petrarch's friends and acquaintances, including Laura, the love of his life, as well as Cardinal Colonna and Petrarch's son Giovanni. The plague inspired *The Triumph of Death*, which he followed with *The Triumph of Love* and *The Triumph of Chastity*.

Although he had achieved fame as a scholar and poet, Petrarch found himself uninterested in the status or profit that would come with an important appointment. He turned down several offers of high posts in the Catholic Church and as a professor at the University of Avignon. Instead, he lived in Milan, where he enjoyed the patronage of Giovanni Visconti, the ruler of the city, and then in the city of Padua, where he also had the patronage of a nobleman and where he built a country house in which to live out his years.

Petrarch's important works in Latin include *On Contempt for the Worldly Life*, *Metrical Epistles*, *On Solitude*, and the *Eclogues*. He was the first author to find inspiration in Christian piety as well as classical scholarship; his life was devoted to balancing the intellectual life of a scholar and the spiritual pursuits of a man of the church. This outlook had great influence on other writers of Italy and Europe and looked forward to the humanism of Renaissance art and scholarship.

SEE ALSO: Dante Alighieri; humanism

Philip II
(1527–1598)

King of Spain from 1556 to 1598. Born in Valladolid, he was the son of Isabella of Portugal and Charles V, ruler of the Holy Roman Empire as well as Spain, southern Italy, Sicily, the Low Countries, and Spain's

Phillip II, King of Spain.

colonies in the Americas. Charles named Philip his regent in Spain in 1543, when he also arranged his son's marriage to Maria of Portugal, who died giving birth to Philip's first son, Don Carlos, in 1545. Charles then arranged the marriage of Philip to Mary, the daughter of King Henry VIII of England, in 1554. He also made his teenage son the nominal ruler in the duchy of Milan, the Franche-Comte, Sicily, and Naples before abdicating all of his titles, leaving the Holy Roman Empire in the name of his brother Ferdinand I. Raised and tutored as a devout Catholic, Philip found the largely Protestant nation of England hostile and uncongenial, and returned to Spain in 1555. For the rest of his life, Philip remained within the borders of his kingdom, having little interest in following his father's example of frequent travel through far-flung domains.

At the start of Philip's reign, Spain was involved in open warfare with France, a brewing rebellion in the Low Countries,

and threats to Spanish trade and shipping in the Mediterranean from North African pirates and the navy of the Ottoman Empire. Although England had allied with Spain in the war against France, the campaign turned into a pointless stalemate and was finally ended by the Treaty of Cateau-Cambresis in 1559, which was followed by Philip's marriage to Elizabeth of Valois, the daughter of the king of France. The succession was thrown into doubt when Philip's son Don Carlos showed himself unfit to inherit the throne; when evidence came to light implicating Don Carlos was plotting against Philip, the king had him arrested. Don Carlos died under mysterious circumstances in 1568, and may have been executed on Philip's orders.

In 1571 Philip joined a grand alliance, including Venice and the Papacy, that defeated the navy of the Ottoman Empire at the Battle of Lepanto, off the western coast of Greece. But in the Low Countries, Philip badly miscalculated the determined opposition of Protestant towns and nobles against rule by Catholic Spain. By raising taxes, imposing Catholic prelates, and disregarding the authority of local councils, his policies inspired a full-scale revolt. The occupation of the Low Countries would end badly for Spain, as the northern Protestant countries ultimately won independence as the United Provinces (the modern Netherlands).

Philip's rivalry with Elizabeth, the queen of England who had spurned his offer of marriage, prompted him to assemble a massive fleet, known as the Spanish Armada, for a full-scale assault on the English coast. He ordered the ships to link with Spanish troops in the Low Countries, with the mission of disrupting England's support for the Protestant rebels and, ultimately, the Catholic conquest of England itself. In 1588 the Armada sailed to the

British Isles but was defeated by storms and by the skilled English captains who had the advantage of lighter and more maneuverable ships.

Philip did have success in Portugal, where after the death of the childless King Henry, he pressed a claim to the monarchy through his mother, Isabella of Portugal. Spanish armies invaded Portugal and the country was annexed to Spain in 1580. Spanish colonists built outposts in Florida and in the Philippines, an archipelago named for the king. Philip also oversaw the building of the Escorial, a royal palace near Madrid, where he spent most of his time. Although he had raised a splendid monument to the wealth and power of the Spanish monarchy, he had emptied Spain's treasury with the many foreign wars, and the expense of the ill-fated Spanish Armada. Income from the American colonies dwindled, Philip's taxes remained a heavy burden on the people, and farmers suffered a series of droughts and poor harvests. After his reign Spain entered a period of slow decline from which it would never completely recover.

SEE ALSO: Charles V; Spanish Armada

Pico della Mirandola, Giovanni (1463–1494)

Italian scholar and philosopher, whose writings became the most important philosophical testaments of Renaissance humanism. Born into a noble family, the son of the Count of Mirandola and Concordia, he was a precocious young student of Latin and Greek, and left home for Bologna at the age of fourteen to study canon law, the law of the church. He gave up this coursework and moved to Ferrara, where he studied philosophy, and then to the University of Padua, where he studied the teachings of the ancient Greek thinkers

Plato and Aristotle. In Florence he met Angelo Poliziano and the monk Girolamo Savonarola, who would later establish a puritanical dictatorship over the city. In 1485 Pico journeyed to Paris, where he took part in lively scholarly debates over the nature of philosophy and the teachings of the medieval Scholastics. After returning to Italy, he was soon embroiled in a scandal after abducting the wife of a member of the Medici clan, the powerful ruling house of Florence. He was arrested and thrown into prison, but eventually saved from execution by Lorenzo de' Medici, whose friendship and patronage he had won in Florence.

Pico's studies in Italy and Paris had led him to the conclusion that it was possible to discover the underlying agreements of Plato, Aristotle, and all the medieval religious philosophers—Christian, Muslim, and Jewish—and bring these competing schools of thought into harmony. He wrote out a series of *900 Conclusions*, which was published in 1486 and which he intended to defend in a grand conclave of the best scholars of his day.

As an introduction to the *900 Conclusions*, Pico wrote his famous essay *Oration on the Dignity of Man*. But his plans for a council of scholars, before which he would defend the points of his work, were blocked on the orders of Pope Innocent VIII, who appointed a church council that studied and rejected most of Pico's arguments. When Pico responded with his *Apology*, which in large part defended his original arguments, the pope responded by denouncing his entire body of work. Sensing danger in the church's formal disapproval of his thinking, and the pope's accusations of heresy, Pico fled Italy for Paris, but was arrested in France on the orders of the pope's representatives and imprisoned in the fortress of Vincennes, near Paris. Eventually he was released He received the protection of Lorenzo de' Medici, who settled him in an estate near the village of Fiesole, where he wrote another controversial tract, *Heptaplus, A Sevenfold Account of the Six Days of Genesis*. In 1493 he received a formal pardon from Pope Alexander VI for his transgressions against orthodox church doctrine. During this period he also wrote *Disputations Against Divinatory Astrology*, which attacked the precepts of astrology. When Girolamo Savonarola took control of Florence and decreed the destruction of works of art, philosophical writings, and all other worldly vanities, Pico surrendered his money and property and burned all of the poetry he had written. He did not take monastic vows, however, and died in 1494 of a sudden illness, brought on in the opinion of some historians by poison. On the day of his death, King Charles VIII of France entered Florence and overthrew the Medici dynasty.

SEE ALSO: Medici, Lorenzo de'; Savonarola, Girolamo

Piero della Francesca (1415–1492)

Italian painter and a master of the early Renaissance. The son of a shoemaker, who died before he was born, he grew up in the small village of Borgo San Sepolcro near the Tuscan town of Arezzo. He moved to Florence to train as a painter and helped older painters with the decoration of several churches in that city. He worked for a noble patron, Sigismondo Malatesta, for whom he painted a famous portrait, as well as for the pope in Rome. He spent much of his adulthood in the town of San Sepolcro and Arezzo, where he was hired to paint the choir of the church of San Francesco, where he painted a famous fresco cycle known as the *The Legend of the True Cross*, which was inspired by traditional legends surrounding the cross on which Christ was crucified. The orderly arrangement of figures give these pictures a sense of calm rationality, a new sensibility that made a break with traditions of Gothic painting and its direct appeal to the emotions. *The Flagellation*, a renowned work of the early Renaissance, presents three mysterious figures in the foreground over whom art historians have been arguing for five centuries.

For the Duke of Urbino, Federigo da Montefeltro, Piero completed a double portrait of the duke and his wife, as well as a famous altarpiece, *Madonna with Saints and Donor*. Piero's great skill and knowledge of mathematics and linear geometry allowed him to construct masterful paintings with the use of foreshortening and perspective, which gives a three-dimensional appearance to the flat surface of a painting. He wrote a treatise, *De Prospectiva Pingendi*, on the art of perspective, and works on mathematics, including *Treatise on the Abacus*, in which he covered the subjects of geometry, algebra, and the problems of perspective.

SEE ALSO: Montefeltro, Federigo da

Piero di Cosimo (1462–1521)

Italian painter. Born in Florence, where he lived his entire life, he trained in the workshop of Cosimo Rosselli, whose name he took as his own (his given name was Piero di Lorenzo). In 1482 Cosimo traveled to Rome with Rosselli to assist in the painting of the Sistine Chapel. There Cosimo painted a landscape background for Rosselli's fresco of *The Sermon on the Mount*.

Cosimo specialized in painting scenes from classical mythology, such as *The Death of Procris*. His vivid imagination inspired the creation of original figures, half human and half animal, set in a naturalistic landscape and serving as symbolic representations of ideas and emotions. Inspired by the ancient Roman writer Vitruvius, Cosimo painted imaginary scenes from a time when the human race led a simpler existence; these works include *Hunting Scene, Return from the Hunt, Discovery of Honey*, and *Discovery of Wine*. Such works, which were painted outside the tradition of religious painting, came under official disapproval during the reign of the fanatic Dominican monk Girolamo Savonarola in Florence. Cosimo reacted by taking up Christian subjects, including *The Immaculate Conception* and *The Holy Family*. Cosimo also was well known in Florence as a portrait painter, with his most famous work in this vein being the *Portrait of Simionetta Vespucci*, a picture of the mistress of Giuliano de' Medici. He also trained many of the best Florentine artists of his time, including Andrea del Sartro.

SEE ALSO: Florence; Sartro, Andrea del; Savonarola, Girolamo

piracy

Piracy on the open seas dates back millennia, and was a common plague of merchant shipping in ancient Greece and Rome. Through the Middle Ages, Mediterranean pirates commonly hijacked cargoes as well as individuals, selling them into slavery or holding them for ransom. With small or nonexistent navies, weak central governments could do very little to suppress piracy. In the sixteenth century, with the rise of the Ottoman Empire, piracy in the Mediterranean posed even greater dan-

gers. These corsairs, or Barbary Coast pirates, had been operating for centuries using fast, shallow-drafted ships that could outrun any large warship, and take shelter in bays or rivers where military ships could not go. Piracy was an important industry in Tunis, Algiers, and other Barbary Coast cities, where syndicates of wealthy investors sponsored voyages and divided the profits as well as hostage ransoms. The corsairs posed a constant threat to coastal towns in Sicily, Spain, and the southern coasts of Italy, and even raided in the Atlantic Ocean as far north as Iceland. Their piracy was often supported by ruling sultans, who protected the corsairs in port and built holding cells for hostages, who at one point numbered tens of thousands in the city of Algiers.

At the same time, piracy was spreading to the Caribbean and the Atlantic as new colonies were founded in the Americas, and treasure fleets transporting gold to Europe presented tempting targets. As nations competed for colonies and resources, the European monarchies began sponsoring pirates called privateers to undertake raids against the ships of their rivals. One of the most successful was Sir Francis Drake, commissioned a privateer by Queen Elizabeth I of England. Drake raided Spanish ports in the Caribbean and California, and fought in the queen's service during the campaign of the Spanish Armada in 1588.

The buccaneers, as they were also known after the French cooking grill known as a *boucan*, were hired by the governments of England, the Netherlands, and France for the purpose of harassing Spanish shipping to and from Spain's American colonies. The buccaneers formed a powerful military faction in the Caribbean region, and established protected bases in the Bahamas, Tortuga, Jamaica, and later Panama. Under Henry Morgan, pirate bands captured the major cities of Spanish-held Panama, including Portobelo and the city of Panama, a crucial link in the transportation of silver and gold from the Andes region to Spain. Their ranks were often increased by mutineers from British military ships, who escaped a miserable and dangerous existence for the chance to share in captured gold and loot.

Piracy also thrived in Asian waters. The Chinese pirate Pinyin Zheng Zhilong, after leaving the service of the Portuguese at Macau, raided Dutch shipping in the East Indies. Cheng Ch'eng Kuon seized the entire island of Formosa from the Portuguese, using it as a base for a long campaign of piracy in the South China Sea—a region that remains a dangerous hotbed of piracy in the twenty-first century.

Pirckheimer, Willibald (1470–1530)

German author and humanist, and patron of Albrecht Dürer and other leading German artists of the city of Nuremberg. He was born in Eichstätt, a town in the southern state of Bavaria, and studied law in Italy as a young man. His experience in Italy brought him into contact with the humanism of the Renaissance, in which scholars were studying the ancient writers and inspiring a rebirth of art and philosophy. His abilities crossed many different fields, and brought him the notice of the Holy Roman Emperor. In 1499 Pirckheimer commanded a company of infantry in the Swabian War between the emperor and the independence-minded Swiss.

After his return to Germany, Pirckheimer had settled in Nuremberg, where he became a prosperous lawyer and a leading public official, a man of letters and, notably, the patron of Dürer. Pirckheimer gathered one of the largest personal libraries in Germany and translated ancient Greek and Latin books, including the *Geography* of the astronomer Ptolemy, into German. He wrote influential essays on art, humanistic thinking, and on the various controversies dividing the Protestant church. As a close friend of Dürer, he helped the artist make important journeys to Italy, where Dürer came under the influence of Italian Renaissance art and philosophy.

SEE ALSO: Dürer, Albrecht

Pisanello (ca. 1395–1455)

Italian artist of the early Renaissance, known for portraits, frescoes, and for medals he designed to commemorate important people and events. Born as Antonio Pisano in Pisa, he was the son of Pucio di Giovanni and Isabetta Giovanni, who raised him in Verona after the death of his father. He was trained as an artist in Verona in the studio of Stefano di Verona, an artist whose strong influence can be seen in an early work of Pisanello's called *Madonna of the Quails*. By 1415 he was working as an assistant to Gentile da Fabriano, who had a strong influence on his style. The two artists completed frescoes for the Grand Council Hall in the palace of the Doge in Venice. According to the Renaissance historian Giorgio Vasari, Pisanello also made a close study of the work of Paolo Uccello, and learned from him the art of drawing and painting horses. While employed by the Gonzaga family, the rulers of Mantua, Pisanello completed the *Annunciation*, a fresco for the Church of San Fermo. In the Pellegrini Chapel of the Church of Sant' Anastasia he painted *Saint*

George and the Princess of Trebizond; in the ducal palace of Mantua he painted *Scenes of War and Chivalry*. These are the only frescoes Pisanello completed that have survived to the present day.

Pisanello moved to Rome in later years and completed frescoes in the Basilica of Saint John Lateran that had been left unfinished by Gentile da Fabriano on his death. He returned to Verona in 1432 and spent the rest of his life traveling from one aristocratic court to the next, seeking patronage and enjoying a reputation as one of the most skilled painters in Italy. In Florence, he completed portraits of the emperor Sigismund and a *Portrait of a Man*. In the city of Ferrara he painted two famous works, *Portrait of Lionello d'Este* and *Madonna with Saints Anthony and George*.

Pisanello is known for his skillful drawings and his rendering of clothes, hats, fabric, and elegant costumes. He was also skilled at drawing animals, birds, and from nature, a talent he shared with Paolo Uccello. In 1439, he designed a medal for the Byzantine emperor John VII Paleologus, who was in Italy to attend the Council of Ferrara. He was renowned for his skill at designing and casting medals. Rather than stamping the medals with a press, which was the traditional method, he cast them from bronze and created the designs and portraits in relief, in which the design emerges from the flat surface of the surrounding material. He cast other commemorative medals for Filippo Visconti, Francesco Sforza, King Alfonso V of Naples, Sigismondo Malatesta, the ruler of Rimini, and for the wedding of Lionello d'Este and Maria of Aragon.

SEE ALSO: Uccello, Paolo

Pius II
(1405–1464)

Pope from 1458 to 1464, a determined opponent of the conciliar movement and the Ottoman Turks. Born as Eneo Piccolomini in Corsignano, in Tuscany, he was the son of a poor noble, Silvio de Piccolomini. He attended the University of Siena and in Florence, where he learned classical languages and literature. While later studying law in Siena, a bishop invited him to join him at the Council of Basel, where he remained for several years. He served several bishops as a secretary and by 1435 was working for Cardinal Albergati, who sent him on a secret diplomatic mission to Scotland. On returning to the city of Basel, he won a seat on the council, which was negotiating to end the schism in the church, and won appointment to several ceremonial posts. His enjoyment of life's more sensual pleasures prevented him from taking the vows of the clergy, however. He favored study of the classics and writing poetry, and in 1442 was named an official poet laureate by Emperor Frederick III, who also appointed him to a position at the imperial court in Vienna. Piccolomini wrote novels, verse, and plays, but in search of a more secure life he finally agreed to join the church.

In 1445 Piccolomini traveled to Rome and in the next year was ordained as a deacon. He was appointed as the bishop of Trieste in 1447 and in 1450 bishop of Siena. Frederick sent him on important diplomatic missions, while Pope Calixtus III also rewarded his service with an appointment as a cardinal in 1456. Piccolomini used his appointments to gather benefices—profitable estates and property— and soon grew wealthy.

In 1458, he succeeded Calixtus III as pope, taking the name of Pius after the phrase "pius Aeneas" in the poetry of Virgil. After the Fall of Constantinople in 1453, he was determined to face down the threat of invasion of Europe by the Ottoman Turks. In 1459, the first year of his reign, he summoned the rulers of Europe to a congress in Mantua to plan a campaign against the Turks. The princes gathered at the congress were reluctant to coordinate their forces, however, and Pius's attempt to gather armies and money for a campaign against the Turks came to nothing. Pius believed the councils at Basel and elsewhere had contributed to a decline in the authority of the Papacy, and became a powerful advocate against the conciliar movement. He issued the bull Execrabilis in 1460 that condemned the councils and proclaimed that anyone appealing to a council as an authority higher than the pope would be excommunicated from the church.

Pius still was determined to fight the Turks, personally if necessary. He gathered an army of crusaders and led them across the mountains of central Italy to the port of Ancona, on the Adriatic Sea. Already ill and his body weakened through the many years of sensual pleasures before he joined the church, he died in Ancona before the crusade could set out.

See Also: Council of Basel; Fall of Constantinople

Pizarro, Francisco (1476–1541)

Spanish conquistador who subdued the Incan Empire of the South American Andes and founded Peru as a colony of Spain. Born in Trujillo, Estremadura, a poverty-stricken region of western Spain, he was the son of a poor farmer. Like many young men with few prospects in the kingdom, he saw the discoveries of

Francisco Pizarro. © Archive Photos, 530 W. 25th Street, New York, NY 10001.

Christopher Columbus and those who followed to the New World as an opportunity for riches, glory, and status. In 1510, he joined an expedition to Colombia led by Alonso de Ojeda. In 1513, he accompanied Vasco Nunez de Balboa on his expedition across the Isthmus of Panama, when Balboa became the first European to sight the Pacific Ocean. After arresting Balboa on the orders of Pedrarias de Avila, Pizarro settled in Panama on an estate granted to him.

Convinced that an opportunity for great wealth lay in the undiscovered regions to the south, Pizarro joined with Diego de Almagro and a priest, Fernando de Luque, and set off for the western coasts of South America. The two undertook journeys of exploration in 1524 and 1526. He returned to Spain in 1528 and won the commission of Emperor Charles V to found a new colony in South America. Accompanied by several members of his family, he set out again in 1530 with a force of 180 men, including 4 members of his own family, and landed at Tumbes, on the Pacific coast of South America. Pizarro marched from the coast to the Incan capital of Cajamarca. Weakened by civil war and a struggle between competing factions for the monarchy, the Incans were unable to mount an effective resistance against the invaders. After agreeing to negotiate with the Incan emperor, Atahuallpa, Pizarro took the ruler captive. Atahuallpa bargained for his freedom by promising the Spaniards an entire room full of gold, but on delivery of the ransom, Pizarro had Atahuallpa executed. A Spanish force under Diego Almagro captured the ancient capital of Cuzco, effectively overthrowing the Incan Empire, and in 1535 Pizarro founded the colonial capital of Lima.

Rivalry broke out among the founders of the colony established by Pizarro. Almagro, feeling cheated by the division of spoils ordered by Pizarro, seized Cuzco and war broke out. In 1538, Almagro was captured after losing the Battle of Salinas, and Pizarro ordered his execution. Pizarro's greed and unjust actions alienated many of the colonists, and the followers of Diego Almagro took their vengeance by assassinating Pizarro in 1541.

SEE ALSO: Cortes, Hernán; exploration

plague

The generic term plague covers a host of epidemic diseases, with the most familiar being a rapidly spreading, often-fatal infection caused by *Yersinia pestis*. The *Yersinia pestis* bacillus causes a variety of symptoms, with the most common being a painful swelling of the lymph nodes that causes an abnormal growth known as a bubo in the groin or under the armpits (from "bubo" comes the term "bubonic plague"). In the Middle Ages, the bacillus was spread by a flea hosted by rats, the common companions of peasants as well as city-dwellers. The plague spread rapidly, sometimes killing as much as 80 percent of the local population, leaving entire regions depopulated, and causing a breakdown of civil order. The plague outbreak of 1347–1349, also known as the Black Death, was the worst in history and reduced the population of Europe by about one-third. Mortality was especially high among the aged, but a second wave in the 1360s, known as the "children's plague," had a higher mortality rate among the young. The population of the continent fell dramatically in the fourteenth century, which was also a time of widespread famine and, in France, the devastating effects of the Hundred Years' War.

The plague played an important role in ending traditional medieval society. By eliminating so much of the labor force, the epidemic drove up wage rates. This gave serfs an opportunity to defy the manorial system, in which they were tied to the estates of the landowners, and become free-roaming peasants. Many peasants moved to the cities to take up artisanal trades in the cities.

The plague turned the social order upside down and inspired important works of art and literature. Plague played a central role in the *Decameron* of Giovanni Boccaccio, a collection of stories told by a group of young men and women who flee a plague-ridden town for the safety of the countryside. The plague also prompted new writings and historical tracts concerning the history and nature of contagious disease, a first step toward the modern understanding of disease and its causes.

Plague outbreaks continued during the Renaissance, striking cities seemingly at random. Cities were affected more than rural areas; some regions of Europe and cities were spared, while others were devastated. The plague continued to strike Europe at regular intervals through the Renaissance and did not subside until the early eighteenth century, when a final serious outbreak occurred in the French port of Marseille.

The plague forced cities to organize new methods of combating epidemics. Italy led the way during the early Renaissance in fighting plague through civic organizations. The disease prompted Florence and other cities to create civic organizations and committees responsible for new public health measures, such as the enforcement of sanitary laws, the prompt disposal of the dead, and the quarantining of plague-stricken houses. Special hospitals were set up to treat plague victims, and a new system of quarantining ships was set up in ports, which isolated crew, passengers, and cargo for a certain period (usually a month) in order to make sure the ship was not carrying any epidemics. Larger urban administrations became permanent, as cities placed authority in health officials drawn from the citizenry.

Most believed the plague to be the workings of God's wrath for the sins and corruption of humanity. In places where the plague struck, it was common for the citizens to hold public displays of repentance for their sins. At the same time, scientists and doctors were taking the first steps in understanding how the plague was transmitted. They examined victims and watched the progress of the disease, comparing cases and taking note of preventive measures that seemed to work. In this way, the plague helped medical science to progress to its modern era of diagnosis, treatment, and prevention.

SEE ALSO: Boccaccio, Giovanni; medicine

Plato
(ca. 428 B.C.–348 B.C.)

Ancient Greek philosopher who influenced European philosophy and science through the Middle Ages and the Renaissance. Born in Athens, he was the son of a noble family and was given a good education. As a young man he came under the influence of Socrates, a renowned philosopher and debater. Plato experienced firsthand the turmoil of politics in his native city and, after the execution of his friend Socrates on a charge of corrupting the youth of Athens, spent time voyaging to Sicily, then the home of several Greek colonies. When he returned to Athens he founded a school known as the Academy. He began writing dialogues, accounts of debates and conversations among the teachers and philosophers of Athens, with Socrates given an important role. Plato's major work, however, is *The Republic*, an account of an ideal society in which the virtuous and talented hold leadership and all classes cultivate the virtues of wisdom, courage, and moderation.

Plato's school in Athens survived until the seventh century A.D., and Platonic philosophy remained a dominant strain of thought in the Mediterranean world. While the Roman Empire was at its height, Neoplatonism emerged in the Greek city of Alexandria, founded by several prominent scholars and commentators and based on Plato's metaphysical ideas. Although the philosophy and science of Aristotle dominated the Middle Ages, Plato's writings were also well respected, and in the fifteenth century Platonism was revived in the scholarly investigations of Marsilio Ficino and other Renaissance students of the classical world. Plato's belief in the immortality of the soul, and the ideal "Platonic" love that existed on a spiritual and not physical plane, attracted Renaissance philosophers and poets who were seeking new ideas complementary to the accepted doctrines of Christianity. Platonism also took an important place in the writings of Giovanni Pico della Mirandola, who attempted a synthesis of many different philosophical and religious traditions, including Platonism, Christianity, and the kabbalah system of Judaism. *The Republic* inspired the writing of *Utopia*, an account of an ideal society written by Sir Thomas More. Plato's concept of the universe also made a contribution to the works of Renaissance astronomers such as Johannes Kepler.

SEE ALSO: classical literature; Ficino, Marsilio; Neoplatonism; Pico della Mirandola, Giovanni

Pliny the Elder
(23 A.D.–79 A.D.)

Roman naval commander and naturalist whose works were regarded as the authority on the natural world during the Renaissance. Born Gaius Plinius Secundus in the town of Como, in northern Italy, he was schooled in Rome by the poet Publius Secundus. He trained to become a lawyer but remained devoted to the study of philosophy and the natural sciences.

Pliny served in the Roman army as a cavalry commander in western Germany, along an important frontier between Roman territory and the lands of the unconquered German barbarians. He also traveled in Gaul (modern France) and Spain. After serving for about ten years, he returned to the capital and the practice of law. During the reign of the emperor Nero, he wrote a history of Rome's German wars in twenty books, a work that Roman historians considered the best authority on the subject but which was eventually lost. In the year A.D. 70, under the emperor Vespasian, he served in southern Gaul and later in Spain as a procurator. He visited northern Africa and made a close study of human and natural environment in the Roman domains. On his return to Rome Pliny began work simultaneously on a history of Rome as well as *Naturalis Historia*, or *Natural History*, a collection of books covering the sum of human knowledge of the natural world. He dedicated the work to his patron and ally, the emperor Titus, and completed it in 77. To return the honor Titus appointed him commander of a naval squadron at Misenum, on the Bay of Naples. On August 24 of the year 79, Pliny witnessed the eruption of Mount Vesuvius, which destroyed the cities of Pompeii and Herculaneum. He set out to rescue a company of people trapped on a shore near the eruption, but on touching land he was either asphyxiated by poisonous fumes or suffered a stroke or heart attack (the true cause of Pliny's death has been the subject of speculation by historians for centuries).

Pliny was devoted to study and a prolific author, who wrote dozens of books on a great variety of subjects: military affairs, education, grammar and rhetoric, music, art, and Roman history. *Natural History*, however, remains the only work of his to have survived into modern times. The book contains sections on the structure of the universe; on the societies of Europe and Asia, and Africa; on animals; on botany; and on medicine. The final books of the work cover geology, the properties of various minerals, and the history of Roman art—the only ancient book to treat this particular subject. The collection was copied extensively in the Middle Ages and was an essential volume in the few libraries of ancient manuscripts that then existed. Rather than undertake scientific investigations of his own, Pliny simply reported on the writings of authorities of his own time and of the past—473 authorities in all. Although it served for centuries as an authoritative collection of scientific knowledge, it also contains many errors of fact and misinterpretations of the author's sources. Pliny's works began to go out of style during the later Renaissance, as new philosophies and scientific theories came into vogue and a new age of scientific investigation began in the experiments of Sir Isaac Newton, Galileo Galilei, and others.

Poliziano, Angelo
(1454–1494)

Italian scholar, humanist, and poet. Born as Angelo Ambrogini in Montepulciano, he was nicknamed "Poliziano" after the name of this town. His father, Benedetto Ambrogini, was assassinated for supporting the cause of the Medici clan in his town; after this event the ten-year-old Angelo was brought to Florence and schooled at the Studium Academy, a school established by the Medici dynasty. He was a student of Marsilio Ficino, a leading humanist and scholar, and learned to write in the classical Latin of ancient Rome. He translated a part of the *Iliad*, the epic poem of the ancient Greek writer Homer, into Latin for the use of Lorenzo de' Medici. He became a close friend of the Florentine ruler and served as tutor to the sons of Lorenzo and as chancellor (manager) of a Medici estate. After a falling out with Lorenzo he lived for a short time in Mantua, but returned to Florence at Lorenzo's invitation and became a lecturer in Greek and Latin rhetoric at the Studium, where students from all over the European continent attended.

In addition to notes on the classical authors, Poliziano published epigrams, odes, and elegies in Latin and also wrote a scholarly work, the *Praelectiones*, on the history of poetry. He wrote the *Nutricia*, didactic (teaching) poems on the works of Virgil and other classical authors, and his book *Centuria Prima Miscellaneorum* analyzed classical texts. Poliziano's Latin and Greek poetry includes *Manto*, an ode to the works of Virgil.

Poliziano also wrote important works in Italian, including the *Stanze per la Giostra*, a series of poems dedicated to the glory of Lorenzo's brother, Giuliano de' Medici. He wrote in different poetic forms, favoring serene, natural worlds and simpler, shorter forms such as the rispetto and the ballata. His play *La Favola di Orfeo* describes the ancient Greek myth of Orpheus, the first poet. *Orfeo*, written for the court of Mantua, was one of the first plays to be written in vernacular (everyday) Italian.

A noteworthy scholar of ancient books, he translated the works of Galen, Hippocrates, and Callimachus in Italian. He also served Lorenzo as a book scout, roaming libraries and monasteries in Italy in search of worthy manuscripts for the Medici library in Florence. For his dedicated service he was rewarded by the Medici with a villa in the town of Fiesole.

SEE ALSO: humanism; Medici, Lorenzo de'

Portugal

Kingdom located on the Iberian Peninsula that led the European exploration of Africa, Asia, and the Americas beginning in the fifteenth century. After the fall of the western Roman Empire in the fifth century, Portugal became part of the kingdom of the Visigoths. After the Moorish invasion of the eighth century, the Christian nobility fled to the northern mountains, and from this remote region they took part in the reconquest of the Iberian Peninsula. Portugal joined the Kingdom of Leon, of northern Spain, and then became a part of the Kingdom of Galicia. Portugal became an independent realm after the Battle of Sao Mamede in 1128, after which Prince Afonso Henriques was declared the Portuguese king. The Christian armies drove the last Moors from the southern region of the Algarve in 1250, after which the capital of the realm was established in Lisbon.

In the early fifteenth century, King John I ordered a fleet of heavily armed vessels to the port of Ceuta, on the Mediterranean coast of North Africa. The conquest of this city marked the starting point for expansion of the Portuguese frontiers thousands of miles across the oceans. Within a few years, Portuguese captains discovered the Azores, Madeira, and the Canary Islands; and passed Cape Bojador on the West African coast, a point beyond which Europeans had never ventured. The trading posts built by the Portuguese in West Africa brought gold, ivory, and slaves to the kingdom and within a century, trade in Africa as well as Asia—which allowed European merchants to bypass caravan routes controlled by Arabs—would make Portugal one of the wealthiest nations of Europe. This age of exploration and conquest was inspired in large part by the efforts of Prince Henry the Navigator, a son of John I who patronized navigators and organized expeditions to distant and unknown realms.

By building a lighter and more maneuverable ship known as the caravel, the Portuguese were able to sail through regions of unfavorable winds, down the western coast of Africa, around the Cape of Good Hope, and into the Indian Ocean. Portuguese navigators founded dozens of port cities in East Africa, India, and the East Indies, all of them serving as depots for a lucrative trade with Asia. When Spain began exploring the Western Hemisphere after the discoveries of Christopher Columbus, however, Portugal saw its monopoly on overseas exploration vanish. The two kingdoms divided the new lands they intended to colonize in the Treaty of Tordesillas.

Renaissance scholarship and artistic movements arrived in Portugal via contacts with Spain and Italy. An important writer of Renaissance Portugal was Joao de Barres, who penned one of Europe's first complete histories of exploration, *Decadas de Asia*. The discoveries of Portuguese navigators also inspired an architectural style known as Manueline, named for King Manuel I. This heavily ornamented style combined late-Gothic motifs and maritime symbols and emblems of foreign discoveries. Churches, monasteries, and public buildings financed by the riches in spices and other foreign trade goods were designed in the elaborate Manueline style by Mateus Fernandes, Diogo de Arrudu, and other prominent architects. The Manueline style extended to sculpture as well as the paintings of leading artists such as Jorge Afonso, Vasco Fernandes, and Gregorio Lopes.

Early in the sixteenth century, Portugal began sending expeditions to Brazil, Persia, Ceylon (modern Sri Lanka), China, and Japan. Portugal established settlements at Goa, India, as well as the Malay Archipelago and Macao, off the coast of China. At home, however, the royal dynasty ended with the death of King Sebastian in 1578, after which Spain invaded Portugal and the Spanish king Philip II declared himself King Philip I of Portugal, uniting the two realms. Portugal remained under Spanish rule until 1640. During this period Portugal began losing its colonies to its Dutch, French, and English rivals; its trading empire was gradually eclipsed by more powerful northern European nations and by the eighteenth century the nation was in economic and cultural decline.

SEE ALSO: Aviz, House of; exploration; Henry the Navigator

printing

In the Middle Ages, books were laboriously copied by hand. They were rare, carefully preserved in monasteries and private collections, and too expensive for all but the wealthiest to own. Few people were literate; books were the preserve of the aristocracy, the members of the church, and university professors.

The first printing technology in Europe used wood-blocks, which were carved with various designs and images that could be transferred to cloth and, at the start of the fifteenth century, to paper. This method was invented by the Chinese and may have been brought to Europe by overland merchant traders, or by Christian missionaries and explorers on their return from China. In the 1440s Johannes Gutenberg, a German goldsmith, developed a method of printing by movable type. Gutenberg transformed a farmer's press, loading small blocks of letter type that he cast from a metal alloy. The type was set into a wooden matrix and then covered with an oil-based permanent ink. Pressing sheets of paper against the matrix created a printed page.

Gutenberg used the press to create elaborately illustrated Bibles, as well as broadsheets, pamphlets, and color prints. The press spread rapidly through western Europe in the late fifteenth century, creating a new industry and revolutionizing communication. Venice, Paris, and the Netherlands became important printing centers; bookshops began selling their wares in every major city. Printing allowed philosophers and scholars to distribute their works all over the continent, and poets to set their verse in a permanent form. Presses were set up in the Spanish colonies in the 1530s; the first in North America was running in Massachusetts in 1638.

Printing shops operated as did many other artisanal industries in Renaissance Europe. The masters selected constructed presses, selected titles to print, and purchased materials. Apprentices mixed inks and cut and prepared paper. Journeymen were responsible for casting type, compositors set the type, and pressmen set up pages and worked the printing press. Journeymen had to serve many years of apprenticeship and had to learn Latin, the language of education, law, religious tracts, and mass communication. Printing technology spread when journeymen moved from town to town in search of new employers and opportunities to set up their own shops.

The publishing industry grew rapidly in the sixteenth century, when the first large publishing houses opened for business. Some were supported by groups of wealthy men who pooled their capital and published books as financial speculations. Others printed and sold books by subscription, in which those willing to buy a book agreed to pay cooperatively for its printing. Some books were printed in installments, in which a short section of the work was printed each time. Installment printing spread out the cost of printing and reduced the financial risk. Specialty printing houses created journals, calendars, almanacs, illustrated prints, political broadsheets, and the first newspapers.

Printing spread literacy and specialized knowledge to a wider cross section of European society. It allowed scientists to share ideas and challenge concepts that had been accepted for more than a millennium. Books allowed thinkers to openly question the authority of the Catholic Church, and unite with like-minded writers across the continent. No longer isolated by long distances and difficult travel, Europeans could garner larger followings for their ideas, and take part in open scholarly and religious debates. By the end of the Renaissance, thousands of books were being printed every year, the first public libraries were operating, and books had moved from a preserve of the aristocracy to the common possession of the middle class.

SEE ALSO: Gutenberg, Johannes; Venice

Prussia

The kingdom of Prussia had its medieval origins in the conquest of pagan tribes by the Order of Teutonic Knights in the thirteenth century. The Knights established their own state in what is now northern Poland, Latvia, Estonia, and the Baltic coastal region of what is now northeastern Germany, and built a seat of power at Königsberg. The Knights paid homage to the Holy Roman Emperor, but they also contended with the kings of Poland, who commanded a powerful medieval army and who defeated them at the Battle of Grunwald in 1410. By the middle of the fifteenth century the Teutonic Knights had come under the authority of the king of Poland.

The duchy of Prussia was organized among the territories of the Knights in 1525 by Albert of Brandenburg, a Protestant and a member of the Hohenzollern dynasty, rulers of the duchy of Brandenburg and the city of Berlin. In 1618, Prussia and Brandenburg were united. The Hohenzollern domains were scattered throughout northern Germany and were the scene of invasion and fighting during the Thirty Years' War. In 1701, Frederick I crowned himself as the first king of Prussia, and the realm remained one of the strongest military powers in Europe until the unification of Germany in the late nineteenth century.

Quercia, Jacopo della (1374–1438)

Italian sculptor who was born in the town of Quercia Grossa and trained in the workshop of his father Piero d'Angelo, a skilled goldsmith and wood-carver. Quercia assisted Nicola Pisano in carving the pulpit of the Cathedral of Siena. As a young artist he was strongly influenced by contemporaries from Florence, including the architect Brunelleschi and the sculptor Donatello (Quercia took part in the competition to design the Baptistery doors but lost this prize commission to Lorenzo Ghiberti). Although trained in the Gothic style of carving, Quercia's study of Roman artifacts and sculpture in the town of Pisa had a strong effect on his methods and his style, and early in his life he began incorporating Roman motifs and figures from pagan mythology in his work. One of his first important commissions was the carving of a monumental tomb for Ilaria del Carretto, the wife of the ruler of Lucca. This work combines Gothic style with elements borrowed from stone sarcophagi dating to Roman times—some of the earliest classical references of the Renaissance. For the cathedral of Lucca he also carved a famous altarpiece known as the *Man of Sorrows*; another important work is the *Seated Madonna* (also known as the *Madonna of the Pomegranate*) that he carved for the Cathedral of Ferrara.

In 1408 Quercia was commissioned by the city of Siena to design a fountain for the Piazza del Campo. The old fountain in this central square was being demolished, after drawing public superstition for its use of a figure of the pagan goddess Venus. Quercia designed a magnificent rectangular structure in marble, adorned with dozens of figures and scenes, with the Virgin Mary, the patron saint of the city, taking a prominent part. In this work Quercia abandoned the stiff poses that were traditional of Gothic sculpture, and carved his figures with strength, movement and liveliness. The fountain, known as the Fonte Gaia, took the artist more than five years to complete and remains one of the most prominent Renaissance artifacts of Siena. The wide public admiration for the fountain earned another commission from the Sienese, who asked Quercia, Donatello, and Ghiberti to create reliefs for the baptismal font in the baptistery of the Siena cathedral.

He was commissioned to design an altar for the Trenta Chapel of the Church of San Frediano in *Lucca*, but had to halt work when he was accused of various crimes of immorality in 1413 and forced to leave the city. His fame as a carver in marble as well as wood survived this setback, however. For the Collegiata in San Gimignano he carved wooden statues of the Virgin and the angel Gabriel. His most famous work was the design of Porta Magna, a main entrance of the Church of San Petronio in Bologna. The doorway is decorated with ten elaborate sculptural reliefs of biblical prophets and scenes, including the creation of Adam, the story of Cain and Abel, and the temptation of Eve. This work inspired Michelangelo Buonarroti in his designs for the Sistine Chapel in the Vatican. The city of Siena asked Quercia to supervise the construction of the city's cathedral in 1435, and also rewarded Quer-cia for his fine work with a knighthood.

SEE ALSO: Brunelleschi, Filippo; Ghiberti, Lorenzo; Michelangelo Buonarroti; sculp-ture; Siena

Rabelais, Francois
(ca. 1483–1553)

Author and physician whose satires *Gargantua* and *Pantagruel* have survived as some of the most celebrated writings of Renaissance France. Born in the Loire Valley region of Touraine, Rabelais was the son of a lawyer. As a boy he became a novice monk and was educated at a Franciscan monastery and later became secretary to Geoffrey d'Estissac. He acquired a wide-ranging knowledge of science, philosophy, medicine, and ancient Greek and Latin. After leaving the monastery he trained as a physician at the University of Montpellier, where he became a lecturer in the classical medical science of Galen and Hippocrates. In 1532 he became a physician in Lyons, where he also worked as an editor and translator of Latin works. In the same year he published the first volume of his *Pantagruel*. Two years later appeared *Gargantua*, a work in which the events occur before those of *Pantagruel* and which as a result is always published as the first of the two volumes.

In fear of the reaction to these satires, Rabelais signed the works as Alcofrybas Nasier, an anagram of his name. In his lengthy novels Rabelais satirized contemporary writings as well as the medieval chivalric romance by describing the outrageous history of a family of giants. The books treat the subjects of religion, war, and the new humanistic thinking that was sweeping away medieval habits of mind and replacing them with the classically in-spired philosophies of the Renaissance. As thinly disguised attacks on traditional scholarship and the intolerance of the church, Rabelais risked his career as well as his life by writing at a time when the Protestant Reformation was sweeping through central Europe but the Catholic hierarchy was still firmly in control in France.

Undaunted by the disapproval of the authorities, Rabelais continued expanding his work. In 1546 he brought out a *Third Volume*, this time signing his real name to the book, which suffered immediate condemnation from the scholarly authorities of the University of Paris. This book offers an account of the character named Panurge. A fourth volume came out in 1548, in which Rabelais described the unfortunate Papefigues, who had fallen victim to the Papimanes—a reference to the tyranny of the Catholic Papacy.

Raleigh, Sir Walter
(1552–1618)

Explorer and historian who helped to establish the first English settlement in North America, helping England to stake its future claim to colonies on the continent. He was the son of a country squire who owned an estate in Devonshire near Plymouth, a harbor on the English Channel. Although he was sent to Oxford for university studies, he left a short time later and then enlisted with a company of English infantry fighting alongside the French Huguenots (Protestants) on the continent of Europe. Historians know little of his career as a soldier, however.

By 1575 Raleigh was living in London but keeping family ties in Devon, which was becoming a center of English efforts to explore and colonize the New World. He joined his half brother, Sir Humphrey Gilbert, on an expedition against the Spanish. This voyage ended in failure, however, and Raleigh made efforts to secure an appointment at the court of Elizabeth I. In 1579, he helped to put down a rebellion in Ireland, where he dealt ruthlessly with Irish Catholics and ordered a massacre of several hundred enemy mercenaries. For his service he was rewarded with towns and estates in County Munster, where he promoted English settlement in Ireland as a way of keeping the rebellious island under English control.

Raleigh returned to England in 1581 and received lucrative patents, or licenses, from the queen. He was granted a knighthood in 1584 and in the next year became a warden of productive tin mines in western England. After Elizabeth granted him forty thousand acres in Ireland, Raleigh brought in English farmers and introduced cultivation of tobacco and the potato. Seeking to establish lucrative settlements in North America, he promoted an expedition to Newfoundland in 1583 and in 1584 a voyage that reached the Atlantic coast of North Carolina. He became a member of Parliament in the same year, and in 1585 sent out a company of settlers under the leadership of Sir Richard Grenville. This group settled on Roanoke Island, but the small colony soon ran afoul of the surrounding Indian tribes and abandoned their homes. As an individual, Raleigh was unable to sustain an entire colonial enterprise on his own, and the effort to colonize Virginia would pass to a joint-stock company that was able to raise money for the venture from several wealthy investors.

On returning to Ireland, Raleigh again took up the cause of English settlement on the island, and became acquainted with the poet Edmund Spenser, whom he helped to win a royal pension and to publish the first three books of his epic poem *The Faerie Queene*. He was losing favor at Elizabeth's court, however, and was prevented several times from taking part in expeditions against the Spanish. On returning from one aborted voyage, he was arrested and thrown into the Tower of London for seducing and secretly marrying Elizabeth Throgmorton, one of the queen's maids. Raleigh retired from the royal court and, finding himself short of money, voyaged to South America in 1594 in search of the legendary gold mines of El Dorado. Failing in this purpose, he returned to England, where he published an account of his voyage, *The Discovery of Guiana*. He returned to the queen's favor after an expedition against the Spanish port of Cadiz in 1596. When the Earl of Essex, the queen's favorite, brought Raleigh along on a voyage to the Azores, the two men quarreled. After returning to England, Essex was accused of conspiring against Elizabeth and was executed under Raleigh's supervision.

Raleigh was appointed governor of the island of Jersey in 1600. But the death of Elizabeth in 1603 and the accession of King James I proved disastrous, as Raleigh found himself out of favor for his political and religious views and had already been forced to sell his Irish estates in order to raise money. He was accused of conspiracy against the king, arrested, put on trial, and sentenced to death. He languished in the Tower of London for thirteen years, working on a *History of the World*, as well as essays and poetry that earned him a reputa-

A detail from Raphael's 1510 fresco "Parnassus."

tion as one of England's finest writers. In 1616 he proposed to the king that he undertake another voyage to South America in search of gold. Although the king was warned by the Spanish that Spain already had valid claims on this territory, James was in need of funds and released Raleigh from prison. The expedition set out in March 1617, but clashed with a Spanish settlement along the Orinoco River in Guiana. Raleigh sailed home, where he was arrested again. The king made good his promise to execute Raleigh should his expedition fail or find itself trespassing on the claims of Spain, and the sentence was finally carried out on October 29, 1618.

SEE ALSO: Elizabeth I; exploration; Spenser, Edmund

Raphael
(1483–1520)

A painter of the Italian Renaissance admired for the balance and harmony of his compositions, and who had a major influence on art of the later Baroque period. Born in the town of Urbino, he was the son of a painter, Giovanni Santi, who was a court painter to the Duke of Urbino, Federigo da Montefeltro. After the death of his father in 1494, the eleven-year-old Raphael took on greater responsibility for managing the Santi workshop, and quickly developed a reputation as one of the best painters in Urbino. His earliest known works are paintings done for the Church of San Nicola in the nearby town of Castello. In 1500 Raphael apprenticed to the painter Pietro Vannucci, also known as Perugino, under whom he developed a striking, expressive personal style in a series of religious paintings, including the *Marriage of the Virgin*, and the *Mond Crucifixion*. Ambitious and hardworking, he moved to Florence in 1504, and soon came under the influence of Leonardo da Vinci's paintings as well as the works of Fra Bartolommeo. The *Mona Lisa* of Leonardo served as a model for Raphael's portraits of Agnolo and Maddalena Doni, which he completed in 1505. In Florence, Raphael painted a series of Madonnas in which he adopted Leonardo's sfumato method of soft contours as well as Leonardo's typical pyramid composition, with complex groups of figures rising to a single point. His most famous work from this period, the *Entombment*, borrowed ideas from Michelangelo's painting *Battle of Cascina*.

In 1508 Raphael left Florence for Rome, where he was engaged by Pope Julius II to decorate a series of rooms known as the Stanza della Segnatura. These fresco paintings, which the artist completed in 1511, were based on the subjects of theology, philosophy, poetry, and law. They include *The Triumph of Religion* and *The School of Athens*, one of the most important works of the late Renaissance, in which classical philosophers gesture and pose in a setting of opulent grandeur. Over the following years Raphael also painted frescoes in the Stanza d'Eliodoro that include *The Expulsion of Heliodorus, The Miracle of Bolsena, The Repulse of Attila from Rome* by Leo I, and the *Liberation of St. Peter*. In his studio he completed a series of famous Madonnas, including the *Sistine Madonna, The Madonna of the Chair, Madonna with the Fish*, and the *Alba Madonna*.

The work he completed at the Vatican spread Raphael's name and fame throughout Italy. In Rome, he presided over one of the city's busiest and most successful workshops. Raphael hired a large staff of assistants to complete the frescoes in the Stanza dell'Incendio and the Vatican loggias between 1514 and 1519. In this period he also created a series of ten cartoons (designs) of the lives of Saint Peter and Saint Paul for tapestries that were to decorate the Sistine Chapel. These drawings were sent to workshops in Brussels, Belgium, where they helped to spread his fame and painting style to northern Europe.

In the meantime, the pope engaged Raphael as his chief architect after the death of Donato Bramante in 1514. Raphael designed chapels in Sant' Eligio degli Orefici and Santa Maria del Popolo in Rome, and a small section of the new Basilica of Saint Peter. He also designed several aristocratic palaces, adopting for them the classical style of Donato Bramante, adding detailed ornaments and flourishes that would become typical of later Renaissance and Baroque architecture.

In Rome Raphael also created several masterpieces of Renaissance portraiture, including famous paintings of Baldassare Castiglione, Pope Julius II, and the latter's successor, Pope Leo X. He collaborated with Marcantonio Raimondi in his printing shop to produce such engravings as *The Massacre of the Innocents* and *Lucretia*. These inexpensive prints were made by the thousands and circulated throughout Italy, making Raphael's name and works known to commoners as well as aristocrats. His largest painting, *The Transfiguration*, was still unfinished in 1520, when Raphael died suddenly at a young age and of mysterious causes.

SEE ALSO: Julius II; Leo X; Leonardo da Vinci; Michelangelo Buonarroti; painting

Reformation, Catholic

The Catholic Reformation, or Counter-Reformation, was the effort by the Catholic Church to stem the tide of Protestantism that was sweeping across northern Europe by the middle of the sixteenth century. In response to charges of corruption and the greed for wealth and power, the church undertook reforms and established new institutions, including the Inquisition, to counter the Protestants. This campaign was begun by Pope Paul III, who convened the Council of Trent in 1545. Over the next eighteen years, the Council made important changes to the structure of the Catholic Church, reaffirmed church doctrine in questions of the Mass and the sacraments, and reformed the training of priests. The Council of Trent rejected Protestant Reformation leader Martin Luther's doctrine of justification by faith alone, leaving no room for compromise with Protestants on the central issue of the nature of faith. It was followed by the creation in 1559 of the Index of Prohibited Books, which controlled the exposure of Catholic believers to new ideas and unorthodox philosophies. In the meantime, new religious orders such as the Capuchins were founded in order to preach among the common people.

The Counter-Reformation was a military and political effort as well. Catholic monarchs, including Emperor Charles V, fought against Protestant princes in Germany and central Europe. King Philip II of Spain campaigned against Protestant rebels in the Low Countries and dispatched the Spanish Armada against England. Ignatius Loyola established the Society of Jesus, or Jesuits, to return Protestants to the Catholic fold and gather new converts among the people of newly discovered colonies in Asia and the Americas. Jesuit schools throughout Catholic Europe instructed students in the faith.

The Catholic Reformation was supported by many prominent scholars, including Sir Thomas More of England and Desiderius Erasmus, who opposed the Protestants' complete rejection of Catholic authority. The movement, however, also represented a reaction against the humanist ideas that had inspired Renaissance scholars, artists, and writers. The views of scientists such as Galileo Galilei and Nicolaus Copernicus were condemned, even as the church eliminated the practice of selling indulgences and put a stop to the accumulation of ostentatious luxuries in the papal court in Rome. The Catholic Reformation was successful in bringing many European territories back into the church, including Austria, Poland, Hungary, southern Germany, and Bohemia.

SEE ALSO: Catholicism; Papacy; Reformation, Protestant

Reformation, Protestant

A movement that set Christian religious leaders against the teachings and practices of the Catholic Church, and which reached the height of its influence during the late Renaissance. In essence, Protestants rejected the authority of the pope and transformed the meaning of religious faith, rejecting the traditional role of the priest and the sacraments.

The Protestant Reformation was prompted by the new scholarship that emerged in the early Renaissance. Traditional medieval philosophy attempted to perfect and explain religious doctrine, never to question it. The new humanism introduced debate and investigation into the subject of religious doctrine. Philosophers and writers disagreed on the nature of the soul, on the ideas of sin and salvation, the nature of Christ as a manifestation of God, and the relation of religious and secular authority. This questioning was further spurred by the invention of the printing press and the wider circulation of new books and ideas.

Protestantism also grew out of a drive for reform of Catholic institutions in the fifteenth century. The sale of indulgences (remissions of punishment for sins), the practice of simony (sale of church offices), and the growing wealth and political power of the church set off a reaction among many members of the church. Jan Hus, a reformer from Bohemia, dared to question papal authority and criticize the Catholic hierarchy, for which he was burned at the stake in 1415. The German monk Martin Luther a century later developed his doctrine of justification by faith alone, an idea that eliminated the need for priests, bishops, popes, and the entire Catholic hierarchy in the spiritual life of the individual. Luther's ideas were taken up by Huldrych Zwingli in southern Germany and Switzerland, leading to the establishment of the Reformed Church.

In the time of Martin Luther, a new humanist education was allowing young scholars to question accepted traditions. Luther became a hero in cities throughout Germany, where his followers destroyed Catholic images and refused to take part in Catholic ritual. Protestantism became the majority religion in the 1530s, as local rulers adopted Luther's doctrine to declare their independence from the Catholic emperor. After his petition for a divorce from Catherine of Aragon was denied by the pope, King Henry VIII of England established a Protestant church in his domain—the Church of England—seizing Catholic properties, exiling or executing Catholic leaders, abolishing monastic orders, and rejecting outright the authority of the pope. At the same time, Luther's doctrines spread into the Low Countries and Switzerland, while in France, Protestants known as Huguenots were making up a growing minority in the Christian community.

Eventually the Protestant movement was met by an effort of reform by the Catholic Church and by new institutions designed to combat Protestantism, including the Inquisition, the Index of Prohibited Books, and the Society of Jesus, or Jesuits, a missionary and educational organization. Many territories returned to Catholicism, but the Christian church was left permanently divided, and the rivalry between Catholic and Protestant would play a central role in the devastating Thirty Years' War of the early seventeenth century.

SEE ALSO: Calvin, John; Luther, Martin; Reformation, Catholic; Zwingli, Huldrych

Rome

Ancient capital of the Roman Empire, later the headquarters of the Papacy and an important center of patronage and artistic innovation during the Renaissance. At the fall of the western empire in the fifth century, Rome entered a chaotic period when the city was subject to invasion by barbarian tribes and civil war among its most powerful families, the Colonna and the Orsini. The emergence of the Papacy gave the city prominence in the late Middle Ages. After the schisms within the church were settled in the early fifteenth century, the Papacy was established permanently in the city. The city attracted artists from all over Italy with its ancient ruins and monuments that inspired them to emulate the architectural styles of antiquity.

Pope Nicholas V, whose reign began in 1447, invited scholars and artists to the city and commissioned Leon Battista Alberti to design a new basilica. The new Saint Peter's Basilica was constructed over the next century from the plans of Alberti, Donato Bramante, Michelangelo Buonarroti, Raphael, and several other renowned artists and architects. Pope Sixtus IV established the Vatican Library in 1475, began construction on the Sistine Chapel, and ordered new roads to clear away the city's dark and sinister medieval alleys.

Rome became a major political center as the popes expanded their authority to the Papal States in central Italy and contended for power in northern Italy. The city was occupied by the French in 1494 and in 1527 sacked by the mutinous troops of the Emperor Charles V. In the meantime, several popes gained a reputation for nepotism and corruption, and the city remained a lawless place where murder and riots were frequent occurrences. Under Pope Julius II, Leo X, and Clement VII, Rome became a thriving artistic center of the Renaissance, the home of new churches, palaces, and masterpieces created by Michelangelo, Bramante, and Raphael. At the same time, the popes and the Catholic Church were being directly challenged by the Protestant Reformation sweeping northern Europe. By convening the Council of Trent, Pope Paul III attempted to reform the church and return Protestant territories to the religious authority of Rome. The Catholic Reformation that followed discouraged new scholarship and placed new restrictions on the style and subject of art and literature, with an Index banning certain works entirely and an Inquisition accusing and trying

many for religious heresy. The popes ended the lavish feasts and festivals that had entertained the city, and adopted new costumes and regalia meant to display the church's more devout, somber, and modest character. Under Pope Sixtus V, the Papacy established a large police force and banned all manner of unruly behavior, from prostitution to public assembly to dueling. Pope Sixtus cleared away many old neighborhoods in order to make Rome a more welcoming center for religious pilgrims. By the end of the Renaissance the city had been completely transformed, with new churches and palaces raised in the new style largely inspired by the city's ancient ruins.

SEE ALSO: Julius II; Papacy; Papal States; Sack of Rome

Ronsard, Pierre de (1524–1585)

French poet, born in La Poissoniere as the son of an aristocratic but poverty-stricken family. His father arranged for him to be sent to the court of Francis I as a page boy, where he served the sons of King Francis I. He then served under Princess Madeleine after her marriage to King James V of Scotland. He returned to France and joined a circle of classical scholars around Jean Dorat, who became principal of the College de Conqueret in 1547. The group formed a literary circle known as the Pleiade. He began writing poetry and in imitation of the odes of the Greek poet Pindar wrote *The First Four Books of Odes* in 1550, praising members of the royal family in his lines. His next work, *Amours*, was a tribute to the love sonnets of the Italian poet Petrarch.

Ronsard wrote several essays during the 1560s condemning the civil war in

France between Protestants and Catholics. These include *Discourse on the Misery of These Times*, which satirically criticized the followers of John Calvin, and the *Reproof to the People of France*. When Protestant critics returned fire and accused him of being a poor poet and an irreligious pagan to boot, Ronsard replied with his *Response to Insults and Calumnies*. His fervent support of the king earned him a stipend from King Charles IX, and he joined the king's court as an honored poet.

In 1572 Ronsard brought out *The First Four Books of the Franciad*, a failed attempt to imitate the classical epics and to create a French national myth that traced the lineage of the kings of France back to the Trojan kings of Homeric times. In 1578 he published a collection of sonnets, the *Sonnets for Helene*. Ronsard gained fame in his lifetime and many of his poems were set to music. Using the classic and medieval Italian modes in which Ronsard had worked, the Pleiade group made French a new and vital medium for poetic expression.

SEE ALSO: Rabelais

Rubens, Peter Paul
(1577–1640)

Flemish painter whose elaborate religious and mythological scenes, sensuous portraits, and detailed historical works marked a transition from the Renaissance period to the Baroque. Born in Siegen, Germany, he was the son of a Calvinist Protestant family that fled persecution in their hometown and took refuge in the city of Cologne. In 1589 he moved to the city of Antwerp with his widowed mother, and converted to the Catholic faith. He studied with Tobias Verhaeght, a minor artist, and several other artists of Antwerp, and joined the city's painters guild in 1598.

Peter Paul Rubens' self portrait. GETTY IMAGES.

Like many northern European artists, Rubens looked to Italy for instruction in new styles and methods of painting. He traveled to Venice in 1600 and studied the works of Veronese, Titian, and Tintoretto. Soon afterward he joined the ducal court at Mantua and won the patronage of Vincenzo Gonzaga, the ruler of the city, who helped him travel to Rome, where the young artist found inspiration in the frescoes of Michelangelo Buonarroti and Raphael and the paintings of Leonardo da Vinci and Michelangelo da Caravaggio. Rubens served Mantua as a diplomat as well, traveling to Spain and the court of King Philip III on a mission in 1603. In Spain he began painting portraits, a medium he continued when he returned to Italy.

In Rome Rubens won commissions to paint altarpieces for the Church of Santa Croce and Santa Maria in Vallicella, which he adorned with a picture of the medieval Pope Gregory admiring an icon of the Virgin Mary. Having well absorbed Italian humanism and classicism, he returned to Antwerp in 1609 and began to transform northern European painting. He became a court painter for the governor of the Spanish Netherlands (modern Belgium) and built a studio and workshop in Antwerp, where he completed several important altarpieces for local churches. He became a renowned print designer, working in both metal and wood to create illustrations and title pages for books. A devout Roman Catholic, he showed reverence for traditional biblical scenes but also used shadow and contrasting, vivid colors to give his pictures a dramatic and very modern look.

By the 1620s Rubens was known throughout Europe. His workshop in Antwerp trained several leading painters, including Anthony Van Dyck. Rubens had several assistants complete his design for a major painting, *The Assumption of the Virgin Mary*, which was raised in the cathedral of Antwerp. He was also commissioned by Marie de Médicis, widow of the French king Henri IV, to create a series of works describing her life. The twenty-one paintings of this cycle were to hang in the royal Palace of Luxembourg.

Rubens was also trusted with diplomatic missions by the king of Spain, who sought an agreement with the Dutch Netherlands that would keep Spain in control of its colony. He helped settle a treaty between England and Spain in 1630. This work earned him the honor of a knighthood from King Philip IV of Spain as well as King Charles I of England. For Charles I he created *Allegory of Peace and War*, a huge ceiling painting done for London's Whitehall Palace.

In the 1630s Rubens completed several of his most famous creations, including *The Feast of Venus, The Three Graces*, and *The Judgment of Paris*. Inspired by the country around Antwerp and his estate, the Chateau de Steen, he mastered landscape painting in works such as *Farmers Returning from the Fields*, which took their themes and style from the works of Pieter Brueghel.

SEE ALSO: Brueghel, Pieter; Médicis, Marie de; Titian

Rudolf II
(1552–1612)

Holy Roman Emperor of the Habsburg dynasty from 1576 until his death in 1612, and who also reigned as the king of Bohemia and of Hungary. The son of Emperor Maximilian II and Maria of Spain, Rudolf was educated at the court of King Philip II of Spain, Maximilian's cousin. Philip inspired him with devotion to Catholicism and a determination to stamp out Protestantism in Habsburg lands—a policy that ran counter to the religious tolerance of Maximilian.

On the death of Maximilian in 1576, Rudolf as the eldest son inherited the Habsburg throne. He brought members of the Jesuit sect to Germany, seeking to convert his Protestant subjects. Rather than returning Habsburg territories to Catholicism, however, this policy inspired widespread opposition and outright revolt.

In 1604, a rebellion against Rudolf's policies broke out in Hungary, where the opponents of the Habsburgs, under the leadership of Istvan Bocskay, allied themselves with the Ottoman Turks. After this event Rudolf's brother Matthias seized control of Hungary, Austria, and Moravia, at the invitation of nobles in those lands who sought a more tolerant sovereign. In response, Rudolf offered the Letter of Majesty to the Estates of Bohemia, a promise of religious freedom, in 1609, but two years later he was also forced to surrender this kingdom to Matthias. The conflict between the Catholic Habsburgs and the Protestants in Bohemia was the spark that eventually set off the Thirty Years' War.

Rudolf suffered from fits of depression and insanity, and several times during his reign he was unable to fulfill the duties of his office. After one such bout in 1600 he became a recluse in the city of Prague, the capital of Bohemia, which he had made the Habsburg seat of power. He was an avid student of alchemy and the magical arts, but also a generous patron to the leading scientists of his time, including Johannes Kepler and Tycho Brahe. After moving the Habsburg capital to Prague, in order to evade the assaults of the Turks, Rudolf invited architects and artists to his court and made the Bohemian capital an important cultural center.

See Also: Bohemia; Brahe, Tycho; Thirty Years' War

Russia

The Russian state traces its foundations back to the realm of Kievan Rus, established by Scandinavian Vikings in the ninth century A.D. This state controlled trade in honey, wax, timber, and slaves along the rivers running through the plains and forests of Russia and the Ukraine. Russian culture was heavily influenced by the Byzantine Empire and the Eastern (Greek) Orthodox Church after the Kievan ruler Vladimir I forced the baptism of Kiev's nobles into the new religion in 988.

Kiev eventually weakened through struggles among its ruling dynasty, and power over the Slavic peoples of the steppes and river valleys passed to more northerly cities such as Novgorod, Vladimir, and Suzdal. The process was completed in the thirteenth century, when a wave of "Tatar" (Mongol) horsemen overran Kiev and the Russian princely states. Novgorod survived the onslaught and prospered through trade with the west through the Baltic Sea and northern Europe. The Russian princes paid heavy tributes to the Tatar realm, known as the Golden Horde, and its rulers at the city of Sarai, near the northern shores of the Caspian Sea, until the late fifteenth century. The Tatar princes allowed the princes and the Russian Orthodox Church to remain in authority over Russian economic and cultural life. Russia was cut off from the political and cultural influence of the west. In the thirteenth century, Alexander Nevsky, a prince of Novgorod, successfully defended his domains against a hostile force of Scandinavians and German Teutonic Knights.

The principality of Moscow, founded by a son of Alexander Nevsky, gained considerable power when the Tatars recognized the authority of its rulers over the rest of Russia. When the patriarch (head) of the Russian church made the city his capital, Moscow gained further status and influence. In 1380, the Tatars suffered a crushing defeat at the Battle of Kulikovo, after which their influence on the northern princes and on Russia began to wane. The Moscow prince Ivan III "the Great" defied the Tatars by ending Russian tribute, absorbed several rival principalities into his state, and declared himself emperor of all the Russians. His successor Ivan IV "the Terrible" took the title of "tsar," or emperor. He destroyed the last remnants of the Golden Horde at Kazan and Astrakhan, after which the Russian Empire emerged as the largest and most powerful state in eastern Europe. Ivan codified the laws of Russia, expanded its territory to the west, and ruthlessly subordinated the Russian boyars (nobles) to his will. He also established trade links with western Europe.

Through this time, Russian contacts with the innovations and scholarship of the Renaissance was limited. By its ties to the eastern church, Russia also took no part in the struggle between the western (Catholic) church and the Protestant Reformation. In the early seventeenth century, after a lengthy civil conflict known as the Time of Troubles, the Romanov dynasty emerged. Under the Romanov tsar Peter the Great, a new city was established at Saint Petersburg, on an arm of the Baltic Sea. Peter's intention was to open his state to trade and exchange with the west. Through the seventeenth and eighteenth century artists and architects arrived from western Europe. The Romanov leaders had enormous palaces and country mansions built in imitation of the classically inspired buildings of Renaissance Europe, and began collecting the works of western painters and sculptors.

SEE ALSO: Fall of Constantinople

Sack of Rome

An assault on the city of Rome that occurred on May 6, 1527, by the armies of Charles V, the Holy Roman Emperor. The popes and emperors had been contending for power in the Italian peninsula for centuries, with the other major powers of the continent taking sides in the conflict to advance their own interests. In 1494, France entered the fray by invading northern Italy, making alliances with several Italian cities and briefly occupying the city of Naples. By the early sixteenth century the advantage in this conflict had shifted to the Holy Roman Empire; to offset the imperial armies Pope Clement VII had allied with France in the League of Cognac that also included Milan, Venice, and Florence. A polyglot army of thirty-five thousand Spaniards, Germans, Italians, and French under the command of Charles III, the Duke of Bourbon, was fighting in northern Italy on behalf of the Holy Roman Empire in the spring of 1527. Poorly fed and going for several weeks without pay, these troops mutinied and forced their commanders to march on Rome, which was defended by a small force of five thousand militia, including the Swiss Guard responsible for protecting the pope, and cannon set atop the city's ancient walls.

On the day of the attack, the Duke of Bourbon was killed, leading to a complete breakdown of discipline among the imperial troops. By sunset the attackers were breaking through the gates of the city, while the Swiss Guard took positions on the steps of Saint Peter's Basilica, while Clement escaped through a secret passage to the fortified Castel Sant' Angelo. The remaining defenders quickly surrendered and were massacred, while the armies of Charles V degenerated into a violent mob, killing, raping, and plundering without restraint. The sack continued for three days while the pope remained a prisoner in the Castel Sant' Angelo. For several weeks afterward the leading citizens of Rome suffered the ransacking of their houses and kidnapping for heavy ransom payments. Realizing that the members of the League of Cognac would not relieve the city or stage any kind of counterattack, Clement finally surrendered on June 6, one month after the siege began, he was forced to pay a huge ransom and give up papal territories in northern Italy to the emperor.

The imperial troops finally retreated from Rome in February 1528, leaving the city heavily damaged and the Papacy permanently weakened in its long-standing conflict with the Holy Roman Empire. Clement agreed to formally crown Charles V as emperor in February 1530. In the meantime, Rome's primacy in the artistic and cultural life of the Renaissance came to an end, as important artists fled the city to seek patronage elsewhere. The Sack of Rome also freed the emperor of any need to fight in Italy, Charles V turned with full force against the Protestant princes of Germany.

SEE ALSO: Charles V; Paul III

Salutati, Coluccio
(1331–1406)

Important humanist, scholar, and political leader of Florence, Italy. Born in the village of Stignano, Tuscany, he studied at the University of Bologna and was then appointed as the secretary to Pope Urban IV. Appointed the chancellor of Florence in 1375, Salutati held the post for the rest of his life. As chancellor, Salutati supported Leonardo Brunt in his struggles with the church hierarchy, hosted Manuel Chrysolaras in Florence and granted this important scholar a pension. His patronage of scholars on behalf of Florence provided impetus to classical scholarship.

Salutati opposed Giangaleazzo Visconti of Milan in his efforts to take control of Florence. Salutati waged a war with Milan that lasted for more than twelve years, until the death of Visconti in 1402. Florence remained an independent city and in the next century flourished from its involvement in banking and trade.

Salutati is credited as much for his cultural achievements as for his political ones. A skilled orator and writer, Salutati amassed a large collection of books. He sought out classical manuscripts and discovered the lost letters of Cicero as well as the works of other Roman writers, including Cato and Germanicus. Salutati also supported the merits of pagan classical literature, which was still under assault by the church.

Savonarola, Girolamo
(1452–1498)

Dominican monk whose fiery preaching ignited a movement of cultural reform and puritanism in Florence, and who became a martyr for his cause on the day of his public execution in the city's main square, the Piazza della Signoria. Born in Ferrara, the

A portrait of Girolamo Savonarola, by Fra Bartolommeo.

son of a doctor, Savonarola was trained for a career in medicine but took a stronger interest in the Bible, the writings of Aristotle, and the work of the medieval Scholastics, including Saint Thomas Aquinas. He studied at the University of Ferrara but spurned a career as a scholar by turning to the Dominican order, which he joined in 1475. In this year he began his harsh public criticism of the Papacy, naming it a "proud whore" in his poem *De Ruina Ecclesiae*.

Favoring the solitary and ascetic life, he withdrew to the monastery of San Domenico in Bologna and, in 1481, joined San Marco, a convent in Florence. At the Church of San Lorenzo, he preached against the vice, corruption, and vanity of the church and its leaders as well as the pursuit of riches among the Florentines.

At first, his use of the didactic and obscure language of religious scholars turned listeners away. He left the city in 1487 but returned under the patronage of Count Pico della Mirandola in 1490. He continued his sermons and gained a following by speaking in a more direct and popular manner. His accurate predictions of certain worldly events also earned him a reputation as a prophet.

In 1491 Savonarola became the prior of San Marco. His biting criticism of the Florentine aristocrats and tyrants inspired the anger of Lorenzo de' Medici, the ruler of Florence who advised the monk to control his tongue or suffer the consequences. In 1492, the monk boldly denied Lorenzo absolution of his sins, as punishment for his tyranny over the city. In the same year, Savonarola's accurate prediction of the deaths of Lorenzo as well as Pope Innocent VIII brought him a fearful respect among ordinary citizens. After Lorenzo's son Piero succeeded his father as ruler of the city, Savonarola's influence increased; his prediction of a coming catastrophe as punishment for the city's sins and tyranny found a receptive audience.

In 1494, Piero de' Medici was deposed and Savonarola became the city's ruler, intending to make Florence a pure, republican example for the rest of Italy. Savonarola saved his severest criticism for the Papacy, which he saw mired in luxury and corruption, an institution in dire need of reform. For this reason, he supported the invasion of Italy by the French under King Charles VIII, seeing in this event an opportunity for Florence and the other cities of northern Italy to establish democratic governments and for the Papacy to change its ways. Savonarola personally negotiated with Charles after the king deposed Piero de' Medici, and convinced Charles to moderate his demands. After this event Savonarola became the absolute master of Florence.

In 1495, Savonarola had passed a new constitution establishing republic in Florence. He reformed the tax code, replacing arbitrary levies with a tax of 10 percent on property, assessed against all citizens equally. He made sodomy a capital offense, banned popular entertainments, forced the Florentines to don plain clothing, and organized the famous Bonfire of the Vanities, the destruction of books, artworks, and vain luxuries (mirrors, musical instruments, games, cosmetics, jewelry, fine clothing) in the Piazza della Signoria. The Renaissance of new learning, art, and culture inspired by the antiquities of Greece and Rome represented to Savonarola a return to the paganism of the ancients, and a defiance of the religious piety and purity of medieval times.

Savonarola's sermons on the corruption of the church, as well as his alliance with the French invaders, earned him the enmity of the Duke of Milan and of Pope Alexander VI, who ordered him to cease preaching, an instruction that Savonarola defied. The pope excommunicated the monk in 1497, upon which Savonarola accused Alexander of gaining his title through bribery. Savonarola's power among the commoners and middle class in Florence represented a threat to the established church, to the merchant class of the city, to the Arrabiati (supporters of the Medici family), and most dangerously to the pope. He was also opposed by members of the Franciscan order, rivals of the Dominicans.

The pope excommunicated Savonarola in 1497 and then threatened to put the entire city of Florence under an interdict for Savonarola's continued preaching. The town fathers took the threat seriously and ordered the monk to cease his preaching.

In 1498, when one of Savonarola's followers agreed to a public ordeal by fire, a storm prevented the ordeal from taking place. This greatly angered the Florentines, who were growing weary with Savonarola and his puritanical regime. The entire city suddenly turned against him, rioting at San Marco, killing several of his followers, and demanding his arrest. Savonarola was taken into custody with two of his followers and charged with heresy, sedition, and false prophecies. He was tortured on the rack and reportedly confessed to his crimes. The three men were convicted, sentenced to death, hanged by chains from a cross, and then burned to death in the Piazza della Signoria. Savonarola's remains were crushed into the cinders and thrown into the Arno River, to prevent any relics of his body from being preserved and venerated by those still loyal to him.

SEE ALSO: Alexander VI; Charles VIII; Florence; Medici, Lorenzo de'; Medici, Piero de'

Savoy

A territory in what is now southeastern France that held a strategic position astride the Alpine passes that linked Italy and northern Europe and became an influential state during the Renaissance. The Savoy dynasty was founded in the eleventh century by Humbert aux Blanches Mains (White Hands), who extended his domain into northern Italy. Savoy established a parliament of nobles, clergy, and city representatives in 1264 and a lawmaking assembly in 1329. In 1416 Amadeus VIII, the Count of Savoy, was granted the titles of prince and Duke of the Holy Roman Empire by the Emperor Sigismund. The duchy was one of the first states in Europe to convene a regular assembly of representatives and write a constitution, known as

the Statutes of Savoy, that set down the privileges of its three "estates" of nobility, clergy, and townspeople. In 1559 the capital was moved from Chambery to the northern Italian city of Turin. Savoy remained a prosperous and stable region, a refuge for many seeking shelter from the religious and political turmoil affecting France and Italy during the Renaissance.

SEE ALSO: France

Savoy, Louise of (1476–1531)

Mother of King Francis I and influential figure in the culture and government of Renaissance France. The daughter of Philip II, the Duke of Savoy, and Margaret of Bourbon, Louise was married at the age of twelve to Charles of Valois, the count of Angouleme and cousin of King Louis XII. She had two children, Marguerite de Navarre and Francis, the future king. Louise effectively promoted the interests of her son, bringing him to the royal court of France and arranging his engagement to Claude of France, the daughter of King Louis XII. After the wedding took place in 1514, Louis formally recognized Francis as his heir. In the next year, on the death of Louis, Francis ascended the throne of France and rewarded his mother with the counties of Angouleme, Maine, and Beaufort.

Louise took an active part in diplomacy. After the defeat of the French army at the Battle of Pavia in 1525, she helped to negotiate the Treaty of Cambrai between France and the Holy Roman Empire in 1529. This "Ladies' Peace," signed by Louise and Margaret of Austria, ended a long-standing feud between France and Charles V, the Holy Roman Emperor, over control of Italy.

SEE ALSO: France; Francis I; Margaret of Austria

Saxony

A medieval duchy of northern Germany whose leaders, since 1356, had the privilege of taking part in the election of the Holy Roman Emperors. In 1422, the Wettin dynasty was established by Margrave Frederick II. During the sixteenth century, Saxony became a hotbed of Protestant activism, and the Saxon elector Frederick III extended his protection to Martin Luther, the monk who founded the Protestant movement in Germany. After Luther's open declaration of a radical new doctrine in the Ninety-five Theses, he was summoned to Rome by the pope to answer for his heresy. Frederick intervened, however, and the pope relented, also granting Luther safe passage to the Diet of Worms and sheltered at the Wittenberg Castle. Protestantism first took hold in Saxony under Frederick's successor John, who ordered Luther's new doctrine to be preached in his domains and formed the Schmalkaldic League to defend Saxony against the very Catholic emperor Charles V. John's successor John Frederick was defeated at the Battle of Mühlberg in 1547. Protestantism triumphed in Saxony, however, when Lutheranism became the official religion in the early seventeenth century and all other faiths were banned. Renaissance architects raised new palaces and churches in the capital city of Dresden, and the State Library founded in 1556 became the finest collection in Germany, gathering books and manuscripts from Europe, Asia, and the Ottoman domains.

SEE ALSO: Luther, Martin; Prussia; Reformation, Protestant

Scotland

Kingdom of northern Britain that remained independent of the English king throughout the Renaissance, but also kept close economic and cultural ties with the European continent. Scotland at this time was ruled by the Stuart dynasty, which arrived at the throne of Scotland with the accession of King Robert II in 1371. At this time the kingdom was fragmented in several small, virtually independent earldoms under the authority of local rulers, who paid little allegiance to the national monarch. Through the fifteenth century, the Stuarts managed to impose a measure of central authority on the realm. By the time of James IV, who ruled from 1488 until 1513, the earls had largely submitted to the king.

After study on the continent, several prominent Scottish clerics and scholars had brought home the humanism and intellectual curiosity of the Renaissance. An important group of these scholars had gathered around Desiderius Erasmus in Paris, and several of them took part in the founding of universities at Glasgow, Aberdeen, and Saint Andrews in the fifteenth century. Gradually, literacy and scholarship spread down the social ladder from the nobility to landowners to the middle classes, while the arrival of the printing press opened a new era of scholarship, study, and intellectual debate. One prominent Scottish poet, Gavin Douglas, translated Virgil's *Aeneid* into the Scottish language, which became the dominant medium of government, business, and a burgeoning school of Scottish Renaissance poetry.

By trading its wool and other goods, Scotland was also developing close economic ties with the cities of the Baltic region and the European continent. In the meantime, the Scottish monarchs arranged a series of marriage alliances with various European powers, including Denmark and the Netherlands. Scotland also held to an old alliance with France, which supported Scottish independence from England. In 1503, however, James IV married Margaret, the daughter of King Henry VII of England, thus drawing Scotland closer to England's new Tudor dynasty. Despite this marriage, the people of Scotland remained deeply hostile to the English, and it was this popular sentiment that prodded James to invade England in 1513, an action that led to his death at the Battle of Flodden.

In 1542, on the death of King James V, his one-week-old daughter Mary became the queen of Scotland. At the age of five, Mary was sent to France for her safety while England pursued a takeover of Scotland. Mary returned to Scotland in 1561 but was deposed from the throne in 1567 under accusations of adultery. She was taken captive by her cousin, Queen Elizabeth I, and imprisoned in London for twenty years before being put to death in 1587. In the meantime, her son James was schooled in the ideas of Renaissance humanism by George Buchanan. In this period Scotland threw off its ties to France and to the Catholic Church and adopted the Presbyterian sect founded and led by the Scottish religious reformer John Knox. In 1603, on the death of Elizabeth I, the last Tudor monarch of England, James VI of Scotland established the Stuart dynasty of England as King James I. In 1707 the Scottish and English realms would be united by the Act of Union, which established the Kingdom of Great Britain.

SEE ALSO: James I of England; Knox, John; Tudor dynasty

sculpture

As in painting and architecture, the sculpture of the Renaissance made important breaks with the traditions of the Middle Ages. While Gothic sculpture presented idealized forms, in order to inspire faith and Christian devotion, Renaissance sculptors strived for the classical ideals of harmony, proportion, and realism. Their works broke out of the religious tradition of the Middle Ages, to commemorate politicians, princes, and mercenary captains as well as saints, biblical scenes, and the life of Christ. Renaissance sculptors mastered the demands of monumental public art, decorating churches and public squares with larger-than-life statuary and architectural embellishments. Sculptors of the period also excelled in the medium of bronze, which demanded strength and mastery of the craft of forming and casting metal.

The Florentine sculptor Donatello revolutionized and humanized the art form. This artist decorated the Cathedral of Florence and the Church of Orsanmichele with a work in a new style, one that more accurately depicted the human figure and lent it the ideal proportions of classical sculpture. Donatello introduced the low relief technique, in which figures set in a narrow or confined space are given the illusion of motion and depth through the use of perspective. For the first time, the sculptor took into account the point of view of the observer in designing and placing his works. Donatello's most famous works include reliefs on the altar of the Sanctuary of Saint Anthony at Padua, the *Miracle of the Believing Donkey* and *Miracle of the Irascible Son*, monumental panoramic scenes, and two pulpits in bronze for the Church of San Lorenzo in Florence. His statue of *Judith and Holphernes* has been a landmark of the Piazza della Signoria in Florence since the fifteenth century.

Lorenzo Ghiberti's two sets of baptistery doors, completed over a period of two decades in Florence, were done in bronze relief. The rectangular panels were three-dimensional, sculptural paintings, with the figures set in landscapes and architectural backgrounds. The panels represented a daring technical achievement, with figures foreshortened and emerging from the background in three dimensions. In the work of Donatello and Ghiberti, sculpture came under the influence of ancient Roman art and its treatment of the human body and face. The idealized, unearthly forms of the Middle Ages gradually gave way to the expressive power of movement and the depiction of strong human emotions. Other famous Florentine sculptors were Antonio Pollaiuolo and Andrea del Verocchio, who is best known for the group *Doubting Thomas*, created for the facade of the church of Orsanmichele. Jacopo della Quercia, one of the most skilled Italian sculptors outside of Florence, lived and worked in Bologna.

In the Renaissance, sculpture was a display of wealth and status. Busts decorated halls and outer niches, full figures and equestrian statues were raised in public squares, and members of the nobility competed to patronize the best sculptors and have their names associated with their works. Collectors commissioned copies of Greek and Roman statuary, in marble as well as bronze, a method that kept the best workshops of wealthy cities busy.

Michelangelo dominated the area of sculpture of the sixteenth century. He was considered by many to be a greater master of the medium than Roman sculptors, the highest compliment of the Renaissance. His principle works include *Bacchus*; the *Pietà*; *David*, a work more than fourteen feet high; and *Moses*, created for the tomb of Pope Julius II in San Pietro in Vincoli Church. Four works known as the *Slaves* also created for the same tomb, show bodies partially captured in the stone. The allegorical use of sculpture, rather than its use as representation, led the way to the new Mannerist style that ended the Renaissance.

Sculpture at the close of the Renaissance became complex, elaborate, and lacking in the simple classical virtues widely admired at the start of the era. One of the most famous works of Benvenuto Cellini, a skilled metal caster and jeweler, was a solid gold salt cellar that the artist designed for the French king Francis I. Another Cellini sculpture, the bronze *Perseus*, influenced the following generation of Florentine sculptors, including Giovanni Bologna, the most renowned marble sculptor of the late Renaissance. The Mannerist style developed by this sculptor emphasized movement and balance, with the figures skillfully posed in complex arrangements. Giambologna, as he was known, worked for the Medici dynasty in Florence, creating sculptures for parks and grottoes and miniature bronzes for the decoration of noble households. His most famous works, including *The Fountain of Neptune* (created in Bologna), *The Rape of the Sabine Women* and several versions of *Mercury*, had a lasting influence on later sculptors of the Baroque period.

SEE ALSO: Cellini, Benvenuto; Donatello; Ghiberti, Lorenzo; Michelangelo Buonarroti

Sforza, Caterina (1463–1509)

Countess of the Italian domain of Forli and a formidable rival to the Borgia family, Caterina Sforza was the illegitimate daughter of Duke Galeazzo Maria Sforza, a member of the ruling dynasty of Milan. At the age of ten she was engaged to Girolamo Riario, the nephew and reputed illegitimate son of Pope Sixtus VI. She moved to Rome and bore her husband eight children, while the couple, with the help of the pope, became the rulers of the cities of Imola and Forli. The couple spent lavishly to win the support of the people of these towns, but their heavy taxes and Riario's cruelty and deceit earned them widepsread hatred. A conspiracy by a rival family, the Orsi, against Riario ended with his assassination in 1488; Caterina and her children were taken prisoner but Caterina escaped, promising to turn over the fortress of Forli to her enemies. Once she was released, however, she turned against them and gathered a strong company of supporters, eventually winning back the city and taking bloody vengeance on her enemies. Her second marriage, to Giacomo Feo, came to a tragic end in 1495 when he was murdered while the couple was riding through the streets of Forli. Caterina soon had the conspirators and all their families massacred.

Caterina then allied with Florence through a secret marriage to her third husband, Giovanni de' Medici. After Giovanni's death in 1498, Pope Alexander VI offered a marital alliance between his daughter Lucrezia Borgia and Caterina's son, Ottaviano Sforza. The pope was seeking to expand the papal dominions to Imola and Forli, but when Caterina refused the alliance, Alexander simply issued a decree granting Imola and Forli to his son Cesare Borgia, who then assembled a huge army of mercenaries and French troops and began a siege. Refusing all offers of a truce, Caterina took personal command of her troops and held out in the citadel of Forli until January 1500. She was taken as a prisoner to the Castel Sant' Angelo in Rome, but was released in 1501 and fled to Florence. When the Medici dynasty turned against her, she retreated to the convent of Annelena, where she remained until her death in 1509.

SEE ALSO: Alexander VI; Borgia, Cesar; Sforza dynasty

Sforza, Francesco (1401–1466)

Duke of Milan from 1450 until 1466. The illegitimate son of Muzio Sforza, a condottiere (mercenary), he was born in San Miniato, a village of Tuscany. He was raised in the Basilicata region of southern Italy, where he ruled as the marquis of Tricarico, a title granted him by the king of Naples. On reaching adulthood he followed his father's profession and earned a reputation while in the service of Naples as a skilled and courageous military leader. Francesco served in the forces of Pope Martin V as well as Filippo Maria Visconti, the leader of Milan. He fought against Venice in 1431 and as a reward for his service, Filippo Maria engaged his illegitimate daughter, Bianca Maria, to him.

Sforza felt no strong loyalty to the Visconti clan, however, and while campaigning against the papal territories he changed his allegiance to Pope Eugenius IV, who rewarded him with the title of vicar of Ancona. In the service of Florence and then Venice, he campaigned against Milan in 1438 and 1440. When his territories in southern Italy came under siege by the king of Naples, however, he again allied with the Visconti, and in 1441 married Bianca Maria Visconti.

Sforza's further campaigns against Milan on behalf of Venice convinced Filippo Maria to bribe him again by naming him the commander of the armies of Milan. On the latter's death in 1447, Milan declared a republic. Francesco allied with Venice and the Medici rulers of Florence, then besieged and conquered Milan and proclaimed himself its duke in 1450. In the same year, he made the Peace of Lodi with Cosimo de' Medici, the leader of Florence. Francesco allied with Florence and other northern cities in order to prevent conquest of northern Italy by larger and more unified realms of northern Europe, a threat that came to fruition after his death when the king of France invaded Lombardy to subdue the power of Milan. Francesco's son Ludovico succeeded him and was formally proclaimed Duke of Milan by Emperor Maximilian I of the Holy Roman Empire.

Francesco glorified himself and his new Sforza dynasty by his patronage of sculptors, artists, and architects who raised new monuments and buildings in Milan. He improved the city's finances and made the Milanese court an important center of Renaissance scholarship.

SEE ALSO: Sforza, Caterina; Sforza, Ludovico; Visconti dynasty

Sforza, Ludovico
(1452–1508)

Duke of Milan from 1494 until 1499. The second son of Francesco I Sforza, he was born in the town of Vigevano in the Lombardy region of northern Italy. He was a ruthlessly ambitious Renaissance prince who patronized some of the greatest artists of Europe, including Leonardo da Vinci and Donato Bramante.

On the death of Francesco Sforza in 1466, Ludovico's elder brother Galeazzo became the duke of Milan. When Galeazzo was murdered in 1476, the duchy of Milan passed to his son Gian Galeazzo, then seven years of age. Ludovico was thwarted in his attempt to seize the duchy and exiled from Milan by Gian Galeazzo's chief minister, Cicco Simonetta. Soon returning to the city, *Ludovico* had Simonetta murdered in 1480 and then banished Gian Galeazzo and his mother, Bona of Savoy, from Milan. Gian Galeazzo established a rival court in the city of Pavia and, with the support of his wife Isabella of Castile, the daughter of the king of Spain, continued to make his claim for the duchy.

In search of ways to secure his authority, Ludovico allied himself with King Charles VIII of France, and, in order to glorify and legitimize his reign, he engaged Leonardo da Vinci to create works of art in the city that would include the *Last Supper*, painted for the refectory of the Santa Maria della Grazie monastery.

On the death of Gian Galeazzo in 1494, the way was clear for Ludovico to secure his hold on the duchy. He struck an alliance with King Charles VIII of France and arranged a marriage between his niece and Maximilian I, the Holy Roman Emperor. In return Maximilian officially recognized Ludovico as the Duke of Milan, while the French assembled an army and invaded Italy. In 1495, Ludovico turned against the French, who were eventually defeated and chased from Italy.

In 1499, Charles's successor King Louis XII laid claim to the duchy through his descent from Gian Galeazzo Visconti, a member of the dynasty that had preceded the Sforzas as dukes of Milan. Louis invaded Italy and forced Ludovico to flee Milan. After assembling an army of Swiss mercenaries, Ludovico prepared a counterattack. His forces were defeated at the Battle of Novara in 1500 and he was taken prisoner by the French. Brought to the castle of Loches, in central France, Lu-

The title page of "Much Ado About Nothing" from the First Folio (1623) edition of Shakespeare's plays.

dovico languished in a dungeon for eight years before dying.

SEE ALSO: Leonardo da Vinci; Sforza, Caterina; Sforza, Francesco; Visconti dynasty

Shakespeare, William (1564–1616)

Playwright and poet whose works made his reputation as the most original and brilliant writer of the English language. Born as the son of a glove maker in Stratford-upon-Avon in 1564, Shakespeare came from a middle-class family. He was educated in the local grammar school in the traditional subjects of rhetoric, logic, Latin, and classical literature. After marry-ing Anne Hathaway and starting a family, he left his hometown for London to make his fortune as an actor and author.

Historians know almost nothing about Shakespeare's early years in London but have speculated that he may have been an actor or schoolteacher. By 1592, the year Shakespeare published *Venus and Adonis*, a long mythological poem, he was well known in London literary circles as a poet. Shakespeare was familiar with classical mythology and literature and based one of his early works for the stage, *The Comedy of Errors*, on comic plays by the Roman writer Plautus. Shakespeare's other plays from this early period are *Two Gentlemen of Verona* and *Love's Labour Lost*, comedies of mistaken identity and the trials and tribulations of love. The author's complex plotting and brilliantly inventive language are used to draw large casts of memorable characters, whose very human foibles and eccentricities make them familiar to modern audiences in any language.

At some time in the 1590s Shakespeare joined a repertory company, Lord Chamberlain's Men. At this time, the popular theater was gaining widespread acceptance among all classes of English society, and plays were coming to be accepted as a worthy pursuit of talented writers, including Shakespeare's contemporaries Christopher Marlowe and Ben Jonson. Shakespeare went well beyond the ordinary playwrights of his day, however, in creating epics such as *Henry VI* and *Richard III*, plays that combined theatrical dramatics with recent English history.

The Lord Chamberlain's Men relied on Shakespeare as a writer, financial backer, and actor. In 1599 the company built the Globe Theatre on the south bank of the Thames River, a large stage surrounded on three sides by the audience, and open to the sky. For the company Shakespeare wrote *The Taming of the Shrew*, in which the author combines Italian and English plot devices, the fantasy play *A Midsummer Night's Dream*, as well as *The Merchant of Venice* and *Much Ado About Nothing*. On a request from Queen Elizabeth that he write a romantic story for Falstaff, a character of the two historical plays of *Henry IV*, Shakespeare wrote *The Merry Wives of Windsor*. Other comedies from this period include *As You Like It* and *Twelfth Night*.

In 1593, the theaters of London were closed due to an outbreak of plague, and Shakespeare turned to the writing of poetry. For his patron, the Earl of Southampton, he wrote *The Rape of Lucrece*. Both this poem and *Venus and Adonis* are considered masterpieces in the tradition of the long narrative epic. He also wrote a series of 154 sonnets, fourteen-line poems in which the author explored a wide range of emotions and moods, and described a mysterious "dark lady" whom historians have yet to identify.

Around 1600 Shakespeare wrote tragedies including *Romeo and Juliet, Julius Caesar,* and *Hamlet,* his most famous single work. He treated the ancient Trojan War in *Troilus and Cressida,* and also wrote a bittersweet play of love and sex in *Measure for Measure*. In 1603, on the accession of King James I, the Lord Chamberlain's Men won the support of the crown and became the King's Men. The last productive years of Shakespeare's life saw the writing of historical plays *Antony and Cleopatra, Timon of Athens,* and *Coriolanus,* all based on short biographies by the Greek historian Plutarch, as well as three of Shakespeare's most famous plays, *Macbeth, Othello,* and *King Lear*. These plays, based on traditional English historical tales, reveal a more cynical and pessimistic author,

who describes characters alienated from their surroundings, and who are controlled and ultimately destroyed by their passions and desires. *The Tempest*, believed to be Shakespeare's final play, describes the shipwreck of the magician Prospero, who represents an author looking back on his own works as the strange, magical creations of a powerful imagination.

Shakespeare returned to Stratford at the end of his life and lived a comfortable, prosperous retirement. After his death in 1616, his reputation as poet and playwright spread rapidly in England and on the European continent. In 1623 all of his plays were collected and printed from the author's own manuscripts, a rare act in Renaissance England, where plays were widely considered to be disposable works meant only for the temporary amusement of a mass audience. In all, Shakespeare wrote thrity-eight plays, including many that are still considered the pinnacle of the dramatic art: *Hamlet, Macbeth, Othello, King Lear,* and *The Tempest*. His works have been translated into many languages, have been performed all over the world, and have been remade into operas and movies. Hundreds of lines and phrases from his plays became familiar expressions that have survived into the twenty-first century. In the meantime, Shakespeare became emblematic of the literary achievements of the English Renaissance during which, partially through the popularity of his own works, a relatively obscure and little-used language emerged to become the national tongue of a great empire.

SEE ALSO: Elizabeth I; James I of England; Marlowe, Christopher; theater

ships and shipbuilding

As frontiers of knowledge expanded during the Renaissance, new vessels made it possible for navigators to expand the limits of the known world. Medieval ships were small sailing vessels—some of them powered by oars—that had a limited range and were best suited for use along coastlines and in river mouths. There were very different shipbuilding traditions in northern and southern Europe. Squat and wide ships known as cogs were in use in the Atlantic Ocean and the North Sea, while in Genoa and other Mediterranean ports, rowed galleys and small sailing ships modeled on the Arab dhow were built.

In the late Middle Ages, these two ship types were combined in a hybrid model known as the carrack. This ship, also known in Spain as the *nao*, was built in many European ports in the fifteenth century. It employed a larger sail as well as a bowsprit, a mast extended from the front of the ship. Castles were raised in the bow and at the rear of the ship. The carrack used a rudder built into the stem post, rather than a rudder steered from the side of the ship, and adopted the square mainsail, which had powered the cog and the longship. From the Arabs shipbuilders borrowed a lateen (triangular) sail that was rigged to a rear mizzenmast. As ships and crews grew larger, a third mast was added as well as a second "topsail" on the main mast.

Smaller and more maneuverable ships known as caravels were the key to long-range exploration. They were first used by the Portuguese to navigate down the west coast of Africa, where reefs, tricky currents, strong desert winds, and superstition had limited exploration to Cape Bojador, beyond which sailors believed the world simply ended. The caravel was more maneuverable than the carrack. It was developed from the dhows of the Muslim world, with a long, sloping hull and high, wide poop deck aft (in the rear). The ship could sail close to the wind and was extremely buoyant. Caravels could be rigged with square or lateen sails, depending on the wind conditions, and they could navigate in rivers and shallow waters, which made them useful for coastal exploration. The caravel brought the Portuguese as far as the East Indies and Brazil, and was also used in the first expedition of Christopher Columbus to the Western Hemisphere.

The artillery aboard ships transformed naval warfare, forcing ships to fight longer-range battles of maneuver and tactics that replaced the old strategy of simply grappling an enemy ship and trying to board her for a hand-to-hand fight. The carrack was used as both cargo vessel and warship; its gun ports allowed iron and bronze cannon to be added to the traditional complement of infantry and archers. The caravel was not fast enough, however, for good use as a warship. To meet this purpose, in the sixteenth century Portuguese and Spanish shipwrights pioneered the galleon. The galleon was a carrack turned into a large gun platform. It was an imposing ship, with several decks of guns and cannon firing from the forecastle and aft castle decks. Most galleons had four masts with two lateen-rigged masts in the back. Strong hulls made the ship good for long-distance campaigns, such as the great fleet of galleons and smaller ships known as the Spanish Armada. The galleon had a narrower profile and a low forecastle, making it extremely stable, fast, and maneuverable. It was also less expensive to build than the carrack. Galleons remained in use for three centuries both as military and cargo vessels, and were the forerunners of the large square-rigged, long-distance clipper ships that came into use in the eighteenth century.

SEE ALSO: Columbus, Christopher; exploration; Henry the Navigator; trade

Siena

A city of Tuscany in northern Italy that became an important rival of Florence during the Renaissance. Founded by the ancient Etruscans, Siena came under the control of the Lombards after the fall of the Roman Empire in the middle of the fifth century. The city won its independence in the twelfth century, and gradually expanded the surrounding territory that came under its control. Early in its history as a self-governing commune Siena was an important center of support for the Ghibelline faction that supported the authority of the Holy Roman Emperor in Italy. In 1260 the city defeated a force of Florentines at the Battle of Montaperti, which remains a rallying cry for modern Sienese in their sporting rivalries with the larger city of Florence. In 1270 the city was conquered by the king of Naples, Charles I. Siena joined an alliance of Guelph cities that supported the Papacy against the emperor, while growing wealthy as a center of banking and trade. The aristocratic Petrucci family ruled the city late in the fifteenth century; after this dynasty was overthrown in 1523 the wealthy city was fought over by the Spanish, French, and the Habsburg dynasty. In 1554 Cosimo de' Medici rallied an army and laid siege to the city, which was then under the control of a branch of the Strozzi dynasty. The Florentines defeated the Sienese at the Battle of Marciano in 1554. In 1555, it was invaded by Emperor Charles V, who passed control of the city to Cosimo de' Medici as Duke of Tuscany two years later.

Siena was an important center of painting, sculpture, and architecture, and has several notable works dating from the early Italian Renaissance. The Sienese School of painting flourished through the fourteenth century, with its leading artists Simone Martini, Guido of Siena, and Ambrogio Lorenzetti. On its oval main square, the Piazza del Campo, was built the Palazzo Pubblico, an imposing public building that contains a famous Lorenzetti fresco, *Allegory of Good Government*. The main square also became the site of several medieval palaces and mansions and the tall Torre del Mangia. The Fonte Gaia, an elaborate fountain, was designed for the square by Jacopo della Quercia. The cathedral of Siena was raised over a period of three centuries, and remains one of the most important examples of Gothic architecture in Italy. The neighboring Biblioteca Piccolomini was decorated with fresco paintings by Pinturicchio. The Campo remains the scene of a famous horse race, known as the Palio, that echoes festive contests of skill and strength that were common in the medieval era (although the Palio itself originated in the middle-seventeenth century).

SEE ALSO: Florence

slavery

Slavery, an important institution of the classical world, declined in the Middle Ages as Christianity spread to northern and eastern Europe, and the teachings of the new church prohibited making slaves of those who had converted. Yet the practice never completely died out. From the teachings of Aristotle and others, slavery was considered a natural state for lesser orders of human beings, as well as nonbelievers. Slaves taken as prisoners of war served as household servants and manual laborers in the homes of the wealthy. Their children were commonly born as free persons, sometimes considered the legally adopted sons or daughters of the owners of their parents.

Crusaders took captive Muslims as slaves in the Middle East, and in the early Renaissance human trafficking grew more common in the Mediterranean states of Spain and southern Italy. Muslims captured in North Africa and in battles with the Ottoman Empire were made servants in wealthy and noble families, while Venice and other maritime states used slaves as well as prisoners to row their galley fleets. A few slaves from sub-Saharan Africa were also brought to Europe via caravan routes that linked the Mediterranean with the west African empires, including Ghana and Mali.

The industry of slavery revived with the Portuguese explorations of the west coast of Africa in the fifteenth century. Africans were captured and brought to fortified posts at the coast, then transported to Portuguese colonies to work farming plantations. With the discovery of the Americas, and the encounters with native tribes of the Caribbean, Europeans found another source of slave labor. Without having what the slave-dealing countries considered organized governments, true religion, or profitable occupations, Native Americans were considered properly slaves, who benefited from their service to their masters. A few voices protested this practice, including the Spanish monk Bartolomé de Las Casas, and in Europe, several philosophers including Desiderius Erasmus and Sir Thomas More rejected the doctrine of "natural slavery." In Europe, slavery died out in the late Renaissance, as the new doctrine of equality was taken up by the Enlightenment writers and philosophers. Slavery continued in the overseas colonies, which benefited immensely from slaves imported from Africa and the Americas to work sugar, indigo, and cotton plantations.

SEE ALSO: exploration; Las Casas Bartolomé de

Spanish Armada

Also known as the Great and Most Fortunate Navy, the Spanish Armada was a grand fleet of warships sent by Spain in 1588 to attack England. Spain's goal was to end English interference in the Spanish-controlled Low Countries, and return the English kingdom to the Catholic fold. Philip II, the husband of the late queen Mary I of England, saw the return of the Protestant Church under Queen Elizabeth as a mortal threat to the Catholic Church, which he staunchly defended, and a challenge to Spanish domination in the Netherlands. He sent the Armada under the command of the Duke of Medina Sedonia, whose orders were to bring Spanish soldiers from the Low Countries to the vicinity of London, where a direct threat to the city would change English minds about supporting revolts against Spanish rule in the Netherlands. A secondary aim of the Spanish Armada was to end English interference with Spain's colonial empire in the New World.

In the spring of 1588 the Armada set sail with 130 ships, eight thousand sailors, and eighteen thousand soldiers. In the meantime England was fully informed of Spanish intentions through a network of spies in the Spanish royal court. On July 19 the Armada arrived in the English Channel, intending to rendezvous with a company of twenty thousand Spanish infantry on the continent. An English battle fleet of 55 ships immediately set out from the port of Plymouth, engaging the Armada at skirmishes at Eddystone and Portland. When the Spaniards took harbor at the Isle of Wight, the English commander Sir Francis Drake attacked, chasing the Armada out of the Channel. After passing the southern English coast the Spanish anchored off the port of Calais, where the English attacked with fireships. Greatly fearing these dangerous ships that were packed with explosives and gunpowder, the Spanish scattered from Calais and sailed north to Gravelines, prepared to rendezvous with the Spanish infantry under the Duke of Parma.

At Gravelines, the faster and more maneuverable English ships dodged the heavy Spanish cannons that were used ineffectively by the Armada, and stayed well out of grappling range in order to avoid hand-to-hand fighting. Several Spanish ships were lost, and the Armada retreated from the coast under strong northwesterly winds. With the threat of a land invasion thwarted, the English shadowed the Armada as it sailed up the eastern coast of England, then attempted a return home via the coasts of Scotland and Ireland. With food and water running low, the Spanish commander ran into a heavy storm that destroyed 24 of his ships off the western coast of Ireland. Hundreds of sailors were drowned or captured after swimming to land, where the Irish—always hostile to English power—gave some of them food and shelter.

As the Spanish fleet limped home, the English gathered an armada of their own and prepared for a counterattack. This expedition failed, but the defeat of the Spanish Armada gave a boost to the Protestant cause in Europe and to the prestige of Queen Elizabeth, who at a crucial moment had rallied her country's troops with a stirring speech. England continued its support of the rebellion in the Low Countries and also supported the efforts of priva-

teers and its navy against Spanish interests in the New World.

SEE ALSO: Drake, Sir Francis; Elizabeth I

Spenser, Edmund (1552–1599)

English poet and essayist who was an important figure in the founding of a new English poetic tradition during the Renaissance. The son of a tailor, Spenser was born in London, where he attended the Merchant Taylors' School. He enrolled at Cambridge, where he studied classical Latin and Greek writing, worked as a servant to wealthier students, and translated poetry of the medieval Italian poet Petrarch. After earning a master's degree in 1576, he became secretary to John Young, the bishop of Rochester, in 1578, and joined a literary circle led by Sir Philip Sidney. In Rochester he began work on his first major poem, *The Shepherd's Calendar*, which was published in 1579. A series of twelve poems that imitated the allegorical Latin poetry of Virgil, *The Shepherd's Calendar* disguised praise of Queen Elizabeth and the Tudor dynasty, and biting commentaries on current events in England, with the form of "pastoral" poetry and imagined conversations among shepherds. The success of this volume encouraged Spenser in the laborious endeavor of writing a much larger and more difficult epic poem, *The Faerie Queene*, which would be his major work of poetry.

On considering the meager prospects for poets, Spenser sought to win a secure position in government service, and took up the study of law. In 1580 he gained an appointment as the secretary to Lord Grey, England's lord deputy of Ireland. He spent much of the rest of his life in Ireland where, after helping to put down a rebellion by the Irish natives, he was rewarded with a three thousand–acre country estate in Kilcolman, County Cork, which he intended as a center of English settlement and colonization. In early 1590, the first three books of *The Faerie Queene* appeared in London. Dedicated to Queen Elizabeth, the poem was a celebration of the rise of the English nation and England's identity as a Protestant land that stood in proud independence from the Catholic Church and its medieval institutions. Spenser took as his model the twelve books of Virgil's *Aeneid*, the national epic of ancient Rome. Each of the twelve books of *The Faerie Queene* was to consider one of the twelve moral virtues of Aristotle, as seen through the life and acts of a chivalric knight modeled on the heroes of Arthurian legend. The poem would become a national epic of England, but also a grand allegory that combined Christian morality with ancient philosophies of Aristotle and Plato. For this work Spenser developed a new poetic form, the nine-line "Spenserian stanza," which was taken up by major English poets in the following centuries. Although written in archaic language and relying on the medieval traditions of chivalry, Spenser's inspiration by classical pagan philosophies made his poem a truly Renaissance work.

The Faerie Queene was considered a great work when it was published, but Spenser failed in his efforts to win a lucrative position at court. Having received fame and a substantial income from sales of the work, he returned to Ireland from London in 1591. He published a collection of shorter poems under the title *Complaints*. He also wrote an autobiographical poem entitled *Colin Clout's Come Home Again*, describing his life and fame in London and his attempts to fit in to the life of the royal court. Readers and critics praised

his *Amoretti*, love sonnets in the style of the Italian poet Torquato Tasso, and his *Epithalamion*, an ode to love and marriage that he wrote on the occasion of his wedding to Elizabeth Boyle. His best-known essay, *View of the Present State of Ireland*, supported the policies of Lord Grey and suggested a new program for English administration of Ireland, in which the Irish language and culture would be suppressed and replaced with what was in his view the superior moral and cultural life of the English. As the work was critical of England's policy, it was not published until well after the author's death.

Spenser published three more books of *The Faerie Queene* in 1595, but his ambition to create an epic in twelve books was not accomplished. In 1598 he became the sheriff of Cork. Soon after this a rebellion broke out and he was forced to flee his home, which was destroyed by the rebels. After returning to London and giving a report to the queen on his experience in Ireland, he became ill and died. By this time regarded as one of the finest poets in England, he was buried with honors in Westminster Abbey. *The Faerie Queene* became one of the most influential poetic works in English, and inspired later poets from John Milton to William Wordsworth.

SEE ALSO: Elizabeth I; England; Milton, John; Shakespeare, William

Stampa, Gaspara (ca. 1523–1554)

Italian poet whose sonnets in the style of Petrarch, dedicated to a largely unrequited love, made her reputation as one of the finest poets of the Italian Renaissance. Born in Padua, she moved to Venice at the age of eight with her mother Cecilia, soon after the death of her father, Bartolomeo

Stampa. In Venice, she studied literature and music, and with her sister Cassandra she became an accomplished lute player. Her brother Baldassare was earning some renown as a poet and gathering friends and writers to the family home, which became a popular salon enlivened by music performed by the Stampa sisters. After the death of her brother in 1544, Gaspara continued the salon and she became the center of a literary circle, among whom she earned praise as a poet. Three of her poems were published during her lifetime, but after her death Cassandra collected 311 of her poems into the collection *Rime*. The poems describe Gaspara's love affair with Count Collaltino de Collato that brought her heartbreak and frustration. Her sonnets took their inspiration from Petrarch and his love for the distant Laura.

SEE ALSO: d'Aragona, Tullia; Petrarch; Venice

Strozzi family

A dynasty of aristocratic Florentine merchants who rose to prominence in the thirteenth century, and who are remembered for their long-standing feud with the powerful Medici family. Palla Strozzi (1373–1462) was a patron of scholars of Florence and Padua, who founded the first public library in Florence. Under his leadership the Strozzi banking empire survived a financial crisis in the fourteenth century that left his own and the Medici dynasty as the most powerful business corporations in Italy. Filippo Strozzi the Elder (1428–1491) was an outspoken opponent of the Medici, who was banished from Florence by Cosimo de' Medici and established himself in Naples. After returning to Florence in 1466, he became an adviser to Lorenzo de' Medici and began construction of the Strozzi palace, which remains one of the most imposing mansions of his native city. Having gathered a vast fortune, he commissioned the artist Fra Filippo Lippi to decorate the church of Santa Maria Novella.

His son, who is known as Filippo II Strozzi the Younger (1489–1538), allied himself with the Medici through his marriage to Clarice de' Medici, the daughter of Piero de' Medici. He provided loans to the Medici but his own plans for political power brought him into conflict with the Medici and ultimately his banishment from the city. He led fellow exiles in an uprising against the Medici in 1527. The Republic of Florence was overthrown in 1530, but instead of allying with Alessandro de' Medici, the new dictator of the city, Filippo left for Venice. He organized a group of Florentine exiles who sought to reestablish the republic after the assassination of Alessandro de' Medici in 1537. The conflict ended in a battle at Montemurlo, where he was captured. Thrown into the prison of Fortezza da Basso, he was tortured and he died, either by murder or by suicide.

The sons of Filippo Strozzi distinguished themselves in the service of France. Leone Strozzi (1515–1554) joined the Knights of Malta and then the navy of France, where he rose to the rank of admiral. Leone's brother Piero Strozzi (1500–1558) joined the French army in its campaigns in Italy. For his service he was named a marshal of France in 1554. In 1557 he took part in the French siege of the port of Calais, then in the hands of the English. Their descendant Carlo Strozzi (1587–1671) was an author who wrote several noted books of Florentine history.

SEE ALSO: Florence; Medici, Cosimo de'; Medici, Lorenzo de'

Suleiman
(1494–1566)

Sultan of the Ottoman Empire from 1520 until 1566, under whose rule the empire reached the height of its power and influence, as well as its peak as a center of science, culture, literature, and art. Born in 1494, he was the only son of Sultan Selim I, who appointed him to serve as the governor of the provinces of Bolu and Kaffa. He became the tenth sultan of the empire in 1520 on the death of his father.

An ambitious and capable military leader, Suleiman spent much of his life campaigning on the frontiers of the Ottoman Empire. When an Ottoman company of diplomats was refused tribute by the king of Hungary, Suleiman ordered his army into the Balkan Peninsula, and conquered Belgrade in 1521. He then ordered an attack on the Knights Hospitallers, a Christian military order in control of the Greek island of Rhodes. In 1522, the island surrendered after a long siege.

In 1526 Suleiman returned to Hungary, defeated the Hungarian army at the Battle of Mohacs, and captured Buda, the capital of the Hungarian kingdom. He returned in 1529, drove the occupying Austrian army out of the capital, and installed a Duke of Transylvania, John Zapolya, as his vassal. From Hungary Suleiman led an assault on the Austrian capital of Vienna in the fall of 1529. The siege of the city failed as the weather worsened and the professional soldiers known as Janissaries abandoned the siege.

After Vienna, Suleiman campaigned in Persia and Mesopotamia. Under the leadership of his grand vizier, Ibrahim, the Ottoman armies captured Baghdad and the Persian city of Tabriz in 1534. Suleiman sacked the city of Tabriz in 1536, and in the same year ordered the murder of Ibrahim for his ambition to rule Persia.

Suleiman made important reforms in the administration and laws of his expanding empire. He also made an alliance with the French king Francis I against the Habsburg emperors. This alliance made the Turks a forceful influence in the dynastic rivalries of Europe for the next three centuries.

In the 1540s he fought against European armies in Hungary and Austria. The Ottoman Empire annexed Hungary in 1541 and by 1547 was earning an annual tribute from the Habsburg rulers of Austria. The Ottoman navy captured the North African port of Tripoli in 1551. Under Khair al-Din Barbarossa, the Ottoman Empire reigned over North Africa and the Turkish navy became the most powerful force in the Mediterranean. Turkish ships staged frequent raids on European ports for gold and slaves. Ottoman forces also raided ports on the Red Sea as far as the Indian port of Diu, a colony of Portugal, and annexed the coasts of Arabia to the empire. After warring for several more years with the Persian armies of Shah Tahmasp, Suleiman settled the eastern frontiers of the Ottoman Empire in 1555, including Baghdad and the Persian Gulf port of Basra under their control.

Suleiman was a patron of the arts and literature, and was himself a distinguished poet and writer. A distinctly Ottoman style in the visual arts emerged, and the sultan commissioned the building of several important mosques in the Ottoman capital of Istanbul (formerly Constantinople). Suleiman's private life, however, was marred by constant intrigue and the corruption of his ministers and diplomats. He took as his wife a slave girl, Roxelana, who was given the title of Khurrem Sultan and who gave birth to Suleiman's younger son Selim in 1524. Roxelana intrigued in favor of her sons Selim and Bayezid against their elder half brother Mustapha. In 1553, as Mustapha's own power and influence at the sultan's court reached a dangerous point, Suleiman had him executed. In 1558 Roxelana died, an event followed by a war between her sons Selim and Bayezid. The conflict ended in the defeat and the betrayal of Bayezid by the shah of Persia, who turned him over to Suleiman for execution in exchange for a large payment of gold. While on campaign in Hungary, Suleiman laid siege to the Szigetva, where he died. His son Selim II inherited the Ottoman Empire at the greatest extent of its history.

SEE ALSO: Ottoman Empire

Sweden

A kingdom of northern Europe that reached the height of its power during the late Renaissance. Sweden was the homeland of Scandinavian pagans who held to their traditional gods until the tenth century and were among the last in Europe to be converted to Christianity. A series of clans fought for control of this part of Scandinavia, where kings were elected by councils of nobles rather than inheriting their titles. A new era began when Queen Margaret I of Denmark established the Kalmar Union in 1397, uniting the states of Denmark, Norway, and Sweden under an elected Danish monarch. The Kalmar Union was intended to balance the rising power of the Hanseatic League, a union of cities in Germany and other points in northern Europe. But the kings and nobility of Sweden and Denmark were unfriendly allies and frequently clashed over their respective territory and trade. In the meantime, Sweden developed its own parliament, the Riksdag, comprised of four estates of clergy, nobility, burghers, and farmers. This body frequently contended with the Danish monarchs; the conflict between Danish royalty and Swedish nobility reached a bloody climax in 1520, when King Christian II ordered the execution of hundreds of Swedish nobles in Stockholm.

Forging an alliance with the Hanseatic League, Gustav Vasa broke with Denmark and established Sweden as an independent state. Elected king in 1523, Gustav Vasa defied the Catholic Church, establishing Protestantism as the national church. He made himself the head of the church as well as the state and required all Swedish citizens to attend Sunday church services, which became a useful platform for rallying support. Vasa reformed the tax code and confiscated church lands to shore up the Swedish treasury.

The Bible was first translated into Swedish in 1541, an event that spread literacy throughout the kingdom and gave impetus to the development of a national literature. A nationalist movement known as Gothicism arose during this time, when Swedish writers harkened back to the wars and accomplishments of the Gothic tribes.

King Gustavus Adolphus, who ruled Sweden from 1611 until 1632, founded a Swedish empire in northern Europe and fought for the Protestant princes in Germany during the Thirty Years' War against Sweden's main economic rival, the Holy Roman Emperor. Gustavus Adolphus won an important victory at the Battle of Breitenfelt in 1631, but in the next year he was killed at the Battle of Lutzen. In the meantime, his armies were sweeping through central and eastern Europe, and by the Treaty of Westphalia that ended the war Sweden took possession of much of the Baltic Sea coastlands. This hotly contested area was vital to trade between northern Europe and the interior of Russia, which supplied valuable commodities such as furs, honey, and slaves to the European market. But the growing power of Russia made it increasingly difficult for Sweden to defend, and the kingdom lost most of its possessions south of the Baltic Sea in the Great Northern War with Russia in the early eighteenth century.

SEE ALSO: Thirty Years' War; Vasa, House of

Tasso, Torquato
(1544–1595)

Considered the finest Italian poet of the late Renaissance, Torquato Tasso was the son of Bernardo Tasso, a poet and courtier who served as secretary to the prince of Salerno. When the prince was banished by the King of Naples, Torquato and his family lost their property and were forced to move from Sorrento. Torquato lived in Naples and was educated by the new order of Jesuits, the guardians of doctrine and religious expression of the Catholic Counter-Reformation. He learned Latin and Greek before leaving Naples for Rome, where his father was serving the prince of Sorrento in exile. In 1557, at the age of thirteen, Torquato already enjoyed a reputation as a scholar and poet, and was hired as a tutor to the son of Duke Guidobaldo of Urbino. Tasso studied law and philosophy at the universities of Padua and Bologna. He preferred poetry, however, and first won renown in 1562 with *Rinaldo*, an epic poem of chivalry and courtly manners. He also wrote a didactic work, *Discourses on the Art of Poetry*. He earned a reputation as a critic and theorist on poetry, while his career as a scholar was cut short at the University of Bologna, where he was ostracized for writing satiric verses about students and professors.

In 1565 Tasso entered the service of the d'Este family of Ferrara as a court poet. He completed *Aminta*, a pastoral play in verse and music that combined myth and idealized court life, in 1573. This work

had an important influence on Italian music and the development of opera over the next two centuries. In 1575, Tasso's famous epic poem *Jerusalem Liberated* was first published. Written in the poetic form known as *ottava rima*, in which the poem is divided into eight-line stanzas, *Jerusalem Liberated* used *The Aeneid* of the Roman poet Virgil as its model. Tasso described the First Crusade, the exploits of the Christian knight Godfrey of Bouillon and a fictional hero, Rinaldo, and the romantic idylls of several invented characters. Trained in the strictures of the Jesuit order, however, Tasso worried for the rest of his life about the religious propriety of his work. He submitted the poem to several scholars as well as to the church for review. When the poem drew criticism for its structure, characterizations, and religious tone, Tasso began putting it through a drastic revision that drained his creativity as well as his sanity.

In 1576 Tasso began suffering from a mental illness that some modern historians have identified as schizophrenia. He grew suspicious and paranoid, fearing that the Duke of Ferrara and many others meant to do him harm. Outbursts of violent anger alternated with depression. When he assaulted a servant whom he suspected of spying on him, he was sent to a convent by the duke. He escaped to Sorrento but returned to Ferrara in 1579, where Duke Alfonso was celebrating his wedding. On arriving in Ferrara, however, Tasso violently denounced the duke and for this he was imprisoned in a hospital for the next seven years. His epic poem was published in a pirated edition and for the next several years Tasso revised the work, finally bringing out his own edition in 1580.

Tasso wrote hundreds of sonnets, madrigals, dialogues, and *canzoni* (songs) in verse. His last years were spent traveling from one Italian court to the next in search of patrons and conditions that would allow him the necessary peace of mind to work. He was nominated as the poet laureate of Italy but died just before he was to receive the honor in an official ceremony. In 1600, *Jerusalem Liberated* was translated into English; the poem would have an important influence on the works of Edmund Spenser and John Milton.

SEE ALSO: Ariosto, Ludovico; Milton, John; Spenser, Edmund; Virgil

Saint Teresa of Avila. HULTON ARCHIVE/GETTY IMAGES.

Teresa of Avila
(1515–1582)

A nun and patron saint of Spain, and an author of important religious and autobiographical works, Saint Teresa was born in Avila, Spain, as Teresa Sanchez Cepeda Davila y Ahumada. She was the daughter of Beatriz de Ahumada and Alonso de Cepeda, a wealthy *converso*, or converted Jew. Believing his daughter had few prospects for a successful marriage, he sent her to the Convent of Saint Mary of Grace for her studies. She joined the Monastery of the Incarnation but after falling ill traveled to several towns to visit faith healers. Her sickness worsened in 1539, when she began experiencing hallucinations and paralysis. Eventually she recovered, believing that prayer and the saints had been responsible for her survival. Visions and the conversations with phantoms continued, putting her at the center of a controversy, in which some believed her a witch and

others to be directly inspired by God. Vowing to lead a life of prayer and self-denial, she left the monastery, where the wealthier nuns were free to lead a comfortable life and enjoy material possessions and socialize with men.

Believing the order had grown too worldly and needed reform, Teresa established a more austere branch of the Carmelites in 1560 and then the new Convent of Saint Joseph in 1562. This Order of *Discalced* (barefoot) Sisters, isolated itself from the community and established strict rules of poverty, silence, prayer, simple living, and the most simple clothing (including a ban on footwear, outside of the simple sandals Teresa designed for them). King Philip II of Spain saw such reforms as vital to the task of combating the Protestant movement, and called on the monasteries of his kingdom to lead the way.

Teresa described her visions and her youth in an autobiography, *The Life*, and the philosophy of her new order in *The Way of Perfection*. In 1567, the head of the Carmelite order, Giovanni Rossi, asked her to establish new reformed convents, and for the next decade she traveled through Spain with a companion, Saint John of the Cross, and gained renown throughout the kingdom for her austere spirituality. Male orders of barefoot friars who followed her precepts were also established, and new Discalced Carmelite monasteries were established in foreign countries. In 1571 Teresa returned to the Convent of the Incarnation in Avila as the prioress, and reformed the main order's rules. She then wrote *The Foundations*, a book of instruction for members of the order, and *The Interior Castle*, a book about the process of "mental prayer," which Teresa believed to be a road to direct communication with God. Her strict rules for the "unreformed" Carmelites raised opposition by some leaders of the Catholic Church, some of whom saw silent prayer as a less devout practice than vocal prior. She lost her position as prioress at the Convent of the Incarnation, and for a time was even under investigation by the Spanish Inquisition. In 1578, however, the pope of the church officially recognized her order, which was declared separate twelve years after her death in 1594. Teresa was declared the patroness of Spain by the Cortes (Spanish parliament) in 1617, and in 1622 she was canonized as a saint by Pope Gregory XV; in 1970 she became the first woman to be named "Doctor of the Church." Her writings and philosophy grew in importance among Catholics throughout Europe and Teresa was eventually accepted as one of the major figures of the Counter-Reformation, in which the church returned to its spiritual roots in order to better contend with the rising popularity of the Protestant sects of northern Europe.

SEE ALSO: Catholicism

theater

The medieval religious plays performed for small audiences, blossomed into the theater, the most popular form of entertainment during the Renaissance. The new drama was given impetus by the discovery of ancient Greek and Roman plays, including the works of Terence, Plautus, and Seneca. In Italy, the new tradition of pastoral plays gained popularity along with the tragedies and comedies written on classical models. The Italian love for music and display emerged in the intermezzo, a piece performed between the acts of a serious performance, and the commedia dell'arte, a boisterous and improvised comedic romp with a familiar set of characters that was performed in city streets and squares. Eventually music, drama, and dance would be combined in the new form of opera; which emerged in the sixteenth century in the works of Claudio Monteverdi and other Italian masters.

In France, the leading playwrights included Estienne Jodelle and Alexandre Hardy, who defied the classical style. In the late Renaissance, however, there was a return to ancient forms of tragedy (in the works of Jean Racine and Pierre Corneille), and masterful comedies by Moliere. These playwrights wrote under the influence of Cardinal Richelieu and the Catholic Reformation, which resisted innovation and sought a return to tradition, whether that of religion or of art. The Spanish writer Lope de Vega authored hundreds of plays full of action and drama in the tradition of the medieval chivalric romance. Theater flourished in Spain through the seventeenth century, with the production of *sac-*

ramentales, or one-act religious plays, *comedias nuevas*, or new comedies, and musical shows known as *zarzuelas*.

In England the first outdoor theater was established in London in 1576, and was soon attracting thousands of people, who paid a pittance to stand among the "groundlings" or slightly more for seats in covered sections raised above the stage. Previously, stages had been set up in public squares or marketplaces and were open to all; the Globe and other theaters of the late sixteenth century were the first structures devoted exclusively to public entertainment. Smaller, "private" theaters also operated, offering spectators an indoor venue and seating for all.

Thomas Kyd's *The Spanish Tragedy* was among the most popular plays of the Elizabethan era and set the standard for all later tragedies. The Renaissance drama reached the peak of its poetic and dramatic power in the works of William Shakespeare, as well as his contemporary Christopher Marlowe. Shakespeare was a masterful poet and dramatist who worked in many different forms, including tragedies, comedies, and historical plays. After the Elizabethan era, the English theater entered a period of slow decline until the Puritan government closed the theaters in 1642. The leading dramatist of this "Jacobean" era was the satirist Ben Jonson, who found humor in the follies of ordinary people.

SEE ALSO: de Vega, Lope; Marlowe, Christopher; Shakespeare, William; Tasso, Turquato

Thirty Years' War

An international conflict taking place in northern Europe from 1618 to 1648. The war was fought between Catholics and Protestants and also drew in the national armies of France, Sweden, Spain, Denmark, and the Habsburg dynasty that ruled the Holy Roman Empire. The roots of the conflict lay in the Protestant Reformation of the sixteenth century. The Reformation, strongly opposed by the Catholic Habsburgs, brought religious persecution and civil war to Germany. By the Peace of Augsburg, concluded in 1555, each German prince was free to choose the religious faith—either Lutheranism or Catholicism—to be followed in his own realm.

Religious conflict continued despite the Peace of Augsburg, complicated by the territorial ambitions of the nations surrounding Germany, then a patchwork of small and autonomous duchies, kingdoms, counties, margravates, and city-states. Sweden and Denmark, kingdoms to the north, were seeking new territory in northern Germany, while France was opposing Habsburg power in Germany and the Low Countries. Open warfare between Catholics and Protestants broke out in Swabia, a region of southwestern Germany, in the early 1600s. Protestant Calvinists formed the League of Evangelical Union, while Catholics gathered their forces into the Catholic League.

In 1619, Ferdinand of Styria became Ferdinand II, Holy Roman Emperor. His dedication to Catholicism and determination to stamp out Protestantism prompted a revolt in Prague, the capital of Bohemia. Two of the emperor's representatives were attacked and thrown out of a window after a trial, an act that sparked a general revolt against Ferdinand's authority in Bohemia and Hungary. To quell the rebellion, Ferdinand asked for help from his nephew, King Philip IV of Spain. Although Vienna, the Habsburg capital, came under siege by a Protestant army, Ferdinand won a victory against the Protestant Union at the

Battle of Sablat in 1619. The Protestants of Bohemia responded by declaring Ferdinand deposed as their king and replacing him with Elector Frederick V of the Palatinate.

Spain then sent armies from Flanders to come to the emperor's assistance. Spanish armies marauded through the Protestant cities of western Germany, then joined up with the emperor to put down the rebellion in Austria. At the Battle of White Mountain on November 8, 1620, Ferdinand defeated the Protestant armies under Frederick V, a victory that permanently returned Bohemia to Habsburg control. Spanish armies then captured Mannheim, Heidelberg, and many other cities, executing or driving out their Protestant leaders.

The king of Denmark then came to the rescue of the Protestants by gathering a mercenary army, allying himself with England and France, and invading Germany. The Danes suffered two defeats at the Battle of Dessau Bridge in April 1626 and the Battle of Lutter in August 1626. By the Treaty of Lubeck in 1629, the Danes gave up their alliance with the Protestants and the Danish king was allowed to keep his throne. The Swedish king Gustavus Adolphus then intervened, fearing the growing Habsburg power in northern Germany. A brilliant military tactician, this king won several important battles, including the Battle of Breitenfeld in 1631. The Swedes won again at the Battle of Lutzen, but Gustavus Adolphus was killed in the battle.

The Peace of Prague of 1635 temporarily ended the fighting and granted a truce to the Protestant opponents of the emperor. After this, France entered the war on the Protestant side against the Habsburgs. Catholic Spain invaded France in retaliation. The war caused massive damage and heavy casualties on both sides, and after more battles in Bohemia and southern Germany the Truce of Ulm was signed in 1647. The Peace of Westphalia followed in the next year. Over the three decades of war, Germany was ravaged by fighting, pillaging, and widespread disease and famine. The nation would remain fragmented and weak for more than two centuries. Spain began a long decline that left it one of the weakest nations in Europe, and the republics of the Low Countries permanently broke away from Spanish control. Habsburg authority was also weakened in central Europe, while France, which saw little fighting, emerged as Europe's dominant power.

SEE ALSO: Habsburg dynasty; Reformation, Protestant

Tintoretto, Jacopo (1519–1594)

Venetian painter of the Late Renaissance, who rejected the careful precision of contemporary painters for a freer, more energetic style and who was keenly skilled in the rendering of light, perspective, and sheer drama in his works. Born into a family of twenty-one children, he was the son of a dyer, whose occupation (*tintore*) gave his son the nickname of Tintoretto. He was sent by his father to the workshop of Titian, who soon sent the boy home out of jealousy or contempt for his independent style of drawing. As a result, Tintoretto was largely self-taught as an artist, taking both Titian and Michelangelo Buonarroti as his models. He developed his own method of preparing paintings by constructing three-dimensional clay or wax models, posing them and using light from various angles to get the most dramatic effects.

Tintoretto's first major commission was a painting for the Scuola di San

Marco, an important Venetian confraternity. He decorated the Scuola with paintings based on biblical stories, and his great skill in executing these works built up his reputation in Venice. Three famous works—*The Worship of the Golden Calf, The Presentation of the Virgin,* and *The Last Judgement*—were completed for the Church of the Madonna. Eventually these works were painted over, and most of his other church paintings and frescoes have not survived to modern times. For the Scuola di San Rocco, he contributed magnificent ceiling and wall paintings, including *The Crucifixion, The Plague of Serpents,* and *Moses Striking the Rock.* He was commissioned to paint all of the halls of the Scuola as well as the Church of San Rocco, a work that produced more than fifty paintings and on which the artist was occupied until his death in 1594.

In the meantime Tintoretto completed large frescoes in the Doge's Palace and the Sala dello Scrutinio, a seat of power in Venice, as well as many portraits of Venetian rulers and noblemen. Several large paintings on historical themes, including the Battle of Lepanto, were destroyed in a fire in 1577. Tintoretto's masterpiece, *Paradise,* is an immense canvas 74 feet (22.5m) in length by 30 feet (9m) high. Tintoretto's works reflect a new trend in art, the dramatic use of light and shade to tell a story, as well as exaggerated movements, dramatic poses, and distortion of figures. These would become key features of the art of the Baroque period that followed the Renaissance.

SEE ALSO: Titian; Venice

Titian
(1490–1576)

Painter of Venice who is regarded by many as one of the finest artists of the late Re-naissance, and whose works display a mastery of color, design, and painting technique. Born as Tiziano Vecellio in the village of Pieve di Cadore in northern Italy, he left at the age of nine to make his way in Venice, where he first joined the workshop of a mosaic artist, Sebastiano Zuccati. Titian next apprenticed in the Venetian workshop of Gentile Bellini. He became a close friend of Giorgione, whose works had an important influence on Titian's own. One of his early commissions was a fresco painting for the walls of the German Merchant's Foundation, where he collaborated with Giorgione. At the age of twenty-one Titian decorated the Scuola del Santo of the Confraternity of Saint Anthony in Padua with frescoes of Saint Anthony. Titian's most famous early work is an altarpiece, entitled *Assumption of the Virgin,* a monumental painting completed in the Santa Maria Gloriosa church of Venice.

Other famous early works include *Flora, Madonna of the Cherries, Presentation of the Virgin, Christ and the Tribute Money, Christ Crowned with Thorns,* and *Sacred and Profane Love,* in which the artist contrasts clothed and nude figures of the goddess Venus. These paintings made the artist's reputation in Venice, and word of Titian's mastery was soon spreading throughout Europe. His work was in demand by popes, by the Holy Roman Emperor Charles V, by King Philip II of Spain, and by the Dukes of Ferrara and Urbino, important art patrons of Italy. For Alfonso d'Este, the Duke of Ferrara, Titian completed three famous mythological paintings, *Andrians, Worship of Venus,* and *Bacchus and Ariadne.* For the Gonzaga ruler of Mantua, he painted a *Madonna with a Rabbit* and a series of portraits of Roman emperors, which were eventually destroyed.

Titian's "Sacred and Profane Love" contrasts different types of love through two different depictions of the Roman goddess Venus.

Titian's deep colors, rich textures, and complex, carefully balanced designs give his paintings an air of elegance and serenity. Art historians consider his paintings *Worship of Venus, Bacchus and Ariadne,* and the *Venus of Urbino* as among the finest masterpieces of the late Renaissance, and among the best examples of the "Venetian school" of painting. The many commissions he received made him a wealthy man, and by the 1530s Titian had settled himself into the Casa Grande, one of the finest mansions of Venice, where he entertained a devoted following of students, writers, and nobles.

In 1545, the artist moved to Rome at the invitation of Pope Paul III. In Rome he met Michelangelo and was deeply influenced by the ruins of the ancient city as well as the art of Michelangelo and Raphael. He was offered commissions for

works by prelates of the church and also executed portraits of the popes, including a profound portrait known as *Paul III and His Grandsons,* that explores the complex and mistrustful relationship between the members of a privileged and powerful family. Michelangelo's strong, sculptural figures influenced the figures in Titian's *Christ Crowned with Thorns* and *Martyrdom of St. Lawrence.*

Charles V, who had met the artist in Bologna in 1530 on the occasion of his coronation as Holy Roman Emperor, invited Titian to Germany in 1548. Charles made Titian an honorary count of the Palatine, and Titian repaid the compliment by painting the emperor into *La Gloria,* completed in 1554. An equestrian portrait of the emperor as he rode to victory at the Battle of Mühlberg became one of the most famous royal portraits of the Renaissance. For King Philip II of Spain, he completed several works on mythological themes, including *Perseus and Andromeda, Diana and Callisto*, and *The Rape of Europa*. Several major works, including *Adam and Eve* and the *Martyrdom of St. Lawrence*, were painted for the monastery of San Lorenzo del Escorial near Madrid; in the royal palace of the Escorial Titian painted *Christ Carrying the Cross, The Last Supper*, and *Agony in the Garden*. Titian's last painting is the *Pietà*, a work he intended to decorate his tomb. The painter's original use of perspective, foreshortening, and his technique of blending colors to mask outlines of figures and objects were taken up by painters of the Mannerist and Baroque styles who would dominate art after the end of the Renaissance.

SEE ALSO: Bellini, Gentile; Giorgione; Michelangelo Buonarroti; Tintoretto, Jacopo; Venice

Torquemada, Tomás de (1420–1498)

A notorious prosecutor of the Spanish Inquisition who served the Spanish monarchs Ferdinand and Isabella by ruthlessly ridding their kingdom of non-Christians during the 1490s. It was Torquemada's task to root out all false converters and punish them with imprisonment, public humiliation, expulsion from the kingdom, or death. Born in the town of Torquemada, he was the nephew of a Catholic cardinal, Juan de Torquemada. Raised in Valladolid, Tomás became a friar of the Dominican order and was then appointed as the prior of Santa Cruz, a monastery in Segovia. He became confessor of Isabella, heir to the throne of Castile, while the princess was living in Segovia. In 1474, when Isabella became the queen of Castile, Torquemada followed her to the royal palace, where he became both confessor and adviser.

In 1478, Pope Sixtus IV established the Inquisition, an office meant to root out all religious heresy. The first Inquisition court was established in the southern city of Seville. In 1483, the pope rewarded Torquemada for his service to the church by naming him to the post of General Inquisitor. Over the next few years Torquemada founded Inquisition courts in Valladolid, Seville, Cordoba, Zaragoza, and Avila, established a council of five to hear appeals, and wrote a set of rules and regulations for religious trials that remained in effect until the eighteenth century. But the Inquisition had jurisdiction only over Christians; in the meantime the Jews of Spain, also known as Marranos, were accused of heinous crimes, including the notorious murder of Pedro de Arbues, another member of the Inquisition, in 1485. Frustrated by his inability to arrest and try members of the Jewish faith, Torquemada decided on a show trial as the most effective way to enhance his authority. He had eight Jews rounded up in the town of LaGuardia, and had them tried and convicted of the ritual murder of a Christian child—even though the court had no evidence of the crime and no victim. In 1492, the threat of Jewish ritual murder, as revealed by the LaGuardia trial, persuaded Ferdinand and Isabella to pass the Alhambra Decree, giving all Jews one month to leave Spain; those who remained had to sincerely disavow their faith and convert to Christianity.

Torquemada's Inquisition court arrested suspects denounced by a network of spies, and extracted confessions through torture. The Inquisition seized the property of those it accused, then paraded them through the streets before having them publicly whipped at the doors of a church. Some of the suspects were turned over to the civil authorities for a public execution. A mass execution of this sort, known as an auto-da-fé, or "act of faith," might have a dozen or more victims tied to stakes and burned to death.

SEE ALSO: Ferdinand II of Aragon; Inquisition; Isabella of Castile; Jews

Toscanelli, Paolo
(1397–1482)

An Italian physician, astronomer, mapmaker, and mathematician who is best known for creating a map of the world that may have been used by Christopher Columbus in planning his voyage to the East Indies. Born in Florence, he was the son of a doctor, Dominic Toscanelli. He studied mathematics with Giovanni dell'Abacco in Florence and attended the University of Padua, earning the title of doctor of medicine in 1424. He returned to Florence and earned a reputation as a leading mathematician and astronomer, considered by many people to be the most brilliant scientist of his day.

A skilled astronomical observer, Toscanelli observed and measured the orbits of comets, including the occurrence of Halley's Comet in 1456. In the cathedral of Florence he designed a gnomon, a slab of marble placed high in the left transept of the church that cast a shadow of the sun, allowing an observer to determine noon and measure the occurrence of the winter and summer solstices. From his studies of ancient writers, including Ptolemy, and his conversations with travelers and explorers, Toscanelli created a map of the world that was sent to the king of Portugal in 1474, and explained the possibility of sailing west, rather than around Africa and through the Indian Ocean, to reach the East Indies. The scheme became known to Christopher Columbus, who

corresponded with Toscanelli and who carried a copy of Toscanelli's map and letter with him on his first voyage. Toscanelli miscalculated the size of the globe, however, believing Europe and Asia to cover much more of the earth's surface than they actually do. This misconception convinced Columbus that he had actually reached Asia in 1492, whereas his fleet had in fact only sailed as far as the eastern islands of the Caribbean Sea.

SEE ALSO: Columbus, Christopher; exploration

trade

In the Middle Ages, long-distance trade was rare. Travel was dangerous, and most people lived a subsistent existence on rural estates, where they grew just enough to support their families and pay a landlord for the use of the land. Rare and valuable goods were imported from the Middle East and, in later centuries, via the Silk Road that linked eastern Europe with central Asia. As money was in short supply, most of this trade was carried out by the barter system, in which goods were exchanged for other goods.

The expansion of the banking system, the improvement of roads, and the growth of manufacturing industries and a middle class all contributed to a rise in international trade during the Renaissance. Cities of the Low Countries and northern Italy became the wealthiest in Europe. These regions specialized in the making of cloth, silk, woven tapestries, armor, and other goods in demand throughout Europe. German cities prospered from a trade in silver, England sold its wool and herring, and the Scandinavian countries exported fur and timber. From port cities such as Amsterdam, Genoa, Lisbon, and Venice, merchants and navigators sailed to distant regions of Asia to trade in valuable goods in short supply in Europe, such as silk and spices.

The rise of a middle class went hand in hand with economic growth, and the wider circulation of money played an important role in the artistic flowering of the Renaissance. Prominent families such as the Medici of Florence thrived from loans and letters of credit that made long-distance trade possible. The Medici ran an international conglomerate, with banks, mines, mills, trading houses, and other businesses all over Europe; the vast wealth they acquired allowed them to take power as a hereditary ruling dynasty in Florence. The Medici and other merchant families displayed their wealth by patronizing artists, architects and sculptors, and commissioning new works of art for their homes, palaces, and private chapels.

Italy was well located to serve as a center of international trade. Its ports and manufacturing centers lay between western Europe and the Middle East, along convenient shipping routes through the Mediterranean. Trade was also conducted along the major rivers of the continent, including the Danube, the Rhine, the Loire, and the Rhone. As monarchies grew stronger and unified nations emerged, central governments extended their control of trade through taxes, tariffs, and customs barriers. At the same time, foreign trade helped diminish the feudal system, as the money economy allowed bonded serfs to leave their estates and sell their know-how and skills in the cities.

The age of exploration that began in the fifteenth century, with Portuguese expeditions down the coast of Africa and across the Indian Ocean to southern Asia, spelled the end of Italy's dominance of trade. Portuguese and other navigators opened up new sea routes and established colonies, which allowed Portugal and the rest of Europe to bypass the Italian middlemen who had controlled trade between Europe and the Middle East. Busy shipping lanes across the Atlantic linked England, France, and Spain with their overseas American colonies, which provided raw materials and eventually a hungry market for goods manufactured in Europe. Foreign trade replaced agriculture as the lifeblood of western Europe's economies, and would spur the industrial revolution that began in the eighteenth century.

Tudor dynasty

A series of monarchs that ruled England and Ireland from 1485 until 1603. The Tudor kings and queens reigned as England developed into a powerful and influential state, an important center of Protestant resistance to papal authority, and a leader in Renaissance letters, science, and art. The Tudor line began with a Welsh squire, Owen Tudor, a member of the court of King Henry V. On the king's death Tudor married his widow, Catherine of Valois; his eldest son was Edmund Tudor, who in turn fathered Henry Tudor. During the War of the Roses, this Lancastrian nobleman defeated King Richard III in 1485 at the Battle of Bosworth Field and then was enthroned as the first Tudor king, Henry VII.

The brother of this king, Henry VIII, began his reign in 1509. Henry married his brother's widow, Catherine of Aragon, who gave birth to his first child Mary but failed to provide the new king with a male heir. Falling out of favor with Henry, Catherine was replaced by the king's mistress, Anne Boleyn. When Henry found himself unable to convince the pope to sanction his divorce from Catherine, he declared papal authority ended in his realm and founded the Church of England. He then married Anne Boleyn, who gave birth to a single daughter, Elizabeth. Anne ran afoul of powerful nobles allied with the king and was accused of treason and incest, which brought about her arrest and execution. Henry's third wife, Jane Seymour, died giving birth to the king's sole male offspring, Edward.

At the age of nine, Edward VI succeeded his father in 1547. This young and sickly king died in 1553, leaving the throne to his half sister Mary, daughter of Catherine of Aragon. A loyal Catholic, "Bloody Mary" made futile attempts to return England to the Catholic Church, ordering the seizure and execution of several Protestant nobles and clergymen. Mary died in 1558 without an heir, which brought the accession of her half sister Elizabeth, daughter of Anne Boleyn. Devoted to the memory of her mother, Elizabeth felt determined to reign in the religious conflict and political intrigue that plagued the Tudor court since the time of Henry VII.

Elizabeth restored the Church of England and encouraged playwrights, musicians, and poets at her court. Talented men such as William Shakespeare, Christopher Marlowe, and Ben Jonson flourished during the Elizabethan Age, when England was also home to a leading scientific philosopher, Sir Francis Bacon. During her reign England began to colonize North America, and the English captain Sir France Drake led the first voyage of English ships around the world. She also defeated the attempt by her cousin, the Catholic Mary, Queen of Scots, to overthrow her, and regretfully ordered Mary's execution in 1587. In the next year, an immense armada of Spanish warships was sent by the king of Spain, scattered by storms in the English Channel, marking the rise of English power on the continent and the beginning of a steady decline in the power of Spain.

With Elizabeth remaining unmarried and childless, the Tudor dynasty came to an end with her death in 1603. The throne passed to James I, the king of Scotland and the first monarch of England's Stuart dynasty.

SEE ALSO: Edward VI; Elizabeth I; England; Henry VIII

Uccello, Paolo (1397–1475)

Italian painter born as Paolo di Dono, noted for the original use of perspective in his works. Born in Florence, the son of a barber, he earned the nickname "uccello" (Italian for bird) for his skill at painting birds. In 1407 he became an apprentice to the sculptor Lorenzo Ghiberti, the artist who had won the commission to cast bronze panels for the doors of the Baptistery in Florence. Ghiberti's workshop was a busy, vital artistic center of Florence at a time when the city's painters were leading the way in the new science of perspective. In Uccello's works, perspective became an integral part of a unified picture, used in order to give the scene depth and not to simply separate different elements or stories within the paintings.

In 1414, Uccello became a member of the Compagnia di San Luca, a painters guild, and in the next year he was admitted to the official painters guild of Florence. His early works include commissions to paint frescoes for the churches of Santa Trinita and Santa Maria Maggiore. He was also engaged to paint frescoes on the outdoor walls of the Green Cloister of the Church of Santa Maria Novella. For this work he created scenes of the Creation, the Expulsion from the Garden of Eden, and the Flood. The paintings, which earned widespread admiration among the artists of Florence, showed the influence of Ghiberti and his Baptistry panels, although Uccello developed even greater skill at depicting nature and animals.

Uccello lived and worked in Florence, but he also completed works in Venice, where he created mosaics for the facade of the Basilica of San Marco, Bologna, Prato, and Urbino. In the Duomo (cathedral) of Florence, he painted scenes on a large interior clock and a fresco of the English mercenary Sir John Hawkwood, completed in 1436 and famous for its unusual perspective, which gives the illusion of viewing a three-dimensional sculpture from below.

SEE ALSO: Florence; Ghiberti, Lorenzo

universities

The improved literacy and communications of the Renaissance era went hand-in-hand with an increasing respect for intellectual training for professions such as medicine, theology, and the law. To create well-rounded and educated citizens, major universities were established throughout western Europe: at Ferrara, Turin, and Parma in Italy; Bordeaux and Nantes in France; Copenhagen and Uppsala in Scandinavia; Frankfurt and Tubingen in Germany; Saragossa and Valencia in Spain; and at Kraków, Poland. The University of Paris, which taught the liberal arts and theology, remained the model for institutions throughout northern Europe, awarding bachelor's degrees and training students of the upper classes—all male—in a fundamental classical learning of grammar, rhetoric, and ethics.

For cities and their lords, the university was a mark of prestige. It represented advanced thinking, enlightened rule, the new trend of humanistic learning and scholarship, and the generous patronage of town fathers and aristocrats. Universities competed for renowned professors, who in turn attracted the best scholars. Members of the expanding middle class, at the same time, sought out higher education for their sons, who trained themselves in the law, medicine, and for careers as administrators and diplomats. The University of Bologna in northern Italy became a center for the study of the revived Roman law,

Within the university, students attended lectures by professors, who spoke and debated in Latin. The courses relied on the teachings of ancient philosophers such as Aristotle, Galen, Hippocrates, and the Arab scientist Avicenna. Following the humanistic philosophy, students critically examined classical texts, studying the original language, whether Greek or Latin, in order to get at the intended meaning. This was an important break with medieval higher education, in which professors simply handed down the accepted traditional interpretation of the ancient texts and students were discouraged from critical thinking.

After a course of study, the student was put through a degree examination by professors and scholars, who tested his mastery of the subject and his ability to defend his ideas in open debate. The bachelor's degree enabled further study, while the master's was a license to teach. The doctorate was awarded for scholars devoted to the study of a particular field and the contribution of original knowledge to that field. Most universities during the Renaissance had several hundred students, while the largest at Bologna and Paris had a few thousand. Students within the universities organized themselves according to their homelands. At the largest universities these student unions held considerable power, making demands for better working and living conditions and in some places passing on the hiring of new professors by the university.

See Also: Aristotelianism; humanism

Valois dynasty

A dynasty of thirteen kings of France who reigned from 1328 through 1589. The Valois dynasty began with Philip VI, who succeeded the last king of the House of Capet, Charles IV. At this time England and France were in conflict over French support of a rebellion in Scotland, and over the English king Edward III's claim to the throne of France. The two countries went to war in 1337, a contest that endured for more than a century and brought ruin to cities and estates throughout France. The authority of the kings of France was challenged by powerful French nobles and tested further by the arrival of the Black Death—the bubonic plague that struck France in the late 1340s and killed millions of its citizens. The plague and the war drove many French nobles to break away from the authority of the king, and a peasant rebellion known as the Jacquerie brought further chaos and violence to the kingdom. At the Battle of Agincourt, in 1415, English longbowmen defeated the armies of the king and devastated the French knights.

The French cause and the Valois dynasty found salvation in the person of Joan of Arc, who convinced Charles VII to appoint her commander of the French forces lifting the English siege of Orléans. Although Joan was captured and executed in 1429, the French began scoring victories against the English. Royal authority strengthened under Charles and his successors, who brought Normandy, Burgundy, Guienne, and Brittany under central control. The French nobles were brought to heel through a system of seneschals—representatives who enforced royal laws and decrees—and by the actions of royal courts known as Parlements that were established throughout the nation.

At the end of the fifteenth century, with central authority strengthened and France recovered from the Hundred Years' War, the Valois monarchs Charles VIII and Louis XII involved the kingdom in the many disputes burning in the Italian peninsula. In the end, France was expelled from Italy by an alliance of the Habsburg emperors and the Italian city-states, which fielded effective mercenary armies.

The Valois line continued through the reigns of Francis I from 1515 to 1547 and Henri II, whose reign began in 1547. Francis I was a dedicated patron of writers and artists, and made France a center of the Renaissance. Both Francis I and Henri II strongly resisted the Protestant Reformation, prosecuting Protestant heresy and keeping France within the Catholic Church. The conflict culminated during the reign of Charles IX in a nationwide assault on Protestants in 1572 known as the Saint Bartholomew's Day Massacre. The assassination of Henri II in 1559 touched off a bloody civil conflict known as the Wars of Religion between Catholics and French Protestants, also known as Huguenots. Henri III was murdered in 1589 and left behind no heir, bringing Henri IV to the throne as the first of the Bourbon dynasty.

SEE ALSO: Francis I; Henri III; Henri IV

van der Weyden, Rogier
(1399–1464)

A noted Flemish painter of religious subjects and portraits born as Roger de la Pasture in Tournai, northern France. The son of a knife maker, he apprenticed in the workshop of Robert Campin, and took his artistic influence from Campin and Jan van Eyck. As van der Weyden never signed his paintings, historians have argued for centuries between van der Weyden and Campin as the artists of many important works. In 1432 van der Weyden earned the title of painting master of Tournai. In 1435 he moved to Brussels, seat of the wealthy dukes of Burgundy, where he changed his name to Rogier van der Weyden and where he was appointed as the official city painter. This title brought him commissions to paint portraits of the dukes and members of the local aristocracy, and he was soon prospering. Van der Weyden completed a series of huge wooden panels for the town hall of Brussels, works that were famous throughout Europe before they were destroyed in a bombardment of the city in 1695. By 1440 he had completed *Descent from the Cross*, one of his most famous works, for the guild crossbowmen of Louvain. His best-known works include a *Last Judgment* altarpiece that measures 18 feet (5.5m) in width, as well as the *Braque Triptych, Adoration of the Magi, St. Luke Painting the Virgin*, the Deposition panel and Crucifixion triptych, as well as a *Portrait of a Lady*.

Van der Weyden may have made a pilgrimage to Italy in about 1450, a journey that left important marks on his painting style. Members of the d'Este and Medici dynasties commissioned his portraits, and the duchess of Milan sent one of her favorite artists back to Brussels to apprentice in van der Weyden's busy studio. By the time of his death he was renowned throughout Europe for the way he combined traditional Flemish precision with strong emotional intensity, a quality that made his work more accessible to painters of southern Europe and that made him a key influence on the painters of northern Europe for several generations.

SEE ALSO: van Eyck, Jan; Brueghel family

van Eyck, Jan
(ca. 1385–1441)

Flemish artist who pioneered new methods of painting at the dawn of the Renaissance in northern Europe. Born in the town of Maaseik, he was a court painter for the Duke of Bavaria, the Count of Holland, and later for Duke Philip III the Good of Burgundy, then ruler of one of the wealthiest realms of Europe. Van Eyck served the duke as a diplomat as well as a painter, and traveled on several missions in the duke's service.

Van Eyck ran a busy workshop in the city of Bruges, where he remained for most of his life. His works and his painting technique were copied by many other northern European artists. He was a well-read scholar of ancient writers, notably Pliny the Elder, a Roman naturalist who wrote on the subjects of art and painting. Many of his works carry Latin inscriptions, a sign in his own day of a well-educated man. Historians have counted ten of his works that he signed, an unusual practice in the Middle Ages and evidence that van Eyck enjoyed a high reputation among patrons and collectors.

Van Eyck had a gift for composition, rendering his subjects in great detail with

The central panel of Jan van Eyck's "Ghent Altarpiece." It depicts God the Father enthroned as a Pope with St. John the Baptist and the Virgin Mary on either side. Below them is the Adoration of the Lamb. © ARCHIVO ICONOGRAFICO, S.A./CORBIS. REPRODUCED BY PERMISSION.

careful shading of light and texture. He was also a master of the technical aspects of painting, and was one of the first artists to work with oil paints. He produced large-scale religious works as well as intimate personal portraits. His largest and most famous single work is the *Ghent Altarpiece*, also known as *The Adoration of the Lamb*, an elaborate polyptych, or multi paneled painting, that he completed with the help of his brother Hubert van Eyck. This work was carried out for the Cathedral of Saint Bavon in Ghent. He is also known for a later work, the *Marriage of the Arnolfini*, a wedding portrait rich in

detail and bright coloration. Van Eyck also painted *Madonna with Chancellor Rolin* and a famous *Annunciation*, as well as a self-portrait, *Portrait of a Man in a Turban*. These and other works were known to artists throughout Europe, and van Eyck's attention to naturalistic detail, rich texture, and intense coloration influenced generations of artists in northern Europe.

SEE ALSO: painting

van Hemessen, Catherine (ca. 1527–1587)

Flemish painter, the first documented female painter of the Low Countries and a noted portrait painter. Born in Antwerp, the daughter of Jan Sanders van Hemessen, a minor artist, she studied with her father and eventually joined the painters guild of Antwerp. During the 1540s, she was taken on as a court painter by Maria of Austria, then serving as regent for Emperor Charles V in the Low Countries. She painted portraits, mostly of women set against a plain dark background that strikingly focused the observer's eye on the features and character of the subject. Her own self-portrait of 1548 is known as the first to depict the painter working at an easel. When Maria returned to Spain in 1556, van Hemessen followed her patron and was rewarded with a pension for her work after Maria's death in 1558. She then returned to Antwerp. Only ten of her works have survived to modern times, and there are no works at all from this later period in her life. Historians believe she may have given up painting altogether after her marriage.

Vasa, House of

A royal dynasty with branches in Sweden and Poland, which reigned in the sixteenth and seventeenth centuries. The dynasty was founded in Sweden by Gustavus I. His son John married Catherine Jagellonica, the sister of King Sigismund II of Poland. John's brother, then the king of Sweden, bitterly opposed this marriage and confined the couple to the castle of Gripsholm, where their son Sigismund was born and was educated by fervently Catholic Jesuit priests.

In 1587 Sigismund was elected as King Sigismund III Vasa by the electors of the commonwealth of Poland. When his father King John III died, Sigismund also became the king of Sweden, but his attempts to return Sweden to the Catholic Church was opposed by the parliament of Sweden, which deposed him in 1599. In Poland, Sigismund led an attack on the Baltic state of Latvia, intending to annex it to Poland, in 1600. This provoked war with Sweden and a series of conflicts between the two Vasa dynasties that would continue for more than fifty years.

In Sweden Sigismund was succeeded by Charles IX, his uncle and a Protestant. Gustavus II Adolphus succeeded Charles. An able military commander, Gustavus led a powerful Swedish force against the Catholics in Germany and won key victories during the Thirty Years' War. On his death in battle in 1632 his daughter Christina became the queen of Sweden. Christina converted to Catholicism and abdicated the throne of Sweden in 1654, passing the monarchy to her cousin, Charles X, a member of the Wittelsbach dynasty of Germany. This event brought the Swedish Vasa dynasty to an end.

By the Peace of Westphalia, which ended the Thirty Years' War in 1648, Sweden had gained territory on the southern shores of the Baltic Sea—land that had long been claimed by the kings of Poland. In 1655 two large columns of Swedish troops invaded Poland, bringing Poland as well as Lithuania under Swedish control. The Polish line of the Vasa dynasty had continued through the reigns of Ladislav IV, who was succeeded in 1648 by his brother Jan II Kazimierz. This king escaped the Swedish assault of 1655 and from his refuge in Silesia called on the Polish nation to resist the Swedes. The uprising resulted in the Treaty of Oliwa in 1660, which returned Sweden and Poland to their original borders.

SEE ALSO: Sweden; Thirty Years' War

Vasari, Giorgio (1511–1570)

Painter, architect, and author, whose book *Lives of the Most Celebrated Painters, Sculptors, and Architects* remains an important source of information on the life and works of many Renaissance artists. Born in Arezzo, Tuscany, Vasari studied with Guglielmo de Marsiglia in his hometown before leaving for Florence at the age of sixteen. He apprenticed as a painter in the workshop of Andrea del Sartro in Florence; he also traveled to Rome to study the works of Raphael, and Michelangelo Buonarroti. While a young man he worked as a festival manager, in which he designed decorations and processions for festivals at the courts of Florence, where he won the patronage of Cosimo de' Medici, the Duke of Florence. A skilled painter, he completed portraits of the Medici as well as paintings for the Hall of Cosimo I at the Palazzo Vecchio in Florence and the Sala Regia in the Vatican in Rome. He has a stronger reputation as an architect; Vasari helped to design the famous Villa Giulia in Rome for Pope Julius III and palaces in the towns of Arezzo and Pisa. His major architectural work, however, was the design of the

Uffizi gallery in Florence, formerly the government offices (Uffizi) of Tuscany. In this work he took inspiration from the design of the Vatican by Donato Bramante and by Michelangelo's Laurentian Library in Florence. Vasari designed a loggia, or covered passageway, in the Piazza Grande of Arezzo, where he also worked on the Church of Santi Fiora e Lucilla. He renovated the Churches of Santa Croce and Santa Maria Novella in Florence, replacing medieval features of the churches with a unified design inspired by classical Roman architecture. His many commissions allowed him to prosper and become a leading citizen of Arezzo, where he designed and decorated a mansion and where he attained the post of *gonfaloniere*, or mayor. In Florence he founded the Academy of Design with Cosimo de' Medici and Michelangelo; this institution survives to the present day as the Academy of Fine Arts of Florence.

A tireless traveler, Vasari developed on his wide-ranging journeys a keen instinct for judging works of art and especially paintings. From his wanderings he gathered notes and anecdotes that he worked into his *Lives*, which was first published in 1550 and was expanded for a new edition in 1568 and illustrated with woodcut portraits. The book begins with an introduction on the history of painting, sculpture, and architecture in Italy and then covers the lives of men who revived these arts in the Middle Ages: the painters Cimabue and Giotto, the sculptors of the city of Pisa, and the architect Arnolofo di Cambio. Vasari was close to Michelangelo and reserves his highest praise for this artist, whose works he sees as the culmination of the revival of the art of the classical age. For the second edition Vasari included a wider range of painters who lived outside of his favored city of Florence, including

some Venetians and non-Italians. Vasari's book, which coined the term Rinascita, or Renaissance, provides many valuable insights for modern historians of the Renaissance, although he worked in an antiquated style that combined historical speculation and fiction with facts as he knew them. His book provided inspiration for many authors and poets, including Honore de Balzac, George Eliot, and Robert Browning, who treated the themes of struggling artists and their works, but more importantly established a foundation for the modern field of art history.

SEE ALSO: Florence; Medici, Cosimo de'; Michelangelo Buonarroti

Venice

A city of northeastern Italy that was a leading center of artistic innovation through the Italian Renaissance. Venice was founded in the fifth century by Romans fleeing an invasion of the Lombards, barbarians who were overrunning northern Italy. The settlers built their shelters on a series of low-lying islands that rose above a surrounding lagoon, protected from the tides of the Adriatic Sea by a series of barrier islands. A *doge*, or duke, ruled the island settlements, which remained part of the Eastern Roman (Byzantine) Empire until Venice emerged as an independent city-state in the tenth century. The city extended its control to Dalmatia, the coastland along the eastern fringe of the Adriatic Sea, and began to send expeditions to the east. During the Crusades—medieval campaigns to wrest the city of Jerusalem and the Holy Land from the Muslims—Venice established trading routes with several ports in the eastern Mediterranean. Venetian merchants such as Marco Polo voyaged via the Silk Road and other routes as far as China and other points in East

The Doge's Palace in modern Venice. Brand X Pictures/Royalty Free.

Asia. Venetian merchants grew wealthy through the control of eastern spices and other rare goods in high demand by the aristocrats and royalty of Europe. The city extended its boundaries by annexing Padua and other cities on the Italian mainland, as well as land along the Adriatic coast.

In the late fourteenth century, Venice bested its most important rival, the Italian city of Genoa, in the War of Chioggia, which ended in 1380. After this key event, Venice emerged during the Renaissance as one of the wealthiest states in Europe. Representatives of the Venetian doge and its ruling Council of Ten traveled throughout Europe, playing an important role in the diplomatic conflicts of the age. A fleet of more than three thousand ships ranged the Mediterranean, and Venice had captured several mountain passes through the Alps in order to control routes to north-

ern Europe. Venetian power and wealth also posed a threat to the Papacy; the popes also sought authority over cities of the northern Italian plains and the Catholic Church frowned on the tolerance that allowed religious dissent within Venice itself. In 1508 Pope Julius II formed the League of Cambrai with France, Spain, and the Holy Roman Empire to challenge Venetian might. The league failed in its mission, as Venice recaptured all of the mainland territories it had lost and emerged in the mid-sixteenth century as the strongest state in Italy.

The Venetian republic was founded on the authority of the doge—which eventually became a largely ceremonial office—and of the Great Council, a body of several hundred rulers drawn from among the city's noble families. The Council appointed public officials and elected a Senate, which in turn chose the Council often, a committee entrusted with the state's order and security. An extensive network of spies and informers rooted out dissent and conspiracy within the city, which harshly punished the slightest threat to its oligarchic form of government.

The art and architecture of Venice had their roots in Byzantine style; the Cathedral of Saint Mark raised in the eleventh century is lavishly decorated in marble, mosaic, and gilt. Many major artists, including the Bellini family, Paolo Veronese, Palladio, Titian, and Tintoretto, had their homes and workshops in the city, and decorated Venetian churches, monasteries, and public buildings with many of the most renowned frescoes and canvases of the Renaissance. Venice was also an important early center of the printing industry, and laid claim to the busiest publishing industry in Renaissance Europe. The presses of Venice turned out the first editions of classical Greek and Latin authors who played a vital role as a foundation of the intellectual and artistic life of the Renaissance.

Venice built a huge fleet of merchant ships at its famous Arsenal, one of the largest ship works in Europe. But with the rise of the Ottoman Empire, which conquered the Byzantine Empire in the middle of the fifteenth century, Venice was again contending for control of the eastern Mediterranean. The Ottoman navy cut many of Venice's important links with the East. Despite the victory of a European alliance against the Turkish fleet at the Battle of Lepanto in 1571, Venice began a slow decline that lasted two centuries. Its merchant empire in the east was being surpassed by trade with the New World, which its rivals in Europe were exploiting, while the Turks eventually captured all the Venetian possessions in Greece as well as

Cyprus and the coast of Dalmatia. In 1797 Venice was conquered by Napoléon Bonaparte, and granted by the French to Austria in the Treaty of Campo Formio. This put an official end to Venice's status as an independent republic.

Veronese, Paolo (1528–1588)

Italian artist of the "Venetian school" who is considered one of the most important painters of Venice during the late Italian Renaissance. Born as Paolo Caliari in Verona, he was the son of a stonecutter, and gained the nickname "Veronese" from his native city. Veronese trained in the workshop of Antonio Badile. In 1548, he moved to Mantua, where he took part in the decoration of the city's cathedral. He then arrived in Venice, where he won many important commissions and where he remained for the rest of his life. As a younger artist he was influenced by the works of Giulio Romano and later by Titian.

Veronese became a master of the difficult art of fresco painting, in which paint is applied to wet plaster, with which it dries. He used brilliant colors and rich detail, and was keenly sensitive to the varying textures of fabric, stone, and sky. He was also skilled in the arts of perspective, foreshortening, and illusionistic painting, all of which became important ingredients in the Mannerist style developed in the works of the late Italian Renaissance. Many of his works explore religious and mythological themes, such as *The Temptation of St. Anthony*, completed in 1552. For the Doge's Palace in Venice he completed a famous ceiling painting, *Jupiter Fulminating the Vices*, and other works for the Sala del Consiglio, a major meeting hall of the palace, in 1554. After a fire destroyed a portion of the palace, Veronese helped to reconstruct and redecorate the building with two major works, *Venice Ruling with Justice and Peace* and *Triumph of Venice*. For the architect Andrea Palladio, Veronese painted natural and allegorical scenes on the walls and ceilings of the famous Palladian Villa Barbaro. Veronese adopted the classical building style of Palladio in the backgrounds of several of his large canvases, many of which depict grand processions, majestic assemblies, and lavish feasts.

Over a period of fifteen years, Veronese completed several important decorative works for the San Sebastiano church in Venice. Ceiling paintings illustrate the story of Esther, and employ dramatic foreshortening; the choir of the church is decorated with scenes from the life of Saint Sebastian. Two paintings he did for the organ shutters of the church change as the shutters open and close.

Other famous paintings by Veronese include *Christ Among the Doctors, St. John Preaching*, and *The Supper at Emmaus*. The *Marriage at Cana* is a huge and richly detailed canvas with portraits of Veronese, Titian, Tintoretto, and Jacopo Bassano, depicted as musicians seated at the feet of Christ. Veronese received several commissions to decorate refectories, or dining halls, for Venetian monasteries; these works include the *Feast of St. Gregory the Great* and *Feast in the House of Simon*. But he drew unwanted attention from the Inquisition for one of these works: a *Last Supper*, in which he included clowns, soldiers, dwarfs, and other irreverent figures. In response to this scolding by the religious authorities, he simply changed the name of the painting, one of the largest works of the Renaissance, to *Feast in the House of Levi*. Veronese established a busy workshop in Venice that survived his death under the management of his brothers and sons, and which remained an important influence in the painting of Venice for two centuries.

SEE ALSO: Tintoretto, Jacopo; Titian

Verrocchio, Andrea del (1435–1488)

Sculptor, goldsmith, and painter renowned for his monumental works in bronze. He was born as Andrea di Michele di Francesco di Cioni in Florence and was the son of a brick maker. Historians know very few details of his youth or his apprenticeship as an artist. He joined the workshop of Giulio Verrocchi, whose name he took as his own; he may also have studied with Fra Filippo Lippi. Verrocchio was commissioned in 1465 by the traders guild of Florence to create a work for the church of Orsanmichele. The result was his *Christ and St. Thomas* (also known as the *Doubting of Thomas*), which was finally completed in 1483 and which immediately drew the admiration for its dramatic arrangement and ingenious use of a confined space.

Verrocchio enjoyed a high reputation in Florence and drew many skilled young painters to his workshop, including Perugino, Sandro Botticelli, Domenico Ghirlandaio, and Leonardo da Vinci. As a painter, Verrocchio is best known for his *Baptism of Christ*, in which he was assisted by his young apprentice Leonardo da Vinci, who completed a dramatic natural backdrop and the head of an angel. Verrocchio also completed an altarpiece for the cathedral of Pistoia, a *Crucifixion with Saints, Madonna with Child* (the only painting that he signed), and *Tobias and the Angel*.

He won several important commissions from the Medici rulers of Florence, including funerary monuments to Cosimo de' Medici and monuments to Giovanni, and Piero de' Medici that were placed in the sacristy of the church of San Lorenzo. For the Villa Medici at Careggi, Verrocchio created a sculpture of David, showing the young man just after his victory over Goliath. This work was later sold to the Signoria of Florence and displayed in the main square of Venice for several centuries. Verrocchio also was a skilled sculptor in marble, in which he completed a celebrated *Bust of a Young Woman*. His grandest work was the design for an equestrian monument of the mercenary Bartolommeo Colleoni. This work is known for its dynamic motion, in which the horse raises one of its legs, boldly preparing for a charge into battle. The statue was cast after Verrocchio's death and still rises in the Campo San Giovanni e Paolo in Venice.

SEE ALSO: Botticelli, Sandro; Leonardo da Vinci; sculpture

Vespucci, Amerigo (1454–1512)

Italian navigator whose name was given to the New World. Vespucci was a merchant of Florence who was hired by the Medici rulers of the city to work in Seville, Spain. He supplied essential goods to the expeditions of Christopher Columbus and was later taken on as a navigator by Alonso Ojeda. In 1499, Ojeda reached South America; he and Vespucci separated and Vespucci sailed south from the Caribbean, becoming the first European to reach the mouth of the Amazon River. In 1502 Vespucci joined a second expedition to the New World, this one sponsored by Portugal and which reached Guanabara Bay, the present site of Rio de Janeiro, and the Rio de la Plata, which separates Argentina and Uruguay. Vespucci developed a new system for computing longitude and calculated the circumference of the earth to within 50 miles (80.5km) of the correct figure. Realizing that South America was an entirely new continent and not an unknown part of Asia or the East Indies, Vespucci provided European navigators with a more accurate concept of the distances facing them in their voyages of exploration.

An account of these voyages was read by the German mapmaker Martin Waldseemüller, who worked as a mapmaker for a merchant company of Seville. Waldseemüller came to believe, erroneously, that Vespucci had commanded an expedition of 1497 that was the first to reach the mainland of North America, one year before the same feat had been accomplished by Christopher Columbus. In 1507 Waldseemüller honored Vespucci by using his first name as a label for the new continent in his *Cosmographiae Introductio*, a series of maps. In the meantime, Vespucci was honored with the title of pilot major, a chief navigator for the king of Spain. He died of malaria that he had caught during his second voyage.

SEE ALSO: Columbus, Christopher

Villon, Francois (1431– ?)

French poet, whose entire body of work comprises about three thousand lines of verse but who is considered one the greatest French authors of the fifteenth century. Born in Paris, Villon's given name was Francois de Montcorbier or Francois des Loges. He was taken into the household of Guillaume de Villon, the canon of Saint Benoit le Betourne, who educated him. Villon attended the University of Paris, earning the degree of master of arts in 1452.

In 1455 Villon killed a priest in a street brawl and fled Paris. He joined a roving band of thieves and highwaymen known as the *coquillards*, who were a common threat on the chaotic byways of France in the years after the Hundred Years' War. He was granted leniency by the Paris city officials in the next year, when he completed the *Lais*, forty stanzas of eight lines each, in which he describes his turbulent life and satirically details a legacy for his friends, enemies, and acquaintances. This work is also known as the *Little Testament*. In 1461 he completed the *Grand Testament*, a much longer work that includes two thousand lines in various forms and presents a grand spectacle of personages of the medieval French world in which the poet moved. The *Grand Testament* includes Villon's most famous poem, "Ballade of the Ladies of Yesteryear." In 1462 Villon was arrested and imprisoned in the Chatelet fortress in Paris for the burglary at the College de Navarre in 1446, for which he was again granted a pardon on condition that he make restitution for the crime. When he took part in another street brawl, he was sentenced to death; on appeal his hanging was stayed by an edict of the Paris Parlement. Some time after sentence was passed he composed the "Ballade of the Hanged," in which he describes in vivid detail his fate as an executed criminal. He was sentenced to ten years of exile from Paris; after this event he disappeared, and historians know nothing of his whereabouts for the remainder of his life.

Villon's career as an outlaw prevented him from winning any patronage from the court or the nobility. His poetry is intensely personal, full of satire and a bitter, grotesque sense of humor, describing his life in his own words, and owing nothing to the traditional themes of chivalry and religion that were standard for medieval poets and prose authors. His works were collected and edited by Clement Marot, and the discovery of Villon's poetry by the romantic poets of the nineteenth century made his permanent reputation as one of the great poets of French literature.

Virgil
(70 B.C.–19 B.C.)

Ancient Latin poet of Italy whose epic *The Aeneid* described the mythological founding of Rome, and whose works provided the writers of the Renaissance with their most respected poetic model from the classical world. Born as Publius Vergilius Maro, a descendant of barbarian Celts, he was raised in a small town near Verona, the son of a laborer who managed to give his son a good education. As a young man Virgil made his way to the capital, where he studied rhetoric and philosophy. Although trained to practice law, he was too bashful to make a good impression as a speaker, an essential ingredient for a successful public career in ancient Rome. Instead he turned to books, study, and the writing of poetry.

When his family's farm was confiscated by the Roman government as a reward for its victorious soldiers, the emperor Augustus intervened and returned the property. In thanks for this action, Virgil wrote the *Eclogues*, a group of ten poems that celebrate nature and the serene life of shepherds and the countryside. In the four books of the *Georgics*, Virgil describes in great detail the life and the labor of farmers, modeling his writings on the *Works and Days* of Hesiod, an ancient Greek poet.

The Aeneid, an imposing monument of ancient literature, was written by Virgil on a commission from Augustus for a historical work that would celebrate his own accomplishments in establishing the new empire of Rome. The poem describes the voyages and the battles of the hero Aeneas, a Trojan who wanders the Mediterranean in search of a new home for his defeated companions. Virgil based the twelve books of his epic on the *Iliad* and the *Odyssey* of Homer. He began work in 30 B.C. and continued for the last eleven years of his life, leaving the work unfinished at his death in 19 B.C. Although he ordered the entire poem to be burned, Augustus instead had the poem published in 17 B.C. *The Aeneid* was soon acclaimed as one of the great works of Roman literature, an honor it maintained through the Renaissance and still holds today.

The poem was well known to the manuscript copyists of medieval Europe, where the *Aeneid* was often used as a book of divination. Dante Alighieri, in *The Divine Comedy*, made Virgil his own guide to the circles of Hell and Purgatory. Virgil was studied in universities and was a subject of debate and commentary by scholars, philosophers, and poets, who held up *The Aeneid* as a model of classical clarity and perfection of form.

Visconti dynasty

A noble family of northern Italy who ruled the duchy of Milan and whose members were important patrons of the early Renaissance in that important city. In the twelfth century the clan was granted the title of viscount, which they adopted as the family name. Oddone Visconti, the archbishop of Milan, became ruler of the city by ousting the rival Della Torre clan in 1277. His successor, Matteo I Visconti, controlled Milan with the backing of the Holy Roman Emperor, but the opposition of the Guelph (papal) faction forced him to surrender his title in favor of his son Galeazzo I Visconti in 1322. Luchino Visconti (1292–1349) added Tuscany, Piedmont, and a small canton of Switzerland to the Visconti domains. The rapidly growing power and territory of the Visconti

aroused opposition in northern Italy, and the Visconti lands came under frequent attack by rivals fearing the establishment of a Visconti kingdom stretching across northern Italy.

Galeazzo II (1320–1378), the son of Stefano Visconti, fought with his brother Bernabo against the d'Este and Gonzaga clans, defeating his rivals at the Battle of Casorate. He shared the Visconti realm with Bernabo after the death of Matteo II Visconti. A patron of artists and writers, notably Petrarch, he founded the University of Pavia and extended his family's influence by marrying his daughter Violante to a prince of England and his son Gian Galeazzo to Isabella, the daughter of the king of France. In 1362, he moved to Pavia, allowing his brother Bernabo to rule in Milan, where he contended with the powerful cities of Florence and Venice as well as with the pope.

Gian Galeazzo Visconti (1351–1402) combined the Pavia and Milan realms under his authority and brought the Visconti domain to the height of its wealth, power, and prestige. He added the March of Treviso to the realm in 1387 and also conquered Pisa, Siena, Bologna, and the duchy of Umbria, employing skilled mercenary captains as well as his own skillful diplomacy to avoid open warfare with the coalitions that were constantly forming against him. Through the payment of a large sum of money, he was invested as hereditary ruler of Milan by the Holy Roman Empire, an event that brought about the independence of northern Italy from control by the emperors. Gian Galeazzo's dream of founding a hereditary Visconti kingdom was cut short by his death from the plague. After his death the Visconti territories passed to Giovanni Maria Visconti, whose rule was so violent and corrupt that he was assassinated in 1412. The last Visconti duke, Filippo Maria Visconti, died in 1447, after which Milan came under the rule of his son-in-law, Francesco Sforza.

SEE ALSO: Petrarch; Sforza dynasty

Vitruvius
(ca. 80 B.C.–ca. 25 B.C.)

Roman architect, engineer, and author whose treatise *On Architecture*—written as a guidebook for Roman builders—was widely influential during the Renaissance. Vitruvius was born in the town of Formiae as Marcus Vitruvius Pollio. He may have served in the Roman army of Julius Caesar, working to design fortifications and siege engines in Spain and Gaul (modern France). He flourished during the time of the emperor Augustus, his patron, and to whom he dedicated his work. Historians know of only one building designed by him: a basilica in the town of Fano, which has disappeared completely.

On Architecture was one of the classical works to survive the Middle Ages through the manuscript copying carried out in isolated monasteries, where the ancient works were preserved from the violence and chaos of the time. One of these manuscript copies was discovered in 1414 by the Italian scholar Poggio Bracciolini at the abbey of Saint Gallen in Switzerland. The new technology of printing allowed the book to find a wider audience in southern Europe. The first printed edition was brought out in Rome by Fra Giovanni Sulpitius in 1486; an illustrated edition appeared in 1511, and translations in Italian were first published in 1521. Vitruvius was translated into German, French, English, and Spanish by the end of the sixteenth century.

Vitruvius admired the classical architecture of Greece and saw his own time as a decadent period in which architects were forgetting the Greek tradition of harmony and proportion. Written in about 40 B.C., *On Architecture* is divided into ten books and covers the design of buildings and landscapes, engineering, town planning, and the proportions of the human body. Vitruvius held the qualities of strength, utility, and beauty to be necessary in all structures, which took their ideal proportions from that of the body. As the only architectural book to survive the fall of the Roman Empire, *On Architecture* became the most important source of information for Renaissance architects looking to revive classical forms in their churches, palaces, public buildings, monuments, and design of public spaces. Leon Battista Alberti based his important work on architecture, *De Re Aedificatoria*, largely on the work of Vitruvius.

SEE ALSO: Alberti, Leon Battista; architecture; Bracciolini, Poggio

William I of Orange (1533–1584)

A Dutch noble who founded the dynasty of Orange-Nassau and led the revolt in the Netherlands against rule by Spain. Born in Nassau, a small principality in northern Germany, he was the son of Count William of Nassau, who had converted to Lutheranism. At the age of eleven he inherited the title of Prince of Orange. Although he now owned extensive properties in the Low Countries, he was too young to exercise any authority, and his domain was governed by the Habsburg emperor Charles V as regent. He trained as a cavalry officer and at a young age was given command of a unit in the Habsburg armies. On the abdication of Charles V, he was made governor of Holland and Burgundy by Philip II.

William's reluctance to speak out on the brewing political and religious turmoil in the Low Countries earned him the nickname of "William the Silent." Nevertheless, he strongly opposed Habsburg domination of the nobility and favored the free exercise of religion for Protestants as well as Catholics. He eventually emerged as a leading opponent of Spain's brutal occupation. He retreated to his native Nassau, joined the revolt against the Spanish, and organized naval and ground forces to carry out commando raids on Spanish outposts. William won several victories against the Spanish armies, and his personal flag was adopted by the Dutch as the banner of their resistance movement.

After a key victory in 1572, the rebels organized a parliament and declared William their *stadtholder*, or governor. In 1579 several northern provinces declared the Union of Utrecht, and in 1581 the union officially declared its independence from the king of Spain. In 1584 he was assassinated by a Catholic partisan, Balthasar Gerard, in the town of Delft.

SEE ALSO: Netherlands; Philip II

witchcraft

In the Middle Ages, any practice of magic outside the realm of Christian doctrine was seen as the work of the Devil and punished as witchcraft. Heretics and witches were routinely tried and tortured in order to force their confessions. A common medieval practice was to bind suspects with ropes and throw them into lakes and rivers. If they floated to the surface, they were considered "rejected" by the water and thus guilty as charged. If they remained submerged or drowned, they were declared innocent of witchcraft. Those found guilty were burned at the stake by civil authorities working at the behest of religious courts and inquisitions.

During the sixteenth century, the persecution of witches reached its peak in Europe. The Renaissance wave of witch trials began with a bull issued by Pope Innocent VIII in 1484, which acknowledged the presence of witchcraft, contrary to previous church doctrine. According to the church, witches regularly consorted with the devil and conspired to undermine

Malleus maleficarum malefi
cas et earum heresim vt
phramea potentissi
ma conterens.

The title page of "Malleus maleficarum" or "Hammer of Witches," the Inquisition's 1519 manual on detecting and dealing with witchcraft. SPECIAL COLLECTIONS LIBRARY, THE UNIVERSITY OF MICHIGAN.

church authority. The pope commissioned two German monks, Heinrich Kramer and Jacob Sprenger, to prepare a report on witchcraft. The result was *Malleus Maleficarum*, or The Hammer of Witches, which helped its readers learn to recognize the tell-tale signs and marks of a witch, described the sexual perversions, murders, spell-casting, and other wrongdoing, and demanded that Christians actively search out and destroy witches.

At the church's prompting, witches were rounded up by the hundreds and burned publicly. The witch hysteria was especially strong in Germany and Switzerland, even as the Protestant Reformation

was splitting these regions into two hostile religious factions. In France, a member of the court of King Charles IX announced that ten thousand witches were at his command, which set off a rampant anti-witch hysteria in which thousands of people were accused by friends and family.

In Scotland, a witch panic was set off by King James VI (later King James I of England, the first of the Stuart dynasty). Having traveled to Denmark to marry his bride Princess Anne of Denmark, James and his party were beset by a furious storm. The captain of his ship blamed the storm on witchcraft, to which several Danish women willingly confessed. Back in Scotland, James authorized the torture of suspected witches. Several dozen suspects were burned at the stake before the persecutions died down at the end of the 1500s. Nevertheless, witchcraft remained a capital offense in Scotland until 1735.

SEE ALSO: Catholicism; James I

Wolsey, Thomas (1475–1530)

English churchman and statesman who was chaplain to Henry VII and Henry VIII. Born the son of a butcher in Ipswich, he was educated at Oxford, where he served as a master of Magdalen College. Ordained a priest in 1498, he was appointed as the rector of Limington parish in Dorset. In 1503 he became a chaplain to Sir Richard Nanfan, an English governor of Calais who introduced Wolsey to the royal court. He became the royal chaplain to King Henry VII, who sent him as a diplomat to Scotland and the Netherlands.

After Henry VIII came to the throne in 1509, Wolsey won an appointment as the royal almoner, who was responsible for distributing alms to the poor. He organized an invasion force for an assault on

France in 1513 and in the next year arranged a truce between England and France. He was appointed bishop of Lincoln in 1514, archbishop of York in the same year. Pope Leo X named him a cardinal in 1515. Henry appointed Cardinal Wolsey as the lord chancellor of England in 1515; in this post Wolsey directed foreign policy as well as the affairs of England on behalf of the king, who took little interest in the bothersome day-to-day details of managing a kingdom. Wolsey arranged a general truce in Europe in 1518 and also brought the kings of France and England together at the famous meeting on the Field of the Cloth of Gold in 1520. Wolsey failed in his attempt to make England the arbiter of disputes on the continent, however, and in 1522 advised the king to make an alliance with Charles V,

the Holy Roman Emperor, against France. He fell out of favor with the English populace by levying heavy taxes and forcing loans of money to pay for English military campaigns. More dangerously, he lost the support of the king after failing to persuade the pope to grant Henry an annulment of his marriage to Catherine of Aragon in 1529. This event lost Wolsey most of his titles and offices that had brought him the wealth and power that made him the focus of widespread jealousy and resentment. In 1530, he was placed under arrest for treason after letters he had sent to the king of France were discovered. While on his way to face trial before the king, he fell ill and died in the town of Leicester.

SEE ALSO: Henry VIII; More, Sir Thomas

Xavier, Francis
(1506–1552)

Missionary who converted thousands to Christianity in India, the East Indies, and the Far East. Born Francisco de Jasso y Azpilcueta to a noble family of Navarre, he was the son of a counselor to the king of Navarre. He studied at the University of Paris, where in 1534 became one of the seven founding members of the Jesuit Order founded by Ignatius of Loyola. Xavier traveled to Venice in 1536 and was ordained a priest in 1537. He worked for several years to establish Jesuit institutions in Rome and in 1540 was recruited into a Portuguese mission to Goa, India. The Christianizing mission of the Jesuits was well suited to accompany the voyages to the Indies by Portuguese explorers, who saw as their duty not only the establishment of trading posts and colonies but the harvest of souls for the greater glory of the Christian church. Appointed a papal nuncio, or representative, Xavier left for India and the East Indies in 1542. His persuasive speaking and preaching gained converts at Goa, and he successfully established Christian missions along the coasts of India and in the Malay Archipelago. In 1549 he arrived at Kagoshima, Japan, where he became the first to introduce Christianity. Xavier set up several missions in Japan before returning to India in 1551. He left with a Portuguese embassy for China and in 1552 died on the island of Changcheun while seeking entry to China, then ruled by a Ming dynasty emperor. Xavier's body was collected and laid to rest at a Christian church in Goa, which became a popular shrine and place of pilgrimage for Christians throughout Asia. He was canonized along with Ignatius Loyola in 1622; Xavier eventually became the patron saint of India, the Philippines, Japan, China, New Zealand, and of all Christian missionaries.

SEE ALSO: Loyola, Saint Ignatius

Zwingli, Huldrych
(1484–1531)

Swiss church reformer, a contemporary of Martin Luther who established the Reformed branch of the Protestant movement. The son of a village magistrate, Zwingli was born in the village of Wildhaus in eastern Switzerland. He received an education in the classics at the universities of Basel and Vienna, and was ordained as a priest in 1506, when he became pastor of the town of Glarus. He served as a chaplain to Swiss mercenaries in Italy and in 1516 became vicar of Einsiedeln, an important Benedictine monastery where a large library gave Zwingli opportunity for study and research. Soon after this appointment he began preaching reform of the Catholic Church. Zwingli found no foundation for the Papacy in the books of the Bible and increasingly viewed the Catholic Church as a corrupt and decadent institution.

In 1519 Zwingli was appointed vicar to the Grossmunster church in Zurich. Having studied the New Testament translation of Desiderius Erasmus, he developed his own reformist doctrine, and began preaching criticisms of important Catholic institutions, such as monasticism and the selling of indulgences (remissions of sin). He saw the Catholic Mass as a pagan blasphemy on true Christianity; he rejected the notion of purgatory, the veneration of saints, the practice of fasting during Lent, and the Catholic stricture of priestly celibacy. In 1522, he declared that the Bible, and not the church, provided the authority for all questions of Christian doctrine. Many priests of the city took up his cause, which he set out in the Sixty-Seven Articles in 1523. After witnessing a public debate between Zwingli and a representative of the pope, the city fathers followed his reforming impulse, ordering all priests in the city to comply with Zwingli's instruction and in 1524 removing the statues, relics, musical instruments, and works of art that were now deemed idolatrous from the city's churches. In the next year Zwingli published his major written work, *The Commentary on True and False Religion.*

Zwingli believed, like Martin Luther, in the key Protestant doctrine of justification by faith alone. But he differed with Luther in the question of the presence of Christ in the bread and wine of Mass—with Luther holding that Christ is actually present, and Zwingli that the bread and wine are only symbolic representations of Christ's body and blood. The two reformers debated the question at the famous Marburg Colloquy of 1529. The disagreement created a rift in the Protestant movement between Lutheranism and Zwingli's Reformed branch.

In Zurich, the more radical branch of Anabaptists emerged to challenge Zwingli's authority, while the "forest cantons" of Switzerland that remained loyal to the Catholic Church took up arms against the Protestants. In 1531 Zwingli was mortally wounded at the Battle of Kappel. His body was quartered and burned on a manure pile by his enemies, who were determined that no relics of him would remain to inspire veneration by his followers. In the years that followed, the Zwinglian movement gave way to the new doctrines preached by John Calvin.

SEE ALSO: Luther, Martin; Calvin John; Reformation, Protestant

Chronology

The following are representative of the many significant events of the Renaissance that has occurred throughout history:

1096 Christians launch the first Crusade against the Muslims. By the end of the First Crusade on 1099, Crusaders had established several feudal states in the Near East.

1233 Pope Gregory IX establishes the medieval Inquisition by assembling a formal tribunal with the power to seek out and punish heretics.

1275 Venetian Marco Polo travels to China, where he remains for almost twenty years. During the Renaissance, Polo's various writings were the primary source of Western information about the East.

c. 1300 Immanuel of Rome composes his Notebooks, which contained thirty-eight sonnets in Hebrew.

1306 Italian poet Dante Alighieri begins writing his three-part work *The Divine Comedy.*

1337 England and France begin the Hundred Years' War over control of the French throne.

1347–1350 Bubonic plague, more commonly known as "The Black Death," sweeps through Europe.

1364 The University of Cracow is founded in Poland.

1412 Joan of Arc is born in the French village of Domremy.

1421 Sultan Mehmed II restores the Ottoman Empire.

1432 Donatello creates his most famous work, a bronze statue of David, the first freestanding nude statue sculpted since the time of ancient Rome.

1442 King Alfonso V of Aragon conquers and reunites Sicily and southern Italy into a single kingdom.

1453 Led by sultan Mehmed II, the Ottoman Turks conquer Constantinople, the capital of the Byzantine Empire.

1454 German printer Johannes Gutenberg pioneers a new system of movable type for book printing.

1455 The English houses of York and Tudor begin the War of the Roses.

1487 Religious scholars and legal authorities in Germany compile the *Malleus maleficarum* (the "Hammer of Witches"), a text that explored ideas about witchcraft and argued strongly for its vigorous prosecution.

1492 Italian navigator Christopher Columbus makes his first voyage to the New World, establishing a small settlement on Hispaniola called La Navidad.

1503 Giuliano della Rovere is elected pope. Taking the name Julius II, Giuliano became known as "the warrior pope" for his involvement in several wars involving church lands.

1506 Pope Julius II decides to rebuild Saint Peter's Church. The project will eventually take over eighty-four years to complete and involve many famous artists, architects' and sculpters, including Donato Bramante, Raphael, and Michelangelo.

1512 Michaelangelo completes the ceiling of the Sistine Chapel at the Vatican in Rome.

1517 German priest Martin Luther posts

his famous Ninety-Five Theses on the door of the castle church in Wittenberg, signaling the beginning the Protestant Reformation.

1519 Spanish conquistador Hernan Cortés is selected to lead an expedition to the mainland of North America.

1525 German peasants resist the expansion of nobles' economic rights in what is often referred to as "The Peasants' War".

1527 Armies of the Holy Roman Emperor Charles V sack Rome.

1530 The Medici family is formally granted lordship of Florence, Italy.

1534 King Henry VII is declared supreme head of the Church of England.

1535 French explorer Jacques Cartier sails up the St. Lawrence River—gateway to the Great lakes—in an attempt to find a northerly route to the Spice Islands.

1540 Spanish priest Ignatius of Loyola founds the Society of Jesuits.

1545–1563 The Council of Trent is held in northern Italy. This body of the Catholic Church convened to make decisions about religious doctrine; define ceremonial procedures; and oppose the spread of the Protestant Reformation.

c. 1547 Puritanism begins to emerge in England.

1550s Italian architect Andrea Palladio popularizes the villa design style.

1558 Elizabeth I ascends to the English throne, beginning a forty-five-year reign as queen.

1559 Pope Paul IV places Machiavelli's political treatise *The Prince* on the Index of Prohibited Books.

1562 The French Wars of Religion begin.

1570 Flemish mapmaker Abraham Ortel publishes the first world atlas.

1572 Danish astronomer Tycho Brahe discovers a new star.

1572 Over three thousand men, women, and children are killed in Paris during the Saint Bartholomew's Day Massacre.

1588 The massive Spanish Armada is defeated by the English fleet, marking a high point in Queen Elizabeth I's reign and the beginning of England's maritime dominance.

c. 1590s Operas—or full-length musical dramas—begin to appear on Italian stages. The first operas were heavily influenced by classic Greek mythology.

1594 William Shakespeare joins the Lord Chamberlain's Men, an acting company that performed primarily at a London playhouse known as the Theatre.

1595 The Edict of Nantes grants religious and civil liberties to the Huguenots of France.

1601 English architect Inigo Jones is appointed official surveyor at the court of King James I.

1606 Ben Jonson's dark comedic play *Volpone*, or *The Fox* is first produced for the stage.

1610 Italian physicist and astronomer Galileo Galilei discovers Io, Europa, and Callisto, three of Jupiter's moons.

1611 King James I of England approves a new English translation of the Bible.

1612 Painter Artemisia Gentileschi moves to Florence and becomes the first woman accepted into the prestigious Florentine Academy of Design.

1614 Scottish mathematician John Napier discovers logarithms.

1618 Johannes Kepler publishes his third law of planetary motion.

1624 Peter Paul Rubens paints his self-portrait.

1642 The English Civil War begins.

1657 The Habsburg dynasty effectively ends with the signing of the Peace of Westphalia, which reduced the power of both the Holy Roman Empire and the House of Habsburg.

1667 Poet John Milton writes his epic work *Paradise Lost*.

For Further Research

Jacob Burckhardt, *The Civilization of the Renaissance in Italy*. New York: Barnes & Noble, 1992.

Peter Burke, *The Renaissance: Studies in European History*. London: Palgrave Macmillan, 1997.

J.H. Burns, ed., *The Cambridge History of Political Thought, 1450–1700*. Cambridge, England: Cambridge University Press, 1991.

Ernst Cassirer Paul Oskar Kristeller, and John Herman Randall Jr., *The Renaissance Philosophy of Man*. Chicago: University of Chicago Press, 1948.

Arturo B. Fallico and Herman Shapiro, eds., *Renaissance Philosophy: The Italian Philosphers: Selected Readings from Petrarch to Bruno*. New York: Modern Library, 1967.

Brian Copenhaver, and Charles B. Schmitt, *Renaissance Philosophy*. Oxford, England: Oxford University Press, 1992.

Vincent Cronin, *The Flowering of the Renaissance*. New York: Dutton, 1969.

Robert Reinhold Ergang, *The Renaissance*. Princeton, NJ: Van Nostrand, 1967.

Wallace Ferguson, *Europe in Transition, 1300–1520*. Boston: Houghton Mifflin, 1962.

Wallace Ferguson, *The Renaissance in Historical Thought: Five Centuries of Interpretation*. New York: AMS, 1948.

Paul F. Grendler, *Schooling in Renaissance Italy: Literacy and Learning, 1300–1600*. Baltimore: Johns Hopkins University Press, 1989.

Paul F. Grendler, *The Universities of the Italian Renaissance*. Baltimore: Johns Hopkins University Press, 2002.

Paul F. Grendler, ed., *The Renaissance: An Encyclopedia for Students*. New York: Charles Scribner's Sons, 2004.

Paul F. Grendler et al., eds., *Encyclopedia of the Renaissance*. 6 vols. New York: Charles Scribner's Sons, 1999.

J.R. Hale, *The Civilization of Europe in the Renaissance*. New York: Maxwell Macmillan International, 1994.

J.R. Hale, ed., *A Concise Encyclopedia of the Italian Renaissance*. Oxford, England: Oxford University Press, 1981.

A. Rupert Hall, *The Revolution in Science, 1500–1750*. 3rd ed. London and New York: Longman, 1983.

Denys Hay, *The Italian Renaissance in Its Historical Background*. Cambridge, England: Cambridge University Press, 1977.

Denys Hay and John E. Law, *Italy in the Age of the Renaissance, 1380–1530*. London and New York: Oxford University Press, 1989.

Rudolf Hirsch, *Printing, Selling and Reading, 1450–1550*. Wiesbaden, Germany: Harrassowitz, 1967.

L. Jardine, *Worldly Goods: A New History of the Renaissance*. New York: Nan A. Talese, 1996.

De Lamar Jensen, *Renaissance Europe*. Lexington, MA: DC Heath, 1981.

Paul Johnson, *The Renaissance: A Short History*. New York: Modern Library, 2000.

Thomas DaCosta Kaufmann, *The Mastery of Nature: Aspects of Art, Science, and Humanism in the Renaissance*. Princeton, NJ: Princeton University Press, 1993.

Margaret L. King and Albert Rabil Jr., eds., *Her Immaculate Hand: Selected Works by and About the Women Humanists of Quattrocento Italy*. Binghamton, NY: Medieval & Renaissance Texts & Studies, 1992.

A.J. Krailsheimer, ed., *The Continental Renaissance 1500–1600*. Middlesex, England: Penguin, 1971.

Jill Kraye, *The Cambridge Companion to Renaissance Humanism*. Cambridge, England: Cambridge University Press, 1996.

Paul Oskar Kristeller, *Renaissance Thought: The Classic, Scholastic, and Humanist Strains*. New York, 1961.

John Lynch, *Spain under the Habsburgs. Vol. 1, Empire and Absolutism, 1516–1598*. Oxford, England: Oxford University Press, 1965.

John Larner, *Italy in the Age of Dante and Petrarch: 1216–1380*. London and New York: Longman, 1980.

Joan Marie Lechner, *Renaissance Concepts of the Commonplaces*. New York: Pageant, 1962. Westport, CT: Greenwood, 1974.

Robert Mandrou, *From Humanism to Science 1480–1700*. Middlesex, England: Penguin, 1978.

E. Ann Matter and John Coakley, eds., *Creative Women in Medieval and Early Modern Italy: A Religious and Artistic Renaissance*. Philadelphia: University of Pennsylvania Press, 1994.

Garrett Mattingly, *Renaissance Diplomacy*. New York: Russell & Russell, 1970.

I.D. McFarlane, *Renaissance France, 1470–1589*. New York; Barnes & Noble, 1974.

John Paoletti and Gary Radke, *Art in Renaissance Italy*. 3rd ed. Upper Saddle River, NJ: Pearson & Prentice-Hall, 2005.

J.H. Plumb, *The Horizon Book of the Renaissance*. New York: American Heritage, 1961.

Albert Rabil, ed., *Renaissance Humanism: Foundations, Forms, and Legacy*. Philadelphia: University of Pennsylvania Press, 1988.

Han Rachum, *The Renaissance: An Illustrated Encyclopedia*. London, England: Octopus, 1979.

P.A. Ramsey, ed., *Rome in the Renaissance: The City and the Myth*. Binghamton, NY: Center for Medieval and Early Renaissance Studies, 1982.

Aldo Scaglione, *Knights at Court: Courtliness, Chivalry, & Courtesy from Ottonian Germany to the Italian Renaissance*. Berkeley: University of California Press, 1991.

Charles B. Schmitt et al., eds., *The Cambridge History of Renaissance Philosophy*. Cambridge, England: Cambridge University Press, 1988.

Jerrold E. Seigel, *Rhetoric and Philosophy in Renaissance Humanism: The Union of Eloquence and Wisdom, Petrarch to*

Valla. Princeton, NJ: Princeton University Press, 1968.

Jeffrey Chipps Smith, *The Northern Renaissance*. London: Phaidon, 2004.

James Snyder, *Northern Renaissance Art: Painting, Sculpture, the Graphic Arts from 1350 to 1575*. Englewood Cliffs, NJ: Prentice-Hall, 1985.

John Stephens, *The Italian Renaissance: The Origins of Intellectual and Artistic Change Before the Reformation*. London and New York: Longman, 1990.

Jane S. Turner, ed., *Encyclopedia of Italian Renaissance and Mannerist Art*. 2 vols. New York: Grove's Dictionaries, 2000.

A. Wear, R. K. French, and I. M. Lonie, eds., *The Medical Renaissance of the Sixteenth Century*. Cambridge, England: Cambridge University Press, 1985.

Roberto Weiss, *The Renaissance Discovery of Classical Antiquity*. Oxford, England: Basil Blackwell, 1969.

W.P.D. Wightman, *Science and the Renaissance: An Introduction to the Study of the Emergence of the Sciences in the Sixteenth Century*. Edinburgh and London: Oliver, 1962.

David Wilkins, *History of Italian Renaissance Art*. 6th ed. New York: Prentice Hall, 2006.

Jonathan Zophy, *A Short History of Renaissance and Reformation Europe: Dances Over Fire and Water*. New York: Prentice-Hall, 2002.

Index

A

Academies, 19–20, 54, 76, 112, 126, 160, 317
Academy of Design, 54, 317
Academy of Geneva, 63
Academy of Plato, 19, 205–206, 258
Act in Restraint of Appeals, 95
Act of Succession, 219
Act of Supremacy, 95, 158
Act of Union, 284
Adages (Erasmus), 115
Adoration of the Magi (Leonardo da Vinci), 187
The Aeneid (Virgil), 26, 77, 234, 283, 294, 299, 322–323
Aetia (Callimachus), 62
Afonso V (king, Portugal), 35
Agincourt, Battle of, 313
Agnadello, Battle of, 147, 176
Agricola, Rudolf, 20
Alberti, Leon Battista, 20–21, 41, 144, 198, 247, 273, 324
Alberti, Lorenzo, 20, 27
Alchemy, 21–22
Alexander V (pope), 146, 162
Alexander VI (pope), 22–24, 45–47, 176, 241, 281, 286
Alexander of Macedon, 30
Alfonsine Tables, 33
Alfonso II of Aragon, 123, 124
Alfonso V of Aragon (the Magnanimous), 24, 47, 123, 225
Alhambra palace, 145
Alighieri, Dante, 24–26, 40, 43, 49, 189, 323
The Almagest (Ptolemy), 33, 204
Almagro, Diego, de, 256–257
Almanacs, 32, 230, 231
Ameto (Boccaccio), 43
Ammannati, Bartolomeo, 40
Anatomy, 208, 238
Andrew of Anjou (king, Hungary), 173
Angevin dynasty, 75, 123, 225
Anguissola, Sofonisba, 26
Anjou dynasty, 24, 160, 173
Anne of Brittany, 26–27, 75
Anne of Cleves, 95, 158
The Annunciation (Fra Angelico), 131
Antipopes, 78, 92, 93, 117, 229
Apollonius of Rhodes, 62
Arabs. *See* Muslims

Aragon, 24, 35, 123, 145, 222
Archidoxis (Paracelsus), 242
Architecture, 15, 16, 21, 27–29, 36, 56, 261
  classical, 41, 70, 175
  See also individual architects and buildings
Arena Chapel, 143
Ariosto, Ludovico, 29–30, 101, 107, 125, 144, 223
Aristotle, 14, 30–31, 258, 294
  astronomical theories, 87, 137, 138
Art, 12–17, 70
  Baroque, 16, 64–65, 89, 140, 199, 239, 269, 306
  classical, 41, 223
  humanism in, 21, 47, 109, 142, 238
  See also Classicism; Painting; *and individual artists and works*
The Art of Love (Ovid), 235
Ascham, Roger, 31, 113, 114
Assumption of the Virgin (Titian), 304
Astrology, 32–33, 34, 126, 230–231
Astronomy, 14, 16, 33–34, 154, 242
  See also Aristotle; Brahe, Tycho; Copernicus, Nicolaus; Galilei, Galileo; Kepler, Johannes; Ptolemy; Telescopes
Atlas (Mercator), *233*
De Augmentis Scientiarum (Bacon), 38
Augsburg Confession, 102, 211
Aurispa, Giovanni, 34, 78, 125
Austria, 34–35, 91, 153, 154, 161, 271
Auto-da-fé (act of faith), 166, 307
Averroes, 30
Aviz, House of, 35–36, 156
Aztec empire, 90

B

Babylonian Captivity. *See* Great Schism
Bacchus (Caravaggio), 65
Bach, Johann Sebastian, 220, 239
Bacon, Francis, 37–38, 115, 309
Balassi, Balint, 161
Balboa, Vasco Núñez de. *See* Núñez de Balboa, Vasco
Banking, 14, 135, 190, 245

Florentine, 126, 127, 238, 280, 295, 308
  international, 212, 307
  Medici family, 203–204, 205, 206, 308
Baptism of Christ (Verrocchio/Leonardo da Vinci), 187, 320
Baptistery of Florence, 56, 103, 127, 247, 265, 285, 311
Barocci, Federico, 38–39
Baroque period
  art, 16, 64–65, 89, 140, 199, 239, 269, 306
  music, 58, 218
Barres, Joao de, 261
Bartolommeo, Fra, 39–40, 100, 270
Basel Compact, 44
Basilica architecture, 28
Basilica of Santa Maria del Fiore, 56, 57
Basilica of Santo Spirito, 56–57
Battiferra degli Ammannati, Laura, 40
The Battle of San Romano (Uccello), 247
Belgium, 228
Bellini, Gentile, 40, 41, 65–66, 142, 304
Bellini, Giovanni, 41, 108, 109, 125
Bellini, Jacopo, 41–42
Bellini family, 198, 319
Benedict XIII (pope), 92
Bentivoglio, Giovanni II, 42, 176
Bernini, Pietro, 226
Bible
  Gutenberg, 151
  King James version, 116, 171
  translations of, 69, 297
Biologists, 16
  See also Medicine; Science
Biondi, Flavio, 57
The Birth of Venus (Botticelli), *49*
Black Death, 43, 126, 249, 257, 313
Blood, circulation of, 208
Boccaccio, Giovanni, 26, 42–44, 128, 189, 222
  Decameron, 12, 43, 202, 257
Bohemia, 44–45, 162, 271, 302–303
  Habsburg rule, 35, 153, 154, 161, 205, 275–276
Boleyn, Anne, 45, 113, 158, 219, 308, 309
Bologna (Italy), 32, 42, 168
Bologna, Giovanni, 285
Bonacolsi family, 199

H

I

About the Author

Tom Streissguth has written more than 70 books of nonfiction for young people. His titles include *Life Among the Vikings, Women of the French Revolution, Encyclopedia of the Middle Ages*, and *Eyewitness History: The Roaring Twenties*. He has worked as an editor, journalist, and teacher, and has traveled widely in Europe, the Middle East, and Asia. He currently lives in Florida.

About the Consulting Editor

Konrad Eisenbichler teaches Renaissance Studies at the University of Toronto. A past Director of the Centre for Reformation and Renaissance Studies (1990–2000), he has published widely and extensively on a variety of subjects in early modern studies, from Michelangelo to Savonarola, from teenagers to widows, from confraternities to theatre. His book, *The Boys of the Archangel Raphael. A Youth Confraternity in Florence, 1411–1785* (Toronto, 1998) won the Howard R. Marraro Prize awarded by the American Catholic Historical Association.